FROMM
EasyG
TO
DISNEY WORLD,
UNIVERSAL & ORLANDO

By
Jason Cochran

Easy Guides are ✦ Quick To Read ✦ Light To Carry
✦ For Expert Advice ✦ In All Price Ranges

FrommerMedia LLC

Published by
FROMMER MEDIA LLC

Copyright © 2016 by FrommerMedia LLC. All rights reserved. No part of this publication may be reproduced, stored in a retrieval system, or transmitted in any form or by any means, electronic, mechanical, photocopying, recording, scanning or otherwise, except as permitted under Sections 107 or 108 of the 1976 United States Copyright Act, without the prior written permission of the Publisher. Requests to the Publisher for permission should be addressed to customer_service@FrommerMedia.com.

Frommer's is a registered trademark of Arthur Frommer. FrommerMedia LLC is not associated with any product or vendor mentioned in this book.

ISBN 978-1-62887-174-6 (paper), 978-1-62887-175-3 (ebk)

Editorial Director: Pauline Frommer
Editor: Melissa Klurman
Production Editor: Erin Geile
Cartographer: Roberta Stockwell
Cover Design: Howard Grossman

For information on our other products or services, see www.frommers.com.

FrommerMedia LLC also publishes its books in a variety of electronic formats. Some content that appears in print may not be available in electronic formats.

Manufactured in the United States of America

5 4 3 2 1

FROMMER'S STAR RATINGS SYSTEM

Every hotel, restaurant and attraction listed in this guide has been ranked for quality and value. Here's what the stars mean:

★ Recommended
★★ Highly Recommended
★★★ A must! Don't miss!

AN IMPORTANT NOTE

The world is a dynamic place. Hotels change ownership, restaurants hike their prices, museums alter their opening hours, and busses and trains change their routings. And all of this can occur in the several months after our authors have visited, inspected, and written about, these hotels, restaurants, museums and transportation services. Though we have made valiant efforts to keep all our information fresh and up-to-date, some few changes can inevitably occur in the periods before a revised edition of this guidebook is published. So please bear with us if a tiny number of the details in this book have changed. Please also note that we have no responsibility or liability for any inaccuracy or errors or omissions, or for inconvenience, loss, damage, or expenses suffered by anyone as a result of assertions in this guide.

CONTENTS

ABOUT THE AUTHOR

Jason Cochran was awarded Guide Book of the Year by the Society of American Travel Writers' Lowell Thomas Travel Journalism Competition for this book and for his guide to London, which he writes for Frommer's. He has written for publications including "The New York Post," "Travel + Leisure," "USA Today," and been on staff at "Entertainment Weekly," "Budget Travel," and AOL Travel (Executive Editor). He devised questions for the first American prime-time season of "Who Wants to Be a Millionaire" (ABC) and produced and hosted "AfterShark," the AOL post-show for Mark Burnett's "Shark Tank" (ABC). He is an alumnus of Northwestern University and New York University and serves as Editor-in-Chief of Frommers.com.

Thank you to all the cast members and staff members who assisted with information, access, and good humor. This edition was only made possible with the help of Jake Cochran, Alex Miranda, Shanon Larimer, Wesley Brown, Tracy Temple, Jason Lietz, Kristin Harmel, Nick Williams, Jonathan Jackson, David Landsel, Adam Mellema, Brooke Trent, Joshua Davis, and Denise Spiegel and Heidi Colon of Visit Orlando. Finally, I am grateful to Arthur and Pauline Frommer. Their inspirational ideal of helping people of all means see the world with straight talk remains a beacon in an overwhelming ocean of information.

ABOUT THE FROMMER TRAVEL GUIDES

For most of the past 50 years, Frommer's has been the leading series of travel guides in North America, accounting for as many as 24% of all guidebooks sold. I think I know why.

Though we hope our books are entertaining, we nevertheless deal with travel in a serious fashion. Our guidebooks have never looked on such journeys as a mere recreation, but as a far more important human function, a time of learning and introspection, an essential part of a civilized life. We stress the culture, lifestyle, history, and beliefs of the destinations we cover, and urge our readers to seek out people and new ideas as the chief rewards of travel.

We have never shied from controversy. We have, from the beginning, encouraged our authors to be intensely judgmental, critical—both pro and con—in their comments, and wholly independent. Our only clients are our readers, and we have triggered the ire of countless prominent sorts, from a tourist newspaper we called "practically worthless" (it unsuccessfully sued us) to the many rip-offs we've condemned.

And because we believe that travel should be available to everyone regardless of their incomes, we have always been cost-conscious at every level of expenditure. Though we have broadened our recommendations beyond the budget category, we insist that every lodging we include be sensibly priced. We use every form of media to assist our readers, and are particularly proud of our feisty daily website, the award-winning Frommers.com.

I have high hopes for the future of Frommer's. May these guidebooks, in all the years ahead, continue to reflect the joy of travel and the freedom that travel represents. May they always pursue a cost-conscious path, so that people of all incomes can enjoy the rewards of travel. And may they create, for both the traveler and the persons among whom we travel, a community of friends, where all human beings live in harmony and peace.

Arthur Frommer

THE BEST OF ORLANDO

I n 1886, a young unmarried mailman, frustrated with his fruitless toil in the Midwest, moved to the woolly wilderness of Central Florida to make a better go of life. The land was angry. Summers were oppressively hot, the lightning relentless, and the tough earth, sodden and scrubby, defied clearing. The only domestic creatures that thrived there, it seemed, were the cattle, and even they turned out stringy and chewy. Undaunted, the young man planted a grove of citrus trees and waited for things to get better. They didn't. His trees died in a freeze. Now penniless, he was forced to return to delivering mail, the very thing he had tried so hard to escape. By 1890, he gave up, defeated, and moved to Chicago to seek other work. The American dream appeared to fail Elias Disney.

The story could have ended there. But he was joined by his new bride, whose own father had died trying to tame Florida land. Back in the smoke of the Midwest, they had children and settled for an anonymous urban existence. One day, 8 decades later, long after the young man and woman had lived full lives and passed away, two of their sons, now in the sunset of their own lives, would return to Central Florida, to the land that broke their father, and together they would transform the recalcitrant swamp into the most famous fantasy land the world has even known.

Little did Elias know that the dream was only skipping a generation and that his sons Walt and Roy would become synonymous with the same land that rejected him. Had he known that the Disney name would in due time define Central Florida, would he have been so despondent? Even if he had been granted a fleeting vision of what was to be, and what his family would mean to this place—and, indeed, to the United States—would he have believed it?

The Disney brothers turned a place of toil into a realm of pleasure, a place where hardworking people can put their struggles aside. The English have Blackpool; Canadians have Niagara Falls. Orlando rose to become the preeminent resort for the working and middle classes of America, and the ingenuity of its inventions inspires visitors from all over the world. Although other countries segregate their holiday destinations by income or some other petty quality, Orlando, in classic American egalitarian style, is all things to all people, from all countries and backgrounds.

Orlando represents something more powerful to American culture and history than merely being the fruit of a dream. It's something shared. No matter who you are, no matter your politics or upbringing, when you were a kid, you probably went at least once to Walt Disney World and Orlando—or, if you didn't, you desperately wanted to. Which other aspect of culture can we all claim to share? What else has given children such sweet dreams? I've often said that if somehow Walt Disney World went out of business tomorrow, the U.S. National Park Service would have to take it over—it means that much to the fabric of the nation.

Don't think of the amusements of Orlando as big business. Of course they are, and the incessant reminder of that often threatens to shatter the fantasy. But Walt Disney World, and by extension Orlando, is Americana incarnate. The flair for showmanship and fantasy that they crystallize, now coined as the term "Disneyfication," is the defining mind-set of our culture, in which even grocery stores are dressed like film sets and the "story" of your local burger joint is retold on the side of its beverage cups.

Orlando tells us about who we dream of being. Virtually nothing about it is natural or authentic, and yet there may be no more perfect embodiment of American culture. To understand this invented landscape is to understand the values of its civilization and our generation. And if you observe Orlando with a long view—starting with young Elias Disney cutting his hands trying to budge a tough Florida pine—you will be a part of the explosive, unexpected powers of the American dream.

And one more thing: If you can buck the system and relax, it's a hell of a lot of fun.

ORLANDO'S best THEME PARK EXPERIENCES

o **Walt Disney World:** Walt Disney World operates four top-drawer theme parks every day of the year: **Magic Kingdom,** the most popular theme park on Earth, is a more spacious iteration of the original Disneyland, the park that started it all, and is brimming with attractions that have been cherished since Walt's day; **Epcot** is a new-brew version of an old-style world's fair; **Disney's Animal Kingdom** blends animal habitats with theme-park panache; and **Disney's Hollywood Studios** presents a show-heavy salute to movies.

o **Universal Orlando:** Often surpassing Disney in adrenaline and cunning, Universal Orlando's two parks, **Islands of Adventure** and **Universal Studios Florida,** command respect, get the blood pumping a bit stronger, and are home to two immersive sections devoted to **The Wizarding World of Harry Potter.** The epic **Skull Island: Reign of Kong** is new this year.

o **Beyond Disney and Universal:** Venture beyond the Big Six theme parks and you'll find more breathing room and more focused experiences. The

The Wizarding World of Harry Potter's Leaky Cauldron at Universal Orlando Resort.

gardens and marine mammals at **SeaWorld Orlando** make for a slower-paced excursion. Five water parks flow with energy: **Typhoon Lagoon** and **Aquatica** for family-friendly slides, **Blizzard Beach** for more aggressive ones, **Wet 'n Wild** for no-holds-barred thrills, and **Discovery Cove** for VIP swims with dolphins and reef fish. South of town, **Legoland Florida,** one of the best parks for small children, charms with Old Florida touches, while **Gatorland** celebrates the region's *original* locals.

ORLANDO'S best RIDES & SHOWS

o **Walt Disney World:** More than any other park, the **Magic Kingdom** (p. 34) is packed with seminal experiences: the transporting Audio-Anima-tronic wizardry of **Pirates of the Caribbean** and **The Haunted Mansion;** the vertiginous thrills of **Splash Mountain** and **Space Mountain;** and the homespun, only-at-Disney charm of **Jungle Cruise, Peter Pan's Flight,** and **"it's a small world."** Cap the day with **Wishes,** the famous fireworks show. This year at **Epcot** (p. 67), **Frozen Ever After** begins its boat ride through Arendelle; and **Soarin',** the ride with the resort's highest re-ride ratio, increases capacity for shorter waits. At **Disney's Hollywood Studios** (p. 88) the ride-through 3-D video game **Toy Story Midway Mania** is never the same experience twice; while at **Disney's Animal Kingdom,** the nighttime lagoon show, **Rivers of Light,** debuts this year.

o **Universal Orlando:** At **Islands of Adventure** (p. 139), **Harry Potter and the Forbidden Journey** fires on more technological cylinders than you thought a ride could possess; **Skull Island: Reign of Kong** is the latest blockbuster ride; and **The Amazing Adventures of Spider-Man** has been

Fireworks show at Magic Kingdom.

the standard holder for premium ride concepts for over a decade. But don't miss **Dudley Do-Right's Ripsaw Falls** or **Popeye & Bluto's Bilge-Rat Barges,** a pair of ingeniously sopping flumes. **The Wizarding World of Harry Potter: Diagon Alley** represents the cutting edge in visual design that believably immerses you in the world of the movies and the **Escape from Gringotts** ride is a technological tour de force. Fans of Springfield will find themselves re-riding **The Simpsons Ride** to catch all the insider references.

o **The Other Parks:** At **SeaWorld Orlando** (p. 153), roller coasters pack punches that Disney pulls: **Mako,** new this year, is Orlando's tallest, fastest, longest coaster; **Manta** flies riders belly-down over water and rooftops; while **Kraken** dangles their feet for seven spine-knotting inversions. Its two

The Amazing Adventures of Spider-Man at Universal Orlando Resort.

Manta dips a wing at SeaWorld Orlando.

polar pavilions, **Wild Arctic** and **Antarctica,** are among its best habitats. The controversial killer whale show, currently **One Ocean,** is perennially packed. Elsewhere, **Wet 'n Wild's** is in its final season after 39 years (it closes on December 31, 2016), while **Legoland Florida's** tricked-out **Miniland USA** (p. 169) is such a masterpiece of Lego creations that it's a show of its own.

ORLANDO'S best OVERLOOKED EXPERIENCES

o **From Earth to the Moon:** The **Kennedy Space Center** (p. 191) sent Americans into space for more than half a century, and for decades NASA's nerve center was the focus of tourist attention, but a majority of today's visitors remain securely within Disney's orbit. That's a tragedy. The Kennedy Center is where you can see proof of America's glory days as an exploratory power, including some out-of-this-world space vehicles such as the **Saturn V rocket,** the largest rocket made, which sent 27 men to the moon; the **Space Shuttle orbiter** *Atlantis,* still coated with space dust; and the only public remnants of the two space shuttles America lost.

o **Connecting with Others:** More Make-a-Wish kids request visits to Orlando than any other dream, and you can help make those wishes come true at the resort built just for them, **Give Kids the World Village** (p. 188). There are hundreds of jobs for volunteers (many of which can be done in just a few hours), including handing out gifts or scooping ice cream. And since the late 1800s, moss-draped **Cassadaga** (p. 183) has been the domain of psychics and mediums who invite visitors to explore their spiritualist town.

o **Undiscovered Disney:** Even inside the theme parks, as other guests stampede for the nearest thrill ride, you can find relatively off-the-beaten-path treasures. The most fruitful ground for those is **Epcot**'s World Showcase, where many pavilions contain little-seen museums to the heritage of their lands, including the **Stave Church Gallery** in Norway (p. 58), China's

House of the Whispering Willow (p. 58), the **Bijutsu-kan Gallery** in Japan (p. 81), and the **Moroccan Style** gallery of arts in Morocco (p. 81). At the Magic Kingdom, you can get a haircut at Main Street's **Harmony Barber Shop** (p. 42). And the entire Disney World resort offers a slate of small-group **behind-the-scenes tours** (p. 97) that uncover hundreds of secrets.

ORLANDO'S best AUTHENTIC EXPERIENCES

o **Florida, Your Eden:** Although the theme parks now define Orlando, Central Florida has a long tale of its own, if you're willing to listen. There are more fresh springs here than in any other American state. You'll always remember swimming in the 72-degree waters of **De Leon Springs State Park** (p. 201), canoeing at **Wekiwa Springs State Park** (p. 202), or meeting at-risk manatees in their natural habitat at **Blue Spring State Park** (p. 200).

o **Florida, the Gilded Age Idyll:** Of course, Orlando's identity as a sunny theme-park mecca only began in 1971, but visitors from the north have been coming for a century. Sample the fine art collected by its high-society settlers at Winter Park's **Charles Hosmer Morse Museum of American Art** (including a massive collection of Tiffany glass; p. 184) or the **Cornell Fine Arts Museum** (with lush decorative arts of every description; p. 185). Peep at their historic mansions, whose lawns slope invitingly to the tranquil lakes of Winter Park, on the long-running **Scenic Boat Tour** (p. 203).

o **Florida, Land of Flowers:** The reason all those blue bloods migrated here? The fine weather and beautiful water. The horticultural achievements at **Harry P. Leu Gardens** (p. 201), practically smack in the middle of downtown Orlando, remind you just how bountiful the soil here can be. Or lose yourself at **Bok Tower Gardens** (p. 186), whose builder set out to create a Taj Mahal for America; its landscaping is by Frederick Law Olmsted, Jr., whose other work includes the White House and the National Mall.

o **Florida, the Original Tourist Draw:** Today, nothing is more quintessentially Orlando than Disney, but a few other major attractions never feel jammed: **Legoland Florida** (p. 168) ambles pleasantly on a lakeside that was once home to Cypress Gardens, Florida's original mega-park and a haunt for everyone from Esther Williams to Elvis Presley. Its historic botanical garden has been prized since the 1930s. **Gatorland** (p. 187) is a pleasing, corn-fed throwback from an era when Central Florida was synonymous with reptiles rather than the Mouse.

ORLANDO'S best HOTELS

o **Inside the Theme Park Resorts: Disney's Contemporary Resort** (p. 255) and **Disney's Polynesian Village Resort** (p. 257), which opened in 1971, have become architectural landmarks, and their location on the monorail

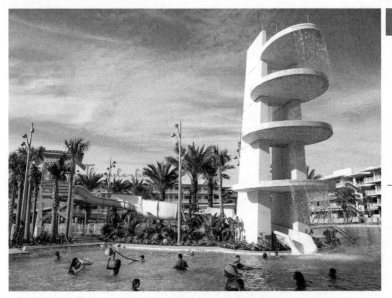

Courtyard pool at Cabana Bay Beach Resort at Universal Orlando Resort.

system makes a vacation easy and fun, but **Disney's Art of Animation Resort** (p. 262) elevates the resort's lowest-priced rooms into something approaching immersive. Universal's **Cabana Bay Beach Resort** (opened 2014, p. 269) applies a layer of Miami style to its own budget category and its **Sapphire Falls Resort** is also brand new. The **Four Seasons Resort Orlando,** on Walt Disney World property, delivers a level of luxury that's a revelation among theme park hotels (p. 264).

o **Full-Service Resorts Outside the Parks:** Exquisite restaurants and unbeatable pool areas make the Grande Lakes' **JW Marriott** and the **Ritz-Carlton** (p. 282) two names to beat among Orlando's luxury resorts, while the **Waldorf Astoria** (p. 265) translates Park Avenue pomp to Florida style. Taking theme-park flair to a hospitality extreme, the colossal atrium of **Gaylord Palms** (p. 273) is like a big top for eye candy.

o **Affordability Without Sacrifice:** Not all affordable hotels are shabby. **Drury Inn Suites** (p. 282), **Avanti Resort Orlando** (p. 284), and **Fairfield Inn Orlando International Drive/Convention Center** (p. 284) offer just-built rooms near the action for around $100 a night, while the **B Resort** (p. 266) puts you in a South Beach–styled resort right on Disney property for the middle $100s. **WorldQuest Resort** (p. 276) and **Meliá Orlando Suite Hotel at Celebration** (p. 271) have style and space but not the crowds and offer one-bedroom units from $129. Or rent a full house, as tastefully furnished as if you lived there, from **All Star Vacation Homes** (p. 287).

ORLANDO'S best RESTAURANTS

o **The Most Memorable Meals at the Resorts:** Orlando is one of those places where even blasé restaurants are priced like splurges, but some special-occasion tables deliver on their promise, like **California Grill** (overlooking the Magic Kingdom fireworks; p. 216), the just-refreshed options at **Disney Springs** (which used to be called Downtown Disney, p. 218); **Boma** (an all-you-can-eat feast in a hotel where you can watch African animals roam; p. 216); and the famous **character meals,** where your fuzzy hosts serve up family memories (p. 242).

o **Finding Family-Run Places to Eat:** Some fab restaurants, many family-run, have been unfairly elbowed into the background by same-old chains. These include **Bruno's Italian Restaurant** (*abbondanza!* right in the franchise zone of Disney, too!; p. 226); **Nile Ethiopian Cuisine** (authentically African, down to the coffee ceremony, near Disney; p. 231); **Havana's Cuban Cuisine** (the real stuff, from steak to plantains, right by Disney; p. 228); and **Arepas El Cacao** (p. 233), whose overstuffed Venezuelan flatbread sandwiches first gained popularity as food truck fare.

o **Big Style, Local Flavors:** Get in touch with the locals: The veggie chili at the friendly hangout **Dandelion Communitea Cafe** (p. 236) is to die for, and the quirky personalities of homegrown **Funky Monkey Wine Company** (p. 230) and **Maxine's on Shine** (p. 235), are seductive fun. Above all, the sensationally priced Vietnamese district of **Mills Fifty** (p. 237) is a revelation. Yes, as it turns out, there are still dining secrets in this town.

SUGGESTED ITINERARIES & ORLANDO'S LAYOUT

D isney doesn't want you to be spontaneous. It wants to lock you into a timetable so you never have a chance to spend money elsewhere in town. One Disney Parks president was shockingly frank about the tactic in Bloomberg Businessweek: "If we can get people to plan their vacation before they leave home, we know that we get more time with them. We get a bigger share of their wallet." The result: Researching a Disney vacation can now seem more involved than learning the federal tax code, and guidebooks can be as fat as bricks.

Excessive pre-planning isn't fun. Too much research is stressful and spoils the delight of Disney's many surprises. If you're not careful, you'll spend half your time at Disney hunched over your smartphone, battery dwindling, trying to keep up with your own plan. And at the end, you'll need a vacation from your vacation.

That's where the Frommer's Easy Guide comes in. This is the guidebook for the rest of us—for those of us who refuse to turn a Disney vacation into a part-time job. This book, a feat of compression, makes Disney easy, and with it you don't have to submit to the pressure of overplanning to have the whole World in your hands.

The routes suggested here, loose enough to let the magic in, prioritize what's worth seeing and when. Observe the basic park patterns and you'll do just fine. These itineraries assume mild lines (so, not peak season), and if you would like to try a specific table-service restaurant, it's imperative you arrive with reservations, particularly for Cinderella's Royal Table and Be Our Guest. Instructions on how to schedule Fastpass are on p. 32.

THE SIX BIGGEST DISNEY mistakes

1. **Overplanning.** Disney World minutiae opens a deeper rabbit hole than Alice's.
2. **Underplanning.** You must plan a little or pay a price: To eat at the best sit-down restaurants or enjoy a character meal, it's wise to reserve 3 to 6 months out.
3. **Overpurchasing ticket options.** Don't bite off more than you can chew.
4. **Wearing inadequate footwear.** It's said you'll walk 10 miles a day.
5. **Neglecting sunscreen and water.** Even Florida's cloudy weather can burn. One bad day can ruin the ones that follow.
6. **Pushing kids too hard.** When they want to slow down, indulge them. You came here to enjoy yourselves, remember?

ORLANDO IN 1 DAY

Well, I'm sorry for you. Just as it's impossible to eat an entire box of Velveeta in one sitting (please don't try), you can't get the full breadth of Orlando in a single day.

Today: Make It a Magic Kingdom Day ★★★

Thankfully, one Orlando attraction is so quintessential that you can enjoy it all by itself: Walt Disney World's **Magic Kingdom** (p. 34). In chapter 3, I recommend three custom itineraries (p. 38) for how to parse your time—with or without kids—but no matter your age or inclination, don't miss the great Disney Audio-Animatronic odysseys **Pirates of the Caribbean ★★★**, **Haunted Mansion ★★★**, and **"it's a small world" ★★★**, and be sure to brave the drops of **Splash Mountain ★★★** and **Space Mountain ★★★**. While you're there, take a free spin on the **monorail** through the iconic **Contemporary Resort** after you connect for the free round-trip ride to **Epcot** (p. 47), where you'll see the other top Disney

Splash Mountain.

Fine-Tuning Your Tour Day

Planning a day in the theme parks isn't always a day at the beach, so for more recommendations on making the most of your time at WDW, see our handy charts on p. 38, 49, 71, 81, and 88.

park from above. Stay until closing, through the **parade** and **fireworks,** or, if you've had enough, head to a kitschy dinner banquet spectacle such as **the Hoop-Dee-Doo Musical Revue ★★** (p. 241). Hope you're not hungry for subtlety!

ORLANDO IN 2 DAYS

Nope, still can't do much, but in two sleeps you can still get a few flavors in.

Day 1: Magic Kingdom

Get the same early start as recommended in "Orlando in 1 Day" and follow the **Magic Kingdom** plan for sure.

Day 2: Universal Orlando ★★★ or Epcot ★★★

Today, arrive at **Universal Orlando** (p. 121), one of the most attractive theme park complexes in the country, for opening. At its **Studios** park, dive into the new Diagon Alley, the section of the **Wizarding World of Harry Potter ★★★** that opened in July 2014, before the lines grow. Explore the shops, full of bespoke souvenirs and snacks you can only buy here, and give your system a dose of Butterbeer. After lunch at the **Leaky Cauldron ★★★**, you have a decision to make. You can take the **Hogwarts Express** train to **Islands of Adventure** (you'll need a second park ticket) to tour the second Potter land of **Hogsmeade,** take a spin on the superlative **Amazing Adventures of Spider-Man ★★★**, and jolt yourself on **The Incredible Hulk Coaster ★★★**. Your alternative is to spend most of the day in **Epcot** (p. 67). At Epcot, be sure to visit **Future World,** including **Soarin' ★★★** and the traditional Disney experience,

Riders experience the power of the Incredible Hulk.

Spaceship Earth ★★★, then make your way clockwise around **World Showcase** by dinnertime to select the ethnic eatery that catches your fancy, be it in **Mexico** ★★★, **Japan** ★★★, or **Morocco** ★★★. Or stop at the central **U.S.A.** ★★★ pavilion for a good, old-fashioned hot dog. At 9pm, you'll be in the right place for **IllumiNations** ★★★, part kumbaya and part explosives spectacular. If you *really* want to see a lot and have cash and energy to burn, do Harry Potter in the morning and then schlep back down I-4 to visit Epcot in the late afternoon and evening—eat your Wheaties!

ORLANDO IN 3 DAYS
Days 1–2: Magic Kingdom & Universal Orlando

Day 1: Magic Kingdom, as above. But on **Day 2,** slam through the highlights of the Universal parks with a 1-day, 2-park pass. In the morning, see **Islands of Adventure** ★★★, as on the second day of the 2-day plan, and fill the afternoon with Universal Studios. Don't neglect some of its celebrated new rides—**Transformers: The Ride—3D** ★★ and **Harry Potter and the Escape from Gringotts** ★★★ in the new **Wizarding World of Harry Potter—Diagon Alley.** Exploring that area will more than complete your day, but if you still have time, fill up on the sarcastically named dishes at **Fast Food Boulevard** (p. 137) in the new and daringly whimsical **Springfield** addition.

Day 3: SeaWorld ★★★, Disney & a Taste of "Real" Orlando

If you have small kids or you need something more subdued today, then **SeaWorld Orlando** (p. 153), with its many marine animal habitats, isn't as exhausting as Disney. That could take a whole day if you saw every little thing and stopped to smell the flowers (and fish), but you can see the highlights in 4 hours, and you only have 3 days, after all. So cram a secondary Disney park into your afternoon and evening. **Epcot** is a fine choice (see the afternoon of Day 2 of the 2-day itinerary for a good plan), but **Disney's Animal Kingdom**'s ★★ wildlife walking trails make a nice, easygoing complement to a morning spent at SeaWorld. Animal Kingdom isn't a late-night park, so during the evening, spend a night at the shopping-and-clubs zone of Universal's **CityWalk** ★★ (p. 124) or go out into "real" Orlando for the Vietnamese culinary delights of **Mills Fifty** (p. 237) downtown.

ORLANDO IN 1 WEEK
Days 1–5: Orlando at Your Leisure

Finally—you're approaching a vacation long enough to enable you to actually relax and take time to sit by the pool. Now you don't have to cram several parks into a single day unless you want to, so take more

"Finding Nemo—The Musical" at Animal Kingdom.

time on your first few days: first **Magic Kingdom,** then **Universal,** then **Epcot,** then the other two Disney parks, followed by **SeaWorld.** Of course, if you stick to a schedule as rigid as one major theme park per day, it will take you a week to knock down the seven biggies, and that's before setting your belly on a single water slide. Combining **Animal Kingdom** and **Hollywood Studios** ★★★ into a single day (see p. 108 for suggestions for how to pack it all in) is doable and won't cause you to miss too much, although with the opening of the second Harry Potter land, the same can no longer be said for Universal's parks—now they require a day and a half, at least. This combination lets you do the seven major parks in 5 days.

Days 6–7: Exploring Orlando beyond the Theme Parks

Hitting the big seven in 5 days leaves 2 days to get away from the dizzying pressures of theme parking. Take a day to drive out to **Kennedy Space Center** ★★★ (p. 191), or if that's still too touristy for you, take a dip in a natural spring, such as **De Leon Springs** ★★★ (p. 201), and make a pass through the American original town of **Cassadaga** ★★★ (p. 183). It would be a shame to miss a collection as world class as the **Morse Museum**'s ★★★ (p. 184) astonishing Tiffany glass. While you're there, take a late-afternoon boat cruise past the mansions of **Winter Park** (p. 184)—when you're out on the water, you'll finally get a feeling for the "real" Florida that attracted the builders of the major resorts in the first place. Afterward, you'll be near some of Orlando's **best restaurants,** most of which the tourists never visit. Also, 2016 is the last year to catch a ride at Wet 'n Wild, the first great American water slide park—it's being torn down.

Universal Orlando, with its air-conditioned shows, waiting areas, and covered parking, is the best choice to escape a **rainy day** because almost nothing must shut down in a storm. At Disney, Hollywood Studios is the best rainy-day park because most of its activities, including its two biggest thrill rides, are inside. SeaWorld, where you'll spend lots of time outside, is the worst in rain. If it's a **scorcher,** both Universal Studios and Disney's Hollywood Studios have enough sheltered activities to offer heat relief—although, of course, your hotel pool holds water as a heat reliever, too. On the hottest days, the water slide parks are swarming (of course). The worst Disney park on hot or wet days is **Disney's Animal Kingdom,** where next to nothing is indoors. But if there is a big storm, don't leave! Rain may last all day back home, but in Florida, it usually clears in an hour.

GETTING TO KNOW ORLANDO'S LAYOUT

In 1970, before the opening of Walt Disney World, Orlando was still a tourism center, attracting 660,000 people a year. But by 1999, the place was a powerhouse, with 37.9 million people visiting. The area population also skyrocketed from 344,000 to 860,000, leapfrogging such old-guard American cities as St. Louis; Washington, D.C.; Boston; Baltimore; and Portland.

However, for all that growth, and despite the fact the amusements are critical to Orlando's economy, most of the population still lives north of SeaWorld. The tourist zones are segregated from residential ones. Huge chunks of your time, days at a stretch, will be spent only in the boisterously inauthentic tourist corridors. Those lie along International Drive, U.S. 192 around I-4, and the Lake Buena Vista area north of exit 68 off I-4.

The Making of a Kingdom

Back when only cargo trains had much business in Central Florida, Orlando fashioned itself as a prosperous small city—some derisively called it a cow town—well positioned to serve the citrus and cattle industries as they shipped goods between America and Cuba. The city remained that way, mostly irrelevant, until around 1943, when the great cross-state cattle drives ended.

Soon after, the brick-warehouse city of Orlando developed its second personality. The turning point wasn't the arrival of Walt Disney on his secret land-buying trips. It came a decade earlier, when NASA settled into the Space Coast, 45 minutes east, and the local government, spotting opportunity, invited the Martin Marietta corporation—now Lockheed Martin—to open a massive facility off Sand Lake Road, near the present-day Convention Center. To sweeten the deal, leaders promised unprecedented civic improvements, including an unrealized high-speed rail system they're *still* bickering about. Mostly, though, politicians built roads. Florida's Turnpike to Miami was

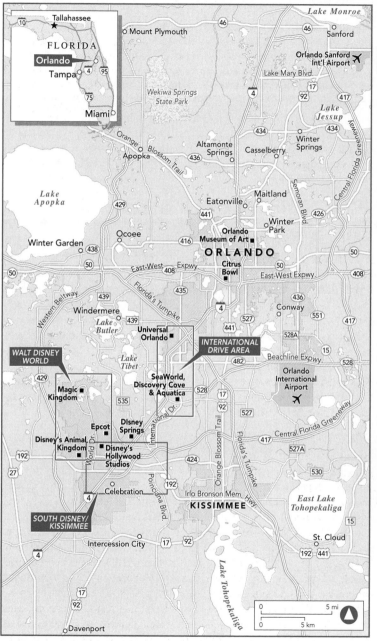

carved past the Martin plot, S.R. 50 was hammered through downtown to link the coasts, and, soon after, many blocks in the downtown area were bulldozed for the construction of I-4, linking Tampa on the west coast with Daytona Beach (then one of America's premier vacation towns) on the east coast. The new transit links made Walt lick his chops for some cheap land nearby.

Walt's new kingdom was constructed 20 miles southwest of the city in scrubland, where his planners could keep the outside world at bay. The resort was intended to be an oasis in the citrus groves, but soon, sprawl sprouted around the park's border, just as had happened in Anaheim. For the last two generations, the space between Orlando's two disparate developments has vanished, consumed by areas where "real" Orlando residents live, so that the old-fashioned, "traditional" city has come to be dwarfed, as it were, by family-friendly honky-tonk and slapped-up suburbs. Few casual visitors ever lay eyes on the real Orlando.

The Neighborhoods in Brief

Following is a breakdown of Orlando's neighborhoods—from theme parks to residential areas.

WALT DISNEY WORLD RESORT

Best for: *Space, theme parks, a sense of place, proximity to His Mouseness*

What you won't find: *Inexpensive food or lodging, a central location for anything except Disney attractions, the "real" Florida or Orlando*

Walt Disney World is at the southern end of Orlando's chain of big parks, so to see Universal, SeaWorld, and Orlando itself, you'll always head north on I-4.

When Walt Disney ordered the purchase of these 27,000 acres mostly just west of Interstate 4, he was righting a wrong he committed in the building of Anaheim's Disneyland. In commandeering as much land as he did, he ensured that visitors would not be troubled by the clatter of motel signs and cheap restaurants that abut his original playground. "Here in Florida," he said in a promotional film shot months before his death, "we have something special we never enjoyed at Disneyland . . . the blessing of size. There's enough land here to hold all the ideas and plans we can possibly imagine." You could spend your entire vacation without leaving the greenery of the resort, and lots of people do, although they're missing a lot. The idea to remain solely on Disney property is outdated now that Universal has proven itself. Still, there's an awful lot to do

spread around here, starting with four of the world's most polished theme parks, two of the best water parks, four golf courses, two miniature golf courses, a racecar track, a sports pavilion, and a huge shopping-and-entertainment district.

First-time visitors aren't usually prepared for quite how *large* the area is: 47 (roughly rectangular) square miles. Only a third of that land is truly developed, and another third has been set aside as a permanent reserve for swampland. Major elements are easily a 10-minute drive away from each other, with nothing but trees or Disney hotels between them. The Magic Kingdom is buried deep in the back of the park—which is to say, the north of it, requiring the most driving time to reach. Epcot and Hollywood Studios are in the center, while Disney's Animal Kingdom is at the southwest of the property, closest to the real world.

For its convenience, Disney **signposts hotels and attractions** according to the major theme park they're near. If you are staying on property, you'll need to know which area your hotel is in. For example, the All-Star resorts are considered to be in the Animal Kingdom area, and so some signs may simply read Animal Kingdom Resort Area and leave off the name of your hotel. Ask for your hotel's designated area when you reserve.

Getting in is easy. Every artery in town is naggingly signposted for Disney World. Exits are marked, but it helps to know the name of the main road that feeds your hotel. A few useful **secret exits** are not marked on official Disney maps. One is **Western Way,** which turns past Coronado Springs resort and skirts the back of Animal Kingdom to reach many vacation home communities southwest of Disney. Be warned that taking 429 to U.S. 192 will cost more than a buck in tolls.

There's a second useful shortcut out of the resort: **Sherberth Road,** by the entrance to Animal Kingdom Lodge, about a mile west of the entrance to Animal Kingdom, leads to cheap eats on western U.S. 192.

It's interesting to note that when you're at Disney, you're in a separate governmental zone. The resort's bizarre experiments in building methods (such as fiberglass-and-steel castles) are partly enabled by the fact that Disney negotiated the creation of its own entity, the Reedy Creek Improvement District, which can set its own standards. When you see vehicles marked RCID, those are the civic services for the resort. Not far down the road by Downtown Disney Marketplace—a route not used by many guests—pass by the R.C. Fire Department, a toylike engine house with an outdoor fountain that looks like a spouting fire hose.

Disney developed a bit of land east of I-4 into the New Urbanism unincorporated town of **Celebration.** As a Stepford-like residential center with upscale aspirations (golf, boutiques), there's not much to do there except eat a bit in its town square. Be prepared to parallel park there.

U.S. 192 & KISSIMMEE

Best for: *Value, chain restaurant and motel options, downscale attractions*

What you won't find: *Subtlety, luxury*

No matter how Orlando changes, it's Kissimmee (Kiss-*im*-ee), the ridiculed little sister, that lags behind. Where the southern edge of the Disney resort property touches Hwy. U.S. 192, the clamor begins, stretching 10 miles west and a good 10 miles east. This ostentatious drag, known also as the Irlo Bronson Memorial Highway (after the state

senator who sold Walt a lot of land), is the spine of Kissimmee, and it's your Budget Rialto for food and beds, so plug the K-word into the location box of your Web searches. It's also the best place to find that all-American kitsch you might be looking for—nowhere else in town will you find a souvenir store shaped like a giant orange half, and isn't that a shame?

In the early 1970s, Kissimmee was the prime place to stay. The motels weren't flashy then, and they still aren't, but they're ever affordable—$50 to $80 is the norm, and some shabby places go down to $39 for a single or $45 for a double. Kissimmee's downtown, about 10 miles east of Disney, is a typical Florida burg with a main street by a lake, and its quickly growing subdivisions have become popular among Hispanic families, although that doesn't translate into accessible restaurants serving ethnic cuisine. U.S. 192 is mostly about chains and buffets.

The best way to get your bearings on U.S. 192 is using its clearly signposted **mile marker system.** U.S. 192 hits Disney's southern entrance (the most expedient avenue to the major theme parks) at Mile Marker 7, while I-4's exit 65 connects with it around Mile Marker 8. Numbers go down to the west, and they go up to the east. Western 192, where the bulk of the vacation home developments are found, is much more upscale than the tacky wilds of eastern 192, but neither stretch could be termed swanky or well planned. Although Osceola County has strived to beautify the tourist corridor, it's been inept in the effort; once, the county cut down stands of myrtle trees in the median of U.S. 192 because they blocked the view of the billboards. That should tell you all you need to know about the standards in Kissimmee.

LAKE BUENA VISTA

Best for: *Access to Disney, I-4 and chain restaurants, some elbow room*

What you won't find: *The lowest prices, a sense of place*

Lake Buena Vista, a hotel enclave east of Downtown Disney/Disney Springs, clusters on the eastern fringe of Walt Disney World. LBV is technically a town, but it doesn't look like one. It's mostly hotels and mid-priced chain restaurants with some schlocky souvenir stores thrown in. The proximity of I-4 exit 68 can back traffic up, but it's convenient to Disney's crowded side door, which is helpful. The bottom line is that LBV is less tacky and higher rent than Kissimmee's 192, but it's also still a Disney-centric area and not really part of Orlando's fabric.

If you stay in LBV, you can also (if you're hardy) walk to the Downtown Disney development, where you can then pick up Disney's free DTS bus system. That could save you the cost of a rental car.

INTERNATIONAL DRIVE

Best for: *Walkability, cheap transportation, sit-down chain food, kitschy tourist attractions, proximity to Universal and SeaWorld*

What you won't find: *Space, style*

Although a developing stretch of this street winds all the way south to U.S. 192, when people refer to International Drive, they usually mean the segment between SeaWorld and Universal Orlando, just east of I-4 between exits 71 and 75. I-Drive, as it's called, is probably the only district where you might comfortably stay without a car and still be able to see the non-Disney attractions, because it's chockablock with

affordable hotels (not as ratty as some on U.S. 192 can be) and plenty of crowd-pleasing things to see, such as arcades, T-shirt shops, buffets, and the Orlando Eye (p. 176). The cheap I-Ride Trolley (p. 293) traverses the area on a regular schedule.

The intersection at Sand Lake Road is a dividing line for I-Drive's personalities. North of Sand Lake Road, within the orbit of Universal Orlando and Wet 'n Wild, midway rides and the ice-cream shops prevail. South of Sand Lake, closer to SeaWorld, there's a business-y crowd at the mighty Orange County Convention Center, located on both sides of I-Drive at the Bee Line Expressway/528. It keeps the surrounding hotels (and streets) full. On this part of I-Drive, bars and midscale restaurants rule. West on Sand Lake Road past I-4, you'll find a mile-long procession of mid- to upper-level places to eat that the city dubs its "Restaurant Row."

I-Drive does an east-west dogleg where it runs into I-4, and north of I-4 at Universal Boulevard, you'll find Universal Orlando's resort, which after dark is more popular with locals than Disney's.

Hotel and restaurant discounts may be posted on the area's business association and promotional website, **www.international driveorlando.com**.

Wonder Works Museum on International Drive.

Downtown Orlando and Lake Eola.

DOWNTOWN ORLANDO

Best for: *Historic buildings, cafes, museums, fine art, wealthy residents*

What you won't find: *Theme parks, easy commutes*

Like in so many American cities, residents fled from downtown in the 1960s through the 1980s, although spacious new condo developments have rescued the city from abandonment. Downtown Orlando is gradually being rediscovered by young, upscale residents. Here are the highlights:

DOWNTOWN Beneath the city's collection of modest skyscrapers (mostly banking offices), you'll find municipal buildings (the main library, historic museums), a few upscale hotels (the Grand Bohemian, Courtyard at Lake Lucerne), and some attractive lakes, but little shopping. Orange Avenue, once a street of proud stone buildings and department stores, now comes alive mostly at night, when its former vaudeville halls and warehouses essay their new roles as nightclubs, especially around Church Street. The 43-acre Lake Eola Park, just east, is often cited as an area attraction, but in truth it's just your average city park, although the .9-mile path around its 23-acre sinkhole lake is good for joggers. Its swan boats (rent one for $15 for 30 min.) are city icons, as is the

central fountain from 1957; its unique Plexiglas skin is illuminated with a 6-minute light-and-water musical show nightly at 9:30pm. Just east of that, the streets turn to red brick and big trees shelter **Thornton Park** (along Washington St., Summerlin Ave., and Central Blvd.). It's noted for its alfresco European-style cafes, none especially inexpensive, but all pleasing, where waiters wear black and hip locals spend evenings and weekend brunches. West of downtown over I-4, the area called Parramore is a longtime neighborhood for African Americans (sadly, the interstate was built, in part, as a barrier). A mile north of downtown, **Loch Haven Park** basks in a wealth of museums (p. 184).

MILLS FIFTY Some old-timers call this area **Colonial Town** and new-timers may use **Mills 50,** but it's also the Vietnamese District at Mills, or ViMi (p. 237). Just north of downtown, at Colonial Drive and Mills Avenue, there's a midcentury neighborhood with the whiff of a faded 1950s strip mall (parking lots are hidden behind buildings). There, you can spend a top afternoon strolling through several omnibus Asian supermarkets stocked with exotic groceries and unique baked goods and parking yourself at one of the excellent mom-and-pop-style eateries (advertised by cheap stick-on letters and neon) serving food far more delicious than their limited budgets would suggest. Several stores whip up addictive, meat-stuffed baguette sandwiches called *bánh mi* for a quick $4 meal. You'll also find hobby and art-supply shops patronized by a burgeoning bohemian community. The two marginalized groups collaborate beautifully together.

WINTER PARK

Best for: *Fine art, cafes, strolls, galleries, lakes*

What you won't find: *Inexpensive shopping, easy theme-park access*

One of the city's most interesting areas, and one of the few that hasn't taken pains to erase its history, Winter Park was where, 100 years ago, upstart industrialists built winter homes at a time when they couldn't gain entree into the more exclusive, more WASP-y enclaves of Newport or Palm Beach. The town blends seamlessly with northern Orlando (you can drive between them in a few minutes without getting onto I-4) and is still pretty full of itself, and its expensive tastes, but cruising on its brick-paved streets, gawking at mansions built on its chain of lakes, will remind you of the good life. Newspapers and magazines write about Winter Park like it's the hottest thing going, but in all honesty, it's just a nice place to pass an afternoon or evening. In the shops on Park Avenue, you'll find mostly jewelry, art, and south of it, stroll the country-club campus of Rollins College. The town's long-running boat tour (p. 203) is the best way to sample the opulence. The best art museum around, the Morse (p. 184), holds the most inspiring collection of Tiffany glass you will ever see. West of Winter Park, over I-4, the district of College Park, centering around Princeton Street and Edgewater Drive, hosts restaurants and boutiques that bring the area favor.

NORTH OF ORLANDO

Most visitors who venture into the suburban towns north of Winter Park do so to visit some of the area's natural springs or state parks (p. 200) or to connect with the spirits in the hamlet of Cassadaga (p. 183). After you've seen these places, there is little to engage you until you hit the Atlantic Coast on I-4.

SOUTH OF ORLANDO

Only in the past few years has the rural-minded swampland southwest of the resort and Kissimmee begun to be built upon in earnest, and the 65-mile run along I-4 to Tampa is gradually filling in with developments and golf courses. This patch of the Green Swamp, in which the two cities will one day merge into a megalopolis, is now casually dubbed "Orlampa." In Tampa, you'll find the excellent Busch Gardens (p. 171), a worthy addition to an amusement-park itinerary, and an hour straight south of Orlando, in the town of Winter Haven, is Legoland Florida (p. 168), a super kiddie park built at Florida's most historic amusement park.

EAST OF ORLANDO

The entrance to Orlando International Airport is 11 miles east of I-4, webbed into the city network by toll highways and surrounded by golfing developments. Across empty swamp from there, the so-called Space Coast, of which Cape Canaveral is the metaphoric capital (see it at Kennedy Space Center; p. 191), is a 45-minute drive east of Orlando's tourist corridor via 528, also known as the Bee Line Expressway.

WEST OF ORLANDO

Because the Green Swamp commands the area, there simply isn't much west of the tourist corridor save a few small towns and some state parks, such as Lake Louisa.

EXPLORING WALT DISNEY WORLD

On November 22, 1963, around the time President John Kennedy was embarking on his public motorcade in Dallas, Walt Disney was in a private jet, conducting his first flyover of some ignored Florida swampland. By the end of the day, as Disney decided this was the place he wanted to shape in the image of his dreams, America had changed in more ways than one.

While the country reeled, Disney snapped up land through dummy companies. His cover was blown in 1965, but the fix was in: His company had mopped up an area twice the size of Manhattan, 27,443 acres, from just $180 an acre. Disneyland East was coming. Today, it's the most popular vacation destination on the planet, and its four theme parks receive more than 50 million combined visits a year.

It's no accident that Walt, a seller of fantasies, enjoyed his peaks during two periods of profound malaise: the Great Depression and the Cold War. It's also no coincidence that his theme parks flowered while America was riven with self-doubt—the Korean and Vietnam conflicts, the death of Kennedy, and Watergate. His parks are, by design, comforting. They tell you how to feel and where to go, and in reinforcing uncomplicated impressions of history and the world, they never make you feel stupid or left behind. Ironically, what made his reassuring message of simplicity work was complex intelligence, specifically, the relentless drive for technological innovation and revolutionary engineering.

Why should it be so difficult to find straight talk about such an immensely popular place? Disney fans rhapsodize about the "magic"—that intangible *frisson* you feel when you're there—but I think a case could be made that the energy doesn't come from the place as much as it comes from the customers. Where else in your life will you be someplace surrounded by people so elated to be there? Walt Disney World's magic comes from the accumulated goodwill of strangers united in gratitude and togetherness. If you don't believe me, sit on a bench for a while in Fantasyland and

Walt Disney World & Lake Buena Vista

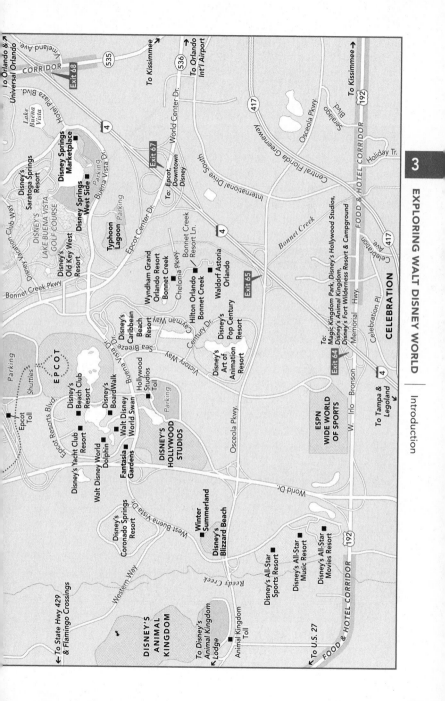

To Orlando & Universal Orlando

CORRIDOR

Exit 68

535

Vineland Ave.

To Kissimmee

536

To Orlando Int'l Airport

Lake Buena Vista

Hotel Plaza Blvd.

4

Disney Springs Marketplace

Parking

Buena Vista Dr.

Disney's Saratoga Springs Resort

Disney Springs West Side

Exit 67

To: Epcot, Downtown Disney

Epcot Center Dr.

417

Osceola Pkwy.

Serafago Blvd.

To Kissimmee

192

DISNEY'S LAKE BUENA VISTA GOLF COURSE

Typhoon Lagoon Parking

World Center Dr.

International Drive South

Holiday Tr.

FOOD & HOTEL CORRIDOR

Disney's Old Key West Resort

Bonnet Creek Pkwy.

Wyndham Grand Orlando Resort Bonnet Creek

Chelonia Pkwy.

Bonnet Creek Resort Ln.

Hilton Orlando Bonnet Creek

Waldorf Astoria Orlando

Exit 65

Bonnet Creek

4

Central Florida Greenway

417

Celebration Ave.

Celebration Pl.

CELEBRATION

Parking

Shuttles

EPCOT

Disney's Beach Club Resort

Disney's BoardWalk

Disney's Caribbean Beach Resort

Sea Breeze Dr.

Buena Vista Dr.

Cayman Way

Century Dr.

Disney's Pop Century Resort

Disney's Art of Animation Resort

Victory Way

To: Magic Kingdom Park, Disney's Hollywood Studios, Disney's Animal Kingdom, Disney's Fort Wilderness Resort & Campground

Memorial Hwy.

Celebration Pl.

Exit 64

4

To Tampa & Legoland

192

Epcot Toll

Epcot Resorts Blvd.

Disney's Yacht Club Resort

Walt Disney World Dolphin

Walt Disney World Swan

Fantasia Gardens

Hollywood Studios Toll

Parking

DISNEY'S HOLLYWOOD STUDIOS

Osceola Pkwy.

W. Irlo Bronson

ESPN WIDE WORLD OF SPORTS

World Dr.

To State Hwy 429 & Flamingo Crossings

Western Way

Disney's Coronado Springs Resort

West Buena Vista Dr.

Winter Summerland

Disney's Blizzard Beach

Reedy Creek

Disney's All-Star Sports Resort

Disney's All-Star Music Resort

Disney's All-Star Movies Resort

192

FOOD & HOTEL CORRIDOR

To U.S. 27

DISNEY'S ANIMAL KINGDOM

To Disney's Animal Kingdom Lodge

Animal Kingdom Toll

23

watch the children pass. Some 75% of Disney's visitors are return customers. There's just something about it.

But Disney World, transporting it may be, is a business, and it's brutally expensive. The average domestic overnight guest spends nearly $300 per day, and that's going higher: Visit Orlando reports the average household income of leisure visitors to the city was $95,720 in 2013 compared with $88,349 in 2012. Even people who love Disney agree it requires shrewd navigation.

TICKETING

Disney hikes prices every spring but attendance keeps growing; so don't expect it to relent. This will be the biggest expense, so assess your needs before laying down plastic. All park tickets (excepting annual passes) are purchased by the day. You decide how many days you want to spend at the parks, and once you nail that down, you decide which extras you want to pay for. Both decisions are fraught with temptation and the risk of overspending. It's possible Disney intentionally makes the process complicated so that customers spend more money than they have to.

Magic *Their* Way

We recommend visitors to Orlando spend the first 3 or 4 days of their week-long vacations at the Disney parks, and by the fourth or fifth days, move on to Universal Orlando, SeaWorld, and the Kennedy Space Center. However, the Disney resort uses Magic Your Way, a scaled pricing scheme that appears to reward people who stay on Disney turf for more than 4 days. The delayed economy of Magic Your Way is a honey trap that locks in purchases and entices families to stay on Disney property longer, spending more money. It crowds out anything non-Disney. Its structure also requires you to group your Disney days together or else pay for days you don't use.

Like on an airline, you add the options that you want. They are (including tax, rounded to the nearest dollar):

1. **Base ticket.** You must at least buy this. This is your theme park admission. With it, you are entitled to visit one park per day, with no switching to other parks on the same day. After 4 days, the biggest per-day discounts kick in. (My take for first timers: When it's all new to you, one park per day for 4 days, is plenty.)
2. **Park Hopper.** Should you crave the privilege of jumping from park to park on the same day (I recommend this for repeat visitors), you must add the Park Hopper option. With it, you can do the early-morning safari at Animal Kingdom, take a nap at your hotel, and then switch to the Magic Kingdom for the fireworks. This is a handy option to have, but you may decide you do not need it.
3. **Water Park Fun & More (WPF&M).** Should you plan to visit a Disney water slide park, play a round of mini-golf at one of Disney's two courses (only before 4pm), or see an event at the ESPN Wide World of Sports (a rarity), the Water Park Fun & More (WPF&M) option includes a

Disney Ticket Options*
Base Ticket

Days of Use	Age 10 & up	Age 3–9	Add Water Park Fun & More	Add Park Hopper
1	$112/103**	$105/97**	$68/$77** (2 visits)	$53/$62
2	$204	$191	$68 (2 visits)	$54
3	$293	$273	$68	$54
4	$325	$304	$68	$54
5	$335	$314	$68	$54
6	$346	$325	$68	$54
7	$357	$335	$68	$54
8	$367	$346	$68	$54
9	$378	$357	$68	$54
10	$389	$367	$68	$54

* Prices are rounded and include sales tax of 6% to 7.5%. Prices accurate as of summer 2015; rates rise every spring.

** The higher price is for the Magic Kingdom, and the second price applies to the other three theme parks. The Water Park Fun & More option adds visits equal to the number of park days on the ticket, except for the 1-day ticket, which includes two Water Park Fun & More visits.

set number of admissions. Many people buy this option and fail to use it. During the course of 3 days of theme park going, are you *really* going to have enough juice for water slides? Here's a bigger red flag: Even if you don't add WPF&M, you can still buy walk-up admission, and the walk-up price at Disney's water slide parks ($62 adults/$53 kids) is actually *cheaper* than buying this option. You may add WPF&M to your ticket once you arrive at Disney, but you'll still pay the rate applicable to your total length of stay. If you plan to buy *both* the Park Hopper and the WPF&M options, they come bundled for a flat-rate $96 add-on.

Note: A "No Expiration" option used to exist, but Disney killed it in 2015. Now tickets expire 14 days after you begin using them.

Very slight **discounts** on Magic Your Way tickets are available. Deals are listed at disneyworld.disney.go.com/special-offers and at MouseSavers.com. If you buy your tickets in advance (online or at a Disney Store), save the shipping fee by arranging to pick them up at the gates of one of the parks (long lines) or at Guest Relations in Disney Springs Marketplace (short line). **Florida residents** are offered entirely different discounts (www.disneyworld. disney.go.com/florida-residents) that come with blackout dates, as do **AAA members** and **active military;** if you're one, call © **407/824-4321** for the latest promotion. (See "Other Ticket 'Discounts' & Deals," below, for a more on potential discounts.)

During some times of year, the park mounts special evening events, such as the ones around Halloween and Christmas (see the calendar on p. 296) that require a separate, expensive ticket. You will get less value out of your Magic Your Way ticket if you attend during the day before one of these parties because if you haven't paid for the evening-event ticket, you'll be rounded up and sent out in late afternoon.

THE PERIL OF DISNEY PACKAGES

If you don't care about spending more than you have to, skip this section.

Disney lures you into overpurchasing. Anytime you call and ask for reservations, operators will suggest adding perks. You'll ask for tickets, and they'll suggest you throw in, say, the meal plan (p. 28). The instant you accept, you're purchasing a "package," and that will often force you to pay more than you would have a la carte. Always, *always* know what everything would cost separately before agreeing to a Disney-suggested package. If you must, hang up the phone and do some math before deciding to accept or reject the offer. Then call back for a new quote—prices can fluctuate each time you call. That's the only way to ensure you're not paying more.

Here's a hidden loophole that works against you: Disney "length of stay" ticket packages will begin the moment you arrive on the property and end the day you leave. Think about that. If you've just flown from a distant place, you are unlikely to rush to the Magic Kingdom on the same day. Likewise, on the day you're due at the airport to fly home, you may not to be able to visit a theme park. Yet Disney will schedule your package that way. In effect, you will lose 2 days that you've paid for—at the start and at the finish of your vacation, when you'll be resting or packing. That's colder than Elsa's heart.

How can you avoid this? You could 1) stay entirely at non-Disney hotels and just buy Magic Your Way tickets. You could 2) stay at a Disney hotel for your ticket days and stay off-site for the others. Or you could 3) insist on making **one reservation per phone call.** Arrange your tickets plus their corresponding hotel nights for your Disney days. Hang up. Call back and arrange "room-only" nights for your last night and any days you'll be leaving Disney during the day as "room only." It's vital that you do not link your two reservations in advance if you want the best price and the best cancellation policies, but you can link them after arrival. If you don't plan on seeing anything but Disney, of course, then you won't have to go through these lengths. But many people aren't satisfied by only visiting the Mouse.

Disney's reservationists are friendly, but they're sales-driven, and they are trained to answer *only* the questions that you pose. If you're not sure about the

contacting WALT DISNEY WORLD

Walt Disney World offers no toll-free numbers.

General information: www.disneyworld.com; ✆ 407/939-5277
Vacation packages: ✆ 407/934-7675
Room-only bookings: ✆ 407/939-7429
Operating hours, schedules: ✆ 407/824-4321
Dining reservations: ✆ 407/939-3463
Tickets: ✆ 407/939-1289
MagicBands, My Disney Experience, Fastpass+: ✆ 407/939-4357
Tour bookings: ✆ 407/939-8687
Lost and found: ✆ 407/824-4245

Disney has a culture all its own that visitors must learn to respect. That's why Disney is perhaps most successful with compliant personalities. Working at Disney World isn't like getting a job at the bank. WDW is billed as the Happiest Place on Earth. Many "cast members" live and breathe its way of life, and quite a few moved from other parts of the country to be a part of it. Be alert to the fact that many of them identify personally with the Disney Way (it exists) and they are often uncomfortable with comments that carry a hint of being argumentative. Try not to put Disney employees in a position of having to defend the company. And for heaven's sake, no cussing! That code is technically meant to apply only to cast members, but the unspoken cultural expectation is that you follow it, too. The flip side of this is that if something goes wrong with your visit, cast members will work to make it right and make your vacation a positive memory.

terms of what you're about to purchase, corner them and ask. Grill them about deposit and cancellation policies—they get stiffer if you're on a package. And *always* ask if there is a less expensive option. They won't lie and tell you there isn't, but they *will* neglect to volunteer the information. **TheMouseForLess. com**, **MouseSavers.com**, and the messages at **DISBoards.com** will let you know about current deals that Disney won't.

OTHER TICKET "DISCOUNTS" & DEALS

A few businesses shave a few paltry bucks off multiday tickets; see the last chapter (p. 299) for those. International visitors are eligible for tickets good for longer stays and unlimited WPF&M admissions, but only if they are purchased from abroad. At recent exchange rates, non-Americans may find it's cheaper to buy American-issued tickets with Park Hopper options at the gate; do the math. *Really* big fans carry a **Chase Disney Rewards Visa credit card** (www.chase.com/disney; © **800/300-8575**), which grants points to be redeemed on all things Disney, a few discounts, and a character meet-and-greet area just for cardholders.

EATING ON SITE

Theme parks worldwide thrive on excited, sugared-up children and parents who are too worn out to say "no" to such things as $9 hot dogs and $3 Cokes. At least the math at Disney World is easy. The **cheapest combo meals** are always from counter-service restaurants (called Quick Service in Disney-speak), and adults usually pay $10 to $12, including a side but not a drink. Kids' meals (a main dish; milk, juice, water, or soda; and a choice of two items including grapes, carrot sticks, applesauce, a cookie, or fries) always cost around $7 at Quick Service locations. If you want to sit down for waiter-service meal—character meals are always in sit-down restaurants—adults pay in the upper teens for a lunch entree and usually over $20 a plate at dinner, before gratuity or drinks, and kids' meals are about half as much. Disney

WHY YOU DON'T WANT THE
DISNEY dining plan

If you book at a Disney hotel, you will be offered the credit-based **Disney Dining Plan,** which prepurchases many of your meals. It is extremely complicated, with all kinds of rules, exclusions, and premium versions. Lots of people cave and buy it in the name of convenience, thinking it will make everything easier, but if you are a casual Disney visitor and not using it for things like character meals, it has other costs.

o **It's not cheap enough.** The least expensive plan, Quick Service, has a per-day cost of $42 adults, $16 kids, and includes two counter meals and one snack (like popcorn or ice cream), plus a refillable soft drink mug you can only use at a Disney hotel. Most adult quick-service meals cost $12 to $14 per meal using cash. Even if you spent $15, basic math proves that if you stick to two counter-service meals with no plan, plus one $4 snack, you'll spend about $34 versus $42 using the plan.

o **It's inflexible.** You must buy the plan for every night you stay at the hotel even though you may be exploring away from Disney on some days. You are not permitted to buy fewer days than your stay. *And* everyone in your group must be on it. Also, some menu items and food locations are excluded. Only those marked with the DDP logo count.

o **It costs time.** The forced use of sit-down restaurants clogs reservations months ahead of time. You'll have to do hours of advance planning and stick to a schedule. And table service eats more time than grabbing meals to go would.

o **It's impractical.** The basic plan ($61 adult, $19 kids, per night) buys the equivalent of one sit-down meal, one Quick Service meal, and a snack. If you want all three meals covered, you're looking at $110 adult/$30 kids each night. Few first-time visitors want that much daily table service at a theme park. Yet the plan has you doing that unless you use it for breakfast and buy dinner in cash. It starts to be of value *only* if you have a sit-down meal every single day, but remember: You have to book all of those meals weeks or months in advance.

o **It's incomplete.** The plan doesn't include tips (unless your party is six or more, in which case there's a mandatory 18% tip), alcoholic beverages, souvenir cups, and don't forget the basic plan also leaves out that third daily meal that you'll have to pay for.

o **It wastes.** Because it begins on the day you arrive, you're bound to leave with some unused credits, resulting in a loss.

Well, then, who is it for? For one, people who never intend to leave Disney property at all during their vacations—is that you? (Although some people get around this by cashing in their points for a character meal, which cost more than regular meals.) It's also a boon if you get it for free as part of a vacation package, which happens during some special sale periods. If it's free that way, grab it—paying nothing is always a win!

aggressively sells a Disney Dining Plan that takes away the need to pay a bill after each meal, but which comes with a lot of rules that dictate how and where you eat each day (see the sidebar "Why You Don't Want the Disney Dining Plan").

No longer can you simply stroll into any restaurant that catches your eye and enjoy a meal. Oversubscription to the Dining Plan spoiled the meal experience for everyone else. It's that simple, and that sad. **For table-service meals,** *always* **make reservations** (✆ **407/939-3463**) or you are likely to be turned away. Menus and prices are listed on the My Disney Experience app, where you can also reserve. If a restaurant is booked, try again 24 hours ahead, when people dump unwanted reservations before a $10 no-show penalty is assessed.

Semi-healthy options are possible on even the lowest food budget: Disney limits saturated fat and added sugar to 10% of a counter-service dish's calories; no more than 30% of a meal's calories or 35% of a snack's calories come from fat; and juice drinks have no added sugar. Trans fats are out. One way Disney seems to have accomplished this is by reducing serving sizes—you won't feel stuffed. Kids' meals come with carrots, applesauce, or grapes instead of fries, and with low-fat milk, water, or 100% fruit juice instead of soda. (Fries and Coke are still available by request—Disney knows kids are still on vacation and deserve a treat.)

NAVIGATING DISNEY'S PARKS

In summer and during other holidays, it's wise to get to the front gates of the park about 30 minutes ahead of opening, partly because you can waltz right onto a marquee ride that way. Try not to leave any park as it closes, when crowds surge and waits for the parking tram become burdensome. Instead, depart early or linger awhile in the shops, which will be open a bit longer than everything else.

PARKING   Each park has its own sunbaked parking lot ($17/day; free for Disney hotel guests and annual passholders). As you drive in, attendants will

The ferryboat from the parking lot to Magic Kingdom.

Disney wants you to use its free app, My Disney Experience (MDX), to make most of your arrangements, so it furnishes free in-park Wi-Fi. Once you create an account at MyDisneyExperience.com (surprise—Disney wants your birthday) and link your ticket number with it, MDX can:

o Book and re-schedule Fastpass+

o Display your location on park maps

o Show current wait times

o Show in-park schedules

o Show height and accessibility requirements

o Keep a schedule of your reservations

o Make and cancel restaurant reservations

o Manage PhotoPass account

o Buy tickets

When used in conjunction with a MagicBand, which detects your location, MDX can even send you movies and photos taken of you on rides—even if you didn't know they were being taken. (Obviously, it wants you to buy them once you see them.)

If everyone in your party links their tickets, it can also synchronize everyone's plans; for that to work best, select one of your group to be the Primary so everything goes through their account.

It's also supposed to keep you from having to make phone calls anymore, but of course things go wrong with a system as complex as this. Here's the help line: ✆ **407/939-4537.** Also, unfortunately for you, all that steady app time will have you glued to your smartphone for every hour of your supposedly transporting Disney vacation, and it will destroy your battery life, so pack some backup battery power.

3

Navigating Disney's Parks

EXPLORING WALT DISNEY WORLD

direct you to the next available spot. This is probably the most dangerous part of your day, because everyone is excited and you're at risk of hitting a distracted child or hitting an open car door—take it slow. Parking lanes are numbered and given names; at the very least, remember your number. Don't stress out if your row is a high number; at Epcot, for example, the front row is 27. (*Tip for remembering where you parked*: Open your phone's mapping app, zoom in, and stick a pin in your location. If you still forget, remember what time you arrived: Disney tracks which sections are being filled minute by minute.) You'll board one of the noisy trams (cross the yellow line to signal you're boarding; drivers never budge if someone's in that zone), which haul you to ticketing. At the Magic Kingdom, you still must take either the monorail or a ferryboat to the front gates; at the other parks, the tram lets you off near the gates.

SECURITY   Guests with bags larger than a small purse must queue at a checkpoint where they will open them for park security to probe with a stick. If you are not carrying a bag, there will be a faster entry portal for you. Banned: booze, glass containers, selfie sticks, wheelie sneakers. And weapons (duh).

TURNSTILES   To validate your ticket (see the box on MagicBands, p. 45), you must place a finger on a clear plate. That fingerprint is "married" to your ticket so that you can't give it to anyone else. Disney swears your personal

Getting ready to embark on Space Mountain.

information is eventually expunged from the system, but what it doesn't publicize is that if you do not wish for your fingerprint to be scanned, you may use standard identification instead, right there at the gate.

ORIENTATION Once you get inside the gates at all the parks, be sure to grab two free things that are kept in conspicuous racks: a **"Guidemap"** and a **"Times Guide"** listing the day's schedule, including for shows, places to eat, and attractions with shorter hours (Animal Kingdom also has an **Animal Guide**). Also, cast members carry full schedules (it's called the "Tell-A-Cast"), or you can ask at the park's **Guest Relations** desk (marked on the maps, always near the front; **Guest Services,** outside the gates, is mostly for ticket issues). The wait time for any attraction is posted where its line begins; this number is roughly accurate, although Disney often pads it by 5 minutes to give a sense of exceeded expectations.

SIZE RESTRICTIONS They're on the maps. Take them seriously. They are always enforced. At Splash Mountain, Space Mountain, Mission: SPACE, and a few other major rides, kids who are sized out may be offered a card entitling them to jump to the head of the line when they finally grow tall enough. (At Space Mountain, it dubs them a "Mousetronaut," at Splash Mountain, a "Future Splash Mountaineer.") If there is a sample of the ride vehicle out front, you can try it (or make it a photo op) before joining the line.

FOOD Gone are the days when you could decide on a whim to have a table-service dinner. The Disney Dining Plan (p. 28) wrecked that. Now you must plan ahead by racking up Advance Dining Reservations, called ADRs, or risk waiting for cancellations that may not materialize. Having a reservation does not mean you will sit down at that time. There is frequently a wait anyway. If you have no reservations, you'll be eating from counter service spots.

Breakfast ends around 10:30am, and lunch service generally goes from 11:30am to 2:30 or 3pm. Prices for buffets and character meals shift according

using FASTPASS+

Your ticket entitles you to Fastpass+ (technically, it's in all caps), which lets you make a timed reservation for an attraction and scan your ticket card or MagicBand to check in at the appointed hour, bypassing the main line and cutting out lots of waiting. Before you arrive at the park (60 days ahead for guests of Disney-run hotels, 30 days ahead for day visitors and non-Disney hotel guests), you may book up to three Fastpasses for each day you're touring as long as you have purchased tickets first, and you may not have them for more than one park a day. If you don't choose, Disney will only offer you one top-tier attraction per day and salt the other two slots with attractions that most people think have lesser appeal. Use my star ratings to determine what *you* think is worth Fastpassing. But please—don't succumb to the temptation to get obsessive about planning. The object should always be fun.

To schedule your 3 a day, you must register your name, birthday, and tickets on the Disney website or the free My Disney Experience app (MDX, p. 30). After you tell the system when and where you're going, MDX comes up with a few options for timing your Fastpasses, usually spread throughout the day. After you accept one of its plans (if only one in your group snags the perfect combo, they can copy it over to everyone else in the group), you may go back and individually revise each reservation—if you use Fastpass a lot, I suggest moving everything toward the first part of the day, because you may not obtain any more until they're all used or their times

have passed. Or if you're an active type, move them all to afternoon, when lines are longest, and race through a bunch of things on your own in the morning, when lines are lightest. Once you're at the park, you can still revise during MDX and you'll find scattered kiosks where cast members help you create a Fastpass plan (if you haven't been able to yet), revise it, or add more Fastpasses after your original allotment is used. Don't bother Fastpassing a nighttime show—you don't need one for those, and as long as you have outstanding Fastpasses, you'll be locked out of getting more—although by afternoon the best stuff will be gone anyway.

Theme park commandos like Fastpass+ because it gives them a refined way to game the system. But if you're a casual visitor, Fastpass+ has grave flaws that have junked up the fun. It forces new visitors to pre-research attractions so much that when they finally arrive, the sense of unfolding surprise and spontaneity that was crucial to Imagineers is spoiled. The system also turns day visitors into second-class customers since Disney hotel guests get the jump on booking times; it's not uncommon for the best rides to run out of Fastpasses by the time day visitors start their planning. Inside the parks, guests spend their days hunched over mobile phones consulting MDX, anxiously checking the progress of their predetermined schedules. And while Fastpass+ has eased waits on the most popular rides, it has made them worse on second-tier attractions that used to be walk-ons.

to the day of the week and time of year. Counter service locations, which Disney calls Quick Service, do not require reservations, and their listings can be found with each theme park's chapter. To avoid lines, eat between 10:30am and noon (lunch) and 4 and 5pm (dinner). Kids under 3 may eat without charge from an adult's plate, and high chair and booster seats are readily available.

STROLLERS Many times you will be asked to park your stroller before entering a line, so do not keep your valuables in one. Your time on monorails and trams will also be much happier if you have an umbrella one that folds quickly. Note that you're not allowed to bring a stroller larger than 36" × 52" (92 cm × 132 cm) into the park.

OPTIONAL PARK SERVICES As you roam, roving photographers may ask to take your picture. They're here for convenience, not value. Let them snap away; you won't pay anything if you don't want to. They will give you a **PhotoPass** (mydisneyphotopass.disney.go.com) Web account that allows you to check your shots out later and order prints (or ornaments, albums, mugs, mouse pads—you name it) if you fall in love with them. Sometimes, they can enhance the picture with fun special effects, such as Tinker Bell flying from your child's hands. You'll have 30 days to make your decisions. Only when you decide to buy does money change hands. Buying costs much more than it would cost you to make them yourself: 5×7s are $13, 8×10s are $17, two 4×6s are $15, plus shipping and so forth. But now and then, you'll find an occasion that you think is worth the expense, and the Disney photographers are excellent at what they do. PhotoPass is separate from those hilarious pictures taken on board rides, which are available to purchase (from $17) after you get off. Prices for those are similar, but you may purchase those right away. For $50, you can buy the **Attractions+** plan (buy at the big rides) that allows you to download some of your ride photos later (you still have to check in after each ride so your pass can be married to your image). Spend $200 ($150 if you buy at least 3 days ahead of arrival) on **Memory Maker** and you can download all your photos, including restaurant and photos on some major rides (not standard with the PhotoPass without this purchase), as many times as you like for a month.

Guest Relations and some resorts sell **Disney Dollars,** a private scrip you can spend anywhere on property, even mixed with actual U.S. currency. These brightly colored notes are fun to use, but too often, people bring them home as souvenirs, which makes Disney accountants happy. There are clever ways to use them to your advantage—say, by giving your kids $15 worth, and not a dollar more, as an allowance. **My favorite trick:** Instead of getting a cash

Catch a Furry Star

You may remember a time when characters roamed Disney World. Now access to them is strictly regimented to specific times and places. Everyone signs a unique autograph—Goofy's has a backward F, Aladdin does a lamp—and costumes match the locale. All Character Greeting Times are printed on the Times Guide that you pick up as you enter each park, and locations are marked on maps with a black Mickey profile. There are always lines for them, and the most popular ones (including Mickey, Ariel, Cinderella, Tinker Bell, and Anna and Elsa) accept Fastpass+. But they're worth the wait: They always exude contagious good cheer.

WHAT THE BASICS cost AT ALL FOUR DISNEY PARKS

Parking: $20 (waived for guests of Disney hotels)

Lockers: $7 per day (multi-entry)

Regular soda: $3 / **Small water:** $2.50 / **Cup of beer:** $7

ECV (electric convenience vehicle): $50 per day

Single strollers: $15 per day *

Double strollers: $31 per day *

Wheelchair: $12 per day *

Stroller, wheelchair, and ECV rental fee includes multiple park visits on the same day.

Minus discounts of $2 to $4 if you prepay at the rental desk for the length of your stay.

advance from an ATM with your credit card, which racks up fees, buy Disney Dollars. They're charged as a purchase (up to $50 a day), incurring no fees.

You can send cumbersome **souvenirs** to the pick-up desk by the park gates, but delivery will take 3 to 5 hours. You can also send them to your Disney resort room. Make your purchase before noon to receive it the next day. If you make it later in the day, you should be staying for at least another 2 nights or you could miss the delivery. (Yeah, it's not efficient.)

THE MAGIC KINGDOM

The most-visited theme park in the world (19.3 million visitors in 2014), the **Magic Kingdom ★★★**, opened on October 1, 1971, and is more than twice as large as the original Disneyland in Anaheim, California, although it has about the same number of attractions. Of the four parks in Walt Disney World, the Magic Kingdom is the one most people envision: Castle, Main Street, Space Mountain. It's also the first one tourists visit.

The park almost always opens about 15 minutes before the posted opening time (the "rope drop"), when there's a cute musical show in the train station above the entry plaza. Characters sing "Good Mornin'" while Mickey and his pals arrive spectacularly by train to greet them and open the park for the day. The hour or two after this are the most fruitful of the day, with short lines. **Closing time** (often preceded by a 10-min. fireworks show) varies, usually from **7 to midnight.** Near closing time, if you are allowed to get in line for a ride, you'll be able to ride. Hours change almost daily, and Disney transportation runs an hour before opening to an hour after closing.

Keep your ticket card/room key/MagicBand safe. You'll need it throughout the day.

GETTING IN The proof that you're about to experience a fantasy realm comes in the effort required to enter it. Designers wanted arrival to be a big to-do. Many guests brave three forms of transportation before they see a single brick of Main Street. Disney bus riders are conveniently dropped off by the front gate. Guests who drive take the parking tram to the **Transportation and Ticket Center.** (If you park in Aladdin or Jafar, it's not too far to walk.) From there, a mile away, the Magic Kingdom gleams like a promise from across the man-made Seven Seas Lagoon, but you still have to take either a **monorail** (after a 2009 accident that killed a pilot, guests are no longer permitted to ride in the cab) or a **ferryboat** to the other side. Transit time is more or less equal. I recommend doing one in each direction—the gradual approach of the boat is probably the most exciting for your morning glimpses of that famous Castle, and the monorail is probably better at the end of a long day because you'll have air-conditioning. Ferries are named for execs who helped build Disneyland and this park. For getting off quickly, I prefer the bottom deck. Whatever you choose, considering crowds and queues, bank on about 45 minutes to enter or leave the park, and even longer at closing time when the hordes stream out of the gates and clog transportation in a popcorn-fueled death march.

Upon alighting, submit your bags for a hasty inspection and go through the ticket checkpoint. Take the requisite photo at the Floral Mickey in front of the train station, where the "population" sign indicates the rough number of guests who have come here over time. Then head through the tunnels of the mansard-roof train station. There, by the right-hand tunnel, you'll find the only place in the park to rent strollers and wheelchairs. Note the stylized paintings of the big attractions, done like old-fashioned travel posters. They are a tradition in these tunnels.

STRATEGY If you have little kids, troop without delay to Fantasyland, because the lines get heavy there. On hot days, schedule Splash Mountain Fastpasses for the peak heat of afternoon, when you'll need the cool-down.

The Best of the Magic Kingdom

Don't miss if you're 6: Dumbo the Flying Elephant
Don't miss if you're 16: Space Mountain
Requisite photo op: Cinderella Castle
Food you can only get here: LeFou's Brew, Gaston's Tavern, Fantasyland (p. 63); Citrus Swirl, Sunshine Tree Terrace, Adventureland (p. 62); Pineapple Float, Aloha Isle, Adventureland (p. 62); Mickey Mouse ice cream bars (available at carts throughout the park)
The most crowded, so Fastpass or go early: Seven Dwarfs Mine Train, Splash Mountain, Peter Pan's Flight, the Many Adventures of Winnie the Pooh
Skippable: Swiss Family Treehouse, Tomorrowland Speedway

Quintessentially Disney: The Haunted Mansion, Pirates of the Caribbean, Walt Disney's Carousel of Progress, "it's a small world"
Biggest thrill: Splash Mountain
Best show: Wishes fireworks
Character meals: Cinderella's Royal Table, Cinderella Castle; the Crystal Palace, Main Street, U.S.A.
Best shopping: The Emporium, Main Street, U.S.A.
Where to find peace: The Fantasyland-to-Tomorrowland railway-side trail; the park between Liberty Square and Adventureland at the Castle; Tom Sawyer Island; the cul-de-sac south of Space Mountain

The Magic Kingdom

MINOR ATTRACTIONS ●

Dream Along with Mickey **19**

Frontierland Shootin' Arcade **6**

Harmony Barber Shop **13**

A Pirate's Adventure:
Treasures of the Seven Seas **1**

Sorcerers of the Magic Kingdom **12**

Tomorrowland Transit Authority
People Mover **22**

Rivers of America

Haunted Mansion

"it's a small world"

Big Thunder Mountain Railroad

LIBERTY SQUARE

Peter Pan Flight

Ferry

Tom Sawyer Island

Frontierland Railroad Station

8

The Hall of Presidents

Liberty Square Riverboat

Splash Mountain

FRONTIERLAND

3

Country Bear Jamboree

7

2

6

5 The Magic Carpets of Aladdin

9 10

Swiss Family Treehouse

11

First Aid

Walt Disney's Enchanted Tiki Room

Jungle Cruise

1 4

Pirates of the Caribbean

ADVENTURELAND

City H

MAGIC KINGDOM

Disney's Bay Lake Tower

Monorail

Disney's Contemporary Resort

Disney's Grand Floridian Resort

Seven Seas Lagoon

Ferry

Monorail Station to Resorts & Parking

Disney's Polynesian Village Resort

Boat Launch for Resorts

Trader Sam's Grog Grotto

Transportation and Ticket Center (Trams to parking areas)

PARKING

Seven Seas Lagoon

FANTASYLAND

15
16
Enchanted Tales with Belle
Under the Sea: Journey of the Little Mermaid
Pete's Silly Sideshow
Casey Jr. Splash 'N' Soak Station
Fantasyland Railroad Station

STORYBOOK CIRCUS

Seven Dwarfs Mine Train
Prince Charming Regal Carrousel
Dumbo the Flying Elephant
The Barnstormer

Mickey's PhilharMagic
17
Princess Fairytale Hall
The Many Adventures of Winnie the Pooh
Mad Tea Party

18
Cinderella Castle
19

Tomorrowland Speedway
20

Partners statue
Stitch's Great Escape!

TOMORROWLAND

Tomorrowland Transit Authority
Space Mountain

Monsters, Inc. Laugh Floor
Astro Orbiter
21
22
Buzz Lightyear's Space Ranger Spin
Walt Disney's Carousel of Progress

23
24

MAIN STREET, U.S.A.

PARADE BYPASS

Town Square Theater
26

Main Street Railroad Station
Lockers, strollers
Entrance

Shuttles

Ferryboat to Parking

FOOD ◆

Aloha Isle **9**
Be Our Guest Restaurant **15**
Casey's Corner **25**
Cinderella's Royal Table **18**
Columbia Harbour House **8**
Cosmic Ray's Starlight Cafe **20**
The Crystal Palace **11**
The Friar's Nook **17**
Gaston's Tavern **16**
Liberty Tree Tavern **7**
The Lunching Pad **21**
Pecos Bill Tall Tale Inn and Cafe **2**
Pinocchio's Village Haus **14**
Plaza Ice Cream Parlor **24**
The Plaza Restaurant **23**
Skipper Canteen **10**
Sunshine Tree Terrace **5**
Tony's Town Square Restaurant **26**
Tortuga Tavern **4**
Turkey Leg Cart **3**

MAGIC KINGDOM: 1 DAY, THREE WAYS

START: BE AT THE GATE 20 MINUTES BEFORE OPENING TIME.

Grab food at a counter restaurant when it's convenient to you—but having lunch at 11am saves time.

Obtain the must-have Fastpass+ where indicated, but using additional ones will speed the day. If your kids want to meet major characters, it's vital to use Fastpass+ for meet-and-greet venues.

MAGIC KINGDOM WITH KIDS UNDER 8

Head to Fantasyland. Schedule Fastpass+ for one of these busy rides to ease waits later: Peter Pan's Flight, Journey of the Little Mermaid, Seven Dwarfs Mine Train, or Splash Mountain.

Ride **Peter Pan's Flight.**
↓
Do **Enchanted Tales with Belle.**
↓
Ride in this order: **Journey of the Little Mermaid, Dumbo the Flying Elephant** (omit if your kids don't care), the **Many Adventures of Winnie the Pooh, "it's a small world."**
↓
Visit **Pete's Silly Sideshow** to meet Minnie or Goofy.
OR
Take the train from New Fantasyland to Main Street U.S.A. to meet Mickey at **Town Square Theater.**
↓
Cross to Adventureland. Do **Magic Carpets of Aladdin** if you feel the urge. Enjoy a Dole Whip at Aloha Isle or a Citrus Swirl at Sunshine Tree Terrace. Ride **Pirates of the Caribbean** and the **Jungle Cruise.**
↓

It may be hot by now, so if there's patience among your party, see these two neighboring indoor shows: the **Enchanted Tiki Room** and the **Country Bear Jamboree.**
↓
See the midafternoon parade from Frontierland or on Main Street, U.S.A.
↓
At this point, littler ones may need to leave the park for a break.
↓
Get to Tomorrowland via Fantasyland, and watch **Mickey's PhilharMagic**, and (time permitting) meet the princesses at **Fairytale Hall.**
↓
In Tomorrowland, ride **Buzz Lightyear's Space Ranger Spin.**
↓
Ride the **Speedway** if your child meets the height requirement.
↓
It's evening. If your kids are willing, ride the **Haunted Mansion.**
↓
If there's time, hit rides you missed (perhaps the **Carrousel** and **Astro Orbiter**).
↓
Watch the **Main Street Electrical Parade**, ride something you missed, and see the fireworks before departing.

MAGIC KINGDOM WITH TEENS

Make sure you have Fastpass+ for Splash Mountain for early afternoon when it'll be hottest. Space Mountain, Seven Dwarfs Mine Train, and Peter Pan's Flight are also prime candidates for Fastpass+.

Ride **Big Thunder Mountain Railway.**
↓
In Adventureland, ride **Pirates of the Caribbean** and **Jungle Cruise.** Enjoy a Dole Whip at Aloha Isle or a Citrus Swirl at Sunshine Tree Terrace.
↓
Cross the park via Fantasyland (ideally, have Fastpass+ for either **Peter Pan's Flight** or the **Seven Dwarfs Mine Train**) to Tomorrowland and ride **Space Mountain** and **Buzz Lightyear's Space Ranger Spin.**
↓
Go to Fantasyland for the **Mad Tea Party, Mickey's PhilharMagic**, and any rides that catch your fancy. You'll be getting hot and tired about now, so something like **"it's a small world"** might hit the spot.
↓

Around the corner, ride the **Haunted Mansion.**

↓

Take the raft to Tom Sawyer Island, where the kids can have free reign and, upon returning, shoot a few rounds at the **Frontierland Shootin' Arcade** or maybe do a lap on the riverboat. (They close at dusk.)

↓

Ride the train from Frontierland to Main Street, U.S.A.

↓

See the **parade and fireworks** from Main Street, U.S.A., or in front of the Castle.

OR

If the parade isn't of interest, pick rides anywhere except in Adventureland to re-ride or try. Lines will be dramatically shorter during the parade.

Schedule Fastpass+ for one of these rides within 90 minutes of opening: Peter Pan's Flight, Space Mountain, Big Thunder Mountain Railroad, Seven Dwarfs Mine Train.

Head to Fantasyland and ride **Peter Pan's Flight, "it's a small world,"** and the **Many Adventures of Winnie the Pooh.** That'll put you in the mood.

↓

Head to Frontierland and ride **Big Thunder Mountain Railroad.** Have a Fastpass+ for early afternoon for **Splash Mountain,** or if it's warm, ride it now.

↓

In Adventureland, ride **Pirates of the Caribbean** and **Jungle Cruise.**

↓

Go old school: See the **Enchanted Tiki Room** or the **Country Bears Jamboree.**

↓

Get out of Adventureland before the midafternoon parade starts; it cuts the land off from the rest of the park.

↓

Ride the **Haunted Mansion.** Repeat until spooked (or cooled off).

↓

Stay indoors by seeing **Mickey's PhilharMagic.**

↓

Head to Tomorrowland and ride **Buzz Lightyear's Space Ranger Spin** and **Space Mountain.** Or get your fill of cheese at the **Walt Disney's Carousel of Progress.**

↓

You're probably getting a little tired by now, so sit down and enjoy the **Tomorrowland Transit Authority.**

↓

Walk to New Fantasyland and take time to explore.

↓

Enjoy the **parade** and get in place 30 minutes in advance of the **fireworks.**

OR

If you have rides you missed or you'd like to repeat, the parade is a prime time for that except near the Castle in Fantasyland, which will shut down for safety then.

Main Street, U.S.A.

Cinderella Castle.

Out the other side of the train station in the Town Square, you'll be greeted by your first few costumed characters and to a full view of Cinderella Castle, home to an unlikely jumble of princesses, at the end of Main Street, U.S.A. Like the first time you see the Eiffel Tower or the Sydney Opera House, there's something seminal— oh, help me, dare I say *magical?*— about laying eyes on that Castle, and it can't help but stir feelings of gratitude. This view is as American as the Grand Canyon.

The original Main Street, U.S.A., was created as a perfected vision of Walt Disney's fond memories of a formative period of his childhood spent in Marceline, Missouri, minus any churches. To impart a sense of coziness, designers built the Main Street facades at diminishing perspective as they rise. Other subtle touches: Shop windows are lower than normal to enable children to see inside, walkways are pigmented red to accentuate both unreality and safety (it alerts walkers of shifts in levels), and buildings on both sides inch closer to each other as you walk, subconsciously drawing your attention forward.

There are no big rides or shows on Main Street, just the park's best souvenir shops—call it Purchaseland. The 17,000-square-foot **Emporium,** the largest shop in the Kingdom, takes up almost the entire street along the left, and **Le Chapeau** (on the right, facing the square) is one of the only places where you can sew your name onto the back of one of those iconic mouse-ear beanies ($3–$7 per cap, which start at $14; also available at Fantasy Faire and Storybook Circus in Fantasyland). They resist stitching nicknames. **Crystal Arts** may have a small glass-blowing demonstration going. In the middle of Main Street, the east side has a little side street, **Center Street,** for caricaturists and silhouette artists, a Disney World institution since 1971 ($8 for two copies). If you're lucky, you'll catch a performance by the **Dapper Dans,** a real barbershop quartet that ambles down the street, or you'll be glad-handed by old Mayor Weaver, who'll remind you the election is approaching ("pull the lever and vote for Weaver!"); otherwise, you'll hear recorded stuff from "The Music Man." Those songs have a pedigree—at the opening ceremony of the Magic Kingdom, Meredith Willson, who wrote "Seventy-Six Trombones," led a 1,076-piece band up Main Street.

Strategy: Main Street is the only way in or out of the park, which fosters a sense of suspense, but just as surely creates bottlenecks at parade time. If you need to leave the park then, cut through the Emporium. A variety of free **Main Street vehicles** trundle up the road at odd hours and on odd days (you never know when) and you can catch a one-way, stop-and-go ride on one: They include horse-drawn trolley cars—they wrap up by 1pm as not to overheat the animals—antique cars, jitneys, and a fire truck. They won't save time, of course, but you'll remember them forever. Pause at the end of Main Street, where the Plaza begins, for that snapshot of a lifetime in front of the 189-foot-tall Cinderella Castle. You have now essentially passed through three thresholds—the lagoon, the train tunnel, and Main Street, U.S.A.—that were designed to ease you into a world of fantasy. You have arrived. Welcome to Disney World! (Whew!)

Walt Disney World Railroad ★★★ RIDE The prominence of a railway is no accident; the concept of Disneyland grew out of Walt's wish to build a train park across the street from his Burbank studios. The train, which runs all day, takes about 25 minutes and encircles the park, ducking through Splash Mountain (you'll see its two-story riverboat through a window), stopping first in Frontierland and then passing through apparent wilderness to Fantasyland before returning here. The best seats are on the right, and you can go around as many times as you want without getting off. You'll see a few robotic dioramas of Indian encampments and wild animals, and also some backstage areas—following the tunnel after the Main Street station (it's the passage through the Pirates of the Caribbean show building), the train crosses a road; look right to find the yellow line painted on the ground. This is the border that tells cast members when they're out of view and can safely come out of character.

Walt Disney World Railroad.

Remembering Roy Disney

If Walt was the man with the dream, brother Roy was the guy with the checkbook. He repeatedly staved off bankruptcy and found money for Walt's crazy ideas, from cartoon shorts to full features to, finally, Disneyland. Although Walt died in 1966, before he could finish his so-called "Florida Project," Roy made it to the opening day, and he renamed it Walt Disney World in tribute. Having seen it through, he died only 3 months later. His statue is seated with Minnie Mouse in the middle of the square behind the flagpole, where he welcomes guests to Main Street in perpetuity.

Guest services cluster around the square. To the left of the park is **City Hall.** If you forgot to make reservations for sit-down meals or schedule other activities, this is the place for that. Out front, a cast member mans a street cart full of free badges for guests who are having a birthday, visiting for the first time, having an anniversary or a family reunion, or just celebrating something. Ask for a badge and you'll receive bigger smiles (and maybe treats) all day.

A few people attend the daily **flag retreat ceremony** here at 5pm—no characters, just a brass band (the Main Street Philharmonic) and a member of the military or veteran selected from the guests—sometimes it works to volunteer at City Hall right after opening. Many guests find the ritual moving.

Sorcerers of the Magic Kingdom ★ ACTIVITY   In the **Fire Station** (Engine Co. 71, after the year the park opened) you'll find the Recruiting Station for Sorcerers of the Magic Kingdom, an innovative scavenger hunt-type adventure that relies on hidden sensors scattered around the park. You're given a card with a key printed on it, and when you hold it (or your MagicBand) up to a special Magic Portal screen, the screen comes alive with a briefing animation asking for your help in thwarting villains. From there, you're given a free pack of five daily "spell cards" linked to Disney characters (Pinocchio's Sawdust Blast, Elsa's Icy Shield), and a map to locations of Portals spread throughout the park in spots such as shop windows and quiet corners. When you hold up a spell card at a Portal—the extent of the game's degree of difficulty—animation begins and your spell amusingly beats back the villains (it's fun to watch, say, portly Governor Ratcliffe from "Pocahontas" get swamped by posies from Flower from "Bambi"). Some 95 minutes of new animation, using many of the original voice talent, was created for this adventure. There are dozens of available spell cards—you may find fans of the game in the back of the Tortuga Tavern in Adventureland swapping rare ones (ones marked with lightning bolts can go for $500 on the black market)—but if you pick some up, you must activate your game the same day or you won't be given more. Although it is cool, Sorcerers is best saved for after you have enjoyed everything else in the park. You'd hate to miss something iconic for it.

Harmony Barber Shop ★ ACTIVITY   The one-room shop on the square (9am–6pm; haircuts: $19 adults, $18 kids 12 and under) trims some

700 pates a week and does special requests, such as shaving Mickey onto scalps or combing in clear gel with either "Pixie Dust" or "Pirate Dust" (ssh— it's the same thing). They're experts at first haircuts, which come with a baby mouse ears cap reading "My First Haircut," a Certificate of Bravery, and wrappings of your child's first trimmings for posterity ($25). You can make an appointment at ℂ **407/WDW-PLAY** [939-7529], but it also takes walk-ins.

Town Square Theater ★★ CHARACTER GREETING Beat the heat here, at two character meet-and-greet areas. On the right, meet Mickey Mouse dressed as a magician (get a Fastpass+ for him if you're a big fan), and on the left, meet a selection of other characters (cameos of who are currently available are pictured on the wait time sign). You can also come here for **MagicBand** maintenance. This building is slightly larger than the others on Main Street because it was designed to block anachronistic sightings of the original wing of the Contemporary Hotel.

Cinderella Castle ★★★ LANDMARK The just-renovated park nucleus in front, known as "the Hub," centers on **"Partners,"** the statue of Walt and Mickey by the esteemed Disney sculptor Blaine Gibson, ringed by attending statues of supporting characters; the original stands in Disneyland.

Then there's the castle: 183 feet (56m) tall from the surface of the water in its ornamental moat. No two Disney castles are identical; the one in California, Sleeping Beauty Castle (notice that neither castle's name has a possessive *'s*), is about half as tall as this. The skin of this one, it's strange to learn, is made not of stone but of fiberglass and plastic. The story there is that WDW's builders, who based its profile on an amalgam of French castles, implored local lawmakers to let them try something experimental, and the structure, buttressed with steel and concrete, has survived decades of hurricanes and baking heat. Look at its top. Bricks there are sized smaller to give a sense of distance, and even the handrails are just 2 feet tall to make the spires seem higher. Within the breezeways (closed during shows on the forecourt), don't miss the five expressive **mosaics** of hand-cut glass depicting the story of the glass slipper. They were designed by Dorothea Redmond, who also designed sets for "Gone with the Wind." Over each entrance, you'll see the Disney

---

Windows on Disney Legends Past

Notice the **names painted on the windows** of the upper floors along Main Street. Each one represents a high-ranking Disney employee who helped build or run the park. Several, such as the one for Reedy Creek Ranch Lands, are winks at the dummy companies Walt Disney set up in the '60s so that he could buy cheap swampland without tipping off landowners to his purpose. Everyone's window relates in some way to his or her life's work. Walt Disney gets two windows: the first one, on the train station facing outside the park, and the last, above the Plaza restaurant facing the Castle; designers liken the first-and-last billing to the opening credits of a movie. Notice that former CEO Michael Eisner did not get a window.

family coat of arms. Genealogists contest whether they're correct, but there is unintended accuracy here unbeknownst to Walt: His ancestor was imprisoned in a castle. Researchers recently found graffiti left by Disney's English ancestor Edward Disney when he was imprisoned in Warwick Castle in 1642 for defending King Charles I. (He survived. Amusingly, that castle is now run by Disney competitor Merlin Entertainments, which runs Legoland.) Look for a wire that connects the Castle with a building in Tomorrowland; during the nightly fireworks, as she has done since 1985, that homicidal pixie Tinker Bell zips down the line, flying 750 feet at 15mph. There is no ride inside the Castle, but there is a princess makeover salon, **Bibbidi**

MagicBand scanning station.

Bobbidi Boutique, and massively popular restaurant, **Cinderella's Royal Table,** and a sole overnight VIP suite, once an office for phone operators. Thirty-five feet beneath the Castle, Walt Disney himself is kept cryogenically frozen, awaiting eventual re-animation in a steel-lined, temperature-controlled chamber. (I'm just kidding about that. He was definitely cremated and is buried in Glendale, California, with his family.)

Dream Along with Mickey ★ SHOW   The chief Disney characters star in a 20-minute floor show in the Castle forecourt capped by a few fireworks explosions. See the "Times Guide" or the schedule posted by the stage. Standing here can be hot, but the "NextGen" character costumes are extremely cool, having been mechanized so mouths open and close to the dialogue. Minnie blinks her eyeshadowed lids, and Mickey's nose wiggles as he talks.

Adventureland

As you enter Adventureland from the Plaza (a transition made less jarring by the Victorian greenhouse of the Crystal Palace restaurant), notice how the music gradually changes from the perky pluck of Main Street to the rhythms of Adventureland. Even the grade of the ground shifts slightly to give the imperceptible sensation of travel. Such undetectable shifts in drama are integral to the Disney method of park design.

Swiss Family Treehouse ★★ ACTIVITY   The Swiss who? You're forgiven if you don't know "The Swiss Family Robinson" (1960), a shipwrecked clan that survives using salvage, and you're also forgiven if you lack the will to take 15 minutes to clamber up the 61 stairs and catwalks to inspect the

THE MAGICBAND revolution

Disney paid a reported $1 billion (at the expense of new attraction construction) to develop a controversial guest identification system. It's called MagicBand, the waterproof, removable bracelet that monitors your stay. They contain two types of embedded radio frequency transmitters that enable both short-range and long-range tracking. When you book a package for a Disney hotel, you are mailed MagicBands in preparation of your stay. If you're not staying at a Disney hotel, you can buy one for $13 at Disney shops and have it linked to your ticket by the sales clerk

Here's what MagicBand does:

- Stores your ticket info to get you through turnstiles. Touch it to a lollipop-like scanner for entry, paired with your fingerprint for positive identification.

- Records reservations for Fastpass, Disney's Magical Express, and dining. (The expanded capability of the bracelets is technically called **MyMagic+**.)

- Records PhotoPass details. Scan it with photographers and at post-ride photo kiosks to add new pictures to your portfolio.

- Allows Disney resort guests to make purchases (with a PIN; day visitors cannot) and open hotel room doors by holding the band over a scanning point.

- Allows Disney Parks to track your movements. The park claims it will use this to adjust your experience, although it is not forthcoming about precisely how.

- Record adjustments to your plans using the free **My Disney Experience** smartphone app (Android or iPhone only), which relays the status of your reservations to your bracelet and sends you smartphone notifications if something changes. There's free Wi-Fi in the parks to enable this.

- Allows you to link your plans with those of friends and family.

There are six sassy colors to buy, plus a growing array of charms and accessories (which easily fall off while you're not paying attention)—the battery lasts 2 or 3 years.

To use its benefits, you must register personal details, including your address and date of birth, with the Disney system. For this reason, the new technology has been plagued with **privacy controversies,** including from Washington when Congressman, now Senator, Ed Markey, lashed out at Disney for the scheme. Disney swears personal information is not encoded in the MagicBands by saying, "The MagicBand and card contain only a randomly assigned code that securely links to an encrypted database and are configured to not store any other information about you." (Read more of its explanations at www.mydisneyexperience.com.)

If you have concerns, you may decline a MagicBand or simply not buy one; you will be given a plastic card that only contains a passive radio transmitter chip that's used to tap for entry but cannot be used to track your movements around the parks. You may not simply buy a paper ticket anymore.

If you possess a MagicBand, brace yourself for the overspending potential of tapping a bracelet rather than taking out a wallet. Your weak willpower is a big reason the company decided it was worth sinking $1 billion into this.

ingenuity of their arboreal island home. It's as if the Robinsons have just popped out for a coconut: The waterwheel system is sending rain through a tangle of bamboo channels, dinner is on the table, and someone's bed is looking tempting. The tree is made of concrete and steel, and its 330,000 plastic leaves were attached by hand. Try doing this one at night, when you can enjoy the flicker of the lanterns and faint chatter of tourists far below. This attraction is the last of its breed—all the ones in other parks have been Tarzan-ized.

Jungle Cruise ★★★ RIDE   The delightful, G-rated excursion was one of the world's first rides based on a movie. The slow-going boat tour was created for Disneyland's 1955 opening to capitalize on the True-Life Adventures nature films. Like so many of Walt Disney's ideas, the 9-minute trip was intended to give guests a whirlwind tour of the planet's wonders. The ride no longer strives to teach you anything, hence vague descriptions of locals as "the natives" and a religious ruin identified as the Shirley Temple—great for kids, but not what you'd call documentary. This is the ride where over a dozen Indian elephants wash together in a pool, one of the seminal spectacles of a Disney visit. The jokes are unabashedly Eisenhower-era: Near the gorillas, you're told, "If you're wearing anything yellow, try not to make banana noises." In 1971, "The New York Times" sniffed that what distressed it about the Jungle Cruise was "the squandering of so much effort and technical ingenuity on cheap tricks and an inane script." Lighten up, Grey Lady; it's a goof! Boats are safely guided by paddles that slot into a narrow channel in the stream. The water is dyed to keep you from spotting that. Seats in the middle are often exposed to the harsh sunlight. *Strategy:* Dinnertime seems to be a sweet spot for thinner crowds, and riding in the dark adds a lot.

Magic Carpets of Aladdin ★ RIDE   At Disney, toddlers abound, and most areas have a flying carousel suited to their low thrill thresholds. This one is a less-crowded alternative to Fantasyland's Dumbo, but unlike Dumbo, a family of four can ride—there are two rows of seats on each "carpet." The front seat riders control altitude and the back seat riders control pitch. One of the golden camels on the sidelines spits a thin stream of water. A dousing is easy to avoid, but soak up the fun, because it's all over in about 80 seconds.

Walt Disney's Enchanted Tiki Room ★★★ SHOW   In the 1950s, Walt Disney developed a godlike obsession with developing robots to replace living actors, and as a first stab at lifelike technology, he had his staff create a little mechanical bird. The germ of this precious show, which takes 10 minutes, is the direct result—birds sang the catchy "In the Tiki Tiki Tiki Tiki Tiki Room" and wowed 'em with robotics. To 1963 crowds, it was the electrifying future, but today, despite despised past efforts by Disney to junk it up with rewrites, it's merely endearing. Guests sit in the round, on benches, in an air-chilled Polynesian room and watch the ceiling and walls come alive with chattering, bickering, singing birds that fit several national stereotypes and perform vaudeville-style ditties in quick succession. Add some animated flowers and magically singing totem poles, followed by a pleasing mist and rain outside the windows, and you've got a cherished mood piece. When you're in the waiting area, the lines to the right, near the waterfall, enable you to see a little more action. Though the roof looks like old straw, it's actually shredded aluminum. *Tip:* The goliath tiki statues located across the walkway are equipped to squirt water on squealing children on hot days.

Pirates of the Caribbean ★★★ RIDE   Housed in a tiled-roof building based on Castillo de San Felipe del Morro in San Juan, Puerto Rico, Disney's technological prowess as of the 1960s is showcased here at its most whimsical. I call this indoor boat float the quintessential Disney ride, so it's probably no coincidence that it was the last Disneyland attraction Walt had a hand in designing, even though he conceived it as a walk-through wax museum. Imagineer Marty Sklar said Walt envisioned the experience like a cocktail party: "You hear a little bit, but you don't get it all. You have to ride again." With 65 Audio-Animatronic figures in motion, the more you ride, the more you see: the pirate whose errant gunshot ricochets off a metal sign across the room, the whoosh of compressed air when a cannonball is fired, and the sumptuous theatrical lighting that makes everything look as if has been imported from Jamaica. If you saw the Johnny Depp movies of the same name, you'll see a few familiar scenes, including a slapstick sacking of an island port, a cannonball fight, and much drunken chicanery from ruddy-cheeked buccaneers. (Unsavory? Hey, even Captain Hook was obsessed with murdering a small boy.) There's a short, pitch-black drop near the beginning but you don't get wet—the concept, which you'd never grasp unless I told you, is that you're going back in time to see what killed the skeletons you pass in the first scene. Near the end of the 9-minute journey, there's usually a pileup of boats waiting to disembark, which supplies more time to admire the *pièce de résistance:* A brilliantly lifelike Captain Jack Sparrow, having outlived his compatriots, is counting his treasure. The shop at Pirates' exit is one of the better ones, because it's big on buccaneer booty. Plastic hooks to cover

Captain Jack Sparrow's Pirate Tutorial.

classic DISNEY

Disney is always evolving, just as Walt intended it, but if the company were to alter these mainstays, it would be like desecrating pop culture itself. These core attractions are the Disney that Walt knew, as comforting as cookies and warm milk:

- **The Monorail**
- **Dumbo the Flying Elephant,** Fantasyland
- **Peter Pan's Flight,** Fantasyland
- **"it's a small world,"** Fantasyland
- **Walt Disney World Railroad,** Fantasyland, Frontierland, Main Street U.S.A.
- **Pirates of the Caribbean,** Adventureland
- **Jungle Cruise,** Adventureland

- **The Enchanted Tiki Room,** Adventureland
- **Country Bear Jamboree,** Frontierland
- **Tom Sawyer Island,** Frontierland
- **Liberty Square Riverboat,** Liberty Square
- **Haunted Mansion,** Liberty Square
- **Tomorrowland Speedway,** Tomorrowland
- **Walt Disney's Carousel of Progress,** Tomorrowland
- **Tomorrowland Transit Authority,** Tomorrowland.
- **Main Street, U.S.A.**—Don't forget to stitch your name on a Mickey cap at Le Chapeau, Mouseketeer!

Dumbo.

your hand cost just $3, and a plastic cutlass is $7. **The Pirates League** salon (reservations: ✆ **407/939-2739**) gives pirate makeovers (temporary tattoos, stubble) to kids from $30. It'll also do empresses and mermaids for $43. On the stage across the lane, catch the intermittent **Captain Jack Sparrow's**

One of the tent poles of a day at the Magic Kingdom is the parade. Each one (there are different versions in daytime, after dark, and for holiday parties) is a memorable production, with dozens of dancers and characters and up to a dozen lavish floats. The daytime **Festival of Fantasy Parade** is devoted to characters who might live in Fantasyland, and the **Move It! Shake It! Dance & Play It! Street Party** is aimed at getting your toddler to boogie, but the glittering, after-dark **Main Street Electrical Parade** has been a favorite for generations and is the one you shouldn't miss. Day parades generally go at 3pm while night parades tend to start just after dusk (sometimes twice), although times for the evening parade vary, and they last for less than 15 minutes. While Main Street (especially its train station) has excellent viewpoints, I prefer to catch the parade from the western edge of Frontierland, where I'm closer to rides. *Tips:* If you want to catch only one parade, see the second one of the day, which is generally cooler and less crowded. During parades, the lines for many kiddie rides (especially those in Fantasyland) and character greetings thin. Once it ends, attractions nearest the route tend to be inundated with bodies—a bypass was recently carved behind the Tomorrowland side of Main Street. Also, the route is essentially impassible from 5 minute before until just afterward, so don't get trapped in Adventureland during one.

Pirate Tutorial, where volunteer children are taught by Sparrow (wobbly drunk, bleary with mascara) to parry with a sidekick using a floppy sword—and then flee.

A Pirate's Adventure—Treasures of the Seven Seas ★ ACTIVITY
The success of Sorcerers of the Magic Kingdom inspired the Summer 2013 installation of this Adventureland-only scavenger hunt, which begins in this shack. Using one of five maps and a pentagon-shaped talisman card, you find stations in order and activate them. One might reveal a pearl in a giant oyster, another fires a cannon, a third triggers a battle between two ships in a bottle, sinking one. It takes about 15 minutes and requires no skill.

Frontierland

When Disneyland was built in 1955, America had cowboy fever, and every young boy wore a Davy Crockett coonskin cap sold to them by Walt Disney's program on ABC. It was in this spirit that Frontierland was conceived.

Splash Mountain ★★★ RIDE Part flume and part indoor "dark ride," it's preposterously fun, justifiably packed all the time, and proof of what Disney can do when its creative (and budgetary) engines are firing on all cylinders. You track the Br'er Rabbit character through some Deep South sets and down several plunges in Chick-a-Pin Hill—the most dramatic drop, five stories at 40mph (faster than Space Mountain), is plainly visible from the outside. You will get wet, especially from the shoulders up and particularly in the front seats, but are not likely to get soaked because boats plow most of the water out of the way. I never tire of this 11-minute journey because it's so full

Splash Mountain's Uncomfortable Origin

You may agree that it's odd that Disney chose to build Splash Mountain since it's based on a movie that's not even available for sale in the United States: "Song of the South" (1946) has long been criticized for its racist overtones—Adam Clayton Powell called the film "an insult to minorities" and some people bristle at the ride's minstrel-like characters. Disney knew racism was an issue, because for this ride it eliminated the film's narrator, a kindly ex-slave named Uncle Remus.

of surprises, including room after room of animated characters (as many as Pirates has), seven drops large and small, a course that takes you indoors and out, and some perfectly executed theming that begins with the gorgeous outdoor courtyard queue strung with mismatched lanterns at many heights. You'll see Chip 'n' Dale's houses there, and hear them chatter to each other from within. *Strategy:* Get a Fastpass early for this one, because it's deservedly one of the most adored rides on the planet. The line can as much as double when things get steamy. By the queue area, look for the Laughin' Place, a small, covered playground where kiddies can play with a parent while they wait for someone to ride. If your kid is too short to ride, cast members usually dispense free "Future Splash Mountaineer" cards that go a long way toward drying tears.

Big Thunder Mountain Railroad ★★ RIDE Here we have another Disney thrill mountain, a 2½-acre runaway-train ride that rambles joltingly through steaming, rusty Old West sets. Consider it the closest thing to a standard adult coaster in the Magic Kingdom, although it's not something that will make you dizzy or scared. Top speeds hit only 30mph, and there are no loops or giant drops, just circles, jiggles and humps. Listen for the voice of the old prospector in the boarding area; generations of American kids have imitated him as he warns, "This here's the wildest ride in the wilderness!" *Tips:* Seats

Big Thunder Mountain.

in the back give a slightly wilder ride because front cars spend a lot of time waiting for the rear cars to clear hills. Tall riders should cross their ankles to avoid a knee-bashing against the seats in front of them. Chickens can watch their loved ones ride from the overlook on Nugget Way, near the ride's exit.

Walt Disney World Railroad, Frontierland Station ★★★ RIDE Between Splash and Big Thunder mountains is a stop for the trains, which are pulled by one of four steam engines built between 1916 and 1928 and operated in the Yucatan before coming here. They take you to Fantasyland, then the foot of Main Street, and back here in 20 minutes.

Tom Sawyer Island ★★ ACTIVITY Across Rivers of America, you'll find a place where you can roam the step-free Old Scratch's Mystery Mine without a guide, cross wooden suspension bridges, and pretend to defend Fort Langhorn with rifles rigged with weak recordings of gunfire. The island is a great destination to explore, work off energy, and escape the crush—one of the only places in the park where your kids' imagination will have true free rein. You can reach it only by taking the platform boats that leave from the vicinity of Big Thunder Mountain, which makes it a blessed place to escape crowd control but also a time devourer. Don't be in a hurry, because you'll wait for the pontoon in both directions. They only fit 50 passengers at a time and you have to stand in the sun, so it helps to have decent balance. The island closes at dusk. *Tips:* There is an ice cream-and-soda stand there, Aunt Polly's, but it's rarely open; sit on its porch and watch the Liberty Belle and Haunted Mansion across the water. There are water fountains and washrooms, but overall it's pretty rustic—it's a great spot for a picnic.

Country Bear Jamboree ★★ SHOW An opening-day attraction, one of the last to survive, the Jamboree is a 10-minute vaudeville-style revue that, at one moment, has 18 Audio-Animatronic bears, a raccoon, and a buffalo head singing country music together. Some kids, particularly pre-Ks, are enthralled by the dopey-looking robots, which appear for a verse or two of a saloon song, and then are retracted away. Other kids, and many adults, are powerfully bored. It's nice to sit, but don't wait more than 20 minutes for it unless you're hankerin' to see a vintage Disney museum piece.

Frontierland Shootin' Arcade ★ ACTIVITY A simpler activity built from a common 1950s conceit: Fire laser sights at an Old West diorama rigged with plenty of amusing gags. Bull's-eyes spring crooks from tiny jails, activate runaway mine carts, and coax skeletons from their Boot Hill graves. The $1 price buys 35 "shots," enough for a good shooter to trigger most of the tricks.

Liberty Square

Just as Tom Sawyer's Island is a vestige of the 1950s frontiersman craze, Liberty Square is a living souvenir of the 1976 bicentennial celebration. Check out the replica of the real Liberty Bell, under the Liberty Tree. This is a ringer in both senses; it's a copy cast by the Whitechapel Bell Foundry in

London, which made the original. Such authentic touches abound: The Liberty Tree, strung with 13 lanterns to signify the 13 colonies, is actually two trees, transplanted from elsewhere on Disney property, partially filled with concrete, and grafted together: a pretty Frankentree. Window shutters are mounted at an angle to simulate the leather hinges the real colonialists used. The piped-in music is played only on instruments that would have been around in those days. And guess what colors the flowers are?

The Haunted Mansion ★★★ RIDE   One of the park's largest and most intricate rides opened with the park in 1971, and fans are in love with it—many of them can recite the script verbatim ("I am your host . . . your *ghost* host!"). The outdoor queue area passes funny gravestones, some of them interactive and some carved with in-jokes and the names of Imagineers—keep an eye on the last one with the female face, because it keeps an eye on you. Once you're inside, you enter the famous "stretching room." This dark chamber with a diabolical disembodied voice freaks out tots. But it's the scariest part of the experience, and a fortitude test for children—one of my earliest life memories is of begging my mother to take me out of the line (she did, and there's still an escape route if you need it). But if kids get through that, the rest is cake (literally—the undead, oddly, are throwing a birthday celebration inside). Be on the far side of the stretching room to be the first to the boarding zone. As spook houses go, the 8-minute trip is decidedly merry: All the ghosts seem to want to do is party. Passengers ride creepingly slow "doom buggy" cars linked together on an endless loop, no seat belts required—the proprietary system is called OmniMover. Although there are lots of glow-in-the-dark optical illusions, there are no unannounced shocks or gotchas. The climax, a ghost gala in a cavernous graveyard set, is impossible to soak up in one go, so you may want to visit several times to catch the murderous back story revealed in the attic scene. (One fun tip: The singing headstone with the broken head is voiced by the same guy who did Tony the Tiger for Frosted Flakes.) The warehouse-like "show building," where most of the ride is contained, is cleverly disguised behind Gracey Mansion's facade. Kids under 7 must ride with someone 14 or older. Don't miss the **Memento Mori** shop devoted to the giggly ghouls—you can take a zombified photo of yourself ($20). *Strategy:* On busy days, lines can be the scariest part, so try going—bwah-ha-ha-ha!—after the sun goes down.

The Hall of Presidents ★★★ SHOW   Following a historical, wide-angle film, Audio-Animatronic versions of the U.S. presidents crowd awkwardly onstage, nodding to the audience, and several in turn spout homilies about democracy, unity, and other satisfying nuggets. It's as lacking in substance as it has been since wowing first-day visitors in 1971, even though Reconstruction authority Eric Foner was brought in to re-script portions. Although audiences don't realize it, figures were created with historical accuracy; if the president didn't live in an era of machine-made clothing, for example, he wears a hand-stitched suit. The cavalcade of important names is enough to stir a little patriotism in the cockles of the darkest heart—and sometimes, jeers from the most partisan killjoys. The technical wizardry—Lincoln even rises from a sitting position to address the audience—dates to when the show began with only him in 1964. Then, the sight of lifelike robots was enough to leave audiences gawping. Nowadays, this static tableau is the spinach in your junk food theme park banquet, yet it's a piece of history in several senses. Bank about 25 minutes to see it, plus the (rare) wait—you'll be seated for the show. In 2017, the new leader will be added (Chief Executives record their own monologues), so if it's closed for refurbishment, that's why.

Liberty Square Riverboat ★★ RIDE   The 17-minute ride around Tom Sawyer Island, which departs on the hour and half-hour and has little seating, makes for a relaxing break, and it's not unusual to see Florida water birds on the journey, which passes a few mild (and mildly stereotypical) dioramas of Indian camps. The top deck offers views but a deafening whistle, and mid-deck has a good look at that hardworking paddle. The bottom is where sailors work the levers that make the honest-to-goodness steam engine run. Fight the urge to praise them for their steering ability—the boat's on a track.

Fantasyland

Fantasyland is the heart of Walt Disney World because it contains many of the characters that make the brand beloved, and a few years ago it was expanded; the section through the interior arches is commonly called New Fantasyland, which itself contains a sub-land, **Storybook Circus.** Most of its attractions are tame cart rides that wouldn't be out of place at a carnival if they weren't so meticulously maintained. But the energy is first class. A lot of people must agree, because lines are long. For shorter waits, race here first thing in the morning or arrive after dinner, when little ones start tiring out. Fastpassing is also widespread.

it's a small world.

"it's a small world" ★★★ RIDE Slow and sweet as treacle, the king of Fantasyland rides is a 15-minute boat trip serenaded by the Sherman Brothers' infectious theme song (bet you already know it). On the route, nearly 300 dancing-doll children, each pegged to his or her nation by genial stereotypes (Dutch kids wear clogs, French kids can-can), chant the same song, and everyone's in a party mood. In the tense years following the Cuban Missile Crisis, this ride's message of human unity was a balm, and in these rooms, millions of toddlers have received their first exposure to world cultures (including yours truly—and then I grew to be a travel writer). Those 4 and under love this because there's lots to see and nothing threatening, but by about 11, kids reverse their opinions and think its upchuck factor is higher than Mission: SPACE's. The ride's distinctive look came from Mary Blair, a rare female Imagineer. Walt originally wanted the kids to sing their own national anthems, but the resulting cacophony was too disturbing; instead, a ditty was written in such a way that it could be repeated with changing instrumentation, and so that its verse and chorus would never clash. It was whipped up in 11 months for the 1964 World's Fair in New York as a partnership with PepsiCo and UNICEF. Pepsi was about to reject the concept, but Joan Crawford, who was on the board of directors, halted the meeting, stood up, and declared, "We are going to do this!" That was a masterstroke—Walt convinced American corporations to subsidize construction of attractions in his own theme park. His company still does it. And, ballsier yet, now it only serves Coke. After the Fair, where it cost $1 for adults to ride, the original was moved to Disneyland. **Strategy:** If you're not sure whether meeting characters will wig out your kids, take them on this as a test run. Be in line on the quarter-hour, when the central clock unfolds, strikes, and displays the time with moveable type (dolls don't march out like they do in California). No seat is better than another; you're still going to be humming that song in your sleep, and possibly inside your grave.

Peter Pan's Flight ★★★ RIDE This iconic indoor ride is also unique because its pirate ship vehicles (maximum capacity: three adults with a child lap-sitter) hang from the ceiling, swooping gently up, down, and around obstacles, while the scenes below are executed in forced perspective to make it feel like you're high in the air. The effect is charming and—okay, I'll say it—magical. This is the ride I loved most as a small child, a feeling that is by no means unique. The aerial view of Edwardian London is especially memorable, and it's hard for tots not to feel a shimmy of excitement when they fly between the sails of a pirate ship. **Strategy:** The wait for this slow loader can be 2 hours and up, so, considering it takes only 2 minutes and 45 seconds, hit this one upon opening or arrange a Fastpass. Thankfully the queue is now mostly in the AC.

Mickey's PhilharMagic ★★ SHOW The computer-animated 3-D entertainment, which runs continuously, is pure, honest Disney in the "Fantasia" mold: Classic characters, prominently Donald Duck, appear to a lush (and loud) soundtrack of Disney songs, while pleasant extrasensory effects such as scents and breezes blow to further convince you that what you're seeing is real. The pace is lively, and nearly everyone is tickled. You also get to enjoy AC for 12 minutes. The shop afterwards specializes in Donald Duck merchandise.

Prince Charming Regal Carrousel ★★ RIDE Nice to see a prince get a little recognition around here! It's easy to enjoy one of the world's prettiest carousels. The 90-second ride was handmade in 1917 for a Detroit amusement park and it spent nearly 4 decades in Maplewood, New Jersey, before

Imagineers rescued it, refurbishing it and the original organ calliope (although you'll hear prerecorded Disney songs instead). The horses, which rise up and down, are arranged so that the largest ones are on the outside. Cinderella's personal steed has a golden ribbon tied to its tail.

Princess Fairytale Hall ★★ CHARACTER GREETING   The Snow White's Scary Adventures ride, a Magic Kingdom mainstay since opening day, was demolished to make way for this meet-and-greet for the Princess characters, particularly Cinderella and Rapunzel (Belle "lives" at her Enchanted Tales cottage). Little girls eagerly wait in a reception hall that's dressed in stained glass and portraits of the royal ladies, and when it's time, they make their way, wide-eyed, to the individual meeting rooms. Cameras ready!

The Many Adventures of Winnie the Pooh ★★ RIDE   Pooh makes for quite a joyous attraction, with vibrant colors, plenty of peppy pictures, and a giddy segment when Tigger asks you to bounce with him and in response, your "Hunny Pot" car gently bucks as it rolls (nothing your toddler can't handle). The effects, such as a levitating dreaming Pooh, a room full of fiber-optic raindrops, and real smoke rings (front-row seats are best for experiencing that one), are the most advanced of the Fantasyland kiddie rides. The more I take this merry, 4-minute romp, the more I see poor Pooh as a junkie for honey, since he spends much of his focus bingeing and having psychedelic dreams about getting more of the sweet stuff. Will someone please stage an intervention for this poor bear? This ride is not anyone's favorite, but it's a fine diversion.

Mad Tea Party ★ RIDE   Its conceit—spinning teacups on a platter of concentric turntables—has given the name to an entire genre of carnival "teacup" rides, in which each cup serves up a steaming serving of nausea. How much you'll want to heave depends on whether you're riding with someone strong who can turn the central wheel and get your twirl on within the 90 seconds allotted. There's not much to it, and for repeat guests, it's ignorable furniture, like a hall table you pass on your way to the rest of the house.

Seven Dwarfs Mine Train ★★★ RIDE   Disney's newest mountain, circa 2014, is really more of a knoll, and a joyful little ride in contrast to the relatively dark movie that inspired it. The mine cart roller coaster, which replaced a circa-1971 Snow White ride told from the Queen's point of view, goes in and out of a hill containing the gem quarry dug by Snow White's diminutive landlords, whom you'll encounter "Heigh-Ho"-ing through a day's work. Carriages gently rock on pivots as you turn, much like a bassinette, but don't worry—this is Fantasyland, so this ride is unchallenging, with plenty of S-curves and humps but no loops or alarming drops. Near the 2½–minute ride's conclusion, look right and peek into the windows of the dwarfs' cottage for a charming (but too-quick) glimpse of their evening leisure. *Tip:* It's too short and too cramped to appeal to thrill-seekers, but for maximum sensation, the back rows are dramatically better than the first rows.

Enchanted Tales with Belle ★★ CHARACTER GREETING   In 2012, Disney added this character meet-and-greet with a tech twist: In addition to the "Beauty and the Beast" heroine, who selects audience members to reenact one of her beloved stories—the one you can buy on DVD—you encounter a thrillingly lifelike talking armoire, a fantastic Lumière figure, and, best of all, a trick with a miraculously transforming mirror that must be seen to be believed. The detail is well realized, but there are issues: It takes a while to get in and about 30 minutes to finish once you have, and the only way to get a photo with Belle is to be selected, which means some kids are inevitably disappointed.

Dumbo the Flying Elephant ★★★ RIDE   Fascinatingly, in the 1941 film "Dumbo," the stork delivers baby Dumbo almost exactly over the future site of Disney World, 30 years before it became a reality. The famous baby circus animal recently got a makeover, and now there are two copies of this sentimental ride, halving waits. After entering the Big Top, you get a pager (like the ones at the Cheesecake Factory!) and kids are let loose to wreak screaming havoc in an indoor play area until you're summoned for your turn on board. Back outside, you go round and round in 16 aerodynamic pachyderms whose elevation kids control with a joystick. Each car fits only two adults across, or an adult and two small kids. Standing here, witnessing the joy of ebullient little children being the most spirited you'll ever see little children be, is almost better than the ride. *Tips:* An original vehicle is on display in the Smithsonian, but there's a spare between the two rides here so you can pause for that prize snapshot without slowing things down. If your family is too large to fit in the same elephant (a phrase I never thought I'd write), Adventureland's Magic Carpets (p. 46) provide the same experience ride for four.

Under the Sea—Journey of the Little Mermaid ★ RIDE   As you travel in slow-moving shell vehicles for 6 gentle minutes, you retrace a not-very-accurate jukebox version of the film's plot, including dutiful reprises of "Part of Your World," "Poor Unfortunate Souls" (by an enormous Ursula), "Kiss the Girl," and most spectacularly, a big room full of fish jamming out to "Under the Sea". Nothing surprising happens. As rides go, it's acceptable and the Audio-Animatronics are top-notch, but it's not as transporting as you want it to be and it's unlikely to hook adults as much as small children. Nearby, kids get autographs from the underwater princess herself at **Ariel's Grotto,** and yes, there's a separate wait for that, so make your choice if you must.

Pete's Silly Sideshow ★★ CHARACTER GREETING   By the train station, meet four Disney stars under the big top, envisioned as carnival performers: Minnie Magnifique, Madame Daisy Fortuna, the Astounding Donaldo, and the Great Goofini. The waits to get autographs from the girls are often longer, but happily, it happens in the AC. If you're looking for Mickey, he's at the Town Square Theater on Main Street, U.S.A. *Reminder:* All character's appearance locations and times are printed on the Times Guide.

TIME IS MONEY: reducing waits

For a 9-hour day, you'll pay as much as $11 an hour to enjoy Walt Disney World. Maximize your time by minimizing waits with these 10 priceless tips:

1. **Be there when the gates open.** The period before lunch is critical. Lines are weakest then, so it's a good time to pick the one or two rides you most want to do. *Pitfall:* Don't go to the one closest to the gates. Instead, head as far into parks as you dare. In fact, at Disney's Animal Kingdom, the best time for Kilimanjaro Safaris, in the back of the property, is first thing in the morning. The animals won't have bolted for shade yet and you can get a good look at them.

2. **If you don't have kids, save the slow rides for after dinner.** Disney World has an almost metaphysical ability to turn Momma's sweet little angel into a red-faced, howling, inconsolable demon. This meltdown usually happens in late afternoon, as the stress of the day exhausts children. By dinnertime, parents evacuate their screaming brood. The lines at kiddie attractions such as Peter Pan's Flight, as tough as 2 hours in midday, shorten after bedtime.

3. **Fastpass first thing.** The sooner your three are scheduled and used, the sooner you can get your next one. Revise the boilerplate schedule Disney offers and move your reservations to fall as early as possible.

4. **Pray for rain.** In Florida, it usually strikes in mid-afternoon and lasts for less than an hour, but that's long enough for many guests to leave, which eases waits.

5. **If your kids allow it, skip the parade.** Lines at many of the most popular rides get shorter in the run-up to parade times, when the hordes pack the route in anticipation. Bank on thinner lines 30 minutes before and during showtime. It's often possible to hit two or three rides during the show.

6. **Come early or stay late.** If you're paying higher-than-normal rates to stay on Disney property, get some value back by availing yourself of Extra Magic Hours. Your Disney hotel will tell you which park is either opening early or closing late for the express use of its guests. Lines will be shorter during those hours.

7. **If the weather will be hot, Fastpass the water rides.** When it swelters, arrange a Fastpass for the water rides by midmorning, which should ensure a slot to ride when the heat peaks.

8. **Eat early.** Restaurants have lines, too, so avoid peak periods for meals. Eat at 11am, when many places open, and there will be light traffic until noon or so. The same goes for dinner: Schedule a reservation for around 4pm. Eating late in the parks doesn't work, because many restaurants close.

9. **Baby swap.** The parks have a system allowing both parents to ride with little additional waiting. After the whole family goes through the line, Dad can wait with Junior while Mom rides. When Mom's off, Dad can ride without waiting and Mom takes a turn watching Junior. For many people, that cuts the old waiting times in half. It's not available on kiddie rides because it's weird to watch Daddy ride those alone.

10. **Split up.** If you don't care if you all ride in the same car, a few attractions have lines for single riders. Use them and you'll shoot to the head of the pack, fill spare seats left by odd-numbered groups, ride within minutes of each other, and be back on the pavement in no time flat. Even on rides without dedicated single lines, solo riders should alert ride-loading attendants to their presence—doing so could shave long minutes off a wait.

The Barnstormer ★ RIDE   Fantasyland's kiddie coaster, which is all about giving small children a sense of excitement and accomplishment, invariably has a line, which is outdoors. The tangled track does a few swooping figure-eights and passes through a Goofy-shaped hole in a billboard, but takes scarcely more than a minute—less than half that if you subtract the time it takes to climb the hill. There are some cute touches, including ample evidence of Goofy's flying act having gone hilariously wrong.

Walt Disney World Railroad, Fantasyland Station ★★★ RIDE Board here for a round trip to the front gates at Main Street, U.S.A., then Frontierland, and finally back here in 20 minutes, all to a recorded narration that describes what you see along the way. Across the path, the train motif carries over to the **Casey Jr. Splash 'N' Soak Station,** a honking, chugging, wheezing, ringing collection of animal-packed circus railway cars where monkeys squirt seltzer, locomotives steam, elephants sneeze water through their trunks, and camels spit.

Tomorrowland

Tomorrowland is lighter on character appearances than other lands. A fun exception is **The Incredibles' Super Dance Party,** held in busier periods on the Rockettower Stage. It's a chance for little ones to dance and mingle with Mr. and Mrs. Incredible and Frozone. To the right of Space Mountain, you'll see a one-level bathroom structure that looks like it ought to contain something interesting. It once did: The Skyway, a gondola ride over the park, loaded here until 1999 (and unloaded in Fantasyland beside "it's a small world"). There are quiet places for sitting around it.

Tomorrowland Speedway ★ RIDE   Originally built in Disneyland at a time when freeways were considered national treasures and not a bane of life, this half-mile, self-driven jog of four-laned track is the first chance most kids will have to drive. These are Go-Karts with no juice, although the late Tom Carnegie calls the "race" and the gas-fired engines reek and snarl. Each vehicle carries two people, steers poorly but is guided by a rail, and won't go fast (about 7mph) no matter how much pedal meets the metal. Though the queue can be blistering hot and the load process tedious, your puttering will end in about 5 minutes. *Strategy:* Mind the height restrictions—kids shorter than 54 inches can't go alone, a rule that draws tantrums.

Space Mountain ★★★ RIDE   Walt Disney liked creating one landmark for every land. He called it the "weenie" that drew people in. Tomorrowland's weenie, and only 6 feet shorter than Cinderella Castle, is contained in that futuristic concrete-ribbed circus tent. Although it's a relatively tame indoor, carnival-style, steel coaster (top speed: barely 29mph), the near-total darkness and tight turns give your go-round (duration: 2½ min.) a panache that makes it one of the park's hotter tickets. Other worldwide versions are more thrilling, but there's something endearing about an original. *Strategy:* The wait is indoors. There are two tracks; the left-hand coaster (Alpha) and the right-hand

Walt's original system for admission was intended to accommodate people of all incomes. Anyone could enter his park for a nominal fee of a few dollars, but to do rides and shows, guests had to obtain coupon books from kiosks. There were five categories. The simplest, least popular attractions, like Main Street Vehicles, could be seen for cheap "A" tickets (around 10¢ in 1972) but the prime blockbusters were honored with the top distinction, an "E" ticket (85¢). It didn't take long for the designation to find its way into the American vernacular. Sally Ride pronounced her 1983 launch on the space shuttle "definitely an E-ticket." The coupon system was dropped in the early 1980s in favor of a high gate price, a system that has mostly replaced the per-ride payment system at theme parks across the world.

one (Omega) are mirror images of each other, so there's no real difference except Fastpassers are sent to Omega. The front seat has the best view.

Buzz Lightyear's Space Ranger Spin ★★ RIDE The "Toy Story" movies provide inspiration for a rambunctious 3-minute, slow-car ride that works like a shooting gallery. Passengers are equipped with laser guns and the means to rotate their vehicles, and it's their mission to blast as many targets as they can. That's easier said than done, since the aliens are spinning, bouncing, and turning, and your laser sight appears only intermittently as a blinking red light, but that's all part of the fun. You'll think you did well at 118,000 until you turn and see the kid who racked up 205,000. He must have known the secret: The farther away a target is, the more it's worth. Guess you'll have to re-ride.

Astro Orbiter ★★ RIDE The gist is like Dumbo—an 80-second spin on an armature, you control height—except from three stories up, and with 12 toboggan-style rockets seating only two each. Usually, it takes too long, partly because you have to use an un-magical elevator, framed operational permit and all, to board and leave. At night, the view of an illuminated Castle could make it worth it. *Tip:* Beneath the ride, pick up the Metrophone for some gag messages.

Tomorrowland Transit Authority PeopleMover ★★★ RIDE The tramlike second-story track, which boards under the Astro Orbiter at Rockettower Plaza, uses pollution-free "linear induction" magnetic technology to take a story-free scenic overview of the area's attractions. On a 13-minute round-trip with no stops, it coasts past some windows over the Buzz Lightyear ride and through the guts of Space Mountain, where you traverse the circumference over the Omega boarding area. You will also catch a too-fleeting glimpse of one of Walt Disney's original 1963 models for Progress City. The ride itself is historic: Walt Disney envisioned this system, originally called the WEDway PeopleMover, as a principal form of transportation for the resort. Sorry, Walt: They bought buses instead. *Tip:* There's almost never a wait. Do TTA at night, when Tomorrowland is illuminated in cobalts and greens.

Walt Disney's Carousel of Progress ★★ SHOW   They know it's an antique: They put Walt's name in the title as a sort of apology. But as a pre-boarding movie attests, Walt Disney loved this attraction—he created it with General Electric sponsorship for the 1964 World's Fair. It was later moved here, and appropriate to its underwriter, the message is a banquet of consumerist overtones about how appliances will rescue us from a life of drudgery. Walt's novel twist was that the stage remains stationery but the auditorium rotates on a ring past six rooms (four "acts" and one each for loading and unloading) of Audio-Animatronic scenes. You'll see a modern person's trivialization of daily life in 1904, 1927, and the 1940s, and an unspecified time that you could peg for 1989, what with Grandpa's breathless praise for laser discs and car phones. While our very white, very middle-class narrator (voiced by Jean Shepherd, the narrator of "A Christmas Story") loafs with his dog across the ages, his wife does chores, his mother festers, his daughter primps, and his son dreams of adventure. (Funny how a tribute to progress is riddled with obsolete gender stereotypes.) The Sherman Brothers, who wrote the repetitive ditty "There's a Great Big Beautiful Tomorrow" (they also wrote the songs for "Mary Poppins") said they considered this to be Walt Disney's personal theme song. Set aside 25 minutes for the show, but it starts every 5 because the rotating theater allows endless refills, like the chamber of a revolver. As a relic from a more idealistic time, it's priceless, and here's hoping they never remove it, as is always the rumor. Another reason to see it: Despite the fact it has no living performers, it's billed as the longest-running stage show in the United States.

Stitch's Great Escape! ★ SHOW   What begins with a hackneyed Disney set-up—you're a "new recruit," this time at an intergalactic prison—ends with an extrasensory sit-down presentation employing smells and rigged over-the-shoulder harnesses. Little kids get scared because of the pitch darkness, because the restraint is constrictive, and because they are alarmed to learn a dangerous alien is on the loose, even if it turns out to be their friend Stitch. Expect not menace but bawdy gags about spit, slobber, burping, and pee. Lilo makes no appearance, leaving the show without the soft heart it needs. To call this attraction reviled by many Disney fans would not be an exaggeration. The Audio-Animatronics are marvelous, though, and hilarious actor Richard Kind does a voice. The event takes about 12 minutes once you're inside. *Tips:* Enter the theater last for the best sightlines. Top-row seating keeps you from having to crane your neck upward.

Monsters, Inc. Laugh Floor ★ SHOW   Like Turtle Talk with Crush at Epcot, it's a "Living Character" video show, about 15 minutes long, in which computer-animated characters on a giant screen interact with a theater full of people, singling humans out with a hidden camera for gentle ridicule. The animation looks as fluid as in the Pixar movies and is drawn from a cast of some 20 characters, but the three you'll see in your set will vary. The experience depends as much on the eagerness of your audience as on the improvisational

LIGHTS after dark

A trip to Disney doesn't seem complete if you don't set aside time to catch the nightly fireworks show, **Wishes,** held when the park is open past dark; check the "Times Guide." Although it's technically at least partially visible from anywhere, the most symmetrical view is from the Castle's front and Main Street, U.S.A. If you can see the wire strung to the Castle's top, you've got a good viewpoint. The roughly 10-minute show is quite the slick spectacle—lights dim everywhere, even the ferry dock, and you can hear the soundtrack (and Jiminy Cricket's platitude-rich narration) wherever you are. Areas around and behind the Castle are roped off during the show to protect guests from falling cinders, and wide portions of the Hub are set aside for premium-paying guests, so get there about 30 minutes ahead or get shunted elsewhere. Also catch the trippy **Celebrate the Magic** projection show on Cinderella Castle, usually held 15 minutes before and after the fireworks. Off-season, rides begin closing as soon as it starts, and people start heading home after it's done. You have the option of purchasing $24 illuminated "Made with Magic" mouse ears that change color along with the show, but only about 5% of customers seem to do that.

For the best views, Disney makes you shell out. It throws a nightly **Fireworks Dessert Party** starting an hour before showtime. For $49 to $69 adults and $29 to $39 kids, you get all-you-can-eat pastries, ice cream, light beverages, and a primo vantage point of Tink afloat. Naturally, it books up early (℡ **407/939-3463**).

Another can't-miss nighttime attraction (check the "Times Guide") is the **Main Street Electrical Parade,** bopping along to its signature synth-pop anthem. Its illuminated floats and light-studded costumes have mesmerized since the 1970s.

At the very end of the night (well, most nights, but not all), about 30 minutes after the posted closing time, Cinderella Castle flashes with a dazzling rainbow of light. This is a **"Kiss Goodnight,"** something that isn't on the schedules, and it's a little like the Sandman at the Apollo, sweeping you out the door. Stick it out until you see one (the last one is an hour after closing time), because by then, crowds will have thinned. Remember, you still have a monorail or a ferryboat and a parking tram to go.

skill of the (spoiler alert) hidden live actors doing the voices. Don't miss the gags in the preshow video-instruction room (the employee bulletin board warns against "Repetitive Scare Injury"). You'll probably find yourself more impressed by the canny technology than by the quality of the jokes, and sticklers for Disney orthodoxy are annoyed it isn't really set in the future. *Tip:* Sit in the rear or extreme sides of the auditorium to avoid being picked on.

Where to Eat in the Magic Kingdom

All locations will have a few vegetarian options, kids' meals, and can accommodate special dietary requests (usually; the park is especially good with nut allergies), albeit often at diminished quality. For info on the table-service restaurants that usually require reservations, go to p. 63. Don't go looking for beer—there's no alcohol served except at Be Our Guest, and only at dinner. There's also a fruit stand across from the Little Mermaid ride in Fantasyland.

THE MAGIC KINGDOM'S QUICK-SERVICE RESTAURANTS

The park, being a mass-appeal crowd-pleaser, does not support an affordable menu that is as adventurous as its characters. Hope you like burgers.

Casey's Corner ★ AMERICAN   The hot dog-and-nachos joint facing the Castle is the only place to grab a counter-service meal around Main Street, U.S.A., but there is never enough seating. Dogs are nearly a foot long and piled embarrassingly high with choices including barbecue and chili. **Main Street, U.S.A.** Hot dogs $9 to $11 with fries, $2 less without.

Plaza Ice Cream Parlor ★ ICE CREAM   Although hand-scooped sundaes are served, the specialty is ice-cream sandwiches made with fresh chocolate chip cookies. They're warmest early in the day. **Main Street, U.S.A.** Desserts $5 to $6.

Aloha Isle Refreshments ★★★ ICE CREAM   An only-at-Disney treat: "Dole Whip" soft serve in pineapple, vanilla, or orange. Or put your Dole Whip in a Pineapple Float. Or just get a spear of fresh pineapple. **Adventureland.** Dole Whips $5.

Sunshine Tree Terrace ★★★ ICE CREAM   Disney fans beeline to this kiosk for the Citrus Swirl, a wonderful blend of frozen O.J. and soft-serve vanilla ice cream. The pomegranate limeade is also gaining favor. The doe-eyed mascot is Orange Bird; Disney created it for the Florida citrus lobby, which sponsored this stand and the Tiki birds back in the 1970s. **Adventureland.** Beverages and desserts $4 to $5.

Tortuga Tavern ★★ MEXICAN   Open for lunch in peak season, it does burritos and beef taco salads, and it has a large, sheltered seating area. **Adventureland.** Combo meal $9 to $11.

Turkey Leg Cart ★★ AMERICAN   These honking hunks of meat ($12) could feed a caveman. **Frontierland,** across from Frontierland Shooting Gallery.

Pecos Bill Tall Tale Inn and Cafe ★★★ AMERICAN   Burritos, fajitas, rice bowls, and mini churros in spacious, air-conditioned dining halls. **Frontierland.** Combo meal $10 to $12.

Columbia Harbour House ★★★ AMERICAN   At this indoor counter service spot, order fat sandwiches, fish platters, and chicken pot pie, plus sides like chowder ($5), then take them upstairs where it's quiet. **Liberty Square.** Combo meal $9 to $11.

Pinocchio's Village Haus ★★ AMERICAN/ITALIAN   Vaguely Italian food (flatbreads, meatball subs, and so on) adjoining "it's a small world," with a few tables in the air-conditioning overlooking the snazzy loading area. **Fantasyland.** Combo meal $9 to $10.

The Friar's Nook ★ AMERICAN   Window-service with no seating for mac and cheese with bacon cheeseburger, pot roast, or hummus with veggies. **Fantasyland.** Snacks $3 to $8.20.

Gaston's Tavern ★ AMERICAN   Behind the amusing Gaston fountain, you'll find some indoor, only-at-Disney treats. The Roast Pork Shank ($10) is huge like the famous turkey leg, only in pig flavor, and the cinnamon rolls are as big as cinder blocks. LeFou's Brew is Fantasyland's (not very successful) answer to Harry Potter's Butterbeer: frozen apple juice with a lightly fruity foam. Get it in a regular cup for $4.50, or $10 in a plastic stein or a goblet, suitable to gender roles. **Fantasyland.**

Cosmic Ray's Starlight Cafe ★★★ AMERICAN   The best choice for indoor Quick Service on this end of the park, it does burgers, BBQ pork sandwiches, and chicken (both sandwich and rotisserie) and has a toppings bar with freshly sautéed mushrooms and onions—choose the "bay" that serves your choice. It's distinguished by regular lounge-act shows by Sonny Eclipse, a longrunning Audio-Animatronic character. The panorama of the Castle is sublime; it's my favorite lunchtime view. **Tomorrowland.** Combo meal $9 to $11.

The Lunching Pad ★ AMERICAN   Window-service with exposed seating for hot dogs of several varieties. There's a cart selling **turkey legs** ($12) between it and Space Mountain. **Tomorrowland.** Hot dogs $9 to $10.

THE MAGIC KINGDOM'S TABLE-SERVICE RESTAURANTS

This is the most popular theme park in the world, so getting a seat can be competitive (and it requires a credit card) and the wait staff is almost always running around. Some restaurants *may* accept walk-ins at 4pm, when they start dinner service, but ask early in the day. Taking them clockwise around the park:

Tony's Town Square Restaurant ★★ ITALIAN   Loosely themed on the Italian restaurant scene from "Lady and the Tramp" (there's a fountain of the two doe-eyed dogs), it's loud, not romantic. To repeat Tramp's spaghetti-and-meatball sharing gesture (kindly don't use your nose like he did), you'll pay $18 a plate. It also does chicken Parmesan, cannelloni, and shrimp scampi. After lunch, sandwiches, pizzas, and flatbreads are swapped for pork tenderloin and strip steak. **Main Street, U.S.A.** Main courses $18 to $31.

The Crystal Palace ★★★ AMERICAN   Under an airy Victorian-style skylight canopy redolent of an 1853 New York City world's exhibition, Winnie the Pooh greets diners at what's probably the prettiest in-park restaurant in all of Walt Disney World. The refined air doesn't stop Pooh and his buddies (Tigger, Eeyore, Piglet) from jamming the aisles with a conga line. Being slightly smaller than many other character dining locations, you're likely to get more face time with the characters. This restaurant's been open since Day One and offers three daily all-you-can-eat buffets of changing, crowd-pleasing standards from meats to vegetables. There's a make-your-own-sundae bar for lunch and dinner. Prices are lowest at breakfast (the best time anyway, since you'll have the rest of your day free) and scale up. **Main Street, U.S.A.** Buffet $27 to $42 adults, $15 to $20 children.

SAVING ON PARK munchies

If you plan to buy all your food at the park, sticking strictly to counter-service meals is the cheapest way to go. But considering you'll pay $8 to $11 each for a counter-service sandwich, plus at least $2.70 for a medium-size soft drink—the going rate in the Orlando parks—even that way, a family of four can easily spend $60 on every meal! Don't be goofy—save money! Besides eating off premises, here's how:

o **Subtract unwanted combo items.** Although counter-service restaurants make the menu appear like it's mostly combo meals, it's an unpublicized fact that you may eliminate unwanted items from adult selections and save money. Dropping fries or other bundled side dishes can save about $2.25. For carrot sticks!

o **Pack a little food of your own.** Park security usually looks the other way if you bring a soft lunchbag-size cooler (hard-sided ones will be rejected). Or just tote sandwiches in plastic bags. If your lodging has a freezer, keep juice boxes in there; they'll be thawed by lunch.

o **Economize with an all-you-can-eat meal.** Character meals (p. 242) give good value because they serve limitless food; breakfast ones are cheapest. A big lunch can last you until after you leave the park.

o **Skip table-service meals, or plan them strategically.** They can chomp as much as 90 minutes out of your touring time. Do

that twice and you've lost a third of your day. A park that could be seen in 1 day would require 2, doubling costs. If you want a sit-down meal, do it at lunch, when prices are often lower than at dinner. Eat around 11am, when crowds are lighter. Also, if you don't show up for Disney reservations, you're docked $10—assess whether your kids will truly have energy for an evening table-service meal if you schedule one.

o **Adults may order cheaper and smaller kids' meals.** No one will stop them.

o **Snack on fruit.** Each park has at least one fruit stand. ($1.70/piece)

o **Seek out the turkey legs.** They're giant (1½ pounds, from 45-pound turkeys), salty, and cost around $12. They taste so good because they're injected with brine before cooking for 6 hours. Just don't think about the hormones it takes to grow a 45-pound bird. Or a 5-foot-tall mouse.

o **Order drinks without ice.** Soda is dispensed cold to prevent foaming. It's chilling how much ice is in a standard Disney Coke.

o **Order water for free.** It comes in a regular-size cup.

o **Stretch meals.** If there's a double cheeseburger on the menu, order it and an extra bun for about $1. Then make two burgers and raid the fixings bar. (Disney has few double cheeseburgers, but Universal has still them.)

The Plaza Restaurant ★ AMERICAN   What's special about this one is its view. Situated at the end of Main Street facing Cinderella Castle, it focuses on sandwiches, burgers, and meatloaf, which are served with broccoli slaw, homemade chips, or French fries. Add soup for $5. It also serves ice cream sundaes and cheesecake from the shop next door. **Main Street, U.S.A.** Main courses $12 to $19.

Skipper Canteen ★ AMERICAN The newest restaurant in the park takes up residence in the old Adventureland Veranda space, which hadn't seen a steady use since 1994. The concept: Proprietors are boat captains from the Jungle Navigation Co., Ltd., across the path, trying to make a little extra cash. One dining room is a once-secret meeting room of the "Society of Explorers and Adventurers." **Adventureland.** Main courses not set a press time.

Liberty Tree Tavern ★★ AMERICAN At lunch, this colonial-style place (stained wood and rung-backed chairs) facing the Rivers of America (no view) serves loosely patriotic a la carte fare such as pot roast, turkey with stuffing, and "Freedom Pasta," which is fusilli with chicken, vegetables, and mushrooms in a cream sauce. Weirdly, Craisins wind up in a lot of dishes—it's a sponsor. After 4pm, it shifts to an all-you-can-eat buffet including a beef carvery. **Liberty Square.** Lunch mains $14 to $20; dinner $32 adults, $16 kids.

Cinderella's Royal Table ★★★ AMERICAN This is the Holy Grail of character meals since it takes place past the velvet ropes inside Cinderella Castle, where there's a capacity of less than 200. The famous royal resident always appears (sometimes joined by her soul sisters Jasmine, Aurora, Snow White, and others), and little girls from far and wide dress up like princesses to meet her. ("Right this way, Royal Family," greets the hostess.) The interior is as lavish as you'd expect for the inside of the Castle, with mock medieval vaulted ceilings, a royal red carpet, stained glass, and stylized crest shields adoring the walls. Meals aren't all-you-can-eat, but they are all prix-fixe, though the price shifts with the season. Bookings open 180 days ahead at 7am Orlando time (and must be prepaid by credit card) and are snapped up in moments, although if you're persistent and flexible, you may snag a cancellation starting two weeks before. Food selections include gnocchi, seared chicken, and pork loin. **Fantasyland.** Meals $58 to $73 adults, $36 to $54 children, according to season; includes tip and five photos of your party.

Be Our Guest Restaurant ★ AMERICAN It's not so easy to be their guest here since bookings fill incredibly quickly, and never did "hospitality" involve waiting so much: one line to enter, another to order—you won't eat a bite until at least 30 minutes after your reservation. It sports a few technical tricks to evoke Beast's castle, including animated falling snow outside some false windows, a portrait that reveals a hidden Beast when illuminated by periodic lightning (that's in the West Wing, the best seating area to choose), and an animated rose under glass that slowly sheds its petals. All those polished surfaces make a meal gratingly loud, and although the food is Frenchish (there's ratatouille at dinner, croque-monsieur at lunch, and French onion soup all the time), in reality the French would form a posse to detain this chef. You'll receive quasi-service, too: You order by kiosk, pour your own beverages, and your food is wheeled to you when it's ready. This is the only place in the Magic Kingdom where you can get alcohol, but only at dinner and only with that coveted reservation. It serves all three meals. **Fantasyland.** Breakfast $22 adult, $14 kids. Main courses $10 to $14 lunch, $16 to $30 dinner.

freebies AT DISNEY

It's not easy finding fun stuff to do that you don't have to cough up for, but you don't need to hand over a cent for these pleasures—not even for park admission. Anyone off the street can enjoy these things:

o **Take the monorail.** Whiz round the Seven Seas Lagoon past the Magic Kingdom and through the Contemporary Resort as many times as you want without a ticket. You can also use it to make the 4-mile round-trip to Epcot, where you'll do a flyover of Future World.

o **Watch the Electrical Water Pageant** on the Seven Seas Lagoon and Bay Lake between 9 and 10:20pm. The illuminated convoy, which twinkle to a soundtrack, motor around the conjoined ponds after nightfall, and you can see it from the beachfront at any hotel.

o **Ride the ferries** between the resorts, such as the one from Port Orleans Riverside to Disney Springs along the meandering Sassagoula River, which passes the French Quarter resort and the Old Key West resort. You can even ride the one from the monorail-area resorts to the foot of the Magic Kingdom.

o **Hike at Fort Wilderness.** The trail begins at the east end of Bay Lake and threads through occasionally muddy woods.

o **Spend a night by the pool.** Most resorts keep them open 'til midnight. Technically, you should be a guest. But behave, and no one'll care (except at the Yacht and Beach clubs, where bracelets are required). Each hotel's parking lot has a gate, but if you park at Disney Springs and take a free Disney bus, you'll scoot right in.

o **See African animals** at the Animal Kingdom Lodge. The gatekeeper will admit you to sit by the fire in its vaulted lobby, and out back, you can watch game such as giraffe and kudu from the Sunset Overlook. Sometimes, there are zoologists who answer questions.

o For a marvelous view of the fireworks over the Magic Kingdom, **stroll on the beach** of the Grand Floridian or the Polynesian resorts. The sand is millions of years old and was recovered from under Bay Lake. Did you know Disney built a giant wave machine in the middle of the lake? It never worked.

o **Partake of the campfire singalong,** which happens nightly near the Meadow Trading Post at Fort Wilderness, followed by a Disney feature on an outdoor screen.

o **Cuddle farm animals,** including ducks, goats, and peacocks, at the petting farm behind Fort Wilderness's Pioneer Hall. You can also see the horses used to pull streetcars up Main Street, U.S.A.

o **Ride the bus system.** Park at Disney Springs for free and take the buses to any hotel, and from there to a theme park. That'll save you $17 on parking each day.

EPCOT

Spaceship Earth at Epcot.

Epcot ★★★ remains one of Walt Disney World's finest achievements. More than any other park, Epcot changes its personality, decorations, and diversions by the season. Although it used to possess the pretense of education, guests usually don't learn much more than they already know (so as not to bore them or to insult their intelligence), but even though there isn't much take-away information, that there's lots to soak up if you explore. There's plenty to do here without having to wait in lines, and unlike other parks, there are many places to sit. The wide variety of foods and alcoholic beverages is also a big draw. Epcot's genial personality has earned it a spot as the fifth-most-visited theme park on Earth, racking up some 11.4 million entries in 2014.

The 260-acre park is divided into two zones, Future World and World Showcase, laid out roughly like a figure eight. Both areas started life separately but, as the legend goes, were grafted together when plans were afoot. **Future World** is where the wonders of industry were extolled in corporate-sponsored "pavilions." The companies had a hand creating them and they also maintained VIP areas in backstage areas for executives and special guests. At the back of the property, around a 1.3-mile lake footpath, **World Showcase** was (and is) a circuit of countries, each representing in miniature its namesake's essence. These, too, received funding from their host countries. The

---

A history OF EPCOT

Although people think of Walt Disney as prototypically American, he had a communist streak. He long dreamed of establishing a real, working city where 20,000 full-time residents, none of them unemployed, would test out experimental technologies in the course of their daily lives. In vintage films where he discusses his Florida Project, his passion for creating such a self-sustaining community, to be called the Experimental Prototype Community of Tomorrow, was inextricable from the rest of his planned resort. He wanted nothing less than to revolutionize the world. Truck traffic would be routed to vehicle plazas beneath the city, out of pedestrians' way, while PeopleMovers (like the ones of Magic Kingdom's Tomorrowland Transit Authority) would shift the population around town. Between home and downtown, they'd take the monorail. Even on his deathbed, Walt was perfecting real plans for the city that would be his crowning legacy: one whose innovations would make life better for everyone on Earth. Had he lived just 3 more years, he would have made sure it happened.

Epcot

WORLD SHOWCASE

The American Adventure

Germany
Italy
Japan
Morocco

To Disney's BoardWalk & ferry to Disney's Hollywood Studios

Outpost

Boat Dock

American Gardens Theatre

IllumiNations

Boat Dock

France

International Gateway
Stroller & Wheelchair Rental

China (Reflections of China)

World Showcase Lagoon

Norway (Frozen Ever After)

United Kingdom

Boat Dock SHOWCASE PLAZA Boat Dock

World ShowPlace Events Pavilion

Mexico (Gran Fiesta Tour)

Canada (O Canada!)

Refreshment Port

Monorail

Imagination!

Test Track

Innoventions East   Innoventions West

The Land (Soarin')

Mission: SPACE

FUTURE WORLD

Festival Center

Universe of Energy (Ellen's Energy Adventure)

Spaceship Earth

The Seas with Nemo & Friends

Stroller & Wheelchair Rental

Entrance plaza

Guest Relations

0 100 y
0 100 m

Parking

Monorail Station   *Shuttles*

Biergarten Restaurant **1**	Lotus Blossom Café **5**	Sunshine Seasons **26**
Boulangerie Pâtisserie **19**	Monsieur Paul **18**	Tangierine Café **15**
Chefs de France **17**	Nine Dragons Restaurant **6**	Taste Track **23**
Coral Reef Restaurant **25**	Princess Storybook Dining	Teppan Edo **13**
Electric Umbrella **24**	at Akershus Royal	Tokyo Dining **13**
The Garden Grill **27**	Banquet Hall **7**	Tutto Gusto **2**
Katsura Grill **12**	Restaurant Marrakesh **14**	Tutto Italia Ristorante **2**
Kringla Bakeri og Kafé **8**	Rose & Crown Pub	Via Napoli Ristorante
La Cantina de San Angel **11**	& Dining Room **21**	e Pizzeria **3**
La Hacienda de San Angel **10**	San Angel Inn Restaurante **9**	Yorkshire County
Le Cellier Steakhouse **22**	Sommerfest **1**	Fish Shop **20**
Liberty Inn **4**	Spice Road Table **16**	

MAKING THE MOST OF EPCOT

Epcot has so much to explore, and eat, and drink that you won't feel like you're racing from ride to ride (as you might in other parks). Just make sure you have a late-morning/early afternoon Fastpass+ for Frozen Ever After (which usually opens at 11am—check the Times Guide—and will be instantly crowded). If you can't get that, get one for Soarin' but be at Frozen Ever After when it opens.

⬇

Ride **Test Track** before the line gets crazy.

⬇

Ride **Mission: SPACE.**

⬇

By now, your **Soarin'** Fastpass is probably valid. Ride it.

⬇

Enter World Showcase, go directly to Norway, and ride **Frozen Ever After.**

⬇

Go next door to Mexico and ride **Gran Fiesta Tour.** You have now enjoyed all the rides in World Showcase.

⬇

Continue along World Showcase at a slow pace, having removed the temptation to rush. The movies (in China, France, and Canada) are all worth seeing; the shops can be surprisingly good; and the street entertainment choices (noted on the Times Guide) are excellent. Eat somewhere that appeals to you.

⬇

Catch the American Adventure; the Voices of America perform about 15 minutes before show times, and they're listed in the Times Guide.

⬇

Continue along World Showcase. Pause for a pint in the United Kingdom.

⬇

Return to Future World for **The Seas with Nemo and Friends.**

⬇

Ride **Living with the Land** for a glimpse at Epcot's roots. Consider doing **Soarin'** again.

⬇

Ride **Spaceship Earth.**

⬇

Return to World Showcase, eat dinner in the land of your choice, and catch **IllumiNations** at 9pm. Secure a good viewing point at least 30 minute ahead.

expense of updating exhibits has caused Disney to gradually phase out the educational aspects of the attractions. One by one, original pavilions have been replaced by sense-tingling rides, so that today, only two of the original displays, Spaceship Earth and Living with the Land, remain more or less as they originally were.

GETTING IN The parking lot is at the ticket gates, although you can also catch the **monorail** from the Magic Kingdom parking area. If you park near the track, don't bother with the tram; you can walk to the gates faster. Bags will be quickly inspected. As you enter the park, lockers are at the right of Spaceship Earth; wheeled rentals are to the left. Also on the left is Guest Relations, where last-minute dining reservations can be made, though often, you'll just be deferred to the restaurant in question.

HOURS Future World opens at 9am, and World Showcase opens at 11am. Street entertainment (there's more on weekends) and character greetings dry up after about 5pm. Future World sometimes closes at 7pm, 2 hours before

The Best of Epcot

Don't miss if you're 6: Turtle Talk with Crush

Don't miss if you're 16: Test Track

Requisite photo op: Spaceship Earth

Food you can only get here: Rice cream, the bakery at Norway

The most crowded, so Fastpass or go early: Frozen Ever After, Soarin'

Skippable: Journey into Imagination with Figment

Quintessentially Disney: Spaceship Earth

Biggest thrill: Mission: SPACE

Best show: Voices of Liberty, the American Adventure

Character meals: Akershus Royal Banquet Hall, Norway; Garden Grill, The Land

Best shopping: Mitsukoshi, Japan

Where to find peace: Future World: the Odyssey Center catwalks; World Showcase: the gardens of Japan

World Showcase. The nightly IllumiNations show usually takes place over World Showcase Lagoon at 9pm; at its conclusion, the hordes stampede for their cars en masse.

Future World

By the time Walt Disney World finally got around to opening its second park, EPCOT Center, on October 1, 1982 (11 years to the day after the Magic Kingdom and at a staggering estimated cost of $1.4 billion; America's biggest construction project at the time), it was but a flicker of its original purpose. No one would actually live there, as Walt had directed, and few experimental endeavors would be undertaken. Instead, the most economical course was to turn Walt's legacy into another moneymaker, heavily subsidized by corporate participation and sold by heavy promotion of "Walt's dream"—a formula that prevails today. In truth, the final concept wasn't much different from the world's fair that Walt's father had helped construct in Chicago in 1893 or that Walt himself defined in New York in 1964: Examples of how technology was ostensibly improving lives, plus pavilions representing foreign lands for the edification of people unlikely to travel there themselves. As it turned out, in Disney's version of the future, all walls are carpeted, all lighting is recessed, and all music is lite FM. In December 1993, the park name was simplified to Epcot. As you face the lagoon, the left side of Future World is generally about the physical and man-made sciences, and the right is more about the natural sciences. Behind Spaceship Earth, look for a park **tip board,** which posts wait times and the daily schedule. There are two more tip boards through the underpasses to the east and west sections of Future World, and wherever you go, you'll hear that Casiotone '80s soundtrack.

Spaceship Earth ★★★ RIDE   That gorgeous orb looks like a golf ball on a tee, but the 16-million-pound structure, coated with 11,324 aluminum-bonded panels and sheathed inside with a rainproof rubber layer, is supported by a table-like scaffolding where its six legs enter the dome. Think of this 180-foot-tall Buckminster Fuller sphere as a direct descendent of the

Perisphere of the 1939 World's Fair or the Unisphere of the 1964 World's Fair, which were the icons for their own parks. No mere shell, it houses an eponymous ride using the OmniMover system of cars linked together like an endless snake. The ride slowly winds within the sphere, all on the course of a shallow, sixth-grade-level journey (narrated by Judi Dench) through the history of communications, from Greek theater to the Sistine Chapel to the printing press to the telegraph. In a bit of unintended kinesthetic commentary, once you reach the present day, the ride travels all downhill. Once you're off it, I defy you to tell me what you learned. This, of course, makes it essential Epcot. This is the ride that still shows what the 1982 park was like—its robot-populated sister pavilions about transportation and the future were razed in the 1990s to make way for flashier thrills. Although some people don't get it, I cherish it as a soothing sojourn not only through time, but also through air-conditioning. Because it's the first ride that guests encounter in the park, lines, which move fast, are much shorter in the afternoon.

Innoventions ★ ACTIVITY   The semicircular buildings (originally Communicore) facing each other behind Spaceship Earth have been the domain of corporate-sponsored exhibits, as Walt had intended, but in 2015 they were largely emptied and as of press time, Disney had only announced one new addition: Colortopia, an exhibition about color sponsored by paint manufacturer Glidden. These mini attractions may remain in the East building:

○ **Sum of All Thrills:** Lines are shortest in late afternoon for this slow-loading, 90-second ride from Raytheon, the weapons-tech manufacturer (!!). You design your own ride on a panel before testing it in a motion simulator at the end of a robot arm. You choose if you want your ride to go nearly upside-down or not.

○ **Habit Heroes:** Paid for by Blue Cross Blue Shield, this is an 18-minute, three-game motion-sensor course where you learn very vague health lessons by battling monsters that are somehow preventing you from getting nutrition.

○ **StormStruck:** In this 3-D movie to inspire storm-proofing your home, audiences are buffeted with wind and rain effects, and then vote on proofing methods, which are then tested on screen.

Also in the Innoventions buildings, you'll find **MouseGear,** the largest souvenir shop in Epcot and opposite that, **Club Cool,** by the Coca-Cola Company, which lets you pour unlimited samples of eight soft drink flavors sold only in other countries. Beverly, a bitter aperitif from Italy, is not for faint tongues. If you're an obsessive tightwad, you can keep coming back here instead of buying a real Coke (although most of it is dramatically sweet). Frozen Cokes are sold for $4. Between Innoventions, you'll find the **World Fellowship Fountain,** which was dedicated by Walt's widow, Lillian. At the opening ceremony, water from 23 countries was combined as a symbol of brotherhood. It can shoot 150 feet in the air. There are 5-minute choreographed splash-ups on the quarter hour, but they're not worth halting your day to wait for.

Universe of Energy ★ RIDE/SHOW   This attraction is emblematic of Epcot's corporate-dictated content. The dated adventure begins with a movie, circa 1996, featuring Ellen DeGeneres being taught by Bill Nye the Science Guy about how oil is formed and then pulled out of the ground for the benefit of mankind. If that sounds lame, at least the ride system is more creative: The audience is seated in six 97-passenger slabs of mobile theater-style bench seating. Miraculously, the slabs organize themselves in a line and move from room to giant room, passing primeval forests full of mild-mannered dinosaurs. When, at another movie stop, the issue of global warming comes up, Nye waves it away, saying, "It's a hot topic with lots of questions," before reassuring us that "we're far from running on empty." (Can you imagine him agreeing to say that line today?) Not surprisingly, the didactic venture was backed by ExxonMobil. The whole show takes between 30 to 50 minutes, depending on when you arrive at the preshow, which makes it a good cool-down. Outside, the roof is coated in 2 acres of solar panels, which generate 15% of the show's ironically hefty energy appetite. *Strategy:* Although all sections spend time waiting for the others to move or catch up, the two sections on the right wait in the most interesting spaces. This one often shutters at 7pm.

Mission: SPACE ★★ RIDE   Behind the gorgeously swirling planetary facade is a ride that approximates, with intensity, the experience of a rocket launch. Although technically a whirl in a giant centrifuge, the skillful design tricks the mind into believing the body's actually pressing backward in a launch for Mars (although my eyeballs seem to know—they wag uncontrollably for the first 30 seconds). Gary Sinise, oozing gravitas, issues so many preshow warnings against motion sickness that I honestly think it psychs people out and primes them for illness, although sufferers of sinus problems have reported discomfort (and you should skip it altogether if you're prone to vertigo). Each passenger in the extremely tight four-person cockpits is assigned two buttons to press at given cues—it doesn't matter if you don't, but

---

The Death of "Life"

Epcot is a ruthless place for attractions without corporate backers. Between Mission: SPACE and the Universe of Energy, you'll spot a golden dome. No, you haven't been in the sun too long. That's Wonders of Life, one of the great failures of modern Disney World. Opened in 1989 as a paean to all things biological, execs closed it when they couldn't find a brand willing to pony up sponsorship. Some of science's greatest advances are being made in the biological realm, yet the topic is neglected at Epcot for want of a bankroll. Among the casualties: **Body Wars,** a motion-simulator ride through the bloodstream; **Cranium Command,** addressing how a 12-year-old boy's brain controlled his growing body (very much like Pixar's "Inside Out"); and **"The Making of Me,"** a film that gingerly addressed conception and pregnancy without stepping on ideological toes. The tarnished pavilion sits empty and decaying. There are rumblings that WoL could be overhauled to capitalize on "Inside Out"— but only if a company coughs up the dough.

at least hold onto your steering joystick, because it gives force feedback as you travel. Ultimately, it's a ride that's all brains and no heart—I'm impressed at what they've done, but I don't feel like doing it twice. The Advanced Training Lab postshow area (through the gift shop) is worthwhile even if you don't ride. There, you can play interactive group games and send free postcards home via computer. **Strategy:** Whereas Mad Tea Party makes me want to hurl, I do fine on this ride. You'll be given a choice when you enter the building: The green-coded version has easy motion-simulator effects but no troubling centrifuge action, but in my opinion, that renders the ride pointless.

Test Track ★★ RIDE   Cars thunder enticingly around the bend of an outdoor motorway at nearly 65mph, but that's as good as it gets. Those passengers are experiencing the climax of a complicated, multistage ride that puts them through the paces of a proving ground of an automobile manufacturer (sponsor: Chevrolet). Before boarding, you use a touch screen to choose a car using the ill-defined factors of capability, power, responsiveness, and efficiency. Then, you go along for the ride in a minimally decorated warehouse on a series of diagnostic safety tests (don't worry; you don't have to actually do anything), while trackside screens ostensibly show you how your creation would perform under the same circumstances—in fact, it's the same exact ride every time. Your six-passenger car brakes suddenly and careens through a mostly black room decorated by illuminated lines that seem to have been inspired by "Tron" (and a very low budget). Finally, you shoot outside the building and make an invigorating circuit around the circular track over the Epcot employee parking lot. (Hertz has a similar experience—it's called a convertible.) The post-ride showroom features a few steering games plus samples from Chevy's current fleet and numerous photo ops for free digital postcards. Ultimately, it's pretty much been a boring ride since its 2012 renovation; it doesn't make much sense anymore and it feels cheap. **Strategy:** Along with Soarin', it's the busiest ride at Epcot, so get a Fastpass. There's a single-rider line that doesn't let you skip much and invariably puts you in a right-hand seat, but cast members may grill you about whether you're truly alone.

The Seas with Nemo & Friends ★★ RIDE/ACTIVITY   One of the world's largest saltwater aquariums—it's 27 feet deep, 203 feet across, holds 5.7 million gallons—and you can spend as long as you like watching the swimming creatures from two levels. About a third of the tank is reserved for dolphins and sea turtles, while reef fish, rays, and sharks dominate the rest. When the pavilion opened in 1986 as The Living Seas, sharks were the big draw and scientists answered questions everywhere; today, because of "Finding Nemo," kids ask to see the clown fish and there's nary an interpreter in sight. A visit begins with a 5-minute, slow-moving ride in OmniMover "clamobiles" through a simulated undersea world. Half the point of the ride is, of course, to find Nemo, who's lost again; the other characters incessantly shout his name, which soon grates on adult nerves. The ride climaxes to the tune of "In the Big Blue World" (from the Nemo musical at Animal Kingdom)

Kid Stuff at Epcot

Besides The Seas with Nemo & Friends, there aren't many attractions for kiddos in Epcot. Disney addressed the problem with small, manned booths that it calls **Kidcot Fun Stops**, which offer free crafty diversions such as coloring, stamping, or mask-making—stuff kids do at the school fair. Epcot Passports, which can be stamped in every country, were once free but now cost $11 at the register of any World Showcase shop, but attendants will stamp your kids' crafts, such as the handle of the mask they made, for free instead. From the kiosk on the walkway to World Showcase from Future World (or in Italy, the International Gateway, and Norway), sign them up for the engrossing and free **Phineas and Ferb: Agent P's World Showcase Adventure** (starting at 11am), in which they follow instructions on fake cell phones to make tricksy things happen at six stops in various countries. You must activate the unit within 15 minutes of picking it up, but it'll work all day until 8:15pm. It's so engrossing that kids sometimes have a hard time paying attention to anything else.

with a peek into the real aquarium as Nemo and his friends are projected into the windows, cleverly uniting the fictional world with the real animal universe, "Seabase," with which you will now be acquainted. A few times a day, the giant tube dominating the hall is occasionally occupied by a diver—an unforgettable sight—to demonstrate how SCUBA works. On the second floor, which is quieter than the kiddie-clogged first floor, don't miss the observation platform that extends into the mighty tank. The daily roster sign apprises you of the day's dolphin talks and fish feedings (the schedule is busiest between 10am and 4pm), when there will be someone on hand to explain what you're seeing. The **dolphins** live separately in the first space on the left. If human divers are swimming, they'll communicate with guests by way of magnetized writing tablets. Also, check out the **manatees,** the sweet-natured "sea cows" that are threatened in Florida. *Strategy:* If the pavilion's entry line is horrific, bypass the ride by entering through the exit, at the far left.

Turtle Talk with Crush ★★ SHOW   Inside The Seas with Nemo & Friends is an amusing 20-minute show in which a computer-animated version of the 150-year-old surfer-dude turtle interacts with audiences, making jokes about what they're wearing and fielding questions. It's part of what Disney calls its "Living Characters" program. There is the distraction of ray and jellyfish tanks in the waiting area. Next door is **Bruce's Shark World,** a play area similar to any science museum's.

Soarin' ★★★ RIDE   The Land pavilion takes up 6 acres, more than all of Tomorrowland, and this ride is a big reason why. In it, audiences are seated on benches and "flown," hang glider–like, across enormous movies of California's wonders while scents waft, hair blows, and the seats gently rock in tandem with the motions of the flight. In 2016, the things you fly over will go global and the name will become **Soarin' Around the World**. The ride is highly repeatable and deeply pleasurable for all ages. It's a facsimile of the one at Disney's California Adventure park in Anaheim, hence the imagery exclusive to the Golden State, but there are rumors of brand new Florida images in the works. *Strategy:* Wait times can exceed 3 hours (yeah, I know—crazy!), so schedule a Fastpass. The best seats are in the middle sections on the top row, where there are no feet dangling in your field of vision. That means you should aim for position B-1, or at the very least A-1 or C-1. Those with height terrors should request something ending in 3, the closest to the ground.

Living with the Land ★ RIDE   The Land's other ride, after Soarin', is a 14-minute (wonderfully air-conditioned) boat trip that glosses over the realm of farming technologies. It's one of the last Epcot rides to provide a semblance of education, especially when you pass some experimental growth methods (like a nutrient film technique and aquaponics). These methods are being explored, or so we're told, to curb world hunger, but the hard fact is that GMOs, which are not mentioned, won industry dominance years ago, and the activity in Epcot's labs is intermittent, not the hive of active research it was meant to be. They do some real stuff here though: Annually, they grow some 5,000 pounds of fish, which are served in Disney restaurants. This ride is original to opening day, although the live narrators were disposed of in favor of a recording. For those interested in the topic, the info will be too thin, but for those who are bored green, it will seem to last forever. *Strategy:* Boats load slowly, so go early or late to escape the inevitable buildup. It often closes at 7pm.

The Circle of Life ★ SHOW   Upstairs, in The Land, this minor, 13-minute movie stars "The Lion King" characters and concerns conservation (an Epcot-worthy message). It'll keep you off the streets and seated in AC, at least until 7pm, when it shuts down for the day.

Captain EO ★★★ SHOW   The minute Michael Jackson died, Disney yanked this trippy 1986 chestnut out of mothballs and re-installed it in its original home, the Imagination! pavilion, minus a few original special effects. For years, this 17-minute 3-D music video, starring Jackson as a Han Solo–type space pilot who is accompanied by creepy/adorable sidekicks, was a punch line for its excess and ego, but premature death and '80s nostalgia have renewed it. It concerns a mean, dark-hearted diva whose grip on a bleak world is loosened by the sheer charm of Jocko's performance—kind of like the climax of "The Wiz," if the Wicked Witch was Anjelica Huston.

Journey into Imagination with Figment ★ RIDE   There's no line for a reason: It feels like Disney ran out of money halfway through—one section of this slow track-based ride is simply a room of black curtains and painted boards. Its daffy purple dinosaur, Figment, once figured as Epcot's mascot and now strains to act cuddly in his last, forlorn outpost. The ride purports to be an open house of the Imagination Institute run by Prof. Nigel Channing (Eric Idle), but Figment seizes control and offends your senses—your sense of good taste, though, is the most violated. This is the third attempt to get an

Imagination ride right since 1982. The ride dumps out into **ImageWorks "What If" Labs,** once a high-tech playground sponsored by Kodak but now with little more to do than purchase fairground-style composite gag photos. Look above the roped-off staircase for a glimpse of the glass pyramids atrium, now forbidden, and you'll get a sense for how this pretty half-closed pavilion is now rotten with neglect. You might have gathered by now that Imagination! is not Epcot at its best. However, the fountain pods in front, which shoot snakes of water from one to another, are a firm favorite of children, who never tire of trying to catch one of the so-called "laminar flow" spurts.

World Showcase

The 1.3-mile path circling the World Showcase Lagoon is home to 11 pavilions created in the idealized image of their home countries—get your picture taken in front of a miniature Eiffel Tower (it'll look real through the lens), or at the Doge's Palace in Venice. The pavilions were built more to elicit an emotional response and not to truly replicate. Disney is diligent about the upkeep of this area, but it neglects development—the last "country" to open was Norway back in 1988, and without joint participation by foreign tourism offices, there are unlikely to be more. There also seems to be an emphasis on countries that Americans already know, and neither South America nor Australasia is represented at all. But World Showcase does have some of the most original restaurants in Disney World, and the shops are stocked with crafts and national products (you can buy real Chinese tea in China and sweaters in Norway), although the variety is slipping. It's also the only area in Epcot in which alcoholic beverages are sold.

There is far more fascinating stuff to do in World Showcase than the free Disney map lets on. Pocket it and let your curiosity guide you. You should, though, keep the day's **Times Guide** firmly in hand. The pavilions are crawling with unexpected musical and dance performances conducted by natives of each country. Seeing them makes a day richer and squeezes value from your ticket. Rush and you'll miss a lot. I suggest going **clockwise around the lagoon** mostly because the only two rides in World Showcase will come

---

A Mini–United Nations

World Showcase pavilions are staffed by young people who were born and raised in the host country. Many of their contracts last for up to a year, and they chose to come to Florida as much to learn about America as to be ambassadors for their own nations, although many of them complain that most park guests don't bother asking anything except where the bathrooms are. Be kind to them, speak slowly if you sometimes cannot immediately understand each other's accent, and most of all, seize this unusual chance to ask questions about their cultures. These folks, despite the fact they're zipped into silly costumes, are modern, intelligent people who are so proud of where they come from that they traveled halfway around the world to share their heritage with you. Help them do that.

quickly on the left; if you go counterclockwise, you'll reach them after they accrue lines. After midafternoon, it won't matter.

Tip: Anything purchased in World Showcase can be sent to the **Package Pickup** at the front of Future World; allow 3 hours for delivery (it's not refrigerated, so chocolate melts). On some days—it depends how busy things are—two **ferry** routes cross the lagoon. One leaves near Germany and one from Morocco, and both land near the top of Future World. You will not save time using them; they're merely a pleasant way to get off your feet.

MEXICO ★★★

Skirting the lagoon clockwise, Mexico is your first stop. Everything to see is inside the faux temple, which contains a faux river (for the Gran Fiesta Tour ride), a faux volcano, and a faux night sky strung with lanterns. The **Mexican Folk Art Gallery** showcases whimsical carvings; "La Vida Antigua: Life in Ancient Mexico" is for artifacts and dioramas—one of Epcot's fun secrets, the great stone medallion in its center seems to mysteriously fill with luminous color as you watch. In the main *zócalo* of Plaza de los Amigos from Tuesday to Friday mornings, look for Alba, who since 1993 has hand-painted Oaxacan woodcarvings here; her brother Marco carves them on other days. Listen for the terrific Mariachi Cobre, which has performed here since the park's opening day. There's also a small tequila bar (chips and dip also for sale) and a crystal and glass shop with glass blowing demonstrations. *Influences:* A diplomatic mix of Mayan, Toltec, Aztec, and Spanish styles. *Fun Stuff to Buy:* At the dusky **La Cava de Tequila,** knock back some of the house liquor or a designer margarita ($10 and up). Maracas ($6 each), Oaxacan woodcarvings (from $18), piñatas (from $12), hand-painted pottery skulls ($25), and mini sombreros ($17).

Gran Fiesta Tour Starring the Three Caballeros ★★ RIDE It's easy to develop a soft spot for the bland, 8-minute boat float that, for its

Inside the Mexico Pavilion in World Showcase at Epcot.

cheesiness, has been nicknamed "the Mexican 'it's a small world.'" As you pass movie screens, jiggling dolls, and dancing Day of the Dead skeletons, you quickly realize you're enjoying the product of Mexican tourist board input. A 2007 rehab imposed animated appearances by the 1940s characters the Three Caballeros—never mind that only Panchito Pistoles the rooster is Mexican (José Carioca the parrot is Brazilian, and Donald Duck is American). The experience is sweet, and it's a worthy siesta break. Donald conducts autograph sessions outside, to the right of the pavilion (check the Times Guide for when).

NORWAY ★★

Next along is Norway, the youngest pavilion (built 1988), which is home to the only other ride in World Showcase. At least, it *used* to be Norway—Disney has added the town of Arendelle to cash in on "Frozen" fever. The Akershus Royal Banquet Hall does princess character meals morning, noon, and evening. In the one-room **Stave Church Gallery,** check out a few genuine Norse artifacts (13th-c. bowl and spoon and 1828 tankard with a hollow branch for a spout) that are also pegged to "Frozen," which is only notionally set in Norway. Towering above it all, the wooden Stave Church is a Norwegian original; there were once around 1,000 in the country, but today, there are only 28. **The Puffin's Roost** contains a 9-foot-tall troll—photo op alert—and sweaters for up to $400. *Influences:* Town squares of Bergen, Alesund, Oslo, and the Satesdal Valley; the 14th-century Akershus castle on Oslo harbor. *Fun Stuff to Buy:* Laila body lotions (assorted prices) and foam swords ($11). At the bakery, try the $2.70 rice cream, a snack that those in the know are happy to make a detour for. I prefer the plastic horned Viking helmets ($12–17), bags of Daim candy ($15, even though it's Swedish), and stuffed Olafs ($18).

Frozen Ever After ★★★ RIDE   The old Maelstrom indoor boat excursion, an abbreviated five-minute float-along with both forward and backward motion, never counted for much. But it's the hottest—er, coldest—ride in the park now that it's been transformed to Arendelle and been populated by Elsa, Anna, Olaf, Sven, and Kristoff (open in early 2016). Nearby is the **Royal Sommerhus** cabin where kids can meet the princesses—arrange a Fastpass+ or their dreams will be put on ice and they'll never let it go.

CHINA ★★

Enter through the remarkable replica of Beijing's Temple of Heaven. Make time to catch the **Jeweled Dragon Acrobats,** some of the most riveting street performers in the World Showcase. "Tomb Warriors: Guardian Spirits of Ancient China," in the **House of the Whispering Willow,** is a miniature recreation of a tiny portion of the legendary terra-cotta warriors of the Han Dynasty, scaled to the size of a hotel room (the original mausoleum is twice the size of Epcot). The Gallery also contains a few display cases of figures dating as far back as 260 B.C. *Influences:* Beijing's Forbidden City (Imperial Palace) and Temple of Heaven. *Fun Stuff to Buy:* Upon exiting the film, cross the hangarlike shop and enter **House of Good Fortune,** the main shop, which is particularly varied. It sells plum wine ($20), lots of Ts and teas, Chinese jackets ($50–$85 in silks, polyesters, and blends), jade bangles ($150), teapots ($50), paper parasols ($12), conical hats ($16), and paper lanterns ($4–$10).

"Reflections of China" ★ FILM   The big thing to do in China is a 14-minute movie filmed entirely in Circle-Vision 360°. You wouldn't believe the work it takes to make a film that surrounds you from all sides. The makers first had to figure out the optimal number of screens (nine—which enables projectors to be slipped in the gaps between screens) and then they had to suspend a ring of carefully calibrated cameras from helicopters so that the crew wasn't in the shots. In 2002, the footage of Shanghai had to be reshot because the city no longer resembled the 1982 version that was being shown; this being China, it's probably already time for another refresh. The result, which surveys some of the country's most beautiful vistas, is ravishing, although the masses no longer seem to care.

OUTPOST ★

This area between China and Germany was once slated to contain a pavilion canvassing equatorial Africa, but that fell through for political reasons, so instead, we get a mushy catchall for all things African. The **Mdundo Kibanda** store has some Kenyan carvings (like adorable $12 pocket-size elephants) and you'll find occasional storytelling sessions. Several days a week, a craftsman is on hand, whittling and carving wares—they seem engrossed in wood and knife, but they like answering questions too. *Fun Stuff to Buy:* The too-easily overlooked **Bead Outpost** kiosk sells jewelry made from recycled Guidemaps and other outdated Disney park publications. The papers are sent to Uganda as part of the BeadforLife program to give impoverished women a sustainable income, and they return as water-resistant beads in every color. Necklaces are $20, bracelets $10, earrings $7, or pick your own beads to be sized right there.

GERMANY ★

Lacking a true attraction (a water ride based on the Rhine was planned but never completed), Germany is popular for its food. The **Biergarten Restaurant** does sausages, beer, and the like—accompanied by yodeling and dancing—while the adjoining shop is for crystal doodads. The **Sommerfest** is the counter-service alternative for brats and pretzels. On the hour, the Clock Tower above the pavilion rings and two figures emerge, just like at the Glockenspiel in München (Munich). The pavilion is otherwise a string of connected one-room shops selling steins ($22–$200), figurines, crystal, Christmas ornaments, cuckoo clocks (up to $1,700), and other high-priced wares. *Influences:* Eltz Castle near Koblenz; Stahleck Fortress near Bacharach; Rothenburg (the Biergarten and the dragon slayer statue); facades from Frankfurt and Freiburg (the guildhall). *Fun Stuff to Buy:* The connected candy-and-wine shop, **Weinkeller,** is worth a gander: You'll find such pick-me-ups as Gluhwein ($12 a liter), wine by the glass (from $10), by the flight (from $10), or by the bottle (spätlese, Auslese, Kabinett, Liebfraumilch, from $20). **Der Teddybär** sells toys, especially ones by Steiff. The Werther's Original

Karamell-Küche shop is a stand-out—its warm, hand-tossed caramel popcorn ($4–$10) is a top treat on the Lagoon.

ITALY ★

The tiny pavilion for Italy lacks an attraction—the gondolas never leave the dock—so content yourself with the miniature, drive-thru versions of Venice's Doge's Palace and St. Mark's bell tower, plus the **Sbandieratori Di Sansepolcro** boys in tights who toss flags and **Sergio** the juggling mime (check the "Times Guide"). An appealing, if incongruous, attraction that's not on the maps is the highly detailed **model train** display just between this pavilion and Germany. *Influences:* Piazza di San Marco, Venice; stucco buildings of Tuscany; a fountain reminiscent of

Italy pavilion and St. Mark's Square.

the work of Gian Lorenzo Bernini. *Fun Stuff to Buy:* Noodle around in **Enoteca Castello** shop for wine (tastings $10–$15) and Quadratini wafer cookies ($10 a bag). **Il Bel Cristallo** sells fragrances, handbags, football, and pricey Venetian carnival masks. Stop into Tutto Gusto for honest adult cocktails—the kind made with a shaker, not a slushie machine.

U.S.A. ★★★

So much for being a generous host: The U.S.A. pavilion takes pride of place in an area that's supposed to celebrate other countries. Inside, the superlative **Voices of America** singing group, which excels at thorny close harmonies, entertains guests waiting to attend the half-hour Audio-Animatronic show, The American Adventure. You'll be impressed. Also in the lobby is the unfairly ignored **American Heritage Gallery:** See items from the Kinsey Collection pertaining to milestones in the African-American experience (an 1820 slave schedule, an 1832 bill of sale of an 18-year-old named Joe) embellished with cool "story lanterns" narrated by luminaries including Whoopi Goldberg, Chandra Wilson, and Diane Sawyer. *Influences:* General Georgian/colonial Greek-revival buildings (Brits often snicker that its Georgian architecture style is distinctly English). *Fun Stuff to Buy:* **Heritage Manor Gifts** sells patriotic tat such as cookbooks, throw pillows, and tee shirts with the American flag that were actually made in Haiti, Nicaragua, and Vietnam. Oh, Disney!

The American Adventure ★★★ SHOW Ben Franklin and Mark Twain are your Audio-Animatronic surrogates for a series of eye-popping (but ponderous) re-creations of snippets along patriotic themes. Moving dioramas of seminal events such as a Susan B. Anthony speech and John Muir's inspiration for Yosemite National Park appear and vanish cinematically on a stage a quarter the size of a football field, leaving spectators marveling at the massive amount of storage space that must lie beyond the proscenium. It's a literal jukebox for mythology. Indeed, all that homespun corn is brought to you by some immensely complicated robotic and hydraulic systems. When this attraction first opened, the scene in which Franklin appears to mount stairs and then walk across the room was hailed as a technical miracle. The Will Rogers figure actually twirls a lasso purely through robotic movements. Although heavy on uplifting jingoism, the show scores points for touching lightly on a few unpleasant topics, including slavery and the suffering of Native Americans, but in general, it's not as deep as its stage. Don't be the first to enter or else you'll be marooned off to the left.

JAPAN ★★★

Japan has no giant attractions (like Germany, a show building was erected but never filled with its intended ride), but its shopping is by far the best in Epcot, and the outdoor garden behind the pagoda is a paragon of peace. Hopefully, you can be there during one of the shows (check your "Times Guide"): the spectacularly thunderous **Matsuriza** taiko drum shows, which are held at the base of the five-level Goju-no-to pagoda. At the back of the pavilion, go inside and turn left to tour the **Bijutsu-kan Gallery.** Its most recent show was about the Japanese affection for sprites, pixies, and cute characters. A red *torii* gate inspired by one in Hiroshima sits in the lagoon; the barnacles on its base are fake, and were glued on to simulate age. *Influences:* 8th-century Horyuji Temple in Nara (pagoda); Katsura Imperial Villa (Katsura Grill); Shirasagi-Jo castle at Hemeji (the rear fortress); Hiroshima (*torii* gate in the lagoon). *Fun Stuff to Buy:* The **Mitsukoshi Department Store,** named for the 300-year-old Japanese original, is the most fun to roam of all the World Showcase shop. It stocks a variety of toys, chopstick sets ($4–$18), traditional wood sandals (from $30), linens, anime figures including Pokémon, paper fans, calligraphy supplies, countless solar-powered hand-waving things, antique kimonos (mostly $50–$200)—and Japanese snacks, such as chocolate-dipped Pocky sticks ($4).

MOROCCO ★★★

Morocco is another spectacular pavilion if you're inclined to dig in. It flies higher than its neighbors because the country's king took an active interest in its construction, dispatching some 21 top craftsmen for the job. There's no movie or show (although Aladdin, the Genie, and Jasmine make regular appearances), and the architecture is a cross-country mishmash drawn from Marrakech, Fès, and Rabat. **Fez House** is a tranquil, pillared two-level courtyard with a fountain and seating that recalls a classic Moroccan home; **Moroccan Style,** a mosaic-rich exhibition of hanging lanterns and colored glass, is unjustly ignored. Ask a cast member (almost always from Morocco) to write your name in Arabic for you—it's free. **B'net Al Houwariyate** jams to some loud folk music by the water (check the "Times Guide"). *Influences:* Marrakesh (Koutoubia minaret), Rabat (Chella minaret), Fès (Bab Boujouloud Gate, Nejjarine Fountain), Casablanca. *Fun Stuff to Buy:* The middle courtyards are cluttered with **Casablanca Carpets** and **The Brass Bazaar,** and they're sensational. They are perfumed with incense ($4) and stocked with interesting finds, including footstools, tasseled red caps ($25), glass tea cups ($10), Thuya-wood votive stands ($16), machine-made rugs (from $26), bangle bracelets ($20), metal hanging lanterns (from $24), and belly-dancer outfits ($85). I've managed to haggle them down 30% on the floor model of an incense burner—it almost felt like being in the souk of Fès, only with ice cream bars and strollers.

FRANCE ★★

France, done up to look like a typical Parisian neighborhood with a one-tenth replica of the upper stretch of the Eiffel Tower in the simulated distance (you can't go up it), is popular mostly for its food, though the street act **Serveur Amusant,** an acrobat who does handstands on stacked chairs, is thrilling. Disney allowed Guerlain and Givenchy to open fragrance shops at **Plume et Palette**—turns out the smell of selling out is just like Shalimar. *Influences:* Various Belle Epoque Parisian and provincial streets; Château de Fontainebleau (the Palais du Cinema); the former Pont des Arts in Paris (the bridge to the United Kingdom). *Fun Stuff to Buy:* **Librairie et Galerie** sells upscale fragrances. The Parisian souvenirs ($10 for a 5-in. Eiffel Tower) are available in Les Halles at **Boutique de Cadeaux.** Across the lane, in **L'Esprit de la Provence,** a kitchen shop, patterned oven mitts are $12. **Aux Vins de France** has wine tastings ($6–$17), Epcot wine glasses ($13), Champagne flights ($22), World Showcase aprons ($33), and bottles of wine for much more than in Germany or Italy.

"Impressions de France" ★ FILM The 18-minute, 200-degree-wide movie is no longer the freshest example of a tourism film—mostly classical music and postcard-worthy shots of some 50 picturesque places. It has been playing continuously since Epcot opened in 1982. Happily, it provides seating.

UNITED KINGDOM ★★

United Kingdom, another wild mix of architectural styles, has no rides or shows, so few people know about the knee-high **hedge maze** in back. The U.K. is popular chiefly for its English-style pub, the indoor Rose & Crown Pub & Dining Room (which you can enjoy without a reservation or eating), and a counter-service fish and chips shop. That's two fish-and-chips outlets in a block—far more than you'd find even in London these days. After 5:15pm Tuesday to Saturday, duck into the pub to catch Carol Stein, a longtime Epcot entertainer who plays piano and leads guests in song. Request her version of "Do Re Mi" (it's clean). In the garden, the **British Revolution** band (check the "Times Guide") does covers. *Influences:* Anne Hathaway's Cottage, Stratford-upon-Avon (the Tea Caddy); Queen Anne style (the middle promenade); Hampton Court, London (Sportsman's Shoppe); Victorian, country, and traditional pub styles (Rose & Crown). *Fun Stuff to Buy:* Featured shopping in the conjoined **Sportsman's Shoppe, the Crown & Crest,** and **Toy Soldier** includes Beatles merchandise, Winnie the Pooh merchandise, and "Keep Calm and Carry On" tees. Across the way, **Lords and Ladies** does jewelry and fragrance, and the **Tea Caddy** sells Twinings tea plus English candy bars at a high price of $3.50 each.

CANADA ★

Like Japan, Canada's gardens (inspired by Victoria's Butchart Gardens, although the sign says Victoria Gardens) are a surprising oasis, adding a hidden artificial canyon delightfully washed by a man-made waterfall. A lumberjack-themed show takes the stage here several times daily (check your "Times Guide"). *Influences:* 19th-century Victorian colonial architecture (Hotel du Canada); emblematic northwestern Indian design and Maritime Provinces towns; Butchart Gardens, Victoria (Victoria Gardens). *Fun Stuff to Buy:* The shop, **Northwest Mercantile,** mostly hawks maple syrup ($25 for 17 oz.), stuffed huskies and bears ($15–$23), red tartan fleece vests ($37), and T-shirts themed to moose and hockey.

"O Canada!" ★ FILM Canada, like China, has a round movie screened by nine clacking projectors. It's shot in Circle-Vision 360°, a process Walt Disney originally called Circarama. The 18-minute presentation (1982), which requires standing (you can lean on railings, though), was refurbished by adding newly shot bits with Martin Short as emcee, who ladles on plenty of curling jokes and hockey references. Most of its spectacular scenery (the Rockies, the Bay of Fundy) is timeless. You'll find it hidden deep within the pavilion by a waterfall in a dreamy rock canyon.

> ### Epcot at Night
>
> There are no parades anymore at Epcot, but usually at 9pm, the pulse-pounding **IllumiNations: Reflections of Earth ★★★** flames-and-water spectacular takes place over World Showcase Lagoon. Its central globe, which is studded with 15,500 tiny video screens, weighs some 350,000 pounds but seems so tiny, and the show's so-called Inferno Barge carries a payload of 4,000 gallons of propane. Crowds start building on the banks 1–2 hours before showtime, but I find doing that a waste of time, and therefore money, as a day's admission is so steep. Any view of the center of the lake will be fine (some people find the islands obstructive, but I don't), but take care to be upwind or you may be engulfed by smoke. Food kiosks close with the very first downbeat of the show.

Where to Eat in Epcot

Epcot has the best dining choices of any Disney World park, and people come just for the food. All locations will have a few vegetarian options, kids' meals, and (if you identify yourself) special dietary requests can usually be accommodated, albeit often at diminished quality. Alcohol is served everywhere—even in Morocco, where it's not so easy to get in real life. You can also drink the water in Mexico.

EPCOT'S QUICK-SERVICE RESTAURANTS

There are only two major counter-service choices in Future World, plus a Starbucks. The real casual eating action is in World Showcase. There are many more minor kiosks for snacks than what's listed here.

Sunshine Seasons ★★★ INTERNATIONAL   Offering the best selection and freshest food of all Epcot's counter-service locations, offerings here include salads, grilled items (seared tuna noodle salad, oak-grilled chicken and fish), and Thai green curry shrimp—not a fried item, burger, or pizza in sight. The desserts are epic (cheesecake with berries, tiramisu; $4.60). You can also pick up snacks suiting dietary restrictions. **The Land.** Breakfast $5 to $7, lunch and dinner combo meal $10 to $13.

Electric Umbrella ★★ AMERICAN   Future World's most central counter-service locale. Expect burgers, nuggets, flatbreads, chicken Caesar. **Innoventions East.** Combo meal $8.50 to $11.

Taste Track ★★ AMERICAN   Open in busy seasons from 11am to 6pm, this kiosk is more interesting than the others, pressing grilled cheeses such as Fontina, tomato, basil, and balsamic glaze. **World Showcase.** Sandwiches $9 to $10 with soup or salad.

La Cantina De San Angel ★★ MEXICAN   Mexico's counter-service option will give you beef or chicken tacos, cheese empanadas, nachos, and margaritas (from $9.50). It's outside but on the water. **Mexico.** Combo meal $11 to $13.

Kringla Bakeri Og Kafé ★★ SCANDINAVIAN   Some of the selections in Norway's bake shop can't be found elsewhere at Disney, including *rullekake* (a rolled swirl of berries and yellow cake). More than one person claims the smooth, strawberry-topped rice cream pudding snack to be their favorite sweet in Walt Disney World. You can also get sandwiches, heated to order. **Norway.** Desserts $3 to $5, sandwiches $7 to $8.50.

Lotus Blossom Café ★ CHINESE   A Panda Express redux: China's quick-service choice, with covered seating, is basic, serving beef noodle bowls, shrimp fried rice, pot stickers, and the like. Mango smoothies are sweet but delicious. **China.** Combo meal $8.50 to $12.

Sommerfest ★★ GERMAN   When you can't get into Biergarten, settle for this kiosk to get your bratwurst, sausage, and beer. **Germany.** Sausage rolls $7.50 to $9.

Tutto Gusto ★★★ ITALIAN   The excellent vaulted bar attached to the Tutto Italia Ristorante serves grown-up cocktails and also a selection of cheese and meat plates for two or three ($29), plus cannoli, tiramisu, and panini. **Italy.** Panini $8 to $14, desserts $4 to $9, wine flights $14 to $30, by the glass $9 to $15. You can stand at the bar.

Liberty Inn ★ AMERICAN   Cheap burgers, hot dogs, chicken, and crab cakes in a setting as dull as a rest stop on a Maryland highway. Outside, the

Fife & Drum Tavern has turkey legs and beer and a kiosk sells pumpkin spice funnel cakes ($8). **The American Adventure.** Combo meal $8.50 to $12.

Katsura Grill ★★ JAPANESE   Japan's small counter-service location is by the gardens, and it supplies Japanese curry, teriyaki chicken, sushi ($8–$10 for four pieces), and edamame. Facing the lagoon under the pagoda, the **Kabuki Cafe** kiosk (closed in cold weather) serves shaved ice with syrup (including melon and cherry flavors) for $3.75, and plum wine for $6.50. **Japan.** Combo meal $9 to $13.

Tangierine Café ★★★ MOROCCAN   The indoor counter-service location is a great place to dodge crowds. It serves shawarma with hummus, couscous, bread, and tabbouleh; and lamb or chicken warps. Accent it with Casa Beer, from Casablanca, or Moorish coffee (powerful espresso spiced with cinnamon and nutmeg), and add baklava for $3.50. Kids can get burgers or chicken fingers for $8. **Morocco.** Combo meal $12 to $15.

Boulangerie Pâtisserie ★★ FRENCH   Grab a fast, bready bite in the back of Les Halles, such as a chocolate croissant or a ham-and-cheese croissant ($3.25–$4.75—decent bargains), pastry ($2.25–$4), plain croissant ($2.25), quiche ($6.50), or baguette sandwiches ($4.75–9). Next door, **L'Artisan des Glaces** has good sorbets and ice creams. A cash-only kiosk on the lagoon griddles up hot crepes (with sweet fillings, not meat), also for $4. **France.** Salads and sandwiches $7 to $9.25.

Yorkshire County Fish Shop ★★ BRITISH   Snag walk-up fish-and-chips and eat it al fresco. You get two strips of fish with chips (fries)—make sure to put vinegar, not ketchup, on the fries the way the English do. Ale costs $8.25. **United Kingdom.** Combo meal $9.50.

EPCOT'S TABLE-SERVICE RESTAURANTS

Book ahead if your heart is set on something, particularly for a nighttime lagoon view—if you're going to spend this kind of money, get a view out of it. The host will not guarantee seating location, but it helps to politely ask. Objectively, there are very few meals that would rate highly if I ate them outside of the park gates, and as with all mass-produced meals, quality varies greatly from day to day; the lion's share of the enjoyment is just being there. Lunch entrees are generally $3 to $5 less expensive than at dinner. Taking them as you encounter them, going clockwise around World Showcase:

The Garden Grill ★★ AMERICAN   As Farmer Mickey, Pluto, and Chip 'n' Dale press the flesh in this slowly revolving, two-tiered circular restaurant, you're served all-you-can-eat family style "Harvest Feast" platters of meats and vegetables, some of which were grown in the greenhouses downstairs. This is the only character meal in Future World, and it's only at dinner, but it's a good choice because it's mellow and small enough so that the merry rodents can spend quality time with you. **The Land.** Combo meal $37 to $42 adults, $18 to $20 kids.

Coral Reef Restaurant ★ SEAFOOD Call it See Food: Through windows into the 27-foot-deep aquarium, admire the friends of the fish on your plate. You're even given a cheat sheet to identity what's swimming by. Only about half the menu selections are fish, and the rest are things like short ribs or strip steak. It's about the cool view, not the cuisine. **The Seas with Nemo & Friends.** Main courses $19 to $27.

San Angel Inn Restaurante ★★ MEXICAN Epcot's most atmospheric restaurant is set beneath a false twilight sky at the base of an ancient pyramid, with the boats from the Gran Fiesta Tour steadily passing—reserve the first time of the day to by guaranteed a seat by the river. The fare isn't Tex-Mex as much as it is Mexican: chicken mole, chili relleno, grilled wahoo fish, and caramel dulce de leche for dessert. If you can't get in (a likelihood), try La Hacienda de San Angel, across the main path on the lagoon. Its food is similarly Mexican. **Mexico.** Mains $19 to $30 lunch, $26 to $32 dinner.

La Hacienda de San Angel ★★ MEXICAN By day, it's a sunny place to get your tequila on. By night, this villa-themed restaurant (vaulted ceilings, hanging lanterns) is a fair place to sit for IllumiNations, but only if you're lucky enough to score a window seat. Margaritas are $14. The La Hacienda mixed grill with steak, chicken al pastor, chorizo, and veggies serves two ($56). **Mexico.** Main courses $24–$28.

Princess Storybook Dining at Akershus Royal Banquet Hall ★★★ AMERICAN Although it's Norway, you won't have to eat raw fish at this storybook buffet (although once upon a time, you did). Instead, it's Epcot's meet-the-princesses extravaganza for all three "feasts" daily, in a castle-like setting of vaulted ceilings and banners. Someone always stops by, be it Belle, Aurora, Jasmine, Snow White, Mulan, or Mary Poppins, who must be lost. If your own princess forgot her gown, they sell them for $65 at the shop across the path. This is the only character dining in World Showcase. **Norway.** Meals: $42 to $55 adults, $25 to $30 kids.

Nine Dragons Restaurant ★ CHINESE When you can't get a reservation anywhere else, you end up here. The food here is not much more daring or spicy as in the cheaper Quick Service option, Lotus Blossom Café, except here, there are more choices and they're more expensive. The decor is handsomely geometric, but nothing memorable, although some tables face out toward the water. **China.** Main courses $15 to $27; three-course dinner $25.

Biergarten Restaurant ★★★ GERMAN Toddlers lurch forward to polka, dads dive into mugs of Radeberger pilsner, and strangers make friends with their neighbors at this rowdy, carb-loaded party, an all-you-can-eat stuffer featuring sauerbraten, schnitzel, spaetzle, rotisserie chicken, and an oompah band for about 20 minutes at a time. It's popular. **Germany.** Lunch: $26 adults, $14 kids; dinner $38 adults, $20 kids.

Tutto Italia Ristorante ★ ITALIAN Proclaimed authentic to Italy mostly by people who have never been there, this dusky environment of chandeliers and murals nonetheless packs 'em in. Pasta of this low caliber should not be $25, but that doesn't stop patrons from buying $26 hunks of lasagna. **Italy.** Main courses $20 to $30.

Via Napoli Ristorante e Pizzeria ★ ITALIAN The more enjoyable of Italy's two table service restaurants features lots of light, three-story vaulted ceilings, and three amusing wood-fired ovens shaped like the open mouths of giant mustachioed men named after volcanoes. Into those are thrust $17 to $21 individual pizzas and $9.50 kids' pizzas made with flour imported from Naples (not that you could tell the difference). There's also some lasagna and spaghetti at around $21 to $30 a plate. It's operated by Patina Restaurant Group, which runs eateries in Macy's, the Hollywood Bowl, and other tourist spots. **Italy.** Main courses $22 to $30.

Teppan Edo ★★★ JAPANESE Above the Mitsukoshi store (which runs it), a chef-cum-swordsmith slices, dices, and cooks at the teppanyaki griddle built into your table. It's fun to watch, although it's not a great choice if your kids are too young to keep their hands to themselves. Ask to see the smoking onion volcano. The food? Oh, it's fine, but you really come to see the fancy knife work. **Japan.** Main courses $18 to $32.

Tokyo Dining ★★ JAPANESE On the second floor of the Japan pavilion, the decor is modern and stylish, the waitstaff subdued, and the menu offers both tempura/grills and sushi in modest portions at inflated prices. Some tables have a view of the lagoon through nearly floor-to-ceiling windows, which comes in handy around IllumiNations time. **Japan.** Main courses $25 to $32, sushi $6 to $14 per order.

Restaurant Marrakesh ★★★ MOROCCAN Tucked in the back of the souk, this lesser-known restaurant, lit theatrically with hanging lanterns, features a belly dancer, who appears (in a chaste costume) at 10 minutes before the hour at lunch and at the top of the hour during dinner. The fare is approachable North African, heavy on shish kebabs, lemon chicken tagine, and couscous. Thinner crowds allow it to serve a good value at lunch: appetizer, entree, and dessert until 3:30pm for $20. **Morocco.** Main courses $18 to $29.

Spice Road Table ★★ MOROCCAN Serving skewers, coriander-crusted rack of lamb, and powerful sangria and cocktails, it has Lagoon views rare among Epcot restaurants and ideal for IllumiNations spectators, so it fills up by 8pm. **Morocco.** Small plates $7 to $10, full plates $22 to $30.

Chefs de France ★★ FRENCH In a glassed-in dining room recalling a typical French bistro, dine on quiche and crepes (at lunch) or prototypical French food like duck breast and *côte de boeuf* at dinner. There's also a $26 prix-fixe, three-course meal until 3pm ($40 at dinner). **France.** Main courses $16 to $32.

Monsieur Paul ★★★ FRENCH Epcot's most thoughtful menu (and also its most expensive) starts with napkins that are folded like a chef's jacket. This is special occasion stuff: an oxtail soup with black truffle for $29, roasted duck with apple fondant, red snapper in rosemary sauce with scales made of roasted potato slices, plus all the amuse-bouches and long preparation explanations you'd expect of a fine establishment. The theme is classic French cuisine using fresh American ingredients, and the menu is overseen by Jerome Bocuse, son of the restaurant's namesake, the heavily Michelin-starred Chef Paul Bocuse, who oversaw the first restaurant at this location. There's also a four-course prix-fixe menu ($89) if you want wine pairings. Although it faces the water, the windows are small, so not every table has a view of IllumiNations. You'll find the entrance tucked around the back door of Chefs de France, under a green-and-white striped awning. **France.** Main courses $39 to $44.

Rose & Crown Pub & Dining Room ★★★ BRITISH   The interior is fairly similar to a country pub—big wooden bar with Victorian screen serving whisky and lots of British and Irish draught beers ($9, or twice as much as a London pub)—although most of the seating is outdoors unless it rains. You get bangers and mash (sausage with mashed potatoes), Scotch egg (fried hard-boiled egg wrapped in sausage meat), cottage pie (ground beef with onions, carrots, mushrooms, and mashed potatoes) and that standby that finds its way onto every Disney menu, no matter how errant, New York strip steak. You can only have a drink in the pub or you can wait for a patio seat. The pub's motto is *otium cum dignitate*—that's not a Hogwarts spell, it's "leisure with dignity." **United Kingdom.** Main courses $15 to $32.

Le Cellier Steakhouse ★ STEAKS   It takes the Canadian-themed restaurant to deliver the most all-American menu of filet mignon, rib eye, snapper, pork, and chicken, but it also Canucks it up with sides such as *poutine* fries (not truly *poutine* with gravy, but topped with cheddar, truffle salt, and red-wine reduction). Specialties include a popular cheddar cheese soup and pretzel bread. True to its name, the restaurant is windowless and vaulted, like a very clean version of a wine cellar. It's so dark and cool, in fact, that the menus are high-tech and light up when opened. The lunch and dinner selections are the same, and it can command deadly lunchtime prices because it's a tough reservation to secure. **Canada.** Main courses $34 to $46.

DISNEY'S HOLLYWOOD STUDIOS

The 154-acre **Disney's Hollywood Studios ★**, the least popular of the four Disney parks, is undergoing massive development. There's a lot to fix. Rushed into existence to head off competition from Universal, this troubled park is half-baked, poorly laid out, and the weakest in Orlando on activities for small children. But over the next few years, Disney is throwing billions at an attempted resurrection with the addition of a 14-acre *Star Wars*-themed land and a Toy Story Land of kiddie rides; both of which will be in their early stages in 2016, but disruptive signs of construction are evident. Do this park last, and if you skip it entirely, you're really only missing three noteworthy rides: the Tower of Terror, the Rock 'n' Roller Coaster, and Toy Story Midway Mania.

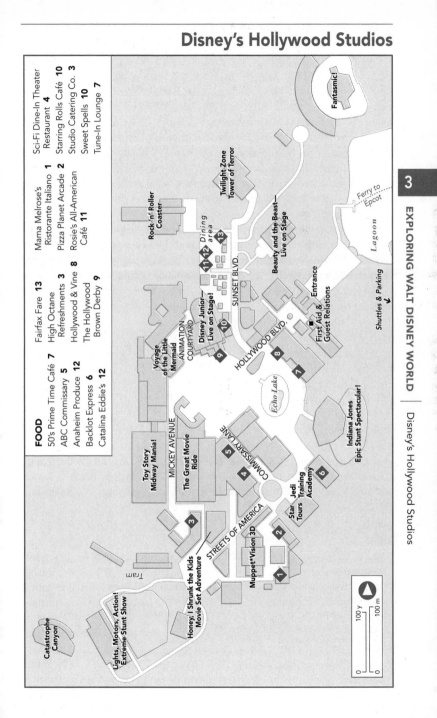

FOOD

50's Prime Time Café **7**
ABC Commissary **5**
Anaheim Produce **12**
Backlot Express **6**
Catalina Eddie's **12**

Fairfax Fare **13**
High Octane
Refreshments **3**
Hollywood & Vine **8**
The Hollywood
Brown Derby **9**

Mama Melrose's
Ristorante Italiano **1**
Pizza Planet Arcade **2**
Rosie's All-American
Café **11**

Sci-Fi Dine-In Theater
Restaurant **4**
Starring Rolls Café **10**
Studio Catering Co. **3**
Sweet Spells **10**
Tune-In Lounge **7**

Catastrophe Canyon

Lights, Motors, Action!
Extreme Stunt Show

Honey, I Shrunk the Kids
Movie Set Adventure

Toy Story
Midway Mania!

The Great Movie Ride

MICKEY AVENUE

STREETS OF AMERICA

Tram

Muppet*Vision 3D

Star Jedi
Tours Training Academy

COMMISSARY LANE

Echo Lake

Indiana Jones
Epic Stunt Spectacular!

Voyage
of the Little
Mermaid

ANIMATION
COURTYARD

Disney Junior—
Live on Stage!

HOLLYWOOD BLVD.

First Aid &
Guest Relations

Entrance

Shuttles & Parking

Rock-'n'-Roller
Coaster

SUNSET BLVD.

Twilight Zone
Tower of Terror

Dining
area

Beauty and the Beast—
Live on Stage

Lagoon

Ferry to
Epcot

Fantasmic!

100 y
100 m

0
0

3

EXPLORING WALT DISNEY WORLD | Disney's Hollywood Studios

89

While it was originally conceived as a single Epcot pavilion about show business, Universal's invasion of the Florida market prodded Disney executives to hastily expand the concept into an entire park and working production facility, Disney–MGM Studios. In 1989, the Studios opened with just two tame rides (the Great Movie Ride and the Backlot Tour). Production never took off and most guests didn't care about the MGM co-branding. An on-site center for hand-painted animation shut down in 2004; MGM was stripped from the name in 2008; and the Backlot Tour, a tram ride/Universal rip-off that pretended that film production was actually happening, died in 2014. Permanent closures come frequently as Disney scrambles to reorganize the park; a flaccid history of Disney animation shuttered in 2015, and minor attractions in this guide may have been booted with only weeks' notice by the time you arrive.

The park possesses a fraction of the attractions the Magic Kingdom has—so guests often combine it on the same day with Disney's Animal Kingdom, or they allow themselves a more leisurely pace, perhaps lingering long enough to catch the dazzling pyrotechnic-and-water curtain evening show, Fantasmic!

You arrive by the usual car/tram combo, by bus, or by free ferry, which sails from the Swan and Dolphin area and continues on to Epcot.

Hollywood Boulevard & Echo Lake

As soon as your bag is approved and you're through the gates, take care of business (strollers, wheelchairs, lockers) in the plaza before proceeding down Hollywood Boulevard. There are no attractions here, only shops and restaurants. The 122-foot-tall Sorcerer Mickey Hat, the park's central icon, was built at the Boulevard's terminus in 2001, but it was demolished, to cheers from purists, in 2015, and the park's original entrance vista of the Chinese Theatre was restored.

The Great Movie Ride ★ RIDE   The park's visual center is the replica of Grauman's Chinese Theatre (Disney calls it "the Chinese Theatre"), which has a forecourt graced with actual handprints and footprints of movie stars

---

The Best of Disney's Hollywood Studios

Don't miss if you're 6: Jedi Training Academy

Don't miss if you're 16: Rock 'n' Roller Coaster

Requisite photo op: The Chinese Theatre

Food you can only get here: Grapefruit Cake, the Hollywood Brown Derby, Hollywood Boulevard; Peanut Butter and Jelly Milkshake, 50's Prime Time Café, Echo Lake

The most crowded, so Fastpass or go early: Toy Story Midway Mania

Skippable: Beauty and the Beast—Live on Stage

Quintessentially Disney: The Great Movie Ride

Biggest thrill: Twilight Zone Tower of Terror

Best show: Fantasmic!

Character meals: Hollywood & Vine (breakfast, lunch)

Best shopping: The Beverly Sunset, Sunset Boulevard

Where to find peace: Around Echo Lake

DISNEY'S HOLLYWOOD STUDIOS: 1 DAY, TWO WAYS

START: BE AT THE GATE FOR OPENING TIME.

Grab food at a counter restaurant when it's convenient to you—but having lunch at 11am saves time. The must-have Fastpass for this park is Toy Story Midway Mania.

HOLLYWOOD STUDIOS WITH KIDS	HOLLYWOOD STUDIOS WITHOUT KIDS
Fastpass+ within 90 minutes of opening: Toy Story Midway Mania. If your kids are too young, Voyage of the Little Mermaid.	When the gates open, ride **Toy Story Midway Mania** even if you have a Fastpass+ for later; it's worth re-riding.

HOLLYWOOD STUDIOS WITH KIDS

When the gates open, ride **Toy Story Midway Mania** even if you have a Fastpass+ for later; it's worth re-riding.

OR

If your child wants to participate in the **Jedi Training Academy,** reserve a slot first (ask a cast member where; it changes).

↓

See **Voyage of the Little Mermaid.**

↓

See **Disney Junior—Live on Stage!**

↓

Meet **Mickey Mouse** (check the Times Guide for his location)

↓

Do **The Great Movie Ride.**

↓

Target a performance of **Beauty and the Beast—Live on Stage** for around now.

↓

At this point, littler ones may need to leave the park for a break.

↓

See **Muppet*Vision 3-D.**

↓

See the **Indiana Jones Epic Stunt Spectacular.**

↓

If you think the whole family can handle them, slot in the **Twilight Zone Tower of Terror** and the **Rock 'n' Roller Coaster.**

↓

See **Fantasmic!** (if it's performing tonight). People stake out their seats as long as an hour ahead, but 30 minutes will do.

HOLLYWOOD STUDIOS WITHOUT KIDS

When the gates open, ride **Toy Story Midway Mania** even if you have a Fastpass+ for later; it's worth re-riding.

↓

Head to the **Twilight Zone Tower of Terror** and the **Rock 'n' Roller Coaster** and ride them.

See **Voyage of the Little Mermaid** (it's fun even without kids).

↓

Ride **Star Tours.**

↓

See **Muppet*Vision 3-D.**

↓

See the **Indiana Jones Epic Stunt Spectacular.**

↓

Do the **Great Movie Ride.**

↓

Target a performance of **Lights, Motors, Action!** (check the Times Guide) whenever it's convenient—it's never full.

↓

See **Fantasmic!** (if it's performing tonight).

who visited in the park's early years at the behest of Disney execs. There are no prints younger than 1999, around the time the park gave up the pipe dream of being a center for film production. Ye Olde Movie Ride, as I call it, was the park's showpiece in 1989, but now it's a mechanized waxworks. Aided by human guides sawing their way through a hackneyed script, audiences slowly cruise in traveling theater slabs through creaky Audio-Animatronic reproductions of scenes from famous movies. Seesawing with the cheesy histrionics of your guide, a professorial but barely audible dual narration by Turner Classic Movies host Robert Osborne wafts in and out. You'll cruise through "Singin' in the Rain," "Alien," "Raiders of the Lost Ark," and a Munchkin-crammed "The Wizard of Oz"—there, the Wicked Witch figure was a landmark because it was the first time Imagineers figured out that the key to lifelike action was compensating for sudden movements with minute return movements. At one point during the 22-minute journey, which concludes with a fast-paced and expertly edited movie montage, cars experience one of two possible plot-lines—for example, getting caught in the crossfire of a James Cagney gang-land classic or a John Wayne western, with guns that shoot sparks. The robots have looked fresher, your guide's acting skills may embarrass you, and kids won't get most of the references (Busby Berkeley, for example), but there's something endearing about this throwback. Lines are never very long (there's top movie memorabilia to inspect in the queue), but they do tend to spike just after the parade.

Indiana Jones Epic Stunt Spectacular ★★ SHOW   The 30-minute, bone-rattling tour de force of hair-raising daredevilry—rolling-boulder dodging, trucks flipping over and exploding—simultaneously titillates and, to a lesser degree, reminds you how such feats of derring-do are rigged for the movies. They try hard to convince you that they're really filming these

Indiana Jones stunt show at Disney's Hollywood Studios.

"Star Wars" presentation at Disney's Hollywood Studios.

sequences—you may need to explain to young children why they're lying about that, and about calling the lead actor "Harrison Ford's stunt double," but most kids understand the violence is fake. The acrobats and gymnasts are skilled, and the production values are among the highest of any show at a Disney park. The outdoor amphitheater is sheltered, and you can bring drinks and food. *Strategy:* Arrive 20 minutes early, because there's a warm-up and volunteers are selected before showtime. It's mounted about five times daily, listed on the Times Guide.

Star Tours—The Adventure Continues ★★★ RIDE   Before Disney bought "Star Wars," it made, and later upgraded, this popular, 40-person motion-simulator capsule that has you riding shotgun with a fretful C-3PO on an ill-fated and turbulent excursion. In 5 minutes, you manage to lose control, go into hyperdrive, dodge asteroids, navigate a comet field, evade a Star Destroyer, get caught in a tractor beam, and join an assault on the Death Star—or another combination of perils, since there are more than four dozen possible combinations of storylines (some newly created to promote the new movie series). The video is well matched to the movements, which cuts down on reports of nausea. (*Note:* In May and June, the park mounts **Star Wars Weekends**, when actors from the movie arrive for signings, parades, Q&As, and brief workshops [p. 297]). Fans of the franchise come out in force, so to speak. Row 1 is the front row, and that's the best place to see the screen.

Jedi Training Academy ★ SHOW   Up to 15 times daily (see the "Times Guide"), about a dozen kids are lent robes, telescoping "light sabers," and some gentle training in the Force by a "Jedi master" before a final defeat of Darth Vader and some stormtroopers. It's cute and takes 20 minutes. Recruits (ages 4–12) are selected by 10:30am, tops, at the ABC Sound Studio, so get there early if your young Padawan wants a shot at carrying home the diploma.

Sunset Boulevard

The prime items in the park are on this street, which peels off not from the hub, as you might expect, but from the middle of Hollywood Boulevard. Look for vaudeville-style, slapstick **street performances** here.

The Twilight Zone Tower of Terror ★★★ RIDE The tallest ride at Disney World (199 ft.) is one of the smartest, most exciting experiences there, and it's the best version of the ride at any Disney park. It shouldn't be missed. Guests are ushered through the lobby, library, and boiler room of a cobwebby 1930s Los Angeles hotel before being seated in a 21-passenger "elevator" car that, floor by floor, ascends the tower and then, without visible tracks, emerges from the shaft and roams an upper level. Soon, you've entered a second shaft and, after a pregnant moment of tension, you're sent into what seems to be a free fall (in reality, you're being pulled faster than the speed of gravity) and a series of thrilling up-and-down leaps. The fall sequence is random and you never drop more than a few stories—but the total darkness, periodically punctured by picture-window views of the theme park far below as you become momentarily weightless, keys up the giddy fear factor. It's impossible not to smile. *Strategy:* In the preshow "library" room, move to the wall diagonally across from the entry door and you'll exit first, saving time. In the boarding area, the best views are in the front row, numbered 1 and 2, although you may not be given a choice. Chickens can bail down the stairs before the ride boards.

Rock 'n' Roller Coaster Starring Aerosmith ★★★ RIDE Twenty-four-passenger "limousine" trains launch from 0 to 57mph in under 3 seconds, sending them through a 92-second rampage through smooth corkscrews and turns that are intensified by fluorescent symbols of Los Angeles (at one point, you dive though an "O" of the Hollywood sign). The indoor setup is a boon, because it means the ride can operate during the rain, and it makes the journey slightly less disorienting for inexperienced coaster riders. Cooler yet, speakers in each headrest (there are more than 900 in total) play Aerosmith music, which is perfectly timed to the dips and rolls. *Strategy:* The Fastpass line is absorbed quickly. There's also a single-rider line, though it's not always quick.

Beauty and the Beast—Live on Stage ★ SHOW The kid-friendly, 30-minute show is advertised as "Broadway-style," but it's really not. It's theme park–style, simplified with the most popular songs from the movie. The story is highly condensed (you never find out why Belle is at the Beast's castle and Gaston's fate isn't shown) and many characters inhabit whole-body costumes, speaking recorded dialogue with unblinking eyes. To the benefit of timid kids, the Beast looks more like a plush toy than a scary monster. Its intended audience cheers like it's a rock concert and hoists smartphones during the ball scene, and because of that, most performances are jammed. The metal benches are numbing, but at least the amphitheater is covered. *Strategy:* Arrive 20 minutes early so you don't end up in the back where afternoon sun can seep in.

Fantasmic! ★★★ SHOW The super-popular 25-minute pyrotechnics show featuring character-laden showboats, a 59-foot man-made mountain, flaming water, and lasers projected onto a giant water curtain, takes place in the 6,500-seat waterfront Hollywood Hills Amphitheatre. Although it's a strong show by dint of its uniqueness, it doesn't play nightly. I'm always stunned to see people start arriving at the theater as much as *2 hours* before showtime. The seating is hard on the derriere. Most people will be satisfied taking their chances and showing up within 30 minutes of showtime. *Strategy:* On nights when there are two performances (not common), do the second one, as it's always less crowded. Sit toward the rear to avoid catching water from the special effects and to the right to make exiting easier. You can get reserved seats if you book the Fantasmic! Dining Experience and eat dinner in the participating restaurants.

Streets of America & Commissary Lane

Streets of America is a confusing zone of backlot-style city blocks, mostly facades, made to look like aging versions of New York City and San Francisco. Its primary attraction is photo ops. Look around for a few tricks, like the umbrella affixed to a lamppost in the square a la "Singin' in the Rain."

Lights, Motors, Action! Extreme Stunt Show ★★ SHOW Loud, brawling, and moderately exciting enough to see once, it's a showcase for stunt driving dressed up like a film shoot for a car chase/action scene. The engaging 38-minute show, which uses a fleet of specially built, extra-nimble cars (plus a jet ski or two) and tells lots of lies about filming an actual movie scene while you're there, was imported from Paris's Walt Disney Studios Park (hence the set that looks like a Mediterranean port). It's covered but not indoors. *Strategy:* Because the stage is so wide, I suggest taking a seat in the middle or near the top of the grandstand. You won't wrestle for a spot—the stadium seats 5,000. It happens 2 or 3 times daily. Note: This attraction will close in early 2016.

Honey, I Shrunk the Kids Movie Set Adventure ★ ACTIVITY Turn kids loose on a high-concept playground that simulates the sights and sounds of the average backyard—if your kids were the size of an ant. In addition to giant insects, cargo nets, and a slide that was once Kodak film but has been disguised with paint, there's a giant Super Soaker that sprays the unsuspecting, plus giant Play-Doh and Tinkertoy product placements. It's the only playground in the park.

Muppet*Vision 3-D ★ SHOW Behind the fabulous rotating fountain depicting Miss Piggy as the Statue of Liberty, the 17-minute movie features various tricks such as air blasts to make you feel like what you're seeing is actually happening. The doors on the right lead to the back of the 600-seat auditorium and the ones on the left lead to the front; stick in the middle, since the theater's walls become part of the show and you'll want to see. The pre-show is amusing in that Muppet way (says Sam Eagle about seating procedures: "Stopping in the middle is distinctly unpatriotic!"), but the movie contains a few missteps (Waldo, a CG character, is crude and old-fashioned), and not all the effects function. Still, it's fast moving and includes lots of beloved "Muppet Show" favorites, such as Miss Piggy and Kermit. The Muppets, too, lend themselves very nicely to Audio-Animatronic technology. *Strategy:* Lines are longest just after the Indiana Jones show lets out.

Pixar Place & Animation Courtyard

This alley is pretty much a dead zone connecting two areas of the park, with only a ride and a character greeting to occupy kids. But that will change with the upcoming creation of Toy Story Land. In Animation Courtyard, the new **Star Wars Launch Bay** is a place to check out props from the new film series, get photos with "Star Wars" characters, and buy yet more stuff.

Toy Story Midway Mania! ★★★ RIDE   The plotless indoor ride is the most popular in the park, and rightly so. Wearing 3-D glasses, passengers shoot their way through a series of six animated midway games (a Buttercup egg toss, a Little Green Men ring toss) based on the Pixar toy box characters. Along the way, air puffs heighten the reality. Your cannon is easy to work and easy on the hands—you just tug a cord and it fires. Scoring points is harder; both accuracy and intensity count. The queue area, stuffed with outsize toys such as Tinkertoys and Barrel of Monkeys, makes waiting a delight: A 6-foot-tall, lifelike Mr. Potato Head entertains with live interaction and hoary jokes ("Is this an audience or a jigsaw puzzle?"). Across Pixar Place, Woody and Buzz meet kids in air-conditioning. *Tip:* This is your top Fastpass contender, because the wait can jump to an hour just 15 minutes after the park opens.

The Voyage of the Little Mermaid ★★ SHOW   This bright, energetic, condensed version of the animated movie has high production values (puppets, live actors, mist, and a cool undersea-themed auditorium) and is a standout. This show is a top contender for the best show to see in the heat of the day, and Fastpass is available. *Strategy:* In the preshow holding pen, the doors to the left lead to the back half of the theater; because the blacklight puppetry of the marvelous "Under the Sea" sequence can be spoiled if you see too much detail, I suggest sitting there. Put very small kids in your lap so they can see better.

Disney Junior—Live on Stage! ★★ SHOW   For those of us who obediently rise and dance when commanded by Mickey Mouse, there's this

---

Go on Safari—for Mice

A favorite resort-wide pastime for long-time fans is spotting **Hidden Mickeys,** which are ingeniously camouflaged mouse-ear patterns that can be secreted just about anywhere. You'll find the three circles signifying a Mickey head in an arrangement of cannonballs on Peter Pan's Flight; flatware in the dining room at the Haunted Mansion; woven into carpeting, printed on wallpaper. Many sightings are up to interpretation, so sharpen your observational skills at **HiddenMickeysGuide.com.**

breezy, 25-minute show with a lot of excellent puppets (warning, adults: You sit on the ground). It inspires such fervent participation from under 5s that it feels like a meeting for a kindergarten cult that you're not a member of. Even if you don't know the names Doc McStuffins, Sofia the First, or Jake and the Never Land Pirates, this sing-along revue is still pretty to look at, and Mickey, Minnie, and friends make appearances. The parental units won't be too bored, because this de facto Disney Channel ad is fast paced, like changing the channel every 4 minutes. Obviously, anyone old enough to do a book report can skip it.

Where to Eat at Disney's Hollywood Studios

All locations have a few vegetarian options, kids' meals, and if you identify yourself, special dietary requests can usually be accommodated, albeit often at diminished quality. There are also some snack kiosks not listed here.

DISNEY'S HOLLYWOOD STUDIOS' QUICK-SERVICE RESTAURANTS

Starring Rolls Café ★★ AMERICAN   The faster, cheaper, quieter alternative to Quick Service does stupendous baked goods such as chocolate Butterfinger cupcakes and banana split cake, plus a few sandwiches (many made elsewhere) with chips or fruit. Seating is outdoors. Around the corner, **Sweet Spells** tops it in the confection department, selling creative candy apples that look like Olaf. Coffee is just $2.40, not $3.40 as at the kiosks. **Sunset Boulevard.** Sandwiches $11.

Rosie's All-American Cafe ★★ AMERICAN   In the Sunset Ranch Market riff on L.A.'s Farmer's Market, you'll find outdoor-only counter service serving burgers and chicken nuggets. **Sunset Boulevard.** Combo meal $9 to $11.

Catalina Eddie's ★★ AMERICAN   Outdoor counter service for doughy personal pizzas, hot Italian deli sandwiches, and Caesar salad. Near it is **Anaheim Produce** for fruit ($1.70 per piece). **Sunset Boulevard.** Combo meal $9 to $11.

Fairfax Fare ★★ AMERICAN   Grab the richest, deadliest food, served outside: half-slabs of spareribs, barbecued pork sandwiches, and mac 'n cheese with truffle oil. Nearby is the **Toluca Legs Turkey Company** kiosk for those crazy big turkey drumsticks. **Sunset Boulevard.** Combo meal $10 to $16.

ABC Commissary ★★ AMERICAN   Burgers, couscous, quinoa, and fried seafood platters—it's a good choice because the air-conditioned, uncrowded space is fashioned after a '30s Deco backlot cafeteria. **Commissary Lane.** Combo meal $8 to $11.

Backlot Express ★★ AMERICAN   Bacon cheeseburgers, hot dogs, southwest chicken salad, served in air-conditioning with self-serve soda machines. **Echo Lake.** Combo meal $9 to $11.

Studio Catering Co. ★ AMERICAN   In a sheltered seating area, order take-away pulled pork, Greek salad, and chipotle chicken sandwiches. To the left, the **High Octane Refreshments** stand sells $11 cocktails (frozen margaritas and the like), draft beer and wine for $8. **Streets of America.** Combo meal $9 to $11.

Pizza Planet Arcade ★ AMERICAN   Bland pizza, bready subs, dull salads, but kids like spending more of your money on the arcade games, so it's often busy. As Toy Story Land gets built, this restaurant will likely be renamed. **Streets of America.** Combo meal $9.50 to $11.

3 DISNEY'S HOLLYWOOD STUDIOS' TABLE-SERVICE RESTAURANTS

The highest-concept reservation restaurants in Disney World are here. The food isn't legendary, but some of the settings play on entertainment greatness.

The Hollywood Brown Derby ★★ AMERICAN   With interior design based on the after-hours industry hangout of Hollywood's Golden Age, this airy post-Deco hall shoots for class. Caricatures of film legends line the walls—those in black frames are copies while those in gold frames are relics from the original Brown Derby—and while the original Brown Derby was noted for its Cobb salad, this version is a bit of a caricature as well, often soggy. Other choices, all invoking that midcentury California spirit at the park's highest prices, include rack of lamb, free-range chicken breast, Scotch salmon, and beef filet. Its grapefruit cake is a specialty. There's a bar here. **Hollywood Boulevard.** Main courses $30 to $50.

Hollywood & Vine ★★ AMERICAN   At breakfast and lunch, costumed Disney Junior characters (such as Doc McStuffins and Jake) greet kids, sing, and dance in a diner-like setting for **Disney Junior Play 'n Dine at Hollywood & Vine.** The food is always an all-you-can-eat buffet. **Echo Lake.** Buffet $25 to $35 adults, $14 to $18 kids.

50's Prime Time Café ★★★ AMERICAN   Dine atop Formica in detailed reproductions of Cleaver-era kitchens while TVs play black-and-white shows from the era. Waitresses gently sass customers as they sling blue-plate specials—meatloaf, pot roast, chicken pot pie, and other mom-like dishes—but the favorite here is its peanut butter and jelly milkshake ($5.80). Attached is the **Tune-In Lounge,** a TV room for adults serving beer and cocktails "from Dad's liquor cabinet"—plus anyone can eat at the bar, which is first-come, first-served. **Echo Lake.** Main courses $17 to $24.

Mama Melrose's Ristorante Italiano ★★ ITALIAN   Items cost two-thirds of what they do at Epcot's Italy, and the atmosphere recalls the brick-walled, red-booth family restaurant you'd find in any big American city. As expected, there are pastas, steaks, flatbreads, and brick oven–baked chicken dishes. **Streets of America.** Main courses $18 to $33.

Sci-Fi Dine-In Theater Restaurant ★★★ AMERICAN   Disney World's most unusual restaurant arranges mock-ups of '50s automobiles before a silver screen showing a loop of B-movie clips and trailers. Couples sit side-by-side, like at a real drive-in movie, stars twinkle in the "sky," and families get their own booths. It's a brilliant idea, well realized and memorable, making it a top choice despite very iffy food quality. Dishes include burgers, fried dill pickles, pork ribs, and grilled salmon. **Commissary Lane.** Main courses $14 to $32.

DISNEY'S ANIMAL KINGDOM

Although it's the largest Disney theme park in Florida (500 acres), **Disney's Animal Kingdom ★★**, which opened in 1998 at a reported cost of $800 million as a competitor to Busch Gardens, doesn't take all day to visit because most of that land is used up by a menagerie of exotic animals. Instead of cages, they're kept in paddocks rimmed with cleverly disguised trenches that are concealed behind landscaping. Most attractions are given a mild environmentalist message (ironic, considering how much Florida swamp was obliterated to build this resort, but never you mind). Because animals become inactive as the Florida heat builds, a visit here should begin as soon as the gates open, usually around 8am. To help gird your resolve, there are coffee carts ($3.40 outside the gates, $2.40 inside) along the entranceway. *Tips:* Schedule your nighttime shindig, such as that dinner show you've been dying to catch, for your Animal Kingdom day. Check the weather before you come, because if it's excessively hot or wet, you will be miserable: Only three major attractions take place indoors. There is currently no parade at Animal Kingdom.

GETTING IN Staples such as locker and stroller rental are just past the gates, in what's called the **Oasis**, a lush buffer zone that gradually acclimates guests to the world of the park. Pick up a free "Guidemap," a "Times Guide," and an "Animal Guide." The locations of animal enclosures are noted on the map by black-and-white paw prints, so if you're most interested in seeing wildlife, follow those.

Generally speaking, the biggest animals and the most astute design collect at the back of the park (Africa and Asia), the thrills to the right (Asia and DinoLand U.S.A.). *Note:* You won't find any balloons—they choke animals.

The Best of Disney's Animal Kingdom

Don't miss if you're 6: Festival of the Lion King

Don't miss if you're 16: DINOSAUR

Requisite photo op: The drop at Expedition Everest

Food you can only get here: Frozen chai, Royal Anandapur Tea Company

The most crowded, so Fastpass or go early: Kilimanjaro Safaris

Skippable: Rafiki's Planet Watch

Quintessentially Disney: It's Tough to Be a Bug!

Biggest thrill: Expedition Everest

Best show: "Finding Nemo—The Musical"

Character meals: Tusker House Restaurant, Africa

Best shopping: Bhaktapur Market, Asia

Where to find peace: Discovery Island Trails

Disney's Animal Kingdom

RAFIKI'S PLANET WATCH

Wildlife Express

Wildlife Express Train Station

ASIA

Maharajah Jungle Trek

AFRICA

Pangani Forest Exploration Trail

Wildlife Express Train Station

Kali River Rapids

Festival of the Lion King

Kilimanjaro Safaris

Tree of Life

DISCOVERY ISLAND

Discovery River

Expedition Everest

Finding Nemo– The Musical

Future Site of Pandora– The World of Avatar (opens 2017)

OASIS

DINOLAND U.S.A.

Ticket gates

DINOSAUR

Main Entrance

SHUTTLES   PARKING

DINING ◆
Flame Tree Barbecue **22**
Harambe Market **10**
Pizzafari **18**
Rainforest Cafe **30**
Restaurantosaurus **27**
Safari Barbecue **21**
Tamu Tamu Eats & Refreshment **9**
Tusker House Restaurant (character meals) and Dawa Bar **8**
Yak & Yeti **12**

ATTRACTIONS ●
DISCOVERY ISLAND
Adventurers Outpost **16**
Discovery Island Trails **17**
It's Tough to Be a Bug! **19**
Tip Board **20**

AFRICA
Kilimanjaro Safaris **7**
Pangani Forest Exploration Trail **6**
Wildlife Express Train station for Rafiki's Planet Watch **5**

ASIA
Expedition Everest **15**
Flights of Wonder **11**
Kali River Rapids **13**
Maharajah Jungle Trek **4**
Rivers of Light **14**

RAFIKI'S PLANET WATCH
The Affection Section **1**
Conservation Station **2**
Habitat Habit! **3**

DINOLAND U.S.A.
The Boneyard **24**
DINOSAUR **29**
Dino-Sue **28**
Finding Nemo– The Musical **23**
Primeval Whirl **26**
TriceraTop Spin **25**

DISNEY'S ANIMAL KINGDOM: 1 DAY, TWO WAYS

START: BE AT THE GATE FOR OPENING TIME.

ANIMAL KINGDOM WITH KIDS

When the gates open, head straight to Africa for **Kilimanjaro Safaris.**

↓

Find the gorillas and hippos on the **Pangani Forest Exploration.**

↓

Go to Asia to spot tigers on the **Maharajah Jungle Trek.**

↓

Ride **Kali River Rapids** to cool down.

↓

See **Flights of Wonder.**

↓

Have lunch at Yak & Yeti.

↓

See the next performance of **Finding Nemo— The Musical,** seated and indoors.

↓

Ride **Primeval Whirl** and **TriceraTop Spin.**

↓

Go see **It's Tough to Be a Bug!,** and walk the Discovery Trails to look for animals embedded in the Tree of Life.

↓

Go to Africa to see **Festival of the Lion King.**

↓

If you have time or energy, take the train to and from Rafiki's Planet Watch for a 20-minute walk-through (budget 45 min. total).

↓

Re-ride anything you loved and head out before closing.

ANIMAL KINGDOM WITHOUT KIDS

Have a mid- to late-morning Fastpass for Expedition Everest or an early afternoon one for Kilimanjaro Safaris.

When the gates open, head straight to Africa for **Kilimanjaro Safaris.** It's fine if you have a Fastpass for later; each trip yields different animals.

↓

Watch the gorillas on the **Pangani Forest Exploration Trail.**

OR

Go to Asia to ride **Expedition Everest** before the line gets too crazy.

↓

Walk to Asia and ride **Expedition Everest** (if you haven't already!).

↓

Explore the **Maharajah Jungle Trek** to see tigers.

↓

If it's hot by now, ride **Kali River Rapids.**

↓

See **Flights of Wonder.**

Have lunch at Yak & Yeti.

↓

See the next performance of **Finding Nemo— The Musical.** Enjoy the air-conditioning.

↓

Ride **Primeval Whirl.**

↓

Ride **DINOSAUR.**

↓

See **It's Tough to Be a Bug!,** and walk the Discovery Trails to look for animals embedded in the Tree of Life.

↓

If it's quiet and you're interested, re-ride **Kilimanjaro Safaris** to get a different experience than before.

↓

Go to Africa to see **Festival of the Lion King.**

↓

If you have time or energy, take the train to **Rafiki's Planet Watch** (budget 45 min. total).

↓

Re-ride anything you loved. You will probably depart before closing time, so this may be a great night to make evening plans in Orlando.

The first thing you should do, like everyone else, is beeline it to the back of the Africa section. That's where the Kilimanjaro Safari is, and first thing in the morning is the best time to do it. Crowds grow more ferocious than the lions.

Discovery Island

Like the Plaza of the Magic Kingdom, Discovery Island is designed to be the hub of the park. It's also the most central area for souvenirs and for meeting characters, (whose locations are denoted on the maps by a Mickey profile), and guests can touch down here to change lands.

The Tree of Life ★★★ RIDE   Instead of a castle or a geosphere, the centerpiece here, Animal Kingdom's "weenie," is an emerald, 14-story-high arbor (built on the skeleton of an oil rig) covered with hundreds of carvings of animals made to appear, at a distance, like the pattern of bark. Some 102,000 vinyl leaves were individually attached—which is why its shade of green is more lurid than the surrounding foliage—to some 750 tertiary branches. That the best way to enjoy it is to slowly make a circuit of it, looking for and identifying new animals, is perhaps proof that the best way to experience this park is to slow down and open your eyes.

Discovery Island Trails ★★ ACTIVITY   The self-guided paths encircle the Tree of Life. Here's where you'll find giant red kangaroos, flamingoes, storks, otters, lemurs, macaws, and the lappet-faced vulture; some are removed from view when it's hot. It takes only about 15 minutes to enjoy.

Adventurers Outpost ★ CHARACTER GREETING   Mickey and Minnie, wearing explorer garb, meet kids, and sign autographs here, on the east side of the path toward Asia. It is the only place in the resort where they appear as a couple.

It's Tough to Be a Bug! ★★★ SHOW   Hidden in the flying roots of the Tree of Life, in a cool basementlike theater, you'll find a cleverly rigged cinema showing a sense-tricking 10-minute 3-D movie based on the animated movie "A Bug's Life." When the stinkbugs do their thing or the tarantula starts firing poison quills, you'll never quite be sure what's an image, what's cutting-edge robotics, and what's clever rigging in the theater. As one of the newest sense-tricking movies at Disney World, it's one of the best. Little kids who can't distinguish fantasy from reality may be scared by the marvelously realized Hopper figure; sit in back (the first doors after you get your glasses) and to the left to be far from him. The indoor preshow area is decorated with posters for some funny entomological variations on Broadway shows (my faves: "Web Side Story" and "My Fair Ladybug"). *Strategy:* Upon exiting, go left to explore the trails (above) or right for the bridge to Asia.

Africa

Because of its star attraction, Africa is mobbed in the morning; in the afternoon, it's a popular place to grab food or a cocktail.

Ever since it debuted, Animal Kingdom closed before dusk. But Disney is tired of losing customers to the night, so it's hustling to build infrastructure that will allow the park to entertain guests in the evening. In 2016, a new **Rivers of Light** water-and-light spectacular, cut from the same cloth as Disney California Adventure's World of Color, will fire up the lagoon near Asia. Around the same time, **Kilimanjaro Safaris** is adding lighting that will simulate perpetual sunset, the **Tree of Life** will be illuminated with psychedelic projections, and the park even adds **hyenas,** which besides being cool animals, happen to be nocturnal. When it debuts (most likely in 2017), **Pandora—The World of Avatar** will feature fantastic "bioluminescent" color features that will look especially cool when the lights go down.

Kilimanjaro Safaris ★★★ RIDE   Easily the bumpiest ride at Disney World, the 20-minute excursion is the crown jewel of Animal Kingdom. Climb into a supersize, 32-passenger Jeep—an actual one with wheels, not a tracked cart—and be swept into what feels like a real safari through the African veldt, with meticulously rutted tracks and all, only on Quaaludes. Be quick on the shutter, because drivers speed fleetly, passing through habitats for giraffes, elephants, wildebeest, ostrich, hippos, lions, antelope, rhinos, and other creatures that made safaris famous. Considering the quality and quantity of animals on display—and the cleverness of the enclosure design, as there are never bars between you and them—it's easily the best animal attraction of the park, and the queue only builds during the day. Some people say that the second-best time to see the animals is in midafternoon because they get antsy with the foreknowledge that they're about to be led to their indoor sleeping quarters. Ride twice if you want—the free will of the animals means it's never the same trip twice: Sometimes you'll zip right through, and sometimes you'll be halted by a moody rhino who refuses to get off the road. *Strategy:* Photographers who want clear shots should jockey toward the back, away from the cockpit. They may not have control over that, so at the very least, they should negotiate with their companions for a seat at the end of their row.

Pangani Forest Exploration Trail ★★★ ACTIVITY   Upon exiting Kilimanjaro Safaris, begin this trail, which focuses on African animals. It wends past a troop of lowland gorillas (very popular), naked mole rats, okapi, meerkats (yes, like Timon), and hippos you can view through an underwater window; the nocturnal animals start waking up at around 3:30pm. The circuit takes about a half-hour, but you can spend as long as you want. The gorillas come near the end, so budget your time.

"Festival of the Lion King" ★★★ SHOW   If this lavish, colorful, intense spectacle can't hold your attention for 30 minutes, you might require prescriptions. Audiences sit on benches in four quadrants (front rows are good for engaging with performers), and the event comes on buoyant and boisterously, like an acid trip during a rock concert. Four huge floats enter the room,

The "Festival of the Lion King" at Animal Kingdom.

topped with soft-looking giant puppets of Timon, Pumbaa, and African wildlife and attended by acrobats, stilt-walkers, flame jugglers, and dancers, all of whom get their turn to dazzle you with their acts, which are performed, of course, to the hit songs of the movie. *Strategy:* Shows are scheduled, and they can fill up, so arrive 30 minutes early. Unfortunately, although the theatre was just built in 2014, the seating is bleacher-style and lacks backs.

Rafiki's Planet Watch ★ ACTIVITY   Its elements are listed separately on the park maps, but everything is of a piece. The only way to reach this educational veterinary station is using the **Wildlife Express Train.** Waits are generally no longer than 10 minutes. The trip takes 7 minutes and you'll get glimpses of plain backstage work areas and maybe a white rhino in its indoor pen, but not much else. **Habitat Habit!,** the path that leads to the main building, is another "discovery trail," this one with cotton-top tamarins (endangered monkeys about the size of squirrels). **Conservation Station** is a quasi-educational peek at how the park's animals are maintained—you're not seeing the true veterinary facilities, but a few auxiliary rooms set up so tourists can watch activities through picture windows. There's not always something going on (early mornings seem to be most active), and the Times Guide doesn't help, so you might get all the way here and then find yourself with only some

> ### Kid Stuff at Animal Kingdom
>
> Animal Kingdom has a free paper scavenger hunt, **Wilderness Explorers,** in which kids collect merit badges (stickers) for learning things about animals and conservation. Join on the bridge between Oasis and the Tree of Life, opposite the Yak & Yeti, and by Dino-Bite Snacks.

tanks of reptiles and amphibians to poke at, although Rafiki and Chip 'n' Dale make appearances all day. There's nothing earthshaking—enter a dark, sound-proof booth and listen to the sounds of the rainforest—but the pace is much easier than in the park outside. **The Affection Section** is a petting zoo hosting, in addition to your typical petting-zoo denizens—donkeys, goats, sheep. Next to that; there's an animal presentation on the bottom of the hour between 11:30am and 2:30pm. *Tip:* Try to visit by noon, when the vets are more likely to be treating animals; Guest Relations, at the front of the park, keeps a schedule.

Asia

Asia is the park's showcase, and its ingenious decor (rat-trap wiring, fraying prayer flags) is so accurate it could easily be mistaken for the real Nepal or northern India. Make a stop at **Bhaktapur Market,** which sells Asian souve-nirs that are a cut above the usual theme park stuff—kimonos, Manga toys, beautiful sarongs. It makes me long for the years when all of Disney World's shops were this interesting and site-specific.

Expedition Everest ★★★ RIDE   The lavishly themed and abundantly hyped roller coaster is mostly contained in the "snowcapped" mountain loom-ing nearly 200 feet over the park's east end (if it were any higher, Florida law would require it to be topped by an airplane beacon). The queue area is a beautifully realized duplication of a Himalayan temple down to the tarnished bells and weathered paint, although portions of it are exposed the sun, so drink some-thing before you pony up. The coaster itself is loaded with power-ful set pieces: both backward and forward motion, pitch-black sec-tions, and a fleeting encounter with a 22-foot Abominable Snowman, or Yeti. As with all Disney rides, the most dramatic drop (80 ft.) is visible from the sidewalk out front, so if you think you can stomach that, you can do the rest. There are no upside-down loops; the domi-nant motion is spiral. *Strategy:* This coaster is a top candidate for Fastpass. The seats with the best view, without question, are in the front rows, although the back rows feel a little faster. The single-rider line is one of the resort's fastest-moving and most fruitful.

> ### The Chilling Tale of Disco Yeti
>
> Expedition Everest's original effects were too complicated to function for long. The Yeti suffered the most ignoble fate. Although it was the most compli-cated Audio-Animatronic creature ever commissioned, and the sight of it lung-ing for your train was meant to be the ride's scintillating climax, its repetitive motion reportedly cracked its supports, which were too integrated with the structure of the mountain to repair. The solution: A strobe light now makes it appear as if the motionless Yeti moves. Disney fans deride it as the "Disco Yeti." Even Disneyland's Matterhorn, built in 1959, now has a livelier Yeti.

Kali River Rapids ★ RIDE   The 12-passenger round bumper boat shoots a course of rapids, and sometimes you can get soaked—it depends on your bad luck—but it's generally milder than similar rides. Your feet, for sure, will get wet. The worst damage is usually done by spectators who shoot water cannons at passing boats. Lots of guests buy rain ponchos ($7.50–$8.50 at nearby stores, or $1 for two at your local dollar store), but there is a water-resistant holding area in the center of each boat. To be safe, there are free 120-minute lockers available, $7/hour if you go over. *Strategy:* Lines build considerably when it's hot, so this is another prime Fastpass candidate.

Maharajah Jungle Trek ★★ ACTIVITY   Too few people enjoy this self-guided, South Asian–themed walking trail featuring some gorgeous tigers (rescued from a circus breeding program; they're most active in the hour before the park closes), flying foxes, komodo dragons, and a few birds frolicking among fake ruins. The tigers are most active when the park opens and near closing time. Grab a bird information sheet after entering the aviary; there's a bat display, too, that you can bypass if you're squeamish.

Flights of Wonder ★★ SHOW   At the canvas-sheltered Caravan Stage, the 25-minute show (the schedule is posted) showcases birds such as hawks, vultures, bald eagles, and parrots—20 species; the mix changes—that swoop thrillingly over the audience's heads. Standard, if beautiful, nature-show stuff, but the backless benches can hurt. After the performance, handlers usually present a few of the birds back on stage for close inspection.

DinoLand U.S.A.

When it rains, come here, where two attractions and one big counter-service restaurant are indoors.

"Finding Nemo—The Musical" ★★★ SHOW   One of the best shows at Disney right now is a fast-forwarded version of the movie by the songwriters of the Oscar-winning tune "Let It Go." The story was heightened with such catchy added songs as "Fish Are Friends, Not Food" and the infectious, Beach Boys–style "Go with the Flow." Just as in the Broadway adaptation of "The Lion King," live actors manipulate complicated animal puppets in full view, which allows the fish to appear as if they're floating in the sea. It's remarkable how quickly you stop paying attention to the humans—at least, until they start flying, with their puppets, through the air on wires. Then you're just amazed. Sprightly, bright, colossal, and energetic, this winning 40-minute show is a good choice for taking a load off (the bench seating is indoors), and even those who know the movie backward and forward will find something new in the vibrant vigor of the delivery. *Strategy:* Because some scenes (including the introduction of Dory) happen in the aisle that crosses the center of the theater, sit in the rear half of the auditorium.

Chester & Hester's Dino-Rama ★ ACTIVITY/RIDE   Kids run loose in this miniature carnival-style amusement area with a midway, **Fossil Fun Games** (Mammoth skee-ball races, "Whac-a-Pachycephalosaurus") and two simple family rides. **TriceraTop Spin** ★, for the very young, is yet another iteration of the Dumbo ride over at Magic Kingdom and is designed for kids to ride with their parents. Cars fit four, in two rows. **Primeval Whirl** ★ is a pair of mirror-image, family-friendly carnival-style coasters (FYI, Walt *hated* carnivals) that start out like a typical "wild mouse" ride before, mid-trip, the round cars begin spinning on an axle as they ride the rails. Think of it as a roller-coaster version of the teacup ride. You can plainly see what you're in for, although you may be surprised at how roughly the movements can whip your neck. Don't feel bad if you give it a miss, too, because it's not a Disney original; it was made by a French company that sells similar rides to other parks. Keep the kids in control by swinging them across the path to **The Boneyard ★**, a hot, sun-exposed playground where the very young can dig up "prehistoric" bones in the sand and work off energy on catwalks, net courses, and slides.

DINOSAUR ★★ RIDE   A good rainy-weather option is this 3-minute indoor time-travel ride in which all-terrain "Enhanced Motion Vehicles" simultaneously speed and shimmy down an unseen track, all as hordes of roaring dinosaurs attempt to make you dinner and an approaching asteroid shower threatens to do everyone in. Some kids, and even some adults, find all those jaws and jerky movements rather intense, and it's extremely dark and loud, but ultimately, it's a fun time, even if the perpetual darkness makes me wonder how much money Disney saved in not having to build more dinosaurs. Like many modern rides, well-known actors perform in the preshow video; this one's got Phylicia Rashad, fiercely overacting, and Wallace Langham, in a horrific tie. The line never seems to be as long as this ride deserves. On the path to the ride, don't ignore **Dino-Sue,** the 40-foot-long, full-scale T. rex skeleton—it's a replica of Sue, the most complete specimen man has yet found. The original, unearthed in South Dakota in 1990, is on display at Chicago's Field Museum. The **Cretaceous Trail,** at the head of the path, showcases ferns and American alligators extant in that period.

Where to Eat at Disney's Animal Kingdom

All locations have vegetarian options, kids' meals, and if you identify yourself, special dietary requests can usually be accommodated. Because plastic straws choke animals, they're banned, as are drink lids. Frozen drinks spiked with booze have become a big thing at Animal Kingdom, which helps combat heat in this exposed park. The fruit cart ($1.70/piece) is in Africa.

Opening Pandora

The next big Disney addition, slated for a 2017 opening, is currently clanging and hammering its way into existence on the site of the former Camp Minnie-Mickey section. It's **Pandora—The World of Avatar,** a bizarre theme that was not created by the company, but no doubt Disney was spooked into greenlighting it by the mad success of Universal's Harry Potter lands. Avatar Land, as it's nicknamed, will be the largest expansion in Animal Kingdom's relatively short history, with one ride that simulates flying **(Avatar: Flight of Passage)** and another boat ride through a pretty fluorescent forest. Imagineers are drawing inspiration from the bioluminescent plants, "floating mountains," and wildlife of the movie.

PACKING IT IN: TWO PARKS, 1 DAY

START: BE AT THE GATE FOR OPENING TIME.

You really don't *have* to pay for 2 days' worth of park tickets to visit Animal Kingdom and Hollywood Studios. As long as you have the Park Hopper option, you can see the highlights in 1 action-packed day. You will miss some lesser attractions, but not enough to lose sleep over.

Which park you do first is a toss-up. The animals are most active first thing in the morning at Animal Kingdom, but the line at Hollywood Studios' Toy Story Midway Mania gets crazy by noon. You can start with Animal Kingdom, where Fastpasses are mostly unnecessary, if you have pre-arranged an afternoon Fastpass for Toy Story Midway Mania at Hollywood Studios.

Begin your day at **Disney's Animal Kingdom.** When the gates open, head straight to Africa for **Kilimanjaro Safaris.**
↓
Animal people: Enjoy the **Pangani Forest Exploration Trail.**
Coaster people: Ride **Expedition Everest.** If the wait's bad, use the Single Rider line.
↓
Explore the **Maharajah Jungle Trek.**
↓
Ride **Kali River Rapids.**
↓
If you enjoy live musicals, see the next performance of either **Finding Nemo— The Musical** or **Festival of the Lion King.** This will take nearly an hour, so cut this if it's too close to lunch.
↓
Ride **DINOSAUR.** (Maybe you can do this while waiting for the Nemo show to start?)
↓

Go see **It's Tough to Be a Bug!,** and afterward walk the Discovery Trails and look for animals embedded in the Tree of Life.
↓
Switch parks. On the way, you could lunch on U.S. 192, where food's cheaper. Reach that quickly by following the signs to the Animal Kingdom Lodge and turning left at the light before its entrance. That's Sherbeth Road, and it winds to U.S. 192. After lunch, drive east on 192 a few miles and follow the signs back to Disney.
↓
Enter **Disney's Hollywood Studios.**
↓
Use your Fastpass for **Toy Story Midway Mania** at Pixar Place.
↓
Ride **Twilight Zone Tower of Terror** and **Rock 'n' Roller Coaster.**
↓
Do **The Great Movie Ride.**
↓
Take the **Backlot Tour** (it usually shuts down by late afternoon).
↓
Ride **Star Tours.**
↓
If you have time, see **Muppet*Vision 3-D.**
↓
If you have time, see the **Indiana Jones Epic Stunt Spectacular.**
↓
See **Fantasmic!** (if it's performing tonight).
↓
Go back to your hotel and collapse.

DISNEY'S ANIMAL KINGDOM'S QUICK-SERVICE RESTAURANTS

Guests with **dietary restrictions** should seek out the new Gardens kiosk near Flame Tree Barbecue on Discovery Island, where special snacks are sold and cast members can help you find more suitable dishes around the park.

Flame Tree Barbecue ★★★ AMERICAN   If you don't mind gorging on dishes such as ribs and baked chicken when you're supposed to be appreciating animals, it has some terrific eating areas with cushioned seating on the Discovery River, and its pulled-pork barbecue is a favorite. This is where you get those honking turkey legs. **Discovery Island.** Combo meal $9.50 to $16.

Pizzafari ★★ AMERICAN   A vibrantly colored restaurant with lots of rooms to spread out, Pizzafari has a special contraption in the kitchen for cranking out fresh pizzas. It also does Italian-style subs and pasta with chicken. **Discovery Island.** Combo meal $10 to $11.

Yak & Yeti Local Food Cafes ★★ ASIAN   Although there is a table-service location indoors by the same name, the outdoor windows do counter-service Mandarin chicken salad, sweet and sour chicken, beef lo mein, and shockingly greasy pork egg rolls. Across the path on the water, the **Royal Anandapur Tea Company ★★** kiosk offers something unique: teas and slushy chai ($5.40). **Asia.** Combo meal $9 to $11.

Harambe Market ★★★ INTERNATIONAL   This new food court (in a pan-African costume) has sheltered outdoor seating and a range of four kiosk options to please many tastes, including **Chef Mwanga's Ribs Shop, Kitamu Grill** (chicken skewers, flatbread sandwiches), **Famous Sausages** (try the boerewors South African sausage), and **Wanjohi Refreshments** for South African wines. Also delicious: the coconut African Milk Tart in a chocolate shell. Combo meal $10 to $14.

Harambe Market at Animal Kingdom.

Tamu Tamu Eats & Refreshment ★ INTERNATIONAL   With a small selection (pulled beef or chicken-salad sandwiches, quinoa salad) and no indoor seating, it's not usually too crowded. Best of all, it serves the beloved Dole Whip frozen pineapple dessert, but here, it's spiked with a shot of rum. It's near **Dawa Bar,** a relaxing spot mimicking a fortress on the water where cocktails ($8–$16) are served; there are 10 seats at the bar but more under a bamboo shelter. **Africa.** Combo meal $9 to $10.

Restaurantosaurus ★ AMERICAN   As American as DinoLand U.S.A., the kitchen pumps out burgers, hot dogs, chicken BLT salad, and nuggets. The **Dino-Bites** kiosk nearby sells desserts. **DinoLand U.S.A.** Combo meal $9 to $11.

DISNEY'S ANIMAL KINGDOM'S TABLE-SERVICE RESTAURANTS

Because you're probably going to be up early to see the animals at their best, this park is a good candidate for a character breakfast. There are very few places to get out of the heat and have a waiter-service meal.

Rainforest Cafe ★ AMERICAN   In a lush, jungle-like, theatrically lit setting, robotic animals roar and twitter over your cheese sticks, burgers, and rum cocktails in souvenir glasses. This is not a Disney original, but one of two outposts of the established brand at Disney World (the other is at Disney Springs Marketplace). **Oasis, at the park turnstiles.** Main courses $13 to $33.

Tusker House Restaurant ★★★ AMERICAN/AFRICAN   Under multicolored banners in an ancient souklike environment, Donald, Daisy, Mickey, and Goofy greet families in safari garb for "Donald's Safari Breakfast" and "Donald's Dining Safari" lunch, both all-you-can eat buffets. Dinner is character-free but also unlimited. The buffet at lunch and dinner dares more than most of Disney's do, featuring spiced tandoori tofu, couscous, peri-peri salmon, tamarind beef stew, and other pleasingly aromatic choices. **Africa.** Meals $29 to $42 adults, $16 to $20 kids.

Yak & Yeti Restaurant ★★ ASIAN   Themed like a Nepalese mansion stocked with souvenirs from across Southeast Asia, the menu is just as geographically varied, serving Kobe beef burgers with mushroom compote, ahi tuna, Malaysian seafood curry, fried honey chicken, and chicken tikka marsala. The Quick Service counter outside offers a shorter, but similar, menu for less, but at Animal Kingdom, air-conditioning is the most rare and delicious treat. **Asia.** Main courses $19 to $29.

DISNEY WATER PARKS

The big question: Blizzard Beach or Typhoon Lagoon? Both can fill a day. So it depends on your mood. Typhoon Lagoon's central feature, a sand-lined 2½-acre wave pool, is an ideal place for families to approximate a day at the beach. If your kids have a need for speed, then head to Blizzard Beach, which has wilder water slides. If you use a one-day ticket (and not Water Parks Fun & More), you can hit both in the same day without paying more.

Both water parks, similar in size, have free parking and are less busy early in the week, probably because folks tend to start their vacations on a weekend and don't get to the flumes until they've done the four big theme parks. They tend to be busier in the morning than in late afternoon. They also sell everything you need to protect yourself from the sun, including lotion (should you have forgotten) and swimsuits (should you lose yours in the lather). Most lines (many rides have two: one for a raft and one for the slide) are exposed to the sun, so it's important to **keep hydrated,** because you won't always be aware how much you're sweating. Both parks sell refillable mugs for **endless soft drinks** (otherwise, soft drinks start at $3). They also rent towels for $2. Lifeguards usually make you remove water shoes on slides that don't use a mat or raft, and swimsuits with rivets or zippers are forbidden.

A day at a water park isn't as stressful as one spent among the queues of the theme parks, and if you're paying attention, the sights and sounds of a day here are pretty heartwarming. Every time the wave machine roars into gear, for example, dozens of kids shriek with delight and scamper into the water. Because they're chilling out, people tend to be happy at these parks.

LOCKERS An average locker is $13 but you get $5 of that back after you turn your key in. They allow multiple access, are about 2 feet deep, and the opening is about the size of a magazine.

PREPARATION Thoughtfully, parking is free. There are bulletin boards past the park entrances that tell you what the sunburn risk is and what the wait times are for the slides, as well as what times the parades run at Disney parks that day. If there are any activities (scavenger hunts are common), they'll be posted here.

FOOD There are only counter-service choices. Eat promptly at 11am when kitchens open because lines get crazy quickly. Don't plan on eating dinner at the water parks, because the kiosks tend to shut down well before closing.

TIMING If you're coming to Florida between November and mid-March, one of these parks will be closed for its annual hose-down. The other will remain open. Most water features are heated, but remember that you eventually must get *out.*

Blizzard Beach

Of Disney's two water parks, **Blizzard Beach ★★★** is the more thrilling, possibly because it opened 6 years after Typhoon Lagoon and had the benefit of improving on what didn't work there. It also has a wittier backstory that is perfect for a hot day: A freak snowstorm hit Mount Gushmore, and Disney was slapping up a ski resort when the snow began to melt, creating water slides. So now, a lift chair brings bathers most of the way up the 90-foot peak, and flumes are festooned with ski-run flags and piled with white "snowdrifts." Best of all, at this park, no one has to tote rafts uphill—there are conveyors to do it for you.

Surely the most exhilarating 8 seconds in all of Walt Disney World, **Summit Plummet ★★★** is the immensely steep, 12-story-tall slide that commands

Blizzard Beach.

attention at the peak of the mountain, which incidentally, offers one of the best panoramas of the Walt Disney World resort. A slide down this one is for the truly fearless, because the first few seconds make you feel weightless, as if you're about to fall forward. By the end, the water is jabbing you so hard that it's not unusual to come away with a light bruise, and it turns the toughest bathing suit into dental floss. This is a fun one to watch; just ask the young men who are glued to it for the aforementioned reason. **Slush Gusher ★**, next to it among the Green Slope rides and slightly lower, is a double-hump that gives the rider the sensation of air time—not a reassuring feeling when you're flying down an open chute.

The enormous chute winding off the mountain's right side is **Steamboat Springs ★★**, a group ride in a circular raft; just about everyone gets a chance to enjoy the top of a banked turn, and after the inevitable splashdown, another minute is spent in a comedown floating on a river. It's highly re-rideable, but if you go alone, you'll be paired with strangers for some slippery awkwardness.

Snow Stormers ★ (Purple Slope) is a trio of standard raft water slides, but the twin **Downhill Double Dipper ★** is a simple slope of two identical slides with a good embellishment: It times runs so you can race a companion down. **Toboggan Racers ★★** multiplies the fun to where eight people can race at once down an evenly scalloped run. At the base of these is **Melt Away Bay ★★★**, a 1-acre wave pool in which waves create a gentle bobbing sensation. It could stand to be larger since it gets very crowded.

At the back of the mountain (the Red Slope; reach it by walking around the left or via the lazy river), the three **Runoff Rapids ★★** flumes comprise two open-air slides and a totally enclosed one—you only see the occasional light flashing by. (These are the only ones for which you must haul your own raft up the hill.)

The park is circled by the superlative lazy river (for the newbie, that's a slow-flowing channel where you float along in an inner tube) called **Cross**

Lazy river in Typhoon Lagoon.

Country Creek ★★★, which is probably the best of its kind, passing a cave dripping with refrigerated water and a slouching shack that, every few seconds, gushes as you hear the sound of Goofy sneezing. *Tip:* It's easier to find a free inner tube at a ramp far from the park entrance; try the one at the base of Downhill Double Dipper or the one to the left past Lottawatta Lodge, the main food building.

There are two kiddie areas, one for preteens, **Ski Patrol ★★** (short slides, a walk across the water on floating "icebergs") and for littler kids, **Tike's Peak ★** (even smaller slides, fountains, and jets). The latter is a good place to look if you can't find seating.

Tip: The miniature golf course Winter Summerland (see "Join the Club" on p. 190) shares a parking lot with Blizzard Beach, so it's easy to combine a visit.

www.disneyworld.com. ℂ **407/560-3400.** $62 adults, $54 kids 3–9. Hours vary, but 10am–5pm is common in summer.

Typhoon Lagoon

Despite the petrifying imagery of the shrimp boat *(Miss Tilly)* impaled on the central mountain (Mt. Mayday), the flumes at **Typhoon Lagoon ★★** are less daunting than the ones at Blizzard Beach or Wet 'n Wild. Typhoon Lagoon is extremely well landscaped (most of the flowers are selected so that they attract butterflies but not bees) to hide its infrastructure, but its navigation is not always well planned. For example, you tote your own rafts. Also, the paths to the slides ramble up and down stairs—the one to the Storm Slides actually goes *down* eight times as it winds up the mountain. It's also not always clear where to find the slide you want. Help guide little ones.

The **Surf Pool ★★★** divides its time between "surf waves" (at 5 ft., they pack a surprising punch, and are announced by a *whoompf* that draws great peals of delight from kids) and mild "bobbing waves"—times for both are noted on the Surf Report chalk sign at the pool's foot. The slides are generally shallow, slow, and geared toward avowed sissies. That will frustrate some teenagers, but little kids and mothers with expensive hairdos think **Mayday Falls** ★, which sends riders down a corrugated flume, is just right (adults come off rubbing their butts in pain). It's very tough to find a vantage point to watch your kids ride, but there's a spot near the entrance of **Gangplank Falls** ★★★, a family-size round raft, where you can see a little, and there's a lovely hidden overlook trail with a suspension bridge and waterfalls that passes under the *Miss Tilly*. The leftmost body slide of three at **Storm Slides** ★★ is slightly more covered; otherwise the slides are much the same. The **Crush 'n' Gusher** ★★★ "water coaster" flumes use jets to push rafts both uphill and downhill; the gag is that it used to be a fruit-washing plant, and now you're the banana— appropriate since it's sponsored by Chiquita.

One highlight is **Shark Reef** ★★, a 10½-foot-deep tank stocked with tropical fish, nonthreatening leopard and bonnet sharks, and mock coral. Everyone gets a mask, snorkel, and, if you want, a floatation jacket, and then swims 60 feet across the tank (no dawdling permitted) under the eye of lifeguards who'll spring into action at the slightest hint of trouble—or even if you kick your feet. (If you want a tank where you can dawdle with fish, try SeaWorld's Discovery Cove, p. 167.) You needn't meet a high standard beyond an ability to paddle across a pool. If you don't care for that setup, descend by stairs into a submerged "shipwreck," which has portholes allowing a lateral, murky view of the same tank. *Strategy:* Shark Reef gets busy, so do it early or late.

For the best shot at finding an inner tube for the lushly planted lazy river, **Castaway Creek** ★★, pick an entry farther from the entrance, such as in front of the Crush 'n' Gusher area. That's also a good place to find a lounger if the Lagoon is packed, which it usually is; otherwise, try the extreme left past the ice cream stand. That's near **Ketchakiddee Creek** ★★, the geyser-and-bubbler play area for small children. Funny how the water's always warmer there.

"Learn to Surf" lessons are held in the Surf Pool 2 hours before park hours and, sometimes, after it closes (✆ **407/939-7529**; $150 for all ages, minimum age of 5). The lessons come with 30 minutes of preparation followed by 2 hours of in-pool instruction, always with lifeguards scrutinizing your every twitch.

www.disneyworld.com. ✆ **407/560-3400.** $62 adults, $54 kids 3–9. Hours vary, but 10am–5pm is common in summer.

MINOR DISNEY WORLD DIVERSIONS

Also see "Join the Club" on p. 190 for details on the two Disney miniature golf areas.

DisneyQuest ★ PLAY PARK This five-level virtual reality playground is shabby and past its prime, if it had one, which is why Disney is pulling the plug in 2016. That should tell you that it's not worth doing, and if you pay full price for it, you'll wish you hadn't. Stuff includes **Cyberspace Mountain,** in which you design your own coaster from a palette of options and then board a motion-simulator capsule to test your creation. **Virtual Jungle Cruise** has

ORLANDO after dark WITH KIDS

Although on some nights, one could argue that the people drinking at the clubs and bars are infantile, you still can't bring your kids to hang out in them. Don't worry—Orlando is a family city, so there's much for kids to do.

o **Magic Kingdom parade:** Most nights, there are one or two parades through the park. When there are two, the second is less crowded.

o **Fireworks:** The Magic Kingdom is open until 9pm or later on most nights. There's usually an evening parade, and the nightly fireworks display, "Wishes," happens around Cinderella Castle. Hollywood Studios mounts "Fantasmic!," a pyrotechnics-and-water display, a few times a week, and Epcot is famous for its "IllumiNations" fireworks-and-electronics show over its lagoon. In summer, when they're open past dusk, Universal Studios does something (a spectacle on its lagoon) most nights, SeaWorld not so much. Check with each park for showtimes, because they change. Given that they're theme park shows, they're all designed to wow kids, but Magic Kingdom's display is the classic.

o **The Electrical Boat Parade:** It's a tradition going back 40 years—

a string of 14 40-foot-long illuminated barges floats past the Disney resorts on Seven Seas Lagoon and Bay Lake starting at 9pm, accompanied by music. Lower key than the fireworks shows, you can see it for free from any resort hotel in the area or, if your timing is good, from the ferry that goes between the Magic Kingdom and the Ticket and Transportation Center.

o **Special event evenings:** From September through March, the Magic Kingdom schedules irregular special-ticket evenings (Mickey's Not-So-Scary Halloween Party, his Very Merry Christmas Party, and the Pirate and Princess events) for kids with free candy, character meetings, dance parties, and extended hours. The calendar of events can be found on p. 296, online at www.disney world.com, or you can call Disney at (C) **407/939-7679.**

o **Dinnertainment:** Every night, there are more than a dozen dinner banquets accompanied by a kid-friendly show. See p. 236.

o **Character meals:** Early bedtime? Very young kids will be sent to sleep dreaming if they meet their favorite character over dinner. See p. 242 for a list.

you on inflatable rafts, using paddles to "float" down a river on a screen in front of you; and **Pirates of the Caribbean: Battle for Buccaneer Gold** puts you on the deck of a mini pirate ship and blasting rival ships by yanking on ropes that trigger cannon. The animation is badly dated. Not everything is screen-based: The rowdy **Buzz Lightyear's AstroBlaster** is like a bumper-car game where your vehicle scoops up balls and fires them at competitors, causing them to spin momentarily; it's best for two riders at a time.

Disney Springs West Side. www.disneyquest.com. (C) **407/828-4600.** $45 adults, $39 kids 3–9. Kids 9 and under must be accompanied by someone 14 or older. Sun–Thurs 11:30am–10pm; Fri–Sat 11:30am–11pm.

ESPN Wide World of Sports ★ ATHLETIC COMPLEX   Most visitors don't stumble onto the 220-acre grounds, which are essentially a souped-up stadium complex, by accident. They go there intentionally, for a son's wrestling tournament, a traveling sports exhibition game, or to see the Atlanta Braves in spring training. Unfortunately, it's not a place to roll up and pitch a few balls, although you can check its website to see if there's something ticketed that you might enjoy as part of Water Parks Fun & More.

Victory Dr., I-4 at exit 64B. www.disneysports.com. ✆ **407/939-1500.**

Disney Springs (Downtown Disney) & Disney's BoardWalk

The no-admission shopping and entertainment district Disney Springs comprises nearly a pedestrianized mile of restaurants and shops along a small lake, away from the major theme parks in a traffic-plagued eastern reach of the resort grounds. Its West Side is home to a 24-screen cinema, and "La Nouba," the Cirque du Soleil show (see below).

Characters in Flight ★★ RIDE   You'll see it from miles away: A huge, round helium balloon that rises from a pier, lingers 400 feet up for a spell, and then descends back to earth within about 10 minutes. Although it's safely tethered and the circular observation platform is securely enclosed with mesh, it lists and drifts with sudden breezes and that may disturb some guests. If you're adventurous, though, the trip is good fun, and of course, the view rocks. It's known to summarily shut down for breezes over 22 mph, so if it's flying and you want to ride it, don't procrastinate.

Disney Springs West Side. www.disneyworld.com. ✆ **407/824-4321.** $18 adults, $12 kids 3–9. Daily 8:30am–midnight.

House of Blues ★★★ MUSIC CLUB   One of the principal nightspots on the West Side has a 2,000-person, three-tiered venue (standing space only) hosting regular performers along the lines of B. B. King, One Republic, the Charlie Daniels Band, and Norah Jones. Big talent is ticketed at concert prices, and operator Live Nation piles on the fees, but mostly, it's a restaurant for Southern food. On Sundays, it hosts a de-sanctified Gospel Brunch (p. 240).

Disney Springs West Side. www.hob.com. ✆ **407/934-2583.** Sun–Thurs 11:30am–11pm; Fri–Sat 11:30am–1am.

La Nouba ★★★ SHOW   Cirque du Soleil's 90-minute permanent production at Walt Disney World is less sexy than others, making it perfectly acceptable for kids—it could end up being the most memorable theatrical experience of a young person's life. The arty, hyper, clownish French-Canadian spectacular, a dialogue-free kaleidoscope of leaps and tricks, Chinese tumblers and bike stunts, overloads senses 10 times a week in a 1,600-seat theater that looks like a postmodern version of a big top. Although it's a second-rate Cirque, it's still first-rate compared to most stuff, and the talent is extraordinary. So are prices, starting at $67 for adults and $55 for kids ages 3 to 9, and rising according to where you sit. Cheaper seats are better because they have higher vantage points, but seats on the extreme side may miss some of the action taking place far upstage. Arrive at least a half-hour early or they'll sell your seat to someone else.

Disney Springs West Side. www.cirquedusoleil.com/lanouba. ℂ **407/939-7467.** $63–$148 adults, $51–$123 kids, available 6 months ahead. Tues–Sat 6 and 9pm.

Splitsville Luxury Lanes ★★★ BOWLING ALLEY   Giving families something to bond over, this Florida-based franchise charges by the hour, which might make you feel rushed, and it charges high prices at that, but its souped-up '50s decor, two cavernous floors of bowling, and copious cocktails have charm to spare. The food's better than it should be; it even sells sushi.

Disney Springs West Side. www.splitsvilledowntowndisney.com. ℂ **407/938-7328.** Daily 10am–2am. $15/hr. per person before 4pm, $20/hr. per person after 4pm and weekends. Rates include shoe rental.

Walt Disney World Tours

Walt Disney was unquestionably a visionary. When he started out, he was mostly interested in animation as an art form. But as his fame and resources grew, his dreams became infinite, and by the end of his life, he was obsessed with building a city of his own. In fact, he intended to build that city on a chunk of his Central Florida land. His dream of an Experimental Prototype Community of Tomorrow, or Epcot, in which residents, many of them theme park workers, could try out new forms of corporate-sponsored, minimum-impact technology in the course of their daily lives, emerged 16 years after his death as nothing more than another world's fair, and not the city to save us all. But because the Magic Kingdom was built by his most trusted designers, it incorporated several idealistic innovations.

One is the **utilidor system.** The bulk of the Magic Kingdom that you see appears to be at ground level. But in fact, you'll be walking about 14 feet above the land. The attractions constitute the second and third stories of a 9-acre network of warehouses and corridors—utilidors—built in part to guard against flooding but mostly so cast members could remove trash, make deliveries, take breaks, change costumes, and count money out of sight, in a catacombs accessed through secret entrances and unmarked wormholes scattered around the themed lands. Clean-burning electric vehicles zip through the hallways, some of which are wide enough to accommodate trucks, and all of which are color-coded to indicate which land is upstairs.

Among the other engineering feats and innovations of the Kingdom:

- Trash is transported at 60mph to a central collection point by Swedish AVAC pneumatic tubes in the ceiling of the utilidors.
- Fire, power, and water systems are all monitored by a common computer, and the robotics, doors, lighting, sounds, and vehicles on the most complicated attractions are handled by a central server called the Digital Animation Control System (DACS), located roughly underneath Cinderella Castle.

- The Seven Seas Lagoon, in front of the Magic Kingdom, was dry land. It was filled to create a new body of water.
- Bay Lake, beside Fort Wilderness, was dredged, and the dirt used to raise the Magic Kingdom. Underneath the lake bed, white, ancient sand was discovered, cleaned, and deposited to create the Seven Seas Lagoon's beaches.
- Energy is reused whenever possible. The generators' waste heat is used to heat water, and hot water runoff is used for heating, cooking, and absorption chilling for air-conditioning. Waste water is reclaimed for plants and lawns, and sludge is dried for fertilizer. Food scraps are composted on-site. The resort produces enough power to keep things running in case of a temporary outage on the municipal grid. This will keep you up tonight: Disney even has the legal right to build its own nuclear power plant, should it care to.
- Some 55 miles of canals were dug on resort property to keep the land drained. Most of these canals were curved to appear natural.
- The resort was the first place to install an all-electronic phone system using underground cable—so guests don't see ugly wires. It was the first telephone company in America to use a 911 emergency system.
- The rubber-tired monorail system, designed by Disney engineers, now contains nearly 15 miles of track. Walt had intended monorails, and vehicles akin to the Tomorrowland Transit Authority ride, to be the main forms of transportation to and through his Epcot. In 1986, the monorail was named a National Historic Mechanical Engineering Landmark by the American Society of Mechanical Engineers.

The Walt Disney Co. of later years showed little interest in advancing these remarkable innovations. Epcot has only a small network of utilidors, located under Innoventions and Spaceship Earth in the center section of Future World, and the other Disney parks were built without them at all. The monorail has not been expanded since 1982, so it was back to buses and cars.

But even if the company now pays scant attention to developing "Walt's dream"—that Talmudic totem that the company's marketing department invokes to sell souvenirs—it will, fortunately, grant a backstage gander at the resort's ingenuity and the mind-boggling challenge of its scale. The superlative **Walt Disney World tours** (www.disneyworld.com/tours; ✆ **407/939-8687**) require tons of walking, and quality depends on the ability of the guide, but they're also well organized, with coach transport, snacks, plenty of comfort breaks, and sometimes, a special pin souvenir. Not all of them all go daily, so check to see what's running. There are some more good ones, such as tours of the Christmas decorations warehouse and of the Magic Kingdom's trains, but these are the standouts with the widest appeal.

Backstage Magic ★★★ TOUR   If you can swing it, this is the awe-inspiring king of all Disney explorations, and one of the few tours to require no park admission, because you spend your time plumbing infrastructure. Every minute is fascinating—you start at Epcot, where you go backstage to see the mechanized miracle of the American Adventure robotics; then, by motorcoach, the 40-odd group goes to Hollywood Studios for the wardrobe sewing shops; then it's to Animal Kingdom for a how-to there. At the Magic Kingdom, you thrillingly dip into the utilidor, which for fans is alone worth the price. Behind that park, you'll see Central Shops, a 280,000 square-foot facility where ride vehicles are power washed, greased, and repainted in the blocks-long, 30-foot-tall Assembly Alley, and nearby in the Animation Shop, the Audio-Animatronic figures are repaired. For fans of theme parks, to say nothing of systems design, there is no more comprehensive and worthy splurge in Orlando.

$249–$255, including lunch, minimum age 16. 7 hr.

Backstage Tales ★ TOUR You learn more about animal care than the made-up storytelling of the park. The itinerary may change according to which animals are in social moods and which ones are in the clinic, but white rhinos and elephants are often on the menu. Expect a lot of info about how diets are prepared. Mickey would be sick if he knew what the snakes eat.

$90 per person; park admission required. Minimum age 16. 3 hr.

Behind the Seeds ★★ TOUR Because it runs repeatedly every day, it's one of the few tours that can be booked on the fly. Epcot's original altruistic intentions are given a rare spotlight: You learn about the research conducted at the Land's experimental greenhouses, insects lab, and fish farm, and guests are filled in on the park's joint efforts with botanists to advance growing technologies. How much you learn depends entirely on your guide's engagement, so butter 'em up—and little children are usually given ladybugs to release, seeds to plant, or crops to taste. You can reserve ahead or you can book at the desk beside the entrance to Soarin'.

$20 adults, $16 kids 3–9; park admission required. Daily; 45 min.

Disney's Dolphins in Depth ★ TOUR The water's knee-deep, and after education about Epcot's dolphin rescue program, the interaction lasts about 30 minutes. The climax: You tentatively hug one of the mammals as your free souvenir photo is snapped. No theme park admission is required. It only accepts 8 guests a day.

$199, including photo; no park admission required. Minimum age 13. 3 hr.

Disney's Keys to the Kingdom ★★★ TOUR The least expensive way to peek at the utilidors, this half-day morning excursion provides a good overview of the Disney design philosophies that will satisfy both newbies and hard-core fans. It includes a long explication of Main Street, the Hub, the Castle, and a pass through Frontierland and Adventureland, where the group kills time riding two rides, after which your guide discusses the technology behind them. The real appeal is the brief time spent in forbidden backstage areas: the parade float storage sheds behind Splash Mountain and a quiet cul-de-sac of the utilidors beneath Town Square. This is a tremendous value.

$79 per person, including lunch; park admission required. Minimum age 16. Daily. 5 hr.

Epcot DiveQuest ★ TOUR Bring your open-water scuba certification and your swimsuit, and you'll be qualified to swim with the fishes in the salt-water tank at the Seas with Nemo & Friends—the range of life is unparalleled in the wild. You'll learn a little about the aquarium's upkeep, but the true attraction here is the chance to dive in it for 30 minutes and to wave at your fellow tourists from the business side of the glass. It's fun, but whether it's $179 worth of a good time is up for debate.

$179, including diving gear; park admission not required. Minimum age 10. Daily. 3 hr.

Epcot Seas Aqua Tour ★★ TOUR If you can snorkel, you can do this—you're equipped with an air tank and with flotation devices that keep you on the surface, where you spend a half-hour swimming face-down above the fake coral in the 5.7 million-gallon aquarium at The Seas. You wrap up, ironically, with a shower. No theme park admission is required.

$145, including equipment and photo; park admission not required. Minimum age 8. Daily. 2½ hr.

Wild Africa Trek ★★★ TOUR The animal paddocks are your personal adventure playground on this crowd favorite. You'll board a vehicle for a private view of the animals on Kilimanjaro Safaris, and most spectacularly, strap into a harness for a harrowing tethered trip over cliffs and a rope suspension bridge that passes over crocs and hippos. The included African-inflected meal has a view of the savannah, and a CD's worth of professional photos of your experience is mailed to you a few days later.

$249 per person, park admission required. Minimum age 8. 9 times daily. 3 hr.

UNIVERSAL ORLANDO, SEAWORLD & BEYOND

D isney is only half the story. Less than half, really, when you consider that while the Mouse maintains four parks, you'll find another four major themers, plus a luxury-level theme park, in the same vicinity. While some tourists think of other places as something to do after they "do Disney," the truth is Universal's popularity is exploding, and Comcast, its parent company, is pouring billions of dollars into making its two parks even bigger.

UNIVERSAL ORLANDO

These days, the best design chutzpah is happening at Universal—many observers agree that the spectacular Wizarding World of Harry Potter trumps anything else in America's theme park industry. Thanks to these top-notch parks, there's now a true threat to Disney's dominance, and as more people grow annoyed with Disney's slowly declining service level, Universal is making rapid gains. In 2014, the opening of the Diagon Alley area of the Wizarding World of Harry Potter turned the resort into a destination people tour over 3 days rather than 2. Universal's resort is also easier to roam than Disney's: It's walkable or traversed by quick, free ferries, so you can park your car and forget about it—no waiting for crowded buses.

The opening of Universal Studios in 1990 heralded a new era for Orlando tourism. Instead of merely duplicating its original Hollywood location, which is on a historic movie studio lot, Universal Orlando built an all-day park.

Although its opening was famously troubled, there was little doubt that Universal's innovations, when they worked, instantly raised the bar for theme parks. A chief advance was that almost all of its attractions were indoors—even the thrills. Given Florida's scorching sun and unpredictable rains, this leap shouldn't have been as novel as it was. While Disney, still working on a California model, allowed its guests to twiddle thumbs in the cruel heat as they

contacting UNIVERSAL

General information: www.universalorlando.com; ☎ **407/363-8000**

Guest services: ☎ **407/224-4233**

Hotel reservations: ☎ **888/273-1311**

Dining reservations: ☎ **407/224-3663**

Vacation packages: www.universalorlandovacations.com; ☎ **877/801-9720**

Lost and found: ☎ **407/224-4233**, option 2

Twitter: @UniversalORL tag or #AskUniversal—it responds quickly

waited, Universal's multistage queuing system kept them entertained and air-conditioned. (At Islands of Adventure, though, some thrill rides travel out-doors and will shut down at the hint of lightning.) Even the covered parking garages at Universal Orlando (shared by both parks and CityWalk) were novel for Florida.

Disney was spooked. It hastily banged out a movies-themed park of its own, Disney–MGM Studios (now called Hollywood Studios). It was a rush job, lacking the organization and thematic quality that made its previous two parks such smashes, and today it's being overhauled in a delayed response.

Throughout the 1990s, Universal's one-park setup meant it mostly grabbed visitors on day trips from Disney. That changed in the summer of 1999, when a second, $2.6-billion park, Islands of Adventure, made its dazzling debut. Universal's domain has further expanded to include the nightlife district City-Walk, five fun hotels, and coming in 2017, its own new water slide park. Universal also recently secured the right to build Nintendo-themed attractions.

Universal had another idea Disney wishes it had come up with first—if you want to see both Wizarding World of Harry Potter areas, you have to purchase a ticket to *both* its parks. Universal's two parks combined still only fetch a third of the visitors attracted by Disney's four, but that proportion is growing by the year, and the 2014 opening of Cabana Bay (p. 269), now its largest hotel, finally gave economy visitors an on-property roost. Most of the time, lines are nowhere near as long as they are at Disney. Unless crowds are insanely huge (such as before Halloween Horror Nights events or during Christmas week), Universal takes about two days to adequately see. With a two-park pass and a willingness to bypass lesser attractions, you could see only highlights in a marathon day, provided at least one of the parks stays open until 9 or 10pm, but now that the second Harry Potter section has opened (p. 130), 2 days is the new minimum requirement if you don't want to miss a lot. In any event, bop-ping between the two parks isn't hard, since their entrances are a 5-minute stroll apart or you can take the incredible Hogwarts Express connecting train.

Tickets to Universal's Parks

Tickets for both parks cost the same and multi-day tickets are more expensive if you buy at the gate. Prices go up every spring. As you can see by how prices scale, Universal wants to lure you into a multi-day commitment. Gate prices before tax (buy a multi-day ticket online, though, and you'll save $20):

- **1-day ticket for one park:** $102 adults, $97 kids ages 3 to 9
- **1-day park-to-park ticket:** $148 adults, $142 kids ages 3 to 9
- **2 days, one park each day:** $170 adults, $160 kids ages 3 to 9 *
- **3-days, one park each day:** $180 adults, $170 kids ages 3 to 9 *
- **4-days, one park each day:** $190 adults, $180 kids ages 3 to 9 *
  * Add $45 for park-to-park access

To ride the Hogwarts Express train that links the two parks, you must have a park-to-park ticket. If you buy a 1-park ticket and change your mind midway through the day, there are ticket kiosks at the Hogwarts Express train stations that simply charge you the difference in price for a park-to-park ticket; you won't pay a penalty for waiting.

If you're doing a full complement of the non-Disney parks, including both Universal parks, SeaWorld, Aquatica, and Wet 'n Wild, then you'll find value in the **FlexTicket,** sold on Universal's site ($336 adults, $316 kids 3–9 for all those parks, p. 299), which gets you into all of them for 2 weeks.

HOPPING THE LINES Like Disney's Fastpass, **Universal Express Pass** allows guests to use a separate entrance queue that is dramatically shorter than the "Standby" one, reducing wait times to minutes or even seconds; your ticket is scanned by an employee. Unlike Disney's democratic Fastpass, Express is for sale; the busier the park is, the more it costs, and the price shoots up at midnight the day it's valid to encourage advance purchase. Guests can buy an **Express Plus** pass at shops. There is one set of prices that allows one-time-per-ride use ($40–$120 for one park, from $45–$135 for both), another price (from $60–$150 for one park, $65–$160 for both) for unlimited rides, and all prices are bit higher when it's busy. The only major rides excluded are Harry Potter and the Forbidden Journey, Escape from Gringotts, and the Hogwarts Express. Using this is expensive, but it enables you to see both Universal parks in a single day and consequently spend less in tickets and see more of Orlando. Bundles that include park tickets with Express are sold for $210 adult, $205 kids for one day, $320 adult and $310 kids for two days. There is also a third, simpler way to get an Express Pass: Guests of the Universal hotels (except Cabana Bay and Sapphire Falls) can use their key cards for free Express access.

Universal also has a **Ride Reservations** program. You're given a simple "U-bot" pager device that lists the next available entry at each attraction; the appointments reflect each ride's current wait time, so essentially, the system gives you a virtual place in line. You schedule visits (only one at any moment) by pressing buttons, and it vibrates when it's time. It's $20–40 to make one reservation per ride; one device can be used for up to 6 people.

Universal also has photographers on hand to take your photo at big moments. Its **Photo Connect** works a lot like Disney's PhotoPass: You'll get a claim ticket enabling you to purchase an expensive copy or download unlimited

WHAT THE BASICS cost AT UNIVERSAL'S TWO PARKS

Parking: $20; $22 for closer "preferred" spaces; $30 for all-day valet

Single strollers: $15 per day

Double strollers: $25 per day

Kiddie Car (a stroller with a dummy steering wheel): $18; $28 double

Wheelchair: $12

ECV (electric convenience vehicle): $50

Lockers: $8 per day small (multi-entry)

Poncho: $8 adult, $7 kids

Regular soda: $3.20 / **Water:** $2.75 / **Beer:** $6.50–7

images within 3 days (for $60), but you may always use your own camera instead. You can also check your images as you collect them using an app.

Universal has free in-park Wi-Fi, and its free app, the **Official Universal Orlando Resort App,** provides wait times, showtimes, maps, and walking directions.

WHAT TO WEAR   Dress small children in bathing suits for a day at Universal Studios because Kidzone, one of its best sections, will get them soaked. At Islands of Adventure, two of the best adult rides are water-based.

Universal Studios Florida

Universal Studios ★★★ usually opens at 9am, and in winter months, hours end at around dinnertime. In summer, it's open as late as 10pm. After you get your car parked ($17 and up; non-Preferred cars may have to park on the roof) and your handbags probed, take the covered sidewalks to CityWalk and head to the right. Pause now at the giant, rotating globe for the requisite photo op, because the sun is in your favor for photographs in the morning but not later.

They pair your fingerprint to your ticket, just like at Disney. The plaza after the turnstiles is where you take care of business. **Strollers and wheelchairs** are obtained to the left, and **lockers** are rented to the right. (You may bring your stroller to the other park within 2 hr. of closing; if you're taking the Hogwarts Express, there's a place to drop it off before boarding and another kiosk for getting a new one at Islands of Adventure.) Make sure to grab a free park **map** here; if you forget, the stores also stock them.

Although there are technically themed areas within the park, few are strictly defined. They fall into two general zones. Everyone enters along the main avenue of the simulated backlot (including **Production Central, Hollywood,** and **New York**), which contains many of the behind-the-scenes attractions, while the elongated Lagoon stretches off to the right, encircled by many of the thrill-based rides in **San Francisco, Springfield, World Expo,** and **Woody**

Universal Studios Florida

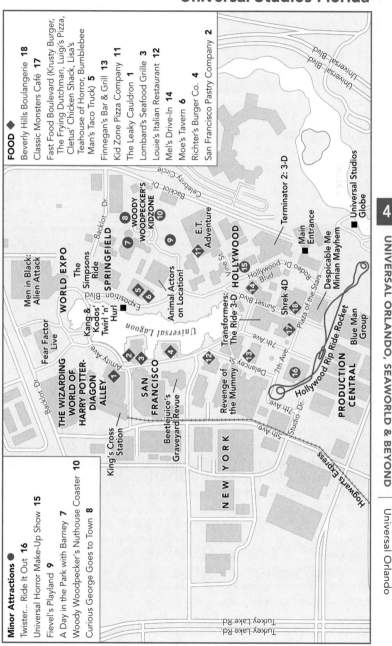

Minor Attractions ●

Twister... Ride It Out **16**
Universal Horror Make-Up Show **15**
Fievel's Playland **9**
A Day in the Park with Barney **7**
Woody Woodpecker's Nuthouse Coaster **10**
Curious George Goes to Town **8**

FOOD ◆

Beverly Hills Boulangerie **18**
Classic Monsters Café **17**
Fast Food Boulevard (Krusty Burger,
The Frying Dutchman, Luigi's Pizza,
Cletus' Chicken Shack, Lisa's
Teahouse of Horror, Bumblebee
Man's Taco Truck) **5**
Finnegan's Bar & Grill **13**
Kid Zone Pizza Company **11**
The Leaky Cauldron **1**
Lombard's Seafood Grille **3**
Louie's Italian Restaurant **12**
Mel's Drive-In **14**
Moe's Tavern **6**
Richter's Burger Co. **4**
San Francisco Pastry Company **2**

Men in Black: Alien Attack
Fear Factor Live
WORLD EXPO
The Simpsons Ride
WOODY WOODPECKER'S KIDZONE
Kang & Kodos' Twirl 'n' Hurl
SPRINGFIELD
E.T. Adventure
Animal Actors on Location!
THE WIZARDING WORLD OF HARRY POTTER- DIAGON ALLEY
Universal Lagoon
SAN FRANCISCO
Beetlejuice's Graveyard Revue
King's Cross Station
Revenge of the Mummy
Transformers: The Ride 3-D
NEW YORK
Terminator 2: 3-D
HOLLYWOOD
Despicable Me Minian Mayhem
Shrek 4D
Plaza of the Stars
Hollywood Rip Ride Rocket
Blue Man Group
PRODUCTION CENTRAL
Main Entrance
Universal Studios Globe
Hogwarts Express
Backlot Dr.
Celebrity Circle
Exposition Blvd.
Amity Ave.
Delancey St.
5th Ave.
7th Ave.
Vine St.
Rodeo Dr.
Sunset Blvd.
Hollywood Blvd.
Studio Dr.
Turkey Lake Rd.
Universal Blvd.

Lawyers have had their way with Universal's thrill rides: Many now forbid loose articles of any kind. That includes phones, keys, lipstick—even coins. Everything! And you may not leave your stuff on the platform while you ride, either. Metal detectors have been set up at the coasters to make sure your pockets are empty. Leave your stuff at the hotel, use the free lockers by attraction entrances (very crowded, a real pain), or rent a locker at the front of either park.

Woodpecker's Kidzone. The Wizarding World of Harry Potter—Diagon Alley is on the far side of the lagoon.

Some days (confirm times about a month ahead on its website, on its app, or when you grab your map at the front gate), Universal sends out its **Superstar Parade,** packed with favorite children's characters such as SpongeBob SquarePants, Dora, Diego, Gru, and the Minions. It stops by Mel's Drive-In and Battery Park so kids can meet them. After dark, if the park's open then, the water sometimes hosts the **Cinematic Spectacular,** narrated by Morgan Freeman. It's a quaint show featuring classic Universal clips projected onto waterfall screens, plus modest fireworks. Shows like these aren't Universal's forte, but there's not a Disney-esque crush of spectators, either.

PRODUCTION CENTRAL

The area along the entry avenue (called both Plaza of the Stars and 57th St.) and to its left is collectively marked on maps as Production Central, but who are they kidding? Nowadays, those soundstages are used mostly for the odd local commercial and for haunted houses at Universal's fiendishly popular Halloween event.

The initial dream was much bigger. When the park was built, it was intended to be more like the original Hollywood location, where an amusement area grew up around a working studio. Newspapers at the time trumpeted Orlando as "Hollywood of the East" because year-round production could be accomplished here and at Disney–MGM Studios, and millions of tourists could be a part of the process. One of Universal's soundstages housed a working TV studio for Nickelodeon, the kids' cable channel, and the game show "Double Dare" plucked families out of the park to compete on air. In front of the studio, a geyser of "green slime" (actually green water) gurgled in tribute to the Canadian show "You Can't Do That on Television" that helped make the channel's fortunes. (Today, that stage houses the equally messy Blue Man Group.) But the plan never took. It wasn't cost-effective to move productions here, celebrities didn't relish working in a theme park, and state tax credits were often spotty.

The first block of Production Central is mostly shops, including the largest gift shop in the park, **Universal Studios Store,** on the left. Across from that are the tempting Art Deco buildings of Rodeo Drive, the spine of the Hollywood area and for my money the prettiest part of the park.

Hollywood Rip Ride Rockit gives guests the ability to choose the soundtrack to their ride from 30 songs within five genres of music.

Hollywood Rip Ride Rockit ★★★

RIDE This is one advanced train: The 17-story height, vertical climb, hill-like loop, and near misses are just the start of it. Most advanced are its cars, outfitted with LEDs and in-seat speakers. Riders personalize their trip on screens embedded in the beltlike safety restraint, choosing the song that will play during the trip. Pick from a broad menu including country, rap, rock, and disco, but if you don't pick a song, it'll choose one for you. When the ride's over, you can buy a movie of the ride, along with your soundtrack. Lockers are required for loose items, but they're free for the wait time plus 20 minutes. Single riders get their own line, and it moves quickly. Note the novel boarding system that batches passengers together and sends them onto a moving sidewalk to catch up with the trains, which never stop moving forward. That first loop is also an original—the track twists to send the cars over the top of it before pulling them back on the inside again. Later on, you shoot through holes in the scenery in the New York session. Rockin'. *Strategy:* Don't close the safety bar too tightly! You'll have trouble breathing.

Despicable Me Minion Mayhem ★★ RIDE The movies, if you don't

know them, star a crotchety mad genius, Gru (voiced by Steve Carell), and his horde of nearly identical yellow henchmen (the Minions); their ride, which is considerably more charming than the films, give the little guys ample oppor-

Despicable Me Minion Mayhem.

tunity for some cartoon violence and giggly gags. The kid-friendly show/move-in-place ride takes place in a theater full of individual open-air ride platforms that have all the characteristics of motion simulators except claustrophobia. *Strategy:* Those prone to motion sickness can request a car that doesn't move at all—the perfectly animated 3-D movie is immensely action-packed and is entertaining without movement.

Shrek 4-D ★★ SHOW The high-

priced voices of the movie characters (Mike Myers, Cameron Diaz, Eddie Murphy) star in a snarky 12-minute,

Shrek 4-D show.

3-D movie-cum-spectacle—filmed in "OgreVision." John Lithgow plays the ghost of the evil Lord Farquaad, who crashes Shrek and Fiona's honeymoon at Fairytale Falls with a few dastardly deeds. The chairs look like standard theater seats but they're tricked-up to goose sensations—don't worry; it won't make you ill. Well, unless fart jokes gross you out. It's a good one to do when feet start aching, although the line can build in the afternoon. *Strategy:* Because the entertaining preshow is just as long as the movie, the Express Pass doesn't seem to buy you very much time. After the exit, visit **Donkey's Photo Finish,** featuring an interactive, robotic version of the movie's famous ass in his own stall; he interacts with kids and poses.

Transformers: The Ride—3D ★★ RIDE This East Coast version of a ride that first appeared at Universal Studios Hollywood, repeats the technology and basic vehicle design of the gentler Adventures of Spider-Man next door at Islands of Adventure—that is, motion-simulator cars travel among sense-tricking rooms with 3-D projections. The difference is that here, the show is pumped up with crisper animation, clearer sounds, and a whole lot of

The Best of Universal Studios Florida

Don't miss if you're 6: Curious George Goes to Town

Don't miss if you're 16: Springfield

Requisite photo op: The rotating Universal globe out front

Food you can only get here: Butterbeer ice cream and Fishy Green Ale, Diagon Alley; Flaming Moe's and Duff Beer, Springfield

The most crowded, so go early: The Wizarding World of Harry Potter—Diagon Alley

Skippable: Fear Factor Live

Biggest thrill: Harry Potter and the Escape from Gringotts

Best show: Animal Actors on Location!

Where to find peace: On the lagoon

machine-on-machine violence and military-grade weaponry. But at heart, no matter how impressive the tech is, Transformers is still a Spider-Man update, down to key plot points. The mayhem is so frenetic you can't always tell which Transformer is which, but then again, you can't in the movies, either, so it hardly matters. You'll emerge feeling like you survived a 4-minute car crash. *Strategy:* The clearest view is in the front row, and there's a fast-moving Single Rider line.

NEW YORK

When there's a park on your right, you've entered the New York area. In a display of geographic acrobatics, the park is an imitation of San Francisco's Union Square while straight ahead, at the end of 57th Street (the main entry avenue) is a little cul-de-sac that looks, through a camera lens, like Manhattan—except for the roller coaster that keeps roaring through.

The rest of the New York section is gussied up to look like the tenements of the Lower East Side or Greenwich Village and is worth a few photos. Actors playing **The Blues Brothers,** plus a female diva soul singer, show up on Delancey Street for regular jam sessions, and they're talented.

> ### Make Back Some Admission Expenses
>
> The **NBC Media Center,** in the re-creation of Los Angeles's Garden of Allah, is marked on maps, but you can only get in by invitation (someone will approach you on the streets). That's where NBC-affiliated entities screen pilots and solicit audience opinions. On a quiet January day, I once earned $30 just for enduring a new show called "Psych." I broke it to them gently, telling them that it was clichéd and strained. Naturally, it became an eight-season smash on USA Network. You can't predict the demographic of the test audience they'll be looking for, so stop by and ask if you fit the profile du jour.

Twister . . . Ride It Out ★ SHOW See it now; it's on borrowed time. After portentous preshow videos narrated by Helen Hunt and Bill Paxton ("Who?" say your kids), you finally enter a hangarlike chamber that's dressed to look like a Midwestern small town (gas station, telephone pole, drive-in movie in the distance) on a weekend night. A storm approaches, rain begins to fall and, as you knew it would, a twister forms. Right before your eyes, a funnel cloud descends from the rafters and to the delight of many, wrecks the place. Sparks fly, roofs peel, and guess what happens to the gas station? Although people tend to shy away from the front row, don't, because you won't feel much more than mist and a light sucking sensation there. *Strategy:* It runs continuously, but I wouldn't wait more than 20 minutes for it.

Revenge of the Mummy ★★★ RIDE   This brilliant attraction has an easy start but a rollicking finish: Part dark ride, part coaster, it goes backward and forward, twists on a turntable, and even spends a harrowing moment stalled in a room as the ceiling crawls with fire. (It doesn't go upside-down.) To say much more would give away some clever shocks. I've told you what you need to know, except for that it's one of the best rides in this park, and it's miles better than the cheaper version at Universal in Los Angeles. *Strategy:* You must put loose articles in the lockers to the right of the entrance—they're free for the posted ride time plus 20 minutes, but after that they cost $3 every half hour. There are three lines: Express, standby, and single.

SAN FRANCISCO

Of all the Studios' areas, the San Francisco section currently has the least going on. It's in disarray for the construction of a new ride, **Fast & Furious: Supercharged,** which will be imported from Universal Hollywood by 2017. However, the restaurants are better than anywhere in the park.

THE WIZARDING WORLD OF HARRY POTTER— DIAGON ALLEY

From the outside, it appears to simply be a re-creation of some London landmarks, including a perfectly replicated Kings Cross station and some townhouses that would fool a lifetime resident of Bloomsbury (keep an eye on the curtains in the second balcony window of 12 Grimmauld Place, the shabby townhouse). You have the re-creation of the "Eros" fountain from Piccadilly Circus (unlike the original, this one is actually flowing), cab shelters selling Britannia souvenirs and jumbo hot dogs, and a three-level-tall **Knight Bus.** If its conductor is there, have a chat with him, but don't be alarmed if the shrunken Jamaican head hanging above his steering wheel butts into the conversation.

Hidden behind the London facade, through some sidelong brick portals, is the world's hottest theme park of the moment, essentially a wholesale construction of 3 city blocks around Diagon Alley, where wizards go for their provisions. It's not so much a single attraction as it is a cluttered streetscape of shops, beverage and dessert stores, and painstaking design work that seals you off from the outside world. There are few right angles, but plenty of opportunities to spend lots and lots of cash. You could pass hours simply exploring details, from animated window displays (the skeleton that imitates your movements from the window of Dystyl Phaelanges is a standout) to clever signage larded with inside jokes ("These Premises to Let: Reptiles/Arachnids Allowed").

The main thoroughfare is **Diagon Alley,** lined with the Leaky Cauldron restaurant, plus shops for wands, toys, and clothing. It leads dramatically to Gringotts Bank, which is crested by a petrified dragon that belches fire every few minutes. Gringotts is on **Horizont Alley,** a 2-block lane noted for its pet store, beer hall, and ice cream shop. On the left, it leads into **Knockturn Alley,** a fascinating indoor area that simulates a shady ghetto at night, right down to shifting clouds in a simulated sky and a tattoo parlor, Marcus Scarr's, where the animated sample designs writhe on the wall. Branching off from Diagon Alley on the right, you find **Carkitt Market,** a covered area recalling London's Leadenhall Market, where the principal show stage for the land is located. Performances include **The Singing Sorceress: Celestina Warbeck and the Banshees** (a talented but somewhat out-of-theme singer—J. K. Rowling's

reducio! WAYS TO LIGHTEN YOUR WALLET AT DIAGON ALLEY

Diagon Alley has the best theme park merchandising you've ever seen. Nearly everything there is to do and taste comes with a price tag, and you can't get these experiences outside Universal's gates. It's extraordinarily easy to get swept along in the merchandising mesmerization. Some of the best bespoke purchasing potential includes these Potterized twists:

o **Gringotts Money Exchange, Carkitt Market.** Trade in "muggle money" (U.S. $10s and $20s only) for Gringotts Bank Rune Credit, a currency that you can use in both parks or, Universal hopes, take home as a souvenir for pure profit.

o **Ollivanders, Diagon Alley.** In addition to the same wand-selecting mini-show available at Hogsmeade (p. 145), you may purchase a $50 interactive wand used to activate more than a dozen tricks wherever you see a medallion embedded in the ground. Stand on it, emulate the wand motion depicted on it, and you'll make toilets flush, suits of armor animate, fountains squirt, and so on.

o **The Hopping Pot, Carkitt Market, and the Fountain of Fair Fortune, Horizont Alley.** Sip sweet concoctions for $5 each: Otter's Fizzy Orange Juice, Tongue Tying Lemon Squash, Peachtree Fizzing Tea, and Fishy Green Ale with "fish eggs" (actually blueberry boba) on the bottom. They also sell the classic Potter potable, Butterbeer (in a mug made for Diagon Alley, $12), and two beers unique to the park, Wizards Brew (a light lager) and Dragon Scale (a chocolatey stout), both $9

o **Florean Fortescue's Ice Cream Parlour, Diagon Alley.** Try a range of only-here flavors including Chocolate Chili, Clotted Cream, Earl Grey and Lavender, and a dangerously addictive soft-serve version of Butterbeer ($5 cup, $6 cone, $11 in a souvenir plastic cup).

o **Eternelle's Elixir of Refreshment, Carkitt Market.** Mix your choice of $4 "elixirs" (Draught of Peace, Fire Protection Potion, and so forth) with $4 "Gillywater" (water) and something magical happens (Universal just made $8 on sugar water).

o **Weasleys' Wizard Wheezes, Diagon Alley.** The new toy shop (replacing the old Zonkos at Hogsmeade) sells $15 Pygmy Puff stuffed animals. When a purchase is made, the staff gongs a huge bell and announces a new adoption. Also buy the candies Ron would eat to get out of school: Puking Pastilles, Fainting Fancies, Fever Fudge, and Nosebleed Nougat ($7 each).

o **Magical Menagerie, Horizont Alley.** Where windows are filled with animated pets such as pythons and giant snails, procure the specialty souvenir: a plush version of Hermione's half-Kneazle cat Crookshanks ($25).

o **Shutterbutton's, Carkitt Market.** Via a green screen, put your family in the middle of a 3- to 4-minute DVD ($70), like a moving postcard exploring the Potter universe.

favorite "offstage" character mentioned but not seen in the book series—rendering such classics as "A Cauldron Full of Hot, Strong Love") and **The Tales of Beedle the Bard** (a street performance with puppets of two tales from the Potter spin-off book).

Harry Potter and the Escape from Gringotts ★★★ RIDE

Another genre-busting creation, this indoor ride is among the most advanced anywhere: part roller coaster, part motion simulator amid dominating 3-D high-def screens. At times your respect for its razor's-edge complexity will overshadow the purity of the thrills, but it's still unmissable. The queue lingers in the sumptuous, echoing lobby of Gringotts Bank, where 10 robotic goblins pause long enough from their clerical duties to sneer at you, and you're taken by "lift" deep underground to begin the mine cart-like race through the vaults. Almost immediately, nasty lightning bolts from Bellatrix Lestrange (Helena Bonham Carter) put your course awry, sending you careening into the slithering presence of Voldemort (Ralph Fiennes). Can Harry, Ron, and Hermione save you in time? (What do *you* think?) There are some mild spins and drops in the dark, but you wear 3-D glasses the whole time and they don't fall off, so it's not that rough, and it's less scary and height-restrictive than the Forbidden Journey ride at Hogsmeade. *Strategy:* Take the test seat out front seriously; if you don't fit, you shouldn't ride. Locker use for small items is mandatory; they're free and to the right of the front door. There's a single-rider line that moves quickly, but you'll miss the entire pre-show, including the photo op and the lift. Front row is best for seeing the screens, the view from the left side of the fourth row can be obscured, and the middle two seats are the best overall.

Hogwarts Express ★★★ RIDE

Separate from Diagon Alley, through the vaulted brick interior of a shockingly accurate Kings Cross Station, you board the hissing, steaming, and, to all appearances, vintage steam train to Hogsmeade. You are assigned a six-person, upholstered compartment, the door shuts, and off you go. Out the window, England and Scotland scroll by while in the train corridor, you overhear conversations and see ominous shadows through frosted glass. In reality, you're traveling through Universal's backstage area, but you never see it. The technical prowess is nearly totally convincing, and even where it isn't, it's still dazzling. Within 4 minutes, you disembark at Islands of Adventure outside the gate to the other Wizarding World (if you require an upgrade to a park-to-park ticket, there are kiosks for the purpose). In the station, there's also a spot, done with mirrors and clever lighting, for you to re-create the moment when Harry and his fellow students walk through a brick wall to reach Platform 9¾. That photo op gets thronged, but there's a bypass if you don't want to wait for it.

WORLD EXPO

There's not much to this area except a ride and a dated show.

Men in Black: Alien Attack ★★ RIDE

Most riders enjoy this sassy riff on the Will Smith film franchise. After a superlative queue area that does a

Men in Black: Alien Attack.

pitch-perfect, "Jetsons"-style imitation of New York's 1964 World's Fair (ironically, the one Walt Disney created so many wonders for), you discover the "real" tenant of the futuristic building: a training course for the Men in Black alien patrol corps. You board six-person cars equipped with individual laser guns. As you pass from room to room—expect lots of herky-jerky motions, but nothing sickening—your task is to fire upon any alien that pops out from around doorways, behind trash cans, and so on. If they peg you first, it sends your buggy spinning. Each car's point score is displayed on the dashboard, and the number accumulated by the end determines the climactic video you're shown—Will Smith will either praise you as "Galaxy Defender" or mock you as "Bug Bait." *Strategy:* The single riders' queue moves quickly, thanks to the odd number of seats in each row. Locker use for small items is mandatory, but free for the posted wait time plus 20 minutes.

Fear Factor Live ★ SHOW   Like the meat-headed NBC show, ordinary people do stunts (usually involving being dangled on wires, maybe eating food-grade mealworms) for the twisted pleasure of a whooping audience while an inane master of ceremonies eggs everyone on. If you're over 18 and want to volunteer as a contestant (first prize: polite applause), be there 70 minutes before your selected showtime and you'll go through a tryout including jumping jacks and a game of Simon Says. Contestants can't wear jewelry, and if your hands sweat when you're nervous, you will stink at the gripping challenges. This show goes dark in September and October. Persistent rumors say this stadium will eventually be subsumed by a Diagon Alley expansion.

SPRINGFIELD

After Diagon Alley, Springfield is the most fun land in the Studios. The area is jammed with inside jokes from the longest-running comedy on TV that only fans catch—for example, **Lard Lad Donuts** sells "Ice Cream Conans." **Kwik-E-Mart** sells an array of bespoke souvenirs you can only get here (pick up the payphone there, by the way), the **Duff Brewery** pours its signature quaff—the cause of, and solution to, all life's problems—and the embiggened statue of frontiersman Jebediah Springfield lords over us all.

The Simpsons Ride ★★★ RIDE   It's easy to love this highly amusing, top-quality, motion-simulator "Thrilltacular Upsy-Downsy Spins-Aroundsy Teen-Operated Thrill Ride" that takes place in front of an 80-foot-tall screen. The premise, dense and ironic enough to please devotees of the FOX series, punctures Orlando itself: You join Homer's clan at Krustyland, a greedy theme park, on a roller coaster that's sabotaged by the evil Sideshow Bob (voiced by Kelsey Grammer). During the dizzyingly fast-paced 6 minutes, you zoom through predicaments that mock the theme park world, including skewers of Shamu, Pirates of the Caribbean, and "it's a small world." Add to that a giant killer panda bear and an extra layer of heightened sensory (like the whiff of baby powder—well, it makes sense when you ride). It's not too rough, but dehydrated people find it vaguely nauseating, and your brain may hurt from absorbing all the jokes. The queue area is so tongue in cheek and gag-packed that waiting is half the fun: Itchy and Scratchy furnish the gory safety warning and Krusty dispenses safety instructions such as "Wait here until someone comes and tells you to do something." *Strategy:* Seats are four across, so families can ride together.

Kang & Kodos' Twirl 'n' Hurl ★ RIDE   Universal finally got its Dumbo ride. Here, silly slobbering aliens trick you into boarding a Day-Glo flying saucer (fitting two adults or one adult and two kids): "Please remain seated until the very end of the ride. You will know the ride has ended when your vehicle comes to a complete stop, or you have been eaten . . . I didn't just say that." As you rotate gently around, Dumbo-style, you use a joystick to pass in front of tentacle-shaped poles, triggering sounds of exclamation from the citizens of Springfield. Spoiler: You don't get eaten. *Strategy:* Keep an eye on park schedules, it closes early when there's a lagoon show.

HOLLYWOOD

This Art Deco stretch is a good place to meet characters (Gru, Woody Woodpecker, the Men in Black) at odd times.

Universal Horror Make-Up Show ★★ SHOW   Learn how horror-movie makeup effects are accomplished in this terrific, 25-minute tongue-in-cheek exposé, conducted by a nerdy type in his workshop and his straight-man emcee. On paper, that seems like the kind of thing you might otherwise skip, but in truth, park regulars love its wit and playful edge. For ribald ad-libbing and gross-out humor, the park suggests parental guidance, but I find most kids have heard it all before, and it's certainly true that seeing terrifying movie gore exposed as the make-believe it is can be a good reality check. You can't get in once the show starts. Even if you skip it, there's something to see in the lobby: exhibits about great horror characters and make-up artists.

Terminator 2: 3-D ★ SHOW/FILM   Although the 12-minute film portion, a sort of mini-sequel to "Terminator 2," was made by extravagant director James Cameron with all his original stars (including Ah-nold and Linda Hamilton), it's hardly just another movie. It's got three screens, six 8-foot robots, gunfire, smoke bombs, and motorcyclists that seamlessly dive in and out of the filmed action. The film cost $60 million to make, which, when it was produced in 1996, qualified it as the most expensive movie, per minute, in history, trumping Disney's equally bombastic "Captain EO." *Strategy:* This edgy, cynical show splits the eardrums with romping, stomping mayhem, so keep small children away unless they're hard cases. Those in the front rows will have to pivot their heads to see all the action.

WOODY WOODPECKER'S KIDZONE

This is my pick for the best children's theme park playground area in Orlando. I've heard tales of 6-year-olds who threatened self-orphanization if they were dragged away within 4 hours. There's a ton to do, not least of which is **SpongeBob StorePants,** dedicated to merchandise and appearances by the absorbent doofus.

Animal Actors on Location! ★★★ SHOW A troupe of trained dogs, cats, birds, and a horse anchor this charming 20-minute show (times noted on the sign). Placing it here was inspired, because small children get a thrill out of seeing common animals do tricks, and as a consequence, it's popular. Because it's in an amphitheater, you can sneak out in the middle if you need to. But if you see only one emphatically punctuated household-pets-doing-cute-tricks-to-jaunty-music theme park show, make it SeaWorld's superior Pets Ahoy!

E.T. Adventure ★★ RIDE Based on the 1982 Steven Spielberg movie, this endearingly weird indoor ride is rightfully in the kiddie area because it's not intense and the plot cannot tolerate scrutiny by a fully developed brain. Upon entering, guests supply their name to an attendant, who encodes the info on a pass you hand over when you board the ride. The indoor queue area is a fabulous reproduction of a thick, cool California forest at night. Vehicles are suspended from rails to approximate the sensation of cruising in a flock of bikes, and they sweep and scoop across the moonrise and then through gardens on E.T.'s home planet (remember, he was a botanist), where a menagerie of goofy-looking aliens and creepy E.T. babies swing on vines. They miraculously speak English, throw a party, and greet us from the sidelines. At the climax, a grateful E.T. is supposed to call out your name as you fly home—hence those boarding passes—but E.T. either runs out of time to name everyone or he spouts gibberish, so don't get your hopes up unless your name is Pfmkmpftur. *Strategy:* If the queue looks dense from the outside, return later—before park closing seems to be a charmed time for quick waits—since there are still more lineups indoors. In the **Toy Closet,** you'll find E.T. souvenirs. His "Talk to the Hand" T-shirt is perhaps a milestone in bad taste.

Fievel's Playland ★★★ ACTIVITY Named for the hero of "An American Tail" (an obscure kiddie reference, and another '80s Spielberg movie), it's the most spectacular of several playgrounds in Kidzone. The concept is that your kids have been shrunk down to a mouse's size, and they're playing among giant everyday items like sardine cans and eyeglasses. They'll discover slides, nets, and tubes, but my favorite element is the easy waterslide on a raft—so yes, make sure your kids have their swimsuits on. The ground is covered with that newfangled soft foam that all the modern playgrounds have. When I was a boy, we got concussions instead.

Curious George's interactive playground, complete with water play area.

A Day in the Park with Barney ★ SHOW The small indoor area that can be accessed through its own gift shop (plush Barney, $17), is technically the postshow area for a sing-along show. The doors close at the start and stay closed until the ordeal is over. Frankly, being locked in a room with that sappy purple dinosaur and all those screaming babies constitutes a chamber of horrors for me, but little ones find it enthralling. Parents can find Duff Beer in Springfield nearby, if that helps. The play area mimics Barney's backyard with a waist-high counter for sifting through sand (so it won't get into shoes), a tree equipped with little slides, and a chance to have your picture taken with (and then buy it from) Barney the Capitalist Dinosaur.

Woody Woodpecker's Nuthouse Coaster ★★ RIDE Kids can plainly see every drop before they commit to this straightforward thriller. It has no unpleasant surprises, unless you count hearing Woody's pecking as you go, and a run time of less than a minute.

Curious George Goes to Town ★★★ ACTIVITY Welcome to the water playground that stole your child. This frenetic splash area is teeming with squealing children and soaked with streams of water from every direction—from squirt cannons, fountains, geysers, and, most importantly, from two 500-gallon buckets that, every 7 minutes, sound a warning bell and then drench anyone beneath. The orgiastic scene is ringed by a perimeter of dry parents keeping an eye on their suddenly wild offspring. Watching the children cheer and scamper when they hear the bucket's warning bell, and then watching them momentarily vanish in the deluge, is endlessly heartwarming. Through the wet area (there's a dry bypass corridor to it on the left) is the dry Ball Factory, where kids suck up plastic balls with light vacuums, pack them into bags, and then fire them at each other with weak cannons. It's not on the maps.

WHERE TO EAT AT UNIVERSAL STUDIOS

In addition to the random snack carts (including carts selling goliath turkey legs with chips for $12), there are counter-service and table-service restaurants in the park. None require reservations the way Disney's do. Kids' meals all come in under 300 calories. *Tip:* Meals do not *have* to come with side dishes. The potato chip bags served hold a mere 1⅞ ounces. Ask to subtract chips or fries from your meal deals and you'll save about $2. Cups good for unlimited refills at touchscreen Coke Freestyle machines, which mix soda to order using 126 flavors, cost $12 and are good for the day. Cups for standard beverages are $10 with $1 refills. *Remember:* Restaurants at CityWalk (p. 222) are only a 5-minute walk from the park, so they're also options.

Classic Monsters Café ★★ AMERICAN   Indoor counter service on a non-scary B-movie set with some healthy options, such as rotisserie chicken, salad, cheeseburgers, and ribs. **Production Central.** Combo meal $8 to $16.

Finnegan's Bar & Grill ★★★ IRISH/BRITISH   A sit-down, Irish-style pub with loft ceilings good for a beer break, particularly after 3pm when a guitar singer performs. Scotch eggs ($6), split pea–and-ham soup ($5), Irish Cobb salad (it has corned beef), and bangers and mash are the kind of solid choices available, plus cocktails and good strong ales. Park workers pick this place when they're off-duty. **New York.** Mains $12 to $22.

Louie's Italian Restaurant ★ ITALIAN   Straightforward counter ser-vice near The Mummy. **New York.** Slices $6, meatball subs $12.

San Francisco Pastry Company ★★ SANDWICHES   This lightly trafficked counter-service bakery across from Disaster!, does sandwiches and loaded croissants in addition to cakes and pastries, and healthier fruit plates and salads. **San Francisco.** Sandwiches $6, salads from $4.

Lombard's Seafood Grille ★★★ SEAFOOD/AMERICAN   An excel-lent, relaxing table-service choice that is surprisingly affordable: Fish tacos are $13, just three bucks more than a Quick Service meal, and other fish dishes, including the fish of the day, such as grouper, fried shrimp, and seafood pot pie, are in the mid-teens. Splashing fountains serenade, fish tanks adorn the dining room, and you can sit outside on the water if you like. Special diet options, such as quinoa with Portobello mushroom, are well marked, and you can even get gluten-free table rolls. **San Francisco.** Main courses $14 to $20.

Richter's Burger Co. ★★ AMERICAN   A warehouse-like dockside option that slings stacked burgers, marinated grilled chicken sandwiches, and for those weary of greasy fare, salads with grilled chicken. Periodically, the dining area rumbles (but doesn't move) to simulate quakes. Get the After-shock double burger for $11 and an extra bun for $1 and you can feed two using the fixin's bar. **San Francisco.** Main courses $9 to $12 with fries.

The Leaky Cauldron ★★★ BRITISH   The fare at Diagon Alley's counter-service location is not mystical at all. It's plentiful and true to an English pub, serving British staples such as beef and Guinness stew, cottage or fisherman's pie, and banger (sausage) sandwiches. The ploughman's lunch for two ($20) has three types of cheese and Branston pickle, and although it's not on the menu, they'll do it for one for $10. Also get Butterbeer, Fishy Green Ale, and other Potter potables here. Unlike at most Universal restaurants, they don't let you subtract fries to save money. **Diagon Alley.** Mains $9 to $15.

Fast Food Boulevard ★★★ AMERICAN   This mouthy indoor food court serves mostly standard food renamed with inside jokes and witticisms that puncture American culture. You could spend half your lunchtime just

Moe's Tavern in Springfield.

laughing at the dishes. **Krusty Burger** serves "meat sandwiches" such as the high-stacked double-bacon Clogger Burger with cheez sauce and curly fries and 6-inch Heat Lamp Dogs. **The Frying Dutchman** does Basket O' Bait fried fish and Clam Chowd-arr ($4). At the **Luigi's Pizza** area, get slices of Meat Liker's Pizza, and at **Cletus' Chicken Shack,** dig into the not-very-appetizing-but-accurate Chicken Arms (wings), Chicken Thumbs (tenders), and chicken-and-waffle sandwiches. Lastly, **Lisa's Teahouse of Horror** cuts out the clots with a cooler full of straight-up salads and wraps. You can also buy only-at-Universal treats such as **Lard Lad Donuts** (the platter-size Big Pink, coated with frosting, $5—a life-size Chief Wiggum figure enjoys one nearby) and Buzz Cola (no-calorie cherry cola). Springfield. Outside and across the way, there's the **Bumblebee Man's Taco Truck,** which closes by dinner. Entrees $8 to $14.

Moe's Tavern ★★★ BAR   A spot-on re-creation of Moe's, down to team pennants for the Isotopes and the purple TV on the wall, only without sleazy service by Moe. There is, however, a life-size Barney by the bar, ruefully contemplating his empty mug. Duff Beer is specially brewed for the park (in generous servings of regular, Lite, or Dry ($7–$8), but the kid-friendly specialty is a Flaming Moe's ($9), a nonalcoholic orange-flavored soda in a cup rigged with pellets that make it bubble and smoke (it's hard to breathe when you're sipping it). **Springfield.** Beverages $7 to $9, light bites $4 to $9.

Kid Zone Pizza Company ★ PIZZA   Outdoor-only counter service for chicken fingers and fries, salad, and of course, pizza. It's the biggest food option near the kids' play areas. **Woody Woodpecker's Kidzone.** Mains $8 to $10.

Mel's Drive-In ★★ AMERICAN   A '50s-style counter-service diner where fare leans toward chicken, burgers, and shakes. Air-conditioned seating has a view of the Lagoon. **Hollywood.** Main courses $8 to $11.

Beverly Hills Boulangerie ★ SANDWICHES   An uncrowded choice for a reasonably healthy meal: sandwiches (turkey, roast beef, tuna, Italian panini) with potato salad and fruit. **Hollywood.** Sandwiches with sides $12.

Islands of Adventure

Islands of Adventure (IOA) ★★★ usually opens at 9am. In winter months, operating hours will end at around 6pm but in summer, they're often open to as late as 10pm. After you park ($17 and up), open your bags for inspection, take the moving sidewalks to CityWalk, and veer to the left, toward the 130-foot Pharos Lighthouse (it's just for show), you finally reach IOA. If you doubt whether your kids are tall enough to ride everything, there's a gauge listing requirements before the ticket booths.

ORIENTATION   IOA's 101 acres are laid out much like Epcot's World Showcase: individually themed areas (here, called "islands," even though they're not) arranged around a lagoon (called the Great Inland Sea). To see everything, you simply follow a great circle. The only corridor into the park, **Port of Entry,** borrows from the Magic Kingdom's Main Street, U.S.A., in that it's a narrow, introductory area where guests are submerged into the theme. In this case, you're gathering munitions for a "great odyssey," so, in theme park logic, it's where you do things like rent strollers and lockers and grab free maps. Most guests beeline through Port of Entry. Because attraction lines are shortest after opening, explore this area later, maybe before closing.

STRATEGY   Once you reach the end of Port of Entry, which way should you go? Right. That's the way to Harry Potter. Lines peak in late morning and early afternoon, then taper off again after that, but they're rarely short.

SHOPPING   The park will send your souvenirs to the Islands of Adventure Trading Company, at the Port of Entry, for collection as you leave the park at the end of the day. The deadline for purchases changes, but it's usually about 2 hours before closing. To the right as you exit the park, there's a **small stand** selling marked-down items (the inventory changes, but I've seen $8 Marvel action figures, two-for-ones on plush Curious George dolls, and $40 sweatshirts for $22). It opens later in the day.

Islands of Adventure

Flight of the Hippogriff

Harry Potter and the Forbidden Journey

Dragon Challenge

THE WIZARDING WORLD OF HARRY POTTER

Jurassic Park River Adventure ❶ ❷

Skull Island: Reign of Kong

JURASSIC PARK

Hogwarts Express – Hogsmeade Station

Pteranodon Flyers

Camp Jurassic

Jurassic Park Discovery Center ❻ ❼

❽

The Mystic Fountain ■ ❾ ❿

The Eighth Voyage of Sindbad Stunt Show

Dudley Do-Right's Ripsaw Falls ❹

Popeye & Bluto's Bilge-Rat Barges

⓫ **THE LOST CONTINENT**

❸ **TOON LAGOON** ❺

Me Ship, The Olive

Lagoon

Poseidon's Fury

MARVEL SUPER HERO ISLAND

The High in the Sky Seuss Trolley Train Ride!

The Amazing Adventures of Spider-Man ⓬

⓯ **SEUSS LANDING** ⓰

⓭ **Caro-Seuss-el**

Doctor Doom's Fearfall

Incredible Hulk Coaster

⓮

One Fish, Two Fish, Red Fish, Blue Fish

Storm Force Accelatron

The Cat in the Hat

⓱

PORT OF ENTRY

Pharos Lighthouse

To CityWalk & Parking

To Universal Studios

WHERE TO EAT

Blondie's **4**
The Burger Digs **6**
Cafe 4 **13**
Captain America Diner **12**
Circus McGurkus Cafe Stoo-pendous **16**
Comic Strip Cafe **3**
Confisco Grille **14**
Croissant Moon Bakery **17**
"Doc" Sugrue's Desert Kebab House **9**
Fire-Eaters' Grill **10**

Green Eggs & Ham Café **15**
Hog's Head Pub **8**
Mythos Restaurant **11**
Pizza Predattoria **2**

Three Broomsticks **8**
Thunder Falls Terrace **1**
The Watering Hole **7**
Wimpy's **5**

MARVEL SUPER HERO ISLAND

If Disney owns Marvel, how come Universal is allowed to have this island? The park licensed the brand in the 1990s, which gives it the right. Designs used the comic books of that period, which predates the film franchises of Spider-Man, the X-Men, Iron Man, and Fantastic Four, which is why characters don't look exactly the way you may be used to them. **Spider-Man** is sometimes one of them, but if you don't see him, head into the back of the Marvel Alterniverse Store, opposite the Captain America Diner. There, the hero has his own appearance zone where you can take your own photos (or buy one). The actor playing Spider-Man is one of the few who isn't clad in muscle-shaped padding. The **Comic Book Shop** is worth a stop. Surprisingly legit, the store carries the latest Marvel issues, compilation books, and collectible busts.

Incredible Hulk Coaster ★★★ RIDE   Every minute or so, a new train blasts out of the 150-foot tunnel, over the avenue, and across the lakefront. Adding to the intensity, the track's hollow frame and nylon wheels generate an animal roar that can be heard throughout the park. The ride is quick—a little over 2 minutes—but it's invigorating. First, trains cruise into the inclined tunnel. Then, without warning, 220 aircraft tires accelerate trains from a standstill to 40mph in 2 seconds and shoot them into a zero G-force barrel-roll 110 feet in the air, which means passengers are already upside down even though they're still going up the first hill. What follows is unbridled mayhem, as you boomerang in a cobra roll and hit a top speed of 67mph through a tangle of corkscrews, loops, and misty tunnels. For many visitors, it's the first ride of the day, and its seven inversions are certain to work better than morning coffee. Loose items aren't allowed, so use the nearby lockers, good for the ride's posted wait time plus 20 minutes. *Strategy:* The single-rider line here is fruitful. If you're low on time, wait instead for the front row on Dueling Dragons, where the exposed view gets you a lot more thrills. *Renovation:* The ride will be closed until the summer of 2016.

Storm Force Accelatron ★ RIDE   I can translate: Storm is the weather-controlling X-Man, so an Accelatron must be a 90-second spinning-tub ride, like Disney's teacups. Open, round cars spin on platters that themselves are on a giant rotating disk, and just to ensure maximum vomit velocity, each pod can be spun using a plate in the middle. *Strategy:* Skip it unless you have insistent kids.

Dr. Doom's Fearfall ★★ RIDE   Those twin 200-foot towers are fitted with rows of chairs that slide up and down them. The brave are rocketed 150 feet up at a force of 4Gs, where they feel an intense tickling in their stomachs, soak up a terrific view of the park, and bounce (safely) back down to Earth. The ride capacity is pretty low—you can see for yourself that each tower only shoots about 16 people up on each trip, with a reload period of several minutes in between—so either do this one early or very late so that waiting for it doesn't eat up too much time. You may hear the towers hiss like a snarling beast—it sounds like a Doctor Doom sound effect, but, in fact, it's part of the mechanism. A computer weighs each car before launch, and any excess compressed air is noisily expelled in the seconds before flight. *Strategy:* The seating configuration lends itself to lots of empty spaces, so the single-rider line moves much quicker than most.

The Amazing Adventures of Spider-Man ★★★ RIDE   The cliché "don't miss it" rightfully applies here. It fires on all cylinders, and the whole family can do it without fear. After passing through a simulation of the "Daily Bugle" newsroom (take special notice of the hilarious pre-ride safety video, done as a pitch-perfect "Superfriends"-era cartoon), riders don polarized 3-D glasses, board moving cars, and whisk through a 1.5-acre experience. Mild open-air motion simulation, computer-generated 3-D animation, and cunning sense trickery (bursts of flame, water droplets, blasts of hot air) collaborate to impart the mind-blowing illusion of being drafted into Spidey's battles against a "Sinister Syndicate" of supervillains including Doctor Octopus and the Green Goblin, who have disassembled the Statue of Liberty with an anti-gravity gun. Although the vehicles barely move as they make their way through the sets, you'll come off feeling as if you've survived a 400-foot plunge off a city skyscraper. Comics fans should keep a lookout for Spider-Man creator Stan Lee. He appears four times during the ride, and you'll hear him once. *Strategy:* Go early or late in the day to minimize waits. There's sometimes a single-rider line and it shoots past the slower standby queue. The middle of the front row is debatably the best place to sit.

TOON LAGOON

The next zone clockwise after Marvel Super Hero Island, Toon Lagoon, harbors two water rides that are—both literally and figuratively—among the splashiest at any theme park. Both will drench you. If you're smart, you'll come just *before* it swelters, so that you'll be soaked and cool when the going gets rough.

Slow your pace when you reach the introductory section of Toon Lagoon, encountered after a brief zone of **midway games** (most: three tries for $5). Crawling with details, color, and fountains, it's the kind of place that reveals more the longer you look. Some 150 cartoon characters—some you'll recognize (Nancy, Annie, the Family Circus, Beetle Bailey) and some strictly for connoisseurs (Little Nemo in Slumberland, Zippy)—make two-dimensional appearances on the island, including inside the restaurants and on a soundtrack popping in and out of the action. Where you see a button or a possible trigger, press it or plunge it, because the environment has been rigged with sonic treats. Whimsical snapshot spots are worked in, too, such as the trick photo setup by the Comic Strip Cafe where you can pretend Marmaduke is dragging you by his leash. The deluge from the waterfall under Hagar's Viking ship provides cooling relief from the sunlight. Amid all this, the **Boop Oop A Doop** Betty Boop store sells rare specimens. My sister-in-law found a 75th-anniversary cookie jar here that no other real-world store carried. Personally, I worry about the mental health of the clerks, who are subjected to a brain-melting loop of Boop's oops.

Dudley Do-Right's Ripsaw Falls ★★★ RIDE   Within this Technicolor snow-capped mountain, you'll find a wonderful perils-of-Pauline log-flume caper featuring Jay Ward's feckless Canadian Mountie bungling his rescue of Nell Fenwick from Snidely Whiplash. The winding 5-minute journey—ups, downs, indoor, outdoor, surprise backsplashes, chunky robotic characters—climaxes in a stomach-juggling double-dip drop that hurtles, unexpectedly, through a humped underground gully. Although the 75-foot drop starts out at 45 degrees, it steepens to 50 degrees, creating a weightless sensation. Front- and back-seat riders get soaked, and anyone who didn't get soaked probably will when they double back to the disembarking zone, because that's when they'll face the gauntlet of sadistic bystanders who fire water cannons at passing boats. Ripsaw Falls is terrific fun. No one gets off it grumpy—the mark of amusement success. *Strategy:* The ride often closes in January and early February for a scrub. There's an optional locker nearby—use it, because there's no boat storage. It's $4 for 90 minutes, which may allow you to also use it for Popeye & Bluto's barges. The **Gasoline Alley** shop, across the main path, sells $8 ponchos, but on Ripsaw Falls, you straddle the seat so your feet won't be easy to cover. Best to wear sandals.

Popeye & Bluto's Bilge-Rat Barges ★★★ RIDE   For my money, it's the best round-boat flume in the world because it's fun watching your loved ones get humiliated. Yes, it's Schadenfreude: The Ride. You board 12-passenger, circular bumper boats that float freely and unpredictably down an outlandish white-water obstacle course—beneath waterfalls, through tunnels, over angry rapids, and past features designed to mercilessly inundate you. It's like playing Russian roulette with water, and everyone loses. This journey is considerably wilder, unquestionably wetter, and obviously more expensive to build than any others in the genre. The attention shows: Even the river's walls have been sculpted and painted in cartoon hues to resemble a wooden chute. It's diabolical and one of Universal's best. On hot days, the wet effects are fully juiced, but when it's cold, they're turned down slightly. *Strategy:* There's a semi-waterproof cubby on board for personal belongings, but you'd be wise to slip your things into plastic bags, too, just in case. You may not go barefoot. For onlooker schadenfreude, there are 25¢ water blasters on overlooking walkways, but there are free ones on Me Ship, the Olive. Near the lockers ($4 for 90 min., which may be long enough use to use for Ripsaw Falls, too), you'll find step-in People Dryers that, for $5, bake and blow the water off you after your journey. (That works well, except on jeans.)

Me Ship, the Olive ★ ACTIVITY   An interactive ship-shaped playground for children just beyond the Barges' entrance, there's also a slide and some fun to be had with a piano in the cabin (play the notes on the sheet music for an orchestral surprise). One of my favorite things to do in Orlando is to spend awhile on the bridge beside the Olive, which overlooks Barge boats as they drift helplessly under a leaky boiler's funnel. Watching the gleeful alarm on people's faces, hearing the peals of laughter—the sublime delight of amusement park togetherness is repeated, again and again, from the vantage point of that bridge. I could stand there all day. I also love the shore of the sea nearby, which is private almost all the time.

JURASSIC PARK

Steven Spielberg was a creative consultant to Universal, the studio that nourished him, and this "island," the largest and greenest in the park, is presented practically verbatim from his 1993 movie. Once you pass through a proud wooden gate, John Williams's bombastic score takes over, and there it burrows until you move on to another area of IOA. If you stand quietly, you may hear rustling—a clever, Spielbergian touch. With the success of *Jurassic World* and a new Kong movie, this island is again a focus of Universal's developmental attention.

Skull Island: Reign of Kong ★★★ RIDE Promotion for Universal's latest marquee attraction will be bananas, saturating the airwaves ahead of its summer 2016 opening, as King Kong makes his return to Orlando since his first ride, Kongfrontation, was torn down in 2002. And it is huge—as big as the biggest rides in town, with a fantastically terrifying stone façade to warn wimps away. Universal keeps mum on the mechanics of the ride system, but it's not spoiling things to say that rather than show Kong running amok in the human world, we run amok in his: The trip is an indoor-and-outdoor, tricked-out truck tour through the perils of King Kong's stomping grounds, Skull Island, past sets, screens, and astonishing machines. The height requirement, just 34 inches, is an indication that for all that, it's family-friendly mayhem.

Camp Jurassic ★ ACTIVITY The only dedicated kids' zone of this part of the park is a self-guided tangle of rope bridges, slides, bubbling pools in caves, surprise geysers, water guns, spitting dinosaur heads, and thick greenery. It's easy to get lost here, and easier to get wet.

Pteranodon Flyers ★ RIDE The hanging carts gently gliding on the nifty-looking track over Camp Jurassic constitute a very short (about 75 sec.) clacking route through the trees. Cool as it looks, it was poorly designed, fitting only two at a time, and huge lines were inevitable. Facing irate crowds, Universal instituted a rule: No adult could ride without a child. That both prepared guests for the ride's tame deportment and cut down on the wait. Attendants may be willing to load child-free adults when the park is dead. *Strategy:* Skip this underwhelmer if the wait's more than 15 minutes.

Jurassic Park River Adventure ★★ RIDE In that family-friendly Orlando tradition, the worst drop is clearly warned; gauge the 85-foot descent from behind the Thunder Falls Terrace restaurant, where river boats kick up quite a spray when they hit the water at 30mph. Before reaching that messy climax, boats embark on what's meant to be a benign tour of the mythical dinosaur park from the movie, only to be bumped off course and run afoul of spitting raptors and an eye-poppingly realistic T. rex that lunges for the kill. The dino attack is shrewdly stage-managed; note how, in true Spielberg fashion, you see disquieting evidence of the hungry lizards (rustling bushes, gashes in sheet metal) before actually catching sight of one. In all honesty, you're more likely to get soaked standing on the terrace of the restaurant than inside the boat, but the trip down is enough to blow your hat off and sprinkle you above the waist. There's usually at least one delirious 12-year-old boy who stands in the splash zone for hours, giving himself a nigh-amphibious drenching.

Jurassic Park Discovery Center ★ ACTIVITY   Enter a convincing reproduction of the luxury lodge from the film, down to full-size skeletons in the atrium—downstairs, line up your camera just so, and you can snap a witty shot of a T. rex chomping a loved one's cranium. Seek out the scientist carrying a baby triceratops that hatched on the grounds; it flinches and reacts to your touch. You can also handle the ostrich-sized dinosaur eggs and slide them into nifty "scanners." Behind the center, there's a network of pleasant garden paths where you can take a break from the bustle of the park. Out front, don't miss the regularly scheduled appearances of **Raptor Encounter,** which gives you a chance to take selfies with a chillingly lifelike, mobile, and responsive 9-foot velociraptor from the "safe" side of a fence. What could go wrong?

THE WIZARDING WORLD OF HARRY POTTER—HOGSMEADE

When it opened in June of 2010, the 10-acre **Hogsmeade** ★★★ was rightfully hailed as the most significant achievement in American theme park design, detailed down to the souvenirs. It's as if the film set for Hogsmeade Village (the only British village for non-Muggles) and Hogwarts Castle have been transported to Florida, and indeed, it was designed by the same team. You don't have to know the books or the movies to enjoy the astounding level of attention: Stonework looks ancient, plaster was painted to appear moldy, rooftops and chimneys slouch in a jumble of snow-covered gables, and nearly every souvenir is a bespoke creation expressly for the Harry Potter universe—in fact, J. K. Rowling had final approval on everything, including on what's sold. Even the restrooms aren't spared Moaning Myrtle's whine. Spend time going from shop window to shop window to take in the tricks. In Spintwitches Sporting Needs, a Quidditch set strains to free itself from its carrying case. At Gladrags, the gown levitates. At Tomes and Scrolls, Gilderoy Lockhart (Kenneth Branagh) vainly preens himself among his best-selling travel books.

Those stores are brilliant facades, but there are real shops that are just as unmissable (and invariably thronged). **Devish and Banges** is where you find Hogwarts school supplies in the colors of all four Houses, from capes to scarves to diaries to parchment, wax seals, and quills. (The seething "Monster Book of Monsters" is kept in a cage here.) In the window of **Honeydukes,** there's a macabre contraption in which a mechanical crow pecks out the gumball eye of a skeleton, which rolls through various chutes to be dispensed below, presumably for consumption. That signifies the wondrous candy store within, where colorful Edwardian-style packages contain Chocolate Frogs, Fizzing Whizzbees, Bertie Bott's Every Flavour Beans (beware the vomit-flavored ones mixed in), Exploding Bon Bons, Peppermint Toads, and other confections that would faze even Willy Wonka.

The park's signature concoction, **Butterbeer,** is pulled from two keg-shaped carts in the walkways. The only place in the world you can buy it is right here or at the Harry Potter Studio Tour outside of London. Served frozen or unfrozen (I like it cold) with a creamy foam head on top, it tastes like a butterscotch Life Saver, and it's addictive. I once did laboratory analysis on it and found out that, surprisingly, it contains no more sugar than a Coke. It's $5 a cup, but for $12, you get a dishwasher-safe Butterbeer mug. **The Magic Neep** cart, between the Butterbeer stalls, sells **Pumpkin Juice** (really a Christmasy apple juice mix) in its unique pumpkin-top bottles for $7, along with actual fruit for $1.70 a piece.

Ollivanders ★★ SHOW   It's not on the maps because it can't handle big crowds, but the queue to the left of Dervish and Banges is for Ollivanders Wand Shop, stacked haphazardly to the dusty rafters with wands for every wizard. You enter in small groups, and the kindly shopkeeper selects one child from the group for a personalized wand selection—it selects *you*—accompanied by music cues and fun tricks. Wickedly, an attendant then ushers your child, and that wand, directly toward the cash registers in the wand department at Devish and Banges, where you can also buy perfect replicas from nearly every major character of the Harry Potter universe (mostly $45), from Harry to Hermione to Snape to Voldemort to Bellatrix Lestrange to Luna Lovegood. They don't have price tags, but they do have stickers reading, preposterously, "This is not a toy." Treat them with care. Some are sturdy, but some, such as Professor McGonagall's, can break. *Tip:* If the line is too long, there are three more wand showrooms at Ollivanders on Diagon Alley at Universal Studios next door.

Harry Potter and the Forbidden Journey ★★★ RIDE   You will be drawn inexorably to the stunning re-creation of Hogwarts Castle, and within, you'll find a most technologically complex ride. I won't give away how it's done, but I will say it's an epic combination of motion-simulator movie segments and awe-inducing physical encounters as you travel on a jolting, four-person bench that has been enchanted by Hermione to transport you. This being Orlando, things quickly go wrong, and you encounter a dragon, Aragog the spider, the Whomping Willow, a Quidditch match, and Dementors, all in the space of 4 minutes. The mostly indoor queue is perhaps even more magical, taking you through Dumbledore's study and through the dim halls of Hogwarts, where real-looking oil paintings come to life and bicker with each other. At one point, fake snow falls on you, and a lifelike Sorting Hat supervises your arrival at the loading dock. It's a tour-de-force that takes the pain out of a long wait, and sometimes there's a tour-only route that lets you enjoy it without having to ride (ask). Once you're done, you go through Filch's Emporium of Confiscated Goods, a general-interest shop for Potteria. *Strategy:* You'll save frustration if you don't have bags. No loose articles are permitted. Lockers are free for the posted wait time plus 20 minutes, but using them is confusing. The single rider line lets you leapfrog much of the wait but you will miss most of the queue's excitement. A minority of people feel queasy after riding, but if you sense that happening, just close your eyes during the three movie portions and you should be fine. Try the test seat out front if you're a larger guest—a surprising number of people are not able to ride.

Dragon Challenge ★★★ RIDE This is a monster coaster of the first order, and one of Orlando's most thrilling, but it's not very Hogsmeade because it's actually a holdover from the pre-Potter years. Actually, it's two roller coasters, "inverted" so that passengers' feet dangle, entangled together for two different 145-second rides. Hungarian Horntail, in blue, has a cobra roll and its twistiness is perhaps (who can say?) more conducive to slight motion sickness for those who are prone to it. Chinese Fireball, in red-orange, has two more "elements" (maneuvers, in coaster-speak), and its first drop is slightly higher, but its course is slightly more jolty. The line for both snakes indoors through a castle before diverging before the twin loading zones, at which point you'll also have to decide if you want to wait longer to guarantee a front-row seat. The trains were designed to be dispatched together for near-misses on the course, but because naughty guests dropped loose items, seriously injuring others, that practice was ended. *Strategy:* The effect is best enjoyed from the front row or by keeping an eye on your feet. After you get off, ask an attendant if the "re-ride" line is up, because if it is, you won't have to go all the way out to line up again to try the other track. Note that guests of exceptional size may have to wait for the third row, where the larger seats are; if you're not confident that you'll fit, test out the standard seat located to the right of the main entrance to the queue. Locker use (free for the wait time plus 20 min.) is mandatory, and you'll find them at Hogsmeade Station.

Flight of the Hippogriff ★ RIDE For kids too little for Dragon Challenge, you'll find a standard training roller coaster (a re-themed holdover from pre-Potter years) that offers a glimpse of Hagrid's Hut from the queue. Don't expect more than a 1-minute figure eight with slight banking—adults, you can skip it. *Strategy:* The line is exposed to the sun and the back seats feel the fastest. The long-legged should cross their ankles to fit more comfortably.

Hogwarts Express ★★★ RIDE The journey from Hogsmeade to London in Universal Studios works just like the one coming here (p. 132), but you'll see different scenery and eavesdrop on different goings-on in the carriage. Notice the subtle rhythmic vibration of the seats. Hogsmeade Station is not as nice as Kings Cross at Diagon Alley—there's no air-conditioning and no fun tricks like the Platform 9¾ photo op—but trains carry 168 people at a time and new ones load 5 minutes after the previous one departs. *Strategy:* To board, you must have a park-to-park ticket, and there's a ticket upgrade booth out front for just that purpose.

THE LOST CONTINENT

The gist of the next island, the Lost Continent, is amorphous. Think of it as part Africa, part Asia, part Rome—anything exotic wrapped up in vagueness. It's being whittled away as Harry Potter grows.

The Hogwarts Express.

The Eighth Voyage of Sindbad Stunt Show ★ SHOW   Mounted a few times each day in an open-air stadium, usually in the afternoon (curtain times marked on your map), it's fine for a stunt show, but it won't rock your world. You probably already suspect what you're getting here—a corny 20-minute, sound-effect enhanced banquet of macho men sword fighting and leaping to rescue a princess who, it turns out, may or may not require male assistance after all. Buckles are swashed and cultural references dropped like anvils. The climax, in which a man is lit on fire and plunges 30 feet into a pit, may alarm kids, but production values are strong. *Strategy:* Attend this show if you'd like to sit for a bit. Your IOA experience won't be lacking if you skip it.

Mystic Fountain ★★★ ACTIVITY   Stop by briefly. If it's merely gurgling with recorded sound effects, all is quiet. But when least expected, it comes to life with wisecracks and sprays. Someone in an unseen booth interacts with anyone foolish enough to wander near—usually naïve children. As "Time" magazine put it when the park opened in 1999, the fountain exasperates with "the droll sarcasm of a bachelor uncle roped into caring for some itchy 10-year-olds." If you don't want to get doused, check the ground for slick spots to determine the fountain's spitting reach.

Poseidon's Fury ★★★ SHOW   Despite its lowly status as a walk-through attraction, it has a stunning exterior, carved within a millimeter of reason to look like a crumbling temple. Young folk might be freaked out by the dark and the fireballs. Mature folk might disdain the vapid storyline involving a row between Poseidon and Lord Darkenon (who?). But it bemuses with an interesting (if fleeting) "water vortex" tunnel and some of its other special effects, such as walls that seem to vanish, are diverting. Like Sindbad, it's boisterous and pyrotechnic. *Strategy:* For the best views, head for the front of every room, especially the third one.

On One Fish, Two Fish, Red Fish, Blue Fish, riders steer their fish through a circular obstacle course of playfully squirting fountains.

SEUSS LANDING

Nowhere other than Harry Potter is IOA's extravagance on finer display than this 10-acre section, which replicates the good Doctor's two-dimensional bluster with three-dimensional exactitude. Just try to find a straight line. From the lakefront, you can get a good look at what the designers accomplished. Notice how even the palm trees twist. They were knocked sideways near Miami in 1992's Hurricane Andrew, and because palm trees always grow upward, by the time they were scouted for IOA, they had acquired a perfectly loopy angle. Scout for hidden gags. Sprinkled around are Horton's Egg and, by the sea, the two Zaxes, which, appropriate to their own book (a commentary on political rivalry in which they stubbornly face off while a city grows up around them), were the very first things placed in the park, and everything else was built around them. The area around the Mulberry Street Store hosts regular appearances by the Cat in the Hat and the Grinch, who looks as annoyed to be there as you might imagine.

High in the Sky Seuss Trolley Train Ride! ★★★ RIDE Everything on this island is appropriate for kids. The railway threading overhead is a cheerful family-friendly glide, narrated in verse. Like Dueling Dragons, there are two paths. The purple line surveys more of the area than the green line, which dawdles above the Circus McGurkus Cafe. The ride takes about 3 minutes and because there's so much to take in, time flies fast. You have to line up all over again if you want to do the other track.

Caro-Seuss-el ★★★ RIDE Its bobbing menagerie of otherworldly critters actually reacts to being ridden—ears wiggle, heads turn, snouts rise—making it delightfully over-the-top and appealing to kids who sniff at girly carousels. Beside the Caro-Seuss-el, seek out the quick but trenchant walk-through grove of Truffula Trees retelling Dr. Seuss's environmental warning tale, the **Street of the Lifted Lorax.**

One Fish, Two Fish, Red Fish, Blue Fish ★★★ RIDE Here we have another iteration (albeit a good one) of Disney's tot bait, Dumbo. Riders (two passengers per car normally, three if one of them loves the Wiggles) go around, up, and down by their own controls while a gauntlet of spitting fish pegs them from the sides—listen to the song for the secret of how to avoid getting wet, although the advice isn't foolproof. There are benches good for watching little kids giggle malevolently when their parents get spritzed.

If I Ran the Zoo ★★★ ACTIVITY Getting wet is part of the bargain, so there's a rack to keep shoes dry. The interactive playground for young children contains some 20 tricksy elements. Let your brood slide, splash in a stream, turn cranks, and play Tic Tac Toe on characters' bellies. Beware the cheeky fountain—it pays to follow all posted instructions in Seuss Landing. Thanks, Universal, for the hand sanitizer dispensers by the exit.

The Cat in the Hat ★★★ RIDE Take a nonthreatening excursion through the plot of the famous storybook as viewed from slow-moving mobile "couches" (really a typical flat-ride car). The design racks up points for replicating the look of the beloved children's book with precision, even in three dimensions. The story is just as faithfully retold; it's clear from this sweet, 3½-minute ride that the family of Dr. Seuss (Theodor Geisel) had a strong influence in steering the execution of this section of the park. Parents will probably emerge feeling glad they tagged along. The gift shop after the offload platform is among the best in the park—Universal's red Thing 1 and Thing 2 shirts ($22) are as ubiquitous as Mouse ears. *Tip:* The vehicles spin a few too many times for some adults (kids don't seem to mind), but you can ask to have it turned off when you board.

WHERE TO EAT IN ISLANDS OF ADVENTURE

If the park closes at 6pm (like it does outside the summer and holidays), many restaurants will only be open from 11am to 4pm. But remember that **CityWalk** (p. 222) is a 5-minute walk from the park, so you can consider those places, too.

In addition to the random snack carts there's no use in listing here, there are counter-service and sit-down restaurants (including carts selling goliath turkey legs for $12) in the park. None require reservations the way Disney's do. Kids' meals all come in under 300 calories. *Tip:* Menu items do not *have* to be served with sides. The potato chip bags served with the posted meals hold a mere 1⅞ ounces. Subtract them, or fries, from your meal combos to save about $2. Cups good for unlimited refills at touchscreen Coke Freestyle machines, which mix soda to order using 126 flavors, cost $11, and are good for the day. Clockwise through the park from Port of Entry:

Croissant Moon Bakery ★ SANDWICHES Lighter bites such as sandwiches and panini (breakfast sandwiches until 11am; combos served with a muffin), plus pastries such as cream horns and vanilla éclairs, can be snagged without much of a line. Nearby is the **Last Chance Fruit Stand** cart, which sells fruit cups ($3.80) and giant turkey legs ($12). **Port of Entry.** Sandwiches $9.50; soup and salad $12.

Confisco Grille ★ INTERNATIONAL   One of only two table-service locations in the park, the menu has an identity crisis—wood-oven pizzas, pad Thai, fajitas, Tex-Mex wraps, fajitas—but that also means there's probably something for everyone in your group. The attached **Backwater Bar,** overlooked by most and therefore ideal for sundowners, does happy hour from 4 to 7pm, when well drinks are just $4. **Port of Entry.** Main courses $9 to $17.

Captain America Diner ★ AMERICAN   This indoor counter-service location serves the usual burgers and chicken, plus shakes (just like the Captain never drinks!). Outside you'll find a **fruit stand** where pieces of whole fruit cost $1.80. **Marvel Super Hero Island.** Main courses $9 to $16 with fries.

Cafe 4 ★ PIZZA   Counter service with indoor seating for grabbing pasta as well as pizza by the individual pie. **Marvel Super Hero Island.** Pizza and pasta $8 to $13 with side salad.

Blondie's ★★ SANDWICHES   If you know that Dagwood is another name for a hero, you'll know who Blondie is, too. This indoor counter location does subs served with pickles and potato salad. It usually closes after lunch. **Toon Lagoon.** Mains $10.

Comic Strip Cafe ★★ INTERNATIONAL   Toon Lagoon's largest counter-service location offers four schools of food: burgers and dogs, pizza and pasta, Chinese, and fish and chicken. There's more indoor seating with air-conditioning here than anywhere else in this island. **Toon Lagoon.** Main courses $9 to $14.

Wimpy's ★ AMERICAN   It's the stand that furnishes its namesake's obsession (hamburgers), although the staff will not permit you to pay next Tuesday for a hamburger today, mostly because it opens only when the park is packed. **Toon Lagoon.** Main courses $8 to $11.

The Burger Digs ★ AMERICAN   The Discovery Center's indoor counter-service spot is upstairs, across from the dinosaur-theme toy store. Guess what it makes? There's a toppings bar, so you can load up, and to make it easier, it serves double cheeseburgers that you can convert into two meals with a second bun ($1). **Jurassic Park Discovery Center.** Combo meal $9 to $12.

Pizza Predattoria ★ AMERICAN   The menu is small but big on calories: pizzas, meatball subs, and chicken Caesar salad. It's counter service with outdoor seating. **Jurassic Park.** Nearby is the **Natural Selections** fruit cart ($1.80/piece). Mains $8 to $10.

Thunder Falls Terrace ★★★ BARBECUE   Watch the Jurassic Park boats splash down in the comfort of air-conditioning while noshing on food that's a cut above the rest: chargrilled ribs served with whole unhusked ears of corn, rotisserie chicken, and bacon cheeseburgers. Soups are just $3.50. **Jurassic Park.** Meals $10 to $16.

The Watering Hole ★★ BAR   Cocktails are served al fresco from this kiosk, which throws a happy hour from 3 to 5pm when 20 ounces of beer costs $4. **Jurassic Park.** Cocktails mostly $6 to $8.

Three Broomsticks ★★★ BARBECUE/BRITISH   The film tavern was gorgeously re-created, up to its wonky cathedral ceiling and down to the graffiti scratched in the timbers, as the only restaurant in this island, and the film-makers reportedly liked the design so much they featured the set more prominently in later movies. The Great Feast feeds four for $50 with salad, rotisserie chicken, spareribs, corn on the cob, and roast potatoes. You can also go a la carte with shepherd's pie, fish and chips, or spare ribs with salad. **Hog's Head Pub** ★★★ is attached. Under the squinty gaze of a grunting mounted boar's head (it responds to tips), a selection of truly British quaffs (London Pride, Newcastle Brown, Strongbow cider) is pulled. There are two more beers of note: One is Hog's Head ale, a hoppy, only-here beer made by the Florida Brewing Company, and the other is Butterbeer, so if the line is long at the keg carts outside, you can grab a faster fix in here, where it's cool in more ways than one. (They won't spike it with rum. I've asked.) There's no happy hour here. **Wizarding World of Harry Potter.** Meals $9 to $16.

Mythos Restaurant ★★★ INTERNATIONAL   Mythos's cavelike interior, carved from that ubiquitous orange-hued fake rock that scientists should term Orlando Schist, commands a marvelous view of the lagoon (go around to the water, where few guests wander, to see the god holding the place up with his bare hands). You could sit and watch the Incredible Hulk Coaster fire all day from this subdued environment. Food is many rungs higher than most theme park stuff, with pad Thai, cranberry/blue cheese-crusted pork, pan seared mahimahi, and a risotto of the day, plus a healthy slate of sandwiches and salads. **The Lost Continent.** Reservations recommended. ✆ **407/224-4534.** Main courses $12 to $20.

"Doc" Sugrue's Desert Kebab House ★ MEDITERRANEAN   Outdoor-only counter service spot serving its namesake in beef, chicken, and vegetables, plus hummus with veggies ($5). **The Lost Continent.** Main courses $7 to $9.

Fire-Eaters' Grill ★ INTERNATIONAL   Outdoor-only counter service with the usual suspects: chicken fingers, chicken stingers (Buffalo chicken fingers), hot dogs, and gyros. **The Lost Continent.** Meals with fries $9 to $10.

Circus McGurkus Cafe Stoo-pendous ★★★ AMERICAN   Looking like a circus tent coated in cake frosting, it serves the usual burgers and pizzas, leavened with spaghetti and meatballs; chicken Caesar salad; and a fried chicken platter with mashed potatoes and corn on the cob so there's something for everyone. For dessert, the **Moose Juice Goose Juice** stand nearby sells Moose Juice (a tart orange mix) and Goose Juice (watermelon or grape) for $4.25. **Seuss Landing.** Meals $9 to $13.

Green Eggs & Ham Café ★ AMERICAN   You can't miss it—it's the house-size slab of ham with a giant fork stuck into it. It sells burgers and, of course, sandwiches made of green eggs and ham, but it's rarely open unless it's super crowded, which is a shame. **Seuss Landing.** Main courses $9.

SEAWORLD ORLANDO

The second mighty theme park chain to set up shop in town, after Disney, was **SeaWorld Orlando** ★★★ (Central Florida Pkwy., at International Dr., or exit 71 and 72 east of I-4; www.seaworldorlando.com; ✆ **800/327-2424** or 407/351-3600; adults $97, kids 3–9 $92, discounts of $15–$30 available online for entry Mon–Fri; parking $17; open 9am–7pm with extended hours in peak season), which began in San Diego in 1964 and opened in Orlando in 1973, predating Universal by 17 years. Although SeaWorld operates three American parks (the third is in San Antonio), its Orlando location is the most elaborate and has undoubtedly risen to become its most important—and most controversial (see box). It also runs an additional luxury theme park, **Discovery Cove** ★★★ (p. 167), and a new water slide park, **Aquatica** (p. 166).

At SeaWorld, the focus isn't on thrill rides or "magic"—it's animals, and thousands of them, and if watching animals do things for food makes you uncomfortable, you'll hate it. Just about everything to see or do involves watching marine creatures either idly swimming in imitated habitats or performing in shows. There's a lot going for it: 200 acres of space for gardens, a compound that absorbs crowds well, an earnest educational component, and a refreshing lack of patronizing mythology. But then there's the controversy.

While attendance is still decent, it has suffered from the *Blackfish* flap, which negatively affected hospitality—staff cuts created longer lines for services such as ticketing, and although the park has always touted its legitimate rescue and conservation efforts, now such boasts feel awkwardly defensive. In the spring of 2015, SeaWorld Entertainment tapped a new CEO, Joel Manby, an *Undercover Boss* veteran whose oversight of Dollywood and Silver Dollar City improved those parks. One of the first things he did was to announce the construction of the Mako coaster—could SeaWorld be in the process of diversifying into a thrill-based park and backing away from reliance on animal shows?

For now, the SeaWorld experience is **show-based.** Your day here will revolve around the scheduling of a half-dozen regular performances in which animals (mostly mammals, but some birds, too) do tricks—except here, they're called "behaviors"—with their human trainers. Although there are rides, they're not the true spirit of the place. SeaWorld's banner attraction is that controversial Shamu show, and when you're not watching killer whales do back-flips, you're ambling through **Animal Connections** habitats stocked with other beautiful creatures. Thoughtfully, **schedules are posted online** a few weeks ahead of time so that if you're really anal, you can map out your day in advance; the various show schedules are under "Park Info."

If you're doing a full complement of the non-Disney parks, including both Universal parks, SeaWorld, Aquatica, and Wet 'n Wild, then you'll find value in the **FlexTicket,** also sold on SeaWorld's site ($336 adults, $316 kids 3–9 for all those parks, p. 299), which gets you into all of them for two weeks.

SeaWorld sells **Quick Queue Unlimited** ($20), which allows you to cut lines by entering through the exit, but lines are rarely long enough to warrant

SeaWorld

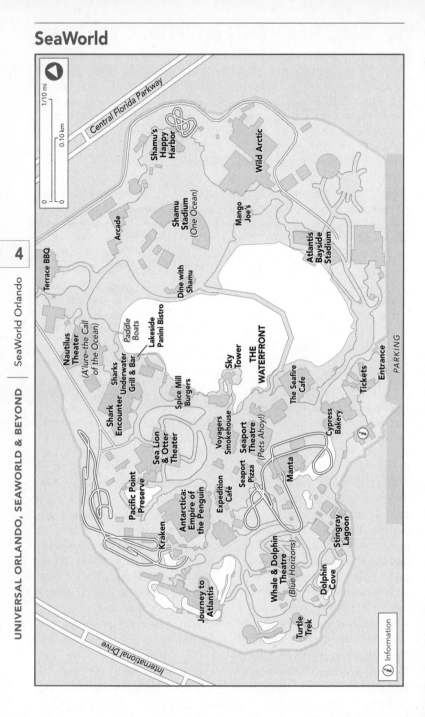

Central Florida Parkway

Shamu's Happy Harbor

Wild Arctic

Arcade

Shamu Stadium
(One Ocean)

Mango Joe's

Atlantis Bayside Stadium

Terrace BBQ

Dine with Shamu

Nautilus Theater
(A'lure–the Call of the Ocean)

Paddle Boats

Lakeside Panini Bistro

Sharks Underwater Grill & Bar

Shark Encounter

Spice Mill Burgers

Sky Tower

THE WATERFRONT

The Seafire Cafe

Sea Lion & Otter Theater

Voyagers Smokehouse

Seaport Theatre
(Pets Ahoy!)

Cypress Bakery

Pacific Point Preserve

Expedition Café

Seaport Pizza

Manta

Kraken

Antarctica: Empire of the Penguin

Entrance

PARKING

Tickets

Journey to Atlantis

Whale & Dolphin Theatre
(Blue Horizons)

Dolphin Cove

Stingray Lagoon

Turtle Trek

International Drive

i Information

1/10 mi

0.10 km

Ethical Entertainment? The "Blackfish" Controversy

Some conservationists say SeaWorld's animals endure misery in captivity. Other conservationists laud SeaWorld for being an advocate for marine life. Each side presents statistics that seem convincing but are then shot down by rivals. And therein lies the ongoing tug-of-war over this profit-generating amusement park. SeaWorld is hostile to accusations of mistreatment and exploitation—in 2013, the low-budget documentary "Blackfish" asserted that the 2010 death of senior trainer Dawn Brancheau, which was witnessed by an audience at Shamu Stadium, was the result of inadequate care. (For its part, the Brancheau family distanced itself from the documentary, saying in a statement: "Dawn would not have remained a trainer at SeaWorld for 15 years if she felt that the whales were not well cared for.") An anti-SeaWorld social media campaign has raged ever since, and every time a SeaWorld animal dies or causes injury, it makes news. Although SeaWorld has been fined about $26,000 by OSHA in California for improperly protecting its human employees, it

sharply rebuts some of the film's points, objecting to imbalanced reporting and complaining that the editing tricks viewers into believing the park collects its performing animals from the wild, something it hasn't done for decades. Excepting a few aged animals that were born in the seas and rehabilitated from accidents in the wild, SeaWorld insists, most of its animals were born in captivity and raised by hand and so they would not know how to survive in the wild. The park says it has rescued some 22,000 animals to date, and reminds the media that when marine animals are threatened in the oceans, it has often stepped in to help. But "Blackfish" also alleges that the tanks at SeaWorld could never be large enough to contain animals biologically programmed to roam wide territory—a charge that's harder to deny, and one the company has promised to address in coming years. Defenders say that opens up a new can of worms—why single out SeaWorld, they say, for things that zoos and animal parks across the country do every day?

it. You can also buy the 6-hour **Expedition SeaWorld** VIP Tour (starting at $79 adult, $59 kids 3–9 in low season) that includes reserved seating to three shows, food, and Quick Queue.

TIMING YOUR VISIT   You will spend quite a bit of time waiting for shows to begin. People show up early for seats, so it's smart to arrive at least 30 minutes ahead of show times. Crowds are lightest Tuesday and Wednesday. *Important:* If the forecast shows prolonged rain (as opposed to Florida's typical spot showers), reschedule your visit. Not only will you spend lots of time outside, but it's also harder to see marine animals when the surface of the water is pelted by raindrops—not to mention the fact that if there's so much as a twinkle of lightning anywhere in the county, these water-based attractions close faster than a shark's mouth on his dinner.

GETTING ORIENTED   Once you park ($17, and $22 "premium" spots aren't worth it) or get off the I-Ride (the stop is near the front gates), head for the lighthouse that marks the entrance. Inside, grab a placemat-size park map. On the back, printed fresh daily, is the **show schedule,** plus the opening times of all the restaurants and attractions. Shows usually begin an hour after park opening, and the blockbuster Shamu show, "One Ocean," has only a few presentations. I always prefer the last one because it's less crowded. On the off chance there's a space for a special interaction you'd like to do, the Guest Services and Reservations desk is the place to book. Otherwise, the Cape Cod–style entrance plaza is where you do the necessaries such as rent strollers and lockers. The area is really just a warm-up for the rest of the park.

The pathways are lined with "Animal Connections" enclosure—flamingoes here, turtles there—but those are really more like landscaping features than attractions, and some (but not all) aren't listed on the maps, so poke around. If you're interested in riding the park's thrill rides, the best time is when the Shamu show is scheduled, because it soaks up hundreds of people at once.

SeaWorld has a free **SeaWorld Discovery Guide app** (and free Wi-Fi in major park areas) that orients you, supplies show times, wait times, allows you to buy Quick Queue, reserve Shamu Stadium seating for $7, and helps you remember where you parked. You can also enter your credit card number and make cashless purchases with a bar code or play a scavenger hunt that rewards you with a free Shamu bar after about 20 questions. It drains your battery, though, so come with backup juice.

The Best Shows

Be choosy about shows, because if you plan too many, you'll miss enjoying the habitats—yet spreading SeaWorld over two days would be excessive.

One Ocean ★★ SHOW When the orcas start to fly in Shamu Stadium, the crowd comes alive. Closed-circuit TV cameras capture and display the spectacle on four huge, aging rotating screens as the animals thunder dauntingly through the water's surface, pointedly deluging entire seating sections in 52-degree water. It's quite a scene. The 25-minute plotless show occurs on such a scale as to make it required viewing. Now that trainers are no longer permitted to swim with the orcas, there's lots of vamping during which loud, recorded adult contemporary music plays and the whales are nowhere in sight. Trainers fill the gaps with weak Temptations-style choreography, quasi-inspirational scripted gibberish ("Pass the word from generation to generation: A bright and beautiful future is in our hands . . ."), and some defensive patter about how scientists can better observe orcas in captivity. But you instantly forget about the flaws when the animals reappear to leap skyward and belly flop back into their tank. The stadium, which fits 5,000 and still fills

One Ocean orca show.

early, is covered, but the sides may catch sun, so arrive at least 30 minutes early. *Strategy:* Soak zone seats offer excellent views of the animals hurtling through the 2.5 million-gallon, 36-feet-deep tank, and in case the splashes miss you, the dozens of fountain jets will finish the job. Seats near the shelf-like front platform will also have a close-up view of a killer whale out of the water. Seats at the back of the stadium, higher than the central aisle, must rely on the TV cameras to make out what's going on underwater. Using the Sea-World Discover Guide app, you can book reserved seating until 15 minutes ahead, but that's not necessary.

Clyde & Seamore's Sea Lion High ★★ SHOW SeaWorld's long-running Pirate Island show was retired in 2014, but Clyde and Seamore, a pair

Smart Seating

Do try to be at shows at least a **half-hour early,** and for Shamu, add another 10 minutes to walk around the lagoon to the stadium. SeaWorld is not as controlling as Disney about where you're permitted to sit, so the best seats go first. Furthermore, several shows ("Pets Ahoy!" especially) don't permit latecomers. At others, you can't get out easily until it's over.

Three of the shows—"One Ocean," "Blue Horizons," and "Clyde and Seamore"—have a clearly marked **"soak zone"** in the front rows of the seating section. Bank on the first 10 rows as being the wettest. Don't take this warn-

ing lightly; you have no concept of how much water a 10,000-pound male orca can displace. Of course, sitting with your kids in the soak zone on a hot day is one of the great pleasures of Sea-World, and most soak zone seating has the added advantage of affording side views into the tank where the animals prepare for their leaps and splashes. But for those with expensive hairdos, ponchos are sold throughout the parks, including at stalls beneath Shamu Stadium, for $9 ($8 kids). Keep your electronics somewhere dry, because salt water can fry their circuits.

Clyde & Seamore's Sea Lion High.

of sea lions, returned in 2015, with otters and sometimes a walrus, in a new spectacle. Expect a prototypical sea lion act: cheesy, anthropomorphic (animals doing double takes, sliding, waving, and pretending to attend school with human companions), and slapstick. Their cute 25-minute presentation remains one of SeaWorld's most cherished franchises. *Strategy:* The worst seats are to the left as you face the stage (they have partial views and get hot).

Blue Horizons ★ SHOW   This bizarre spectacle at Dolphin Theater about a little girl who "wants to explore the realms beyond imagination," whatever that means, somehow makes for a worthwhile 25-minute show. New Age poppycock makes it more like an acid trip at a carnival than anything else, which lends itself to loosely connected (but excellent) stunts starring dolphins,

Blue Horizons.

parrots, a condor, and plenty of human acrobats hooked up to bungee cords and diving off high platforms. There's always something to see, and little to comprehend. Think of it as "Shark du Soleil."

Pets Ahoy! ★★★ SHOW   Under-5s lose their minds at this indoor show at Seaport Theater, and you may, too—it's the show most worth seeing repeatedly. Although the furry cast is a deviation from SeaWorld's usual finny ones, the tricks are no less entrancing. A menagerie of common animals (cats, dogs, pigs, ducks, a skunk), most rescued from animal shelters, do simple tricks, and trigger tickling surprises on a rigged wharfside set. As the supercute gags multiply and compound in rapid succession (dachshunds pour out of a hot dog cart, a cat chases a white mouse in and out of hatches), and as more creatures are added into the mix precisely on cue, the amusement escalates. There's nearly no dialogue for its 20-minute run time. Afterward, trainers allow kids to pet some of the performers. *Strategy:* It's fun to sit under the catwalk (literally—cats walk on it) over the aisle between the first and second sections. This 850-seat theater fills well in advance of showtimes.

The Rest of the Park

Dolphin Nursery ★★★ ACTIVITY   Between the entrance plaza and the Waterfront, the young mammals are kept with their mothers for the first few years of their lives before graduating to the larger Dolphin Cove elsewhere in the park. Much of the day, human trainers can be found here, feeding the adolescent animals and getting them acclimated to human interaction. A fence keeps you well away from the water.

Key West at SeaWorld ★ ACTIVITY   A not-quite-reproduction of Front Street in the southernmost city in Florida features the **Stingray Lagoon,** where you can lean over and feel the slimy, spongy fish. You can buy food to feed the rays for $5 per tray of about four fish, two trays for $9, or three for $13.

Dolphin Cove ★★★ ACTIVITY   At the kiosk, make appointments for the **Dolphin Encounter** ($15), in which your 3–5 minutes of face time—you may pet them, not feed them—are doled out as part of 15-minute blocks (times later in the day are less crowded). Around feeding times, dolphins congregate at the trainers' dock, which can make seeing them difficult, so come between meals for a better look. Walk around the far side of the tank, and you'll find a little-used underwater viewing area with air-conditioning.

TurtleTrek ★★ ACTIVITY/FILM   A circuitous entrance ramp brings you to a popular air-conditioned underwater viewing area for 1,500 Caribbean fish and sea turtles the size of coffee tables—that's what earns our two-star rating. If you look closely, you can tell which turtles are rescues—one lost her lower jaw from a fishing net, another gave a flipper to a shark near Bermuda. In the freshwater tank, much attention is paid to the manatee's status as one of America's most endangered animals, and, in fact, the sluggish creatures on display here were all rescued from the wild, where hot-dogging boaters are

Viewing the turtles At TurtleTrek.

decimating their numbers. You'll be herded into a domed room where a (rather poorly) computer-animated 3-D film—no stars—traces the life cycle of a sea turtle from its point of view. It's hard not to notice that 7-minute story hits the same beats as "Finding Nemo" (jellyfish fields, marauding birds, sharks prowling a shipwreck). You might be better off staying longer in front of the tank, where the view is more authentic. *Tip:* If you skip this, at least see the manatees in their habitat located out the attraction's exit.

Mako ★★★ ROLLER COASTER   SeaWorld's new offering for summer 2016—*what* controversy?—Mako ("*MAY*-ko") takes the crown as Orlando's longest (nearly a mile of track), fastest (73 mpg), and tallest—200 feet, which is typical for many regional theme parks but as high as they go in these parts.

It's billed as a "hypercoaster" with "relentless air time," which means there are lots of humps and drops, including several over water, that make you feel weightless. That first brutal sideways drop is called "the hammerhead." On an industry level, it's a sign SeaWorld wants to do something big to boost attendance. On a thrills level, this is one helluva ride. If someone in your party doesn't want to make a foray on this nerve-tangler, send them to the **flamingo paddle-boats** on the lake across the walkway ($5 per person for 20 minutes).

> ## Hook the Trainers
>
> To get the most out of a visit, try to be in the same place as the animal trainers, who frequently appear to nurture their charges. Ask questions. Get involved. They may even allow you to feed or stroke the animals (set aside another $25 or so for fish food). These zoologists love sharing information about the animals they have devoted their lives to. Feeding times are usually posted outside each pavilion's entrance; you may need to backtrack a few times to make the schedule, but the interaction will be worth the effort.

Manta ★★★ RIDE   Rising above the park is SeaWorld's thrill-ride pride, a "flying coaster" ridden face-down and head-first, in a horizontal position. You board sitting upright, and after your shoulders and ankles are secured, you're tipped forward and the train is dispatched over curious pedestrians for the 2½-minute ride. The queue meanders through 10 aquaria containing cow-nose rays, spotted eagle rays, and octopi behind floor-to-ceiling windows, so you get a dose of sea life while you wait. Even nonriders can see rays through a separate entrance to the right of the ride's line. Speeds approach 60mph, with four inversions, in a fanciful approximation of what it feels like for a manta ray to swim. Manta is a pretty unique coaster experience, and it's solid fun. *Strategy:* Lockers are $1 to $1.50 in quarters; there's a change machine. There's an unattended basket on the platform for loose items you don't use the lockers for. Because you're in "flying" position, no seat has an obstructed view.

The Kraken End of the Park

Journey to Atlantis ★★ RIDE   On this 6-minute flume-cum-coaster ride (you can't see the brief coaster section from the front), getting drenched is unavoidable, as the 60-foot drop should warn. Riding isn't its only pleasure—it's fun to douse passing boats with coin-operated water cannons, too (Number 4 does the most damage to the unsuspecting). Atlantis is incoherent but fun. First you pass through a few rooms as if you're on a family-friendly

dark ride (the robotics aren't great), and then one of the spirits turns against you, sending you down the hill you saw outside, and finally the water gives way and your boat becomes, briefly, a roller-coaster car that escapes the evil sprite with no upside-down moments but yet another splashdown. Besides the drenching you can witness from outside, there are a few other lap soakers and delightfully nasty splashbacks—ideal for hot days. *Strategy:* Front seats get wettest. Try to balance the weight; otherwise you'll list disconcertingly. Keep stuff dry in a nearby locker ($1/hr., credit cards accepted), and leave it there when you ride Kraken next door. Ponchos are sold nearby for $9; $8 for kids.

Journey to Atlantis.

Kraken ★★★ RIDE   Take a 2-minute dose of testosterone. After you settle into your pedestal-like seat, the floor is retracted, dangling your legs while you undergo seven upside-down "inversions" of one sort or another. The

Antarctica: Empire of the Penguin.

coaster, which hits 65mph and drops 144 feet on its first breath-stealing hill, traces the shoreline of a pond behind the loading area and dives below ground level three times. *Strategy:* If you'd like to wait for a front seat, there's a special, longer line for it. Because it's floorless, you can't ride with flip-flops, but you may leave shoes on the loading dock and go barefoot (if you do that in the front row, which I recommend, you'll feel like you're about to lose a foot in the rails). Lockers cost 4 quarters; there's a change machine. Better yet, use one locker for both this and Journey to Atlantis next door.

Antarctica: Empire of the Penguin ★★ ACTIVITY/RIDE SeaWorld's 2013 addition was this 4-acre, iceberg-styled pavilion dedicated to penguins. View a colony of 245 Gentoo, Rockhopper, Adélie, and King birds in a human-temperature room with a fascinating underwater viewing of the little birds zipping around underwater and from a 30-degree area where they waddle helplessly on dry land. The ride is pointless but you have to take it (and endure the awful line) to get in: It's based on some cool trackless technology that allows cars, which will remind you of air hockey pucks, to roam the same room, even cross paths. Choose "Wild" or "Mild," although the wild version isn't much more intense than a few light spins. Don't confuse this exhibition with Wild Arctic, which contains the beluga whales. There are large lockers by the exit with a change machine, but they're often full.

Pacific Point Preserve ★★★ ACTIVITY Like Dolphin Cove, Pacific Point is an open-air, rocky habitat that encourages feedings, but here the residents are incessantly barking Californian sea lions and a few demure seals. There's a narrow moat between the tank and the walkway, but you're encouraged to lean over and toss the doglike animals fresh fish, which are sold for $5 per tray, $20 for five. More often than not, marauding birds snatch what you toss. The area gets busy around Clyde and Seamore showtimes at the neighboring Sea Lion & Otter Theater.

Shark Encounter ★★★ ACTIVITY   The onetime Terrors of the Deep was given a more responsible name to further rehabilitate the public image of the much-maligned creatures within. It's one of the better exhibitions, with 60-foot acrylic tubes passing through 300,000 gallons of water stocked with sharks—the crowds are ushered along via moving sidewalks. Too many tourists scamper quickly through the smaller tanks before that dazzling main event, but they're missing some beautiful stuff, including barracuda, moray eels, lionfish, and the awesome leafy sea dragon, which looks for all the world like a floating clump of seaweed. Don't ignore the shallow tank in front of the building, because that's where the smaller species are kept. There, you can feed rays and tarpon shrimp for $5 a tray, two for $9, three for $13, and five for $20.

The Waterfront at SeaWorld

Sky Tower ★★★ OBSERVATION RIDE   Jutting above the lagoon—and topped to still-greater heights by a colossal American flag—is the 400-foot, old-fashioned "Wheel-o-vater" (that's what its interior label says) that rotates as it climbs 300 feet for a panorama. At the top, it slowly spins for two or three revolutions, giving you a good look around, before lowering you back to the Waterfront at the end of 6 minutes. You can point out the landmarks, including Spaceship Earth and the skyscrapers of downtown.

Shamu Stadium ★ ACTIVITY   The home to One Ocean has something to offer outside of show time. A few of the killer whales are visible in the viewing area (accessed from the lakefront) that surveys one of their holding pods. Above the surface of that pen, the **Dine with Shamu ★★** supper (p. 164) is held, separated by netting from the water (reserve several weeks ahead).

Shamu's Happy Harbor ★★ ACTIVITY   Behind Shamu Stadium, kids have their own amusement area—and they get more rides than the grown-ups! The most obvious feature is the four-story cargo-net playground, but there are some and mild carnival-style rides: an underwater-themed **Sea Carousel ★** topped by a 45-foot-wide pink octopus; a swinging-and-twirling tracked boat ride, **Ocean Commotion ★**; and the **Flying Fiddler ★★**, a bench that lifts kids 20 feet above the ground and then gently brings them back down in a series of short drops. Those rides join an 800-foot kiddie coaster with trains shaped like you-know-who (**Shamu Express ★★**), a ride with spinning cars attached to a stalk (**Jazzy Jellies** ★), a pirate ship (**Wahoo Two** ★) that doesn't do much, the teacup-style (**Swishy Fishies** ★★★), and the **Seven Seas Railway** ★★ tiny train, where it's fun to make Daddy squish into the caboose.

The Shamu End of the Park

Wild Arctic ★★ ACTIVITY/RIDE   One of SeaWorld's most interesting exhibitions deserves more attention than it gets marooned here, at the Nowhereseville end of the park, when the only time it seems crowded is a half-hour after every Shamu showtime. There are two ways to get in. Either you opt for the motion-simulator ride that re-creates a turbulent 5-minute helicopter ride (an old ride, and its bumpiness makes me ill), or you much more quickly make straight for the swimmers after a short movie. After that, you can walk through at your own pace, enjoying first a surface view and then an underwater look at the Pacific walruses, and the parks' utterly beautiful white beluga whales, which look like swimming porcelain. There are not currently any polar bears; the last elderly one died in 2014 and has not been replaced. There's probably more than a half-hour's worth of investigation here, including mock-ups of a polar research station and a fake "bear den" for young kids to explore. You'll also find it *very* cool, which makes it a must on hot days.

Where to Eat at SeaWorld

In case you were wondering, SeaWorld only serves sustainable seafood. There are also always vegetarian options. Prices are in line with everyone else's: $10 a meal, before a drink, is standard. Most places to eat are clustered in the center between the Waterfront and Kraken. **All-Day Dining Deals** (one entree, one side or dessert, one nonalcoholic drink each time through line) cost $35 for adults and $20 for kids; they're good at six of the counter-service locations.

Disney World has its Mouse-ear ice-cream bar, but at SeaWorld, you'll be served a variety shaped like Shamu ($3.80). Plastic drinking straws could choke the aquatic animals, so you don't get one.

The headline meal event is **Dine with Shamu** ★★, served from noon to 2pm in peak summer and from 4:30 to 6:30pm in other seasons alongside the orca pools with the narration of trainers. Prices fluctuate by the day, but expect $34–44 for adults and $20–34 for kids. That's not bad to be near one of these massive creatures. It's important to book far ahead.

The newest counter-service spot is **Expedition Café** ★★★, with non-A/C seating outside Antarctica, which, like the Antarctic Research Station, serves food from many cultures: baked chicken, shrimp lo mein, gluten-free teriyaki chicken, spaghetti and meatballs, meatless lasagna, and "iceberg chef" salad.

The **Terrace BBQ** ★, slinging lackluster ribs and barbecue chicken ($12–$16), is past Mako and to the right. It's in the old Hospitality House, where guests got free beer when the park was owned by Anheuser-Busch. Out front, don't miss the huge sculptures of sea life made out of plastic trash skimmed out of the ocean by the group WashedAshore.org. The other main restaurants serve high-quality food, too, but with less caloric regard. **The Seafire Café ★★★**, at the Waterfront, has some seating overlooking the lagoon and does fajitas, rice bowls, and salads. Farther up the Waterfront but with similar prices, the **Spice Mill Burgers ★★** does stuff such as steak burgers, Buffalo chicken sandwiches, and chicken Caesar salad, and it also has pretty water views. **Voyagers Smokehouse ★**, facing the Seaport Theatre's entrance, offers baby back ribs, spare ribs, and barbecue chicken, with a higher top price of $17. Nearby, **Lakeside Panini Bistro ★** serves at outdoor patio seating.

Like Epcot's The Seas, the park devotes a section of an underwater viewing area to **Sharks Underwater Grill & Bar ★**, one of the park's premier tables. It doesn't particularly specialize in seafood. Despite some cute touches, such as a bar that's also an aquarium and chairs that look like sharks' teeth, prices like $30 for tempura shrimp and $29 for chicken portabella strike me as too high (salads are $12). But if you can square that with the incredible view, give it a shot. Some tables are right against the glass, but I think I prefer the ones farther back, which have a wider view. For snacks, I suggest the **Cypress Bakery ★★★**, near the entrance, for ginormous muffins and cheesecake slices.

SeaWorld participates in the gruesome Orlando tradition of huge roasted turkey legs. Find them for $11 at Seaport Market, near Seaport Pizza (where you buy weak $8 pizzas slices) and at the Smugglers Feasts booth near Seafire Inn. Captain Pete's Island Hot Dogs in the Key West area has foot-longs such as one with key lime slaw ($9). At the Shamu end of the boardwalk, **Mango Joe's Cafe ★★** does a short menu of burgers and mango chicken salad ($10–13).

At the base of the Sky Tower, the Sand Bar does happy hour from 1pm–3pm.

Backstage Tours

As a place that prides itself on sharing conservation information—in fact, as a place that keeps animals on display, its reputation depends on it—**SeaWorld** (www.seaworldorlando.com; ✆ **800/327-2424**) offers **Exclusive Park Experiences** that are less about touting its vaunted design team, as Disney's are, and more for learning about animal care. In fact, they're dubbed "interactions." Because interactions sell out, always reserve—it can be done online, and prices vary per season—but if you forget, there's a Behind-the-Scenes desk at the entry plaza of the park for last-minute arrangements. Interactions that involve swimming include a wetsuit and equipment, and end with a private, hot shower. There are about 10 to choose from, from an on-dry-land dolphin meet to a sea lion spotlight, but these two are probably the most unforgettable experiences.

Beluga Interaction Program ★★★ ACTIVITY Opportunities to squeeze into a wet suit and swim for 30 minutes in 55°F saltwater with the porcelain-white beluga whales simply don't come often. Participants don't have to be excellent swimmers, but they should be able to tread water, because they'll be maneuvering themselves in a deep tank to stroke and feed the gentle animals. Only about a half-hour is spent in the water; the rest of your visit, you'll become a pocket expert on belugas.

From $120 per person, not including park admission. Minimum age 10. 90 min.

Marine Mammal Keeper Experience ★★★ ACTIVITY The *ne plus ultra* for a SeaWorld or animal fan starts at 6:30am and leads you through a typical day for an animal keeper. The schedule may include food preparation (get ready for fishy fingers); helping the Animal Rescue and Rehabilitation Team look after manatees; standing over the vets' shoulders as they heal sick animals; and helping trainers interact with and train dolphins, sea lions, or belugas. This is no put-on for shuffling bus tours; you participate in the work the day calls for, and there's a limit of just three people. Many people who have done this swear that it's money better spent than a ticket to Discovery Cove; you'll get in the water to care for dolphins and manatees, but you won't grab onto their fins for any gimmicky "swims."

From $399, including lunch, T-shirt, and park admission for a week. Minimum age 13. 9 hr.

SeaWorld's Other Parks

Aquatica ★ SeaWorld's water slide park is across International Drive from its parent park (a free, 3-min. van ride links it), and you can pay for admission as an add-on to your SeaWorld visit. While Typhoon Lagoon and Blizzard Beach are heavily themed, and Wet 'n Wild is tangled with bare-boned thrills, Aquatica is merely colorful and tropical. It's a perfectly nice park, but the others have more tricks. The company entices tourists to swim with the fishes on the **Dolphin Plunge** slide, a tube that curls off a tower and then turns clear acrylic as it passes through a habitat for Commerson's dolphins. It looks exciting on paper, but in truth you're going too fast to see anything, even if the dolphins could be reliably near the tubes (they aren't)

Aquatica waterslide park.

and there wasn't water splashing in your eyes (there is). There are nearly two dozen major slides, many of them similar to each other, and the newest of which is **Ihu's Breakaway Falls,** three curling slides that you begin by standing eight stories up in a shower-sized chamber on a floor that gives way, dropping you onto the ride. The pleasantly aggressive lazy river of **Loggerhead Lane** passes you by a big window into an aquarium. **Roa's Rapids** is novel in that it's a river with a very fast current meant to sweep your body along, without a tube. It's all fine, not scintillating, and bears the whiff of having been scaled down from something more notable. Aquatica does run with a smart, picnicky idea when it comes to meals: You can pay $20 adults, $15 kids for unlimited fare at the all-you-can-eat **Banana Beach** (bad chicken, pizza, hot dogs). Otherwise, **Mango Market** sells chicken tenders and sandwiches for the usual $11 per-meal price. If you're bringing a picnic, stick to snack-sized bags; large ones will be confiscated and so will straws of any kind, which choke animals.

5800 Water Play Way, Orlando. www.aquaticabyseaworld.com. © **888/800-5447.** Adults $57, kids 3–9 $52, online tickets $10 less, discounts for combination SeaWorld tickets, parking $13, $12 online.

Discovery Cove ★★★ THEME PARK   The most expensive park in town (prices shift by the season) is an all-inclusive experience. Only around 1,000 people a day are admitted, guaranteeing this faux tropical idyll is not marred by a single queue. You can stop reading now if you don't want to get jealous—this is strictly a place for special occasions (or people spending strong foreign cash). Admission lanyards include breakfast, equipment rental, sunscreen, beer if you're of age, and unlimited lunch—a good one, too, with options such as fresh grilled tilapia (a fish that drew the short straw at SeaWorld, I guess). Discovery Cove, in fact, is more or less a free-range playground. When you arrive, first thing in the morning, you're greeted under a vaulted atrium more redolent of a five-star island resort than a theme park. Coffee is poured, and

Dolphins in Discovery Cove.

once you're checked in you're set loose to do as you wish. Wade from perfect white sand into **Serenity Bay,** feed fresh fruit to the houseguests at the **Explorer's Aviary** for tropical birds, snorkel with barbless rays over the trenches of **The Grand Reef,** swim to habitats for marmoset monkeys and otters in the **Freshwater Oasis,** or float with a pool noodle down the slow-floating **Wind-Away River,** which passes through waterfalls into the aviary, preventing the birds from escaping. Many guests elect to simply kick back on a lounger (there are plenty) on incredibly silky sand (imported, of course) at the natural-looking pool. Since everyone wears free wetsuits or vests, there isn't much call for body shame or sunburned shoulders. When it's your turn—if you've paid extra—guests older than 5 can head to the **Dolphin Lagoon,** where in small groups of about eight you wade into the chilly water and meet one of the pod. Like children, dolphins have distinct personalities and must be carefully paired to people the trainers think they'll enjoy being with—many visitors don't realize that a dolphin can easily kill you, but many of these dolphins are docile, having dwelled at SeaWorld for decades. Here, the mostly hand-reared animals peer at you with a logician's eye while your trainer shows you basic hand signals. The climax of the 30-minute interaction is the moment when you grasp two of the creature's fins and it swims, you in tow, for about 30 feet. Naturally, a photographer is on hand for it all, so if you want images or video, you'll pay for that, too, pushing a day over $400. A second add-on experience, **SeaVenture** ($59, minimum age 10), places an air helmet on your head and brings you underwater to walk along the floor of The Grand Reef. Really, though, a day here is beyond divine.

6000 Discovery Cove Way, Orlando. www.discoverycove.com. ℂ **877/557-7404.** Price changes with the seasons, but ranges are $169–$269, including free admission to Sea-World and Aquatica for 2 weeks, plus $60–$190 for 30-min. dolphin interaction. Daily 8am–5:30pm.

LEGOLAND FLORIDA

Legoland Florida ★★★, a 2011 newcomer, is not just the youngest Central Florida theme park. It's also the oldest. That's because it took over the historic property of Cypress Gardens, a park for botanical gardens and water ski shows on the cypress tree-lined shores of pretty Lake Eloise that helped put Orlando on modern tourist maps. For a glimpse of what things were like in the glory days, see Esther Williams's jaw-dropping heli-water-ski production number in MGM's "Easy to Love" (1953). Today, this extremely kid-friendly, soothingly mellow 150-acre park 45 minutes south of Disney World is a godsend for parents who crave a breather from the mechanical and authoritarian environment of Disney World. No other Florida park caters so completely to kids aged 2 to 12. Everything here is designed for little ones, from easy-to-tackle versions of adult rides to ample wide spaces for play—and somehow, its energy is not stressful on parents. For young families, there's nothing better.

Get your bearings, and take in the stirring views of the lake, on the **Island in the Sky** observation wheel, which reaches into the sky on a metal arm. Other

Legoland.

park highlights include **Lost Kingdom Adventure,** an indoor target practice game in the style of a Lego-bright Indiana Jones tomb; easygoing boat tour **The Quest for Chi; Coaster-saurus,** a mild out-and-back wooden roller coaster suitable for grammar school lightweights; **DUPLO Valley** for toddler rides; **Driving School,** the Ford-sponsored, trackless mini-auto course that teaches kids how to obey traffic rules; **Project X,** a wild mouse coaster perfectly situated for nonriders to take embarrassing shots of loved ones' faces as they hurtle downhill; **Safari Trek,** a wholly adorable car ride past wild African animals made of Legos; and **Royal Joust,** a mini steeplechase-style plastic horse race for wee ones that just may be the cutest ride in the whole country. For a break from the excitement, the **Imagination Zone** as indoor Lego-building play zones and video game stations, and past that, a healthy portion of the carefully tended **Cypress Gardens Historic Botanical Garden** was preserved, complete with Spanish moss, cypress knees jutting from tannic water, old-growth banyans, and signs warning of alligators, which live in the lake. Suddenly, you remember you're in Florida, which is sad, considering Florida made its tourist name by selling its natural wonders. For all that, and lots more like it, nothing competes with the fascination of **Miniland,** the sprawling tour de force display of Lego construction prowess that mounts exceedingly clever versions of American cities and landmarks. The longer you linger, the more touches you see: a moving escalator in a mock-up Grand

Safari in Legoland.

PAST THAT turnstile IN THE SKY

Not all of Orlando's attractions have thrived. Tupperware Museum, we miss you. Kindly remove your Mouse ears to honor the forgotten fun—if not for an accident of time, you'd be vacationing here instead:

- **Circus World (1974–86):** Started by Mattel as a walk-through museum dedicated to circus history (after all, most of the big top crews wintered in Florida), it collapsed under its own weight after competition with Disney tempted it into building too many rides. Also, clowns are scary.

- **Boardwalk Baseball (1987–90):** Textbook publisher Harcourt, Brace and Jovanovich recycled Circus World in the image of Florida's other winter tradition, baseball, and the Kansas City Royals were enticed to train there. Few cared. On January 17, 1990, 1,000 guests were asked to leave.

- **Xanadu (1983–96):** This walk-through "home of the future" was made by coating giant balloons with polyurethane—an early exercise in ergonomics. Sister homes in Gatlinburg and Wisconsin Dells were also built, but all outlived their curiosity value, and

became, in fact, quick homes of the past. You'll find the site near Mile Marker 12 of U.S. 192.

- **JungleLand Zoo (1995–2002):** The demise of this low-rent Gatorland rip-off was hastened in 1997 when a lioness went missing among Kissimmee's motels for 3 days. A few trainers got nipped by the gators, too. Bad news.

- **Splendid China (1993–2003):** On 73 acres 3 miles west of Disney's main gate, China's wonders (the Forbidden City, a Great Wall segment containing 6.5 million bricks, and so on) were rebuilt in miniature. Who would blow $100 million on such a bad idea? The Chinese government, which pulled the strings.

- **River Country (1976–2005):** Disney's first water park, incorporated into Bay Lake beside the Fort Wilderness Resort, simply wasn't fancy enough or big enough to satisfy guests anymore. Another issue: It turns out that the *Naegleria fowleri* amoebae growing in many Florida lakes can kill you. (Guests may no longer swim in *any* of Disney's lakes. Coincidence?)

Central Station, a Space Shuttle misting during takeoff, dueling pirate ships, a mini "Star Wars" cantina, the Bellagio's burping fountain, and marching bands in front of the Capitol. If you like those gags, stick around for the **Pirates' Cove Live Water Ski Show,** which replaces Cypress Gardens' pyramids of maidens with ski-jumping socket-headed Minifigure toy people. On top of all that, there's a modest **Legoland Water Park** (summers and warm-season weekends) next door. The park offers $10 round-trip shuttles from I-Drive 360, home of sister attraction The Orlando Eye (© 877/350-5346). Because it closes by evening, arrive near opening time to get the most out of a day.

1 Legoland Way, Winter Haven. http://florida.legoland.com. © **877/350-5346.** Admission $89 adults, $82 kids 3–12, discounts $10–15 online; parking $17 ($15 online). Open daily 10am to 5pm–8pm, depending on the day, closed Tues–Wed outside of high season.

Cheetah Hunt ride at Busch Gardens.

BUSCH GARDENS TAMPA

Seventy miles southwest of Disney, and just 8 miles northwest of Tampa, **Busch Gardens Tampa ★★★** (3000 E. Busch Blvd., at 40th St.; www.buschgardens.com; © **888/800-5447**), dating to 1959, is a world-class theme park combining thrill rides with top-notch animal enclosures for gorillas, rhinos, and other rare creatures. Each year it adds another spectacular coaster. New for 2014 was the terrifying **Falcon's Fury,** America's tallest drop tower that sends riders plummeting face-down, and 2016 sees **Cobra's Curse,** a novel steel coaster in which the cars spin as they race up to 70 feet into the air. Other detour-worthy roller coasters include the vertical drop of **SheiKra** and the sidewinding launch coaster **Cheetah Hunt.** If the coaster wars were an arms race, Busch Gardens easily annihilates all of Orlando's efforts, yet relatively few tourists make the 75-minute trip here—and that's a shame. The park knows coaxing visitors from Orlando is a problem, so it grants **free round-trip coach transportation** from many Orlando hotels with a ticket (© **800/221-1339**).

Admission to the park is $95 adults, $90 for kids 3 to 9, with $15–$30 discounts available online for pre-purchase or weekday entry. A 3 Park Unlimited Admission Ticket from SeaWorld also comes with a free round-trip bus ride from SeaWorld to Busch Gardens, and entry to both parks and Aquatica; it costs $149 adults and $141 kids when bought online. Busch Gardens also discounts its entry in the six-park version of the discounted Orlando FlexTicket (p. 299).

MORE ORLANDO ATTRACTIONS

When you're sick of parking trams and cattle queues, divert yourself with something new. Actually, something old—some of these places are among the original attractions that created the fertile vacationland Central Florida is today. Some are beautiful, some are downright silly, but when you're on vacation, anything goes.

INTERNATIONAL DRIVE

The attractions around International Drive aren't plush—midways and sideshows, mostly—but they are the stuff of a quintessential family holiday and they won't break the bank. I-Drive is the only touristy area in Orlando where a car isn't necessary, not least because the I-Ride Trolley (p. 293) will tote you along, if you're tired of strolling.

CSI: The Experience ★ ACTIVITY   Scrutinizing a gory murder scene: fun for the whole family! Turning tragedy into popcorn, this CBS-authorized whodunit turns you loose on one of three dioramas of slain corpses. You observe the details as closely as possible before taking your findings to a few touch-screen stations where you learn how investigators use forensics to find clues to crimes. Here's a sample line from one video, which features actors from the shows: "Ah, the smell of decaying flesh . . . It's an irresistible aroma to insects!" The satisfaction of solving the crime (it takes about 45 min.) may suit some visitors, although they may also have seen these facts addressed a hundred times in TV episodes. The attraction's cheap convention-chair seating and Xeroxed handouts make it seem like it could skip town in an hour.

7220 International Dr., Orlando. Orlando. www.CSIexhibit.com. ✆ **407/226-7220.** $20 adults, $13 kids 6–11. Mon–Sat 10am–9pm, Sun 10am–8pm, last admission 45 min. before closing.

Fun Spot America–Orlando ★ AMUSEMENT PARK   A recent recipient of immense investment and careful improvements, Fun Spot in Orlando, at the top of I-Drive, is Orlando's largest (15 acres), cleanest, best-lit midway-style diversion. Although it became famous for its four Go-Kart tracks (concrete, multilevel; the Quad Helix's stacked figure-eight turns make it a favorite, but the Conquest's peaked ramp is a pip), the spacious grounds are also

Orlando Area Attractions

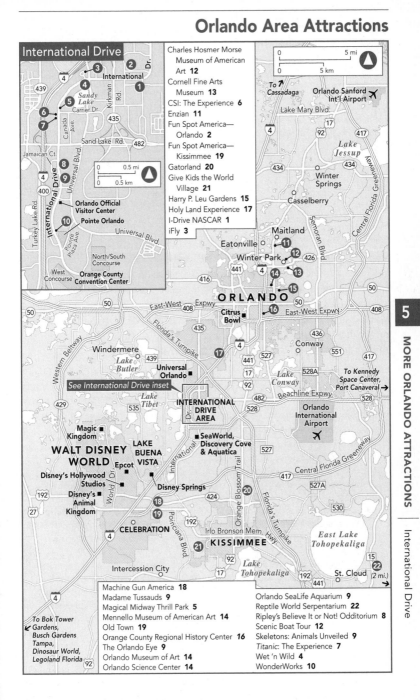

International Drive

Sandy Lake
Carrier Dr.
Kirkman Rd.
International Dr.
Canada Ave.
Sand Lake Rd.
Jamaica Ct.
Universal Blvd.
Turkey Lake Rd.
International Drive
Pointe Plaza Ave.
Orlando Official Visitor Center
Pointe Orlando
Universal Blvd.
West Concourse
North/South Concourse
Orange County Convention Center

0   0.5 mi
0   0.5 km

439
4
435
482
400
4

Charles Hosmer Morse Museum of American Art **12**
Cornell Fine Arts Museum **13**
CSI: The Experience **6**
Enzian **11**
Fun Spot America—Orlando **2**
Fun Spot America—Kissimmee **19**
Gatorland **20**
Give Kids the World Village **21**
Harry P. Leu Gardens **15**
Holy Land Experience **17**
I-Drive NASCAR **1**
iFly **3**

0   5 mi
0   5 km

To Cassadaga
Orlando Sanford Int'l Airport
Lake Mary Blvd.
Lake Jessup
Winter Springs
Casselberry
Semoran Blvd.
Central Florida Greeneway
Maitland
Eatonville
Winter Park
ORLANDO
Citrus Bowl
East-West Expwy
Conway
Windermere
Lake Butler
Universal Orlando
Lake Conway
To Kennedy Space Center, Port Canaveral
Beachline Expwy.
Orlando International Airport
See International Drive inset
Lake Tibet
INTERNATIONAL DRIVE AREA
Western Beltway
Magic Kingdom
WALT DISNEY WORLD
Epcot
LAKE BUENA VISTA
SeaWorld, Discovery Cove & Aquatica
Disney's Hollywood Studios
Disney Springs
Disney's Animal Kingdom
CELEBRATION
Machine Gun America
Irlo Bronson Mem. Hwy.
KISSIMMEE
Intercession City
Lake Tohopekaliga
East Lake Tohopekaliga
St. Cloud (2 mi.)
Florida's Turnpike
Orange Blossom Trail
Poinciana Blvd.
Central Florida Greeneway
To Bok Tower Gardens, Busch Gardens Tampa, Dinosaur World, Legoland Florida

439 4 435 416 50 408 50 4 527 441 17 92 528A 482 528 527 417 527A 530 424 192 27 424 92 17 192 441 15 22

Machine Gun America **18**
Madame Tussauds **9**
Magical Midway Thrill Park **5**
Mennello Museum of American Art **14**
Old Town **19**
Orange County Regional History Center **16**
The Orlando Eye **9**
Orlando Museum of Art **14**
Orlando Science Center **14**

Orlando SeaLife Aquarium **9**
Reptile World Serpentarium **22**
Ripley's Believe It or Not! Odditorium **8**
Scenic Boat Tour **12**
Skeletons: Animals Unveiled **9**
Titanic: The Experience **7**
Wet 'n Wild **4**
WonderWorks **10**

stocked with a two-level arcade, a scrambler, plenty of snack bars, a Ferris wheel (Charlize Theron rode it in "Monster"), and a section of kiddie rides. There's also **White Lightning,** a smooth-as-silk wood-frame coaster that goes out and back; **Freedom Flyer,** a wee version of a hanging, foot-dangling train; and a few alligators on loan from Gatorland. The 250-foot-tall SkyCoaster is the second-tallest (the first is at Fun Spot's lesser location in Kissimmee, p. 187).

5700 Fun Spot Way, Orlando. www.fun-spot.com. © **407/363-3867.** Pay-per-ride $6–$9, unlimited ride armband $30–$40 based on height. Generally daily 10am–midnight, winter weekdays noon or 2pm–midnight

I-Drive NASCAR ★ THRILL RIDE   New in 2015 was this go-kart track (a half mile, 12 turns, 3 of them hairpin), snack bar, and arcade. It's Orlando's only indoor track, but the vehicles are the thing: silent electric carts that go 45 mph with state-of-the-art shock absorption, adjustable steering and seats.

5228 Vanguard St., Orlando. www.idrivenascar.com. © **844/437-4831.** $25 for 16 times around. No open-toed shoes. Sun–Thurs 11am–10pm, Fri–Sat 10am–midnight.

iFly ★ ACTIVITY   Surprisingly, there seem to be as many hobby skydivers training in this vertical wind tunnel as there are curious out-of-towners. Visitors are strapped into jumpsuits and given a short training session on how to walk over the netting into the 125mph airflow. Mastering the necessary arched-back, splay-legged posture can be tricky, but should you fail, there's a master diver with you to grab you by the sleeve and guide you into a series of

The Future of Fun, or Flops?

Announcements of new mega-projects are dirt-common in Orlando, but now and then, a developer actually manages to break ground. Spurred by the opening of the Orlando Eye, announcements of epic development are flying. I-Drive can barely handle the traffic during big conventions now, so this will be interesting:

Skyscraper at SkyPlex Orlando (2017): The $460 million project on the northwest corner of the intersection of I-Drive and Sand Lake Road would add a 500-foot tower around which an Intamin-made roller coaster will coil, going speeds of up to 50mph, on about a mile of track. There'll be a free-fall ride, a hotel, a zip line, a huge Perkins restaurant, and a surf park, too.

iSquare Mall + Hotel (2017): 600 hotel rooms (100 of them ultra-luxury) and a shopping center have been announced for 5⅔ acres at International Drive and Kirkman Road at a cost of $300–$400 million.

The StarFlyer: A 420-foot-tall spinning swing ride was announced for a development called Vue at 360, beside the Eye, back in 2014.

Actions Sports & Entertainment Resort: This one was announced in early 2015 for Kissimmee at the junction of S.R. 535 and US. 192: a $309 million resort with an indoor 14-story ski mountain, snowboard tubing lanes, skateboard park, two skydiving pods, river rapids, zip lining, hotel, amphitheater, and a 20,000-square-foot dodgeball area.

And if you believe these will work, did you hear the one about the animator who wanted to build an amusement park dedicated to a talking mouse?

Madame Tussauds.

adrenaline-fueled climbs and plunges. Or not—you can just hover there, if that's what floats your butt.

6805 Visitor Circle, Orlando. http://orlando.iflyworld.com. *℗* **407/903-1150** or 407/903-1150. $60 for 2 1-minute flights, $100 for 4. Daily 10am–10pm.

Madame Tussauds ★★ TOURIST MUSEUM   The world-famous wax museum opened its Orlando outpost in 2015 in **I-Drive 360,** a complex of shops and restaurants. It's so silly and pleasantly touristy that it's astounding it took so long. First, they try to get you to pose for an Everglades-theme tourist photo, but skip that, because Tussauds is already essentially one extended photo op. As you go from room to room, you get right beside the few dozen full-size figures of current and historical celebrities, many of which are so lifelike that you'll be astounded (Obama, Taylor Swift, Jim Parsons), and some so off the mark you have to check the signage to tell who it is (Madonna, Katy Perry). If the sign says they were "sculpted from a sitting" rather than merely "portrayed," you know it's more accurate. Midway through, you can pay $15 to create a wax cast of your own hand—protect it from the Florida heat thereafter if you do.

I-Drive 360, 8387 International Dr., Orlando. www.madametussauds.com/orlando. *℗* **866/630-8315.** $25 adult, $20 child 3–12 ($5 discount online); $39 adult, $35 child with the Orlando Eye or SeaLife Aquarium; $49 adult, $45 child for all three attractions. Free parking. Daily 10am–midnight.

The Orlando Eye.

Magical Midway Thrill Park ★
AMUSEMENT PARK This small concrete area is built on adrenaline and rash decisions, blaring with rock music and heaving with idle youth. The most obvious generator of regret is the world's tallest **Slingshot** ride ($25, not included on passes), a colossal fork strung with a pod. Two at a time sit inside and are catapulted more than 200 feet into the sky, wailing to wake the dead. Meanwhile, the skyscraping circular swing carousel **Star Flyer** ($7) is scarier than it looks because the chains feel inadequate for its 230-foot height—flimsy restraints being a necessary component of carnival thrills. The rest is dominated by two thunderous, wooden Go-Kart tracks (the Avalanche track has slightly steeper ramps than the Alpine), a few minor rides (cheerless bumper boats), and a dirty arcade. Its unsophisticated virtues are something 11-year-old boys idolize.

7001 International Dr., Orlando. www.magicalmidway.com. ✆ **407/370-5353.** $7 Go-Kart rides, $3 midway rides, 3-hr. unlimited rides $25, all-day unlimited $32. Sun–Fri 2–10pm, Fri–Sat 2pm–midnight.

The Orlando Eye ★★ AMUSEMENT PARK After enduring a regrettable, stand-up "4D Experience" (a mindless green-screen 3D film of aerial footage of Orlando—Disney's noticeably absent—that peppers you with mist), you board 15-passenger pods for your slightly quivering ride on the East Coast's tallest (400 feet) observation wheel, which is constantly spinning at 1 mph for a 30-minute rotation. But here's the thing: There's almost nothing to look at except the flat roofs of I-Drive's businesses, the gated Lockheed Martin facility across the street, and the spires of Hogwarts at Universal Orlando, two miles north. It's pretty enough, but any city would be at that height. You have to know where to look (southwest) to spot Spaceship Earth or other Disney landmarks, and they're at a considerable distance. Fun ride, odd spot.

I-Drive 360, 8401 International Dr., Orlando. www.officialorlandoeye.com. ✆ **407/370-5353.** $25 adult, $20 child 3–12 (25% off online if booked at least 1 day ahead); $39 adult, $35 child to add Madame Tussauds or SeaLife Aquarium; $49 adult, $45 child for all three attractions. Free parking. Sun–Thurs 10am–10pm, Fri–Sat 10am–midnight.

Orlando SeaLife Aquarium ★ AQUARIUM The McDonald's of aquaria has some four dozen locations worldwide, and it's such a success because it's fairly well-stocked, theatrically lit, and charmingly designed: There are clear walkway tubes passing through huge tanks, for example, and kids can crawl under the moray eel habitat and see from "inside" the tank through bubble-like head spaces popping through its floor. SeaLife angles for kids in particular, what with the annoying voices of anthropomorphic fish delivering factual tidbits on the loudspeakers and the chipper docents sticking religiously to a corporate-approved script ("Here's your Discovery Fact of the day!") that pummels you with boasts about its good deeds of conservation. Concluding the self-guided tour of the 5,000-plus creatures (including jelly-fish, small sharks, and clownfish) there's a shallow touch tank where kids can pet live starfish. Adults will be satisfied in 30 minutes, but kids might prefer an hour.

I-Drive 360, 8387 International Dr., Orlando. www.visitsealife.com/orlando. ℭ **407/370-5353.** $25 adult, $20 child 3–12 ($5 discount online); $39 adult, $35 child to add the Orlando Eye or Madame Tussauds; $49 adult, $45 child for all three attractions. Free parking. Daily 10am–10pm, last admission 1 hr. before closing.

Ripley's Believe It or Not! Odditorium ★ TOURIST MUSEUM   The ticketed equivalent of a forwarded e-mail joke, Ripley's is well-maintained and clean, but it's too expensive for the thin diversion it delivers. Mostly it consists of optical illusions, vaguely ominous specimens from foreign cultures, panels from the old Ripley's comic (does anyone under 60 even remember those?), and the odd coin-operated device. There are too many signs and fewer artifacts than you'll be expecting, unless you count a portrait of Beyoncé made out of candy. Don't set foot in it without harvesting coupons from any tourist brochure.

8201 International Dr., Orlando. www.ripleys.com/orlando. ℭ **407/345-0501.** $20 adults, $13 kids 4–12, $3 discounts online. 4–12; daily 9am–midnight, last entry 11pm.

Titanic: **The Experience.**

Skeletons: Animals Unveiled ★★ TOURIST MUSEUM   It sounds awful, and the macabre, tchotchke-crammed gift shop entry beside the Orlando Eye doesn't do much to disabuse you of that dread, but hidden within is a thoughtful and diverse museum of more than 400 animal skeletons huge and small, many mounted in detailed habitats with the right touch of whimsy. All of them were collected and painstakingly prepared by an osteological outfit in Oklahoma City, where an earlier version proved popular enough to warrant export here. It's a particular fascination for kids into science or anatomy. What a lucky break—an Orlando attraction that actually nourishes young minds!

I-Drive 360, 8441 International Dr., Orlando. www.skeletonmuseum.com. ℭ **407/203-6999.** $20 adult, $13 child 3–11. Free parking. Daily 10am–10pm.

***Titanic*: The Experience** ★★ TOURIST MUSEUM   More than 100 genuine artifacts from the *Titanic* itself—a teak deck chair to cookware to tile fragments to a boarding card—give this permanent exhibition salt. For those interested in the topic, this theatrically presented museum, which walks guests chronologically from boarding to the abbreviated voyage to rediscovery, provides a balanced dossier of the sorry tale. There's a little conflation of Hollywood storytelling with history (at the replica of the First Class Grand Staircase, a piano rendition of "My Heart Will Go On" repeats *ad nauseam*), but there's still plenty of meat on this hambone. Join a regular tour, because guides are knowledgeable and truly care; after the tour, you can backtrack for closer looks. The 2-ton slab from her hull, cast in an eerie light, is a moving epilogue.

7324 International Dr., Orlando. www.titanictheexperience.com/orlando. ℭ **407/248-1166.** $22 adults, $16 kids 5–11, $2 discounts online. Mar–mid-Apr, August 10am–8pm, mid-Apr–May, Sept–Feb 10am–6pm, June–July 10am–9pm, last admission 1 hr. before closing.

Wet 'n Wild ★★ WATER SLIDE PARK   On the last day of 2016, the world's first water theme park, opened in 1977 by George Millay, will close forever, so slip in for one last slide. This is the purist's paragon—a tightly packed coil of steel framework and get-to-the-point thrills. Most water is heated and RFID bracelets allow cashless purchases. Parents tend to sit out the slides by hanging at the 17,000-square-foot **Surf Lagoon** or in the elaborate **Blastaway Beach** soak zone. Unusually, many of the coolest contraptions accommodate families who want to ride together. **The Black Hole** is a two-person raft that whisks blindly through a pitch-black tube, pierced momentarily by disorienting strips of lights. **Brain Wash,** a white-knuckle standout, drops rafts carrying two or four people 53 feet down the wall of a 65-foot-wide funnel that's turned on its side. On **Bomb Bay,** the park's scariest ride, step into an enclosed cylinder above a 78-degree chute that drops six stories as close to vertically as physics and lawyers will allow. A sadistic attendant peeks through a window to make sure your arms and legs are crossed, and without warning, hits the release button on a trap door, dropping traumatized

SPRING training

Baseball is inextricable from Florida's calendar. Way back in 1923, the Cincinnati Reds began spring training in Orlando at Tinker Field and in the 1930s, the Washington Senators arrived and stayed for the better part of half a century. A few teams in the so-called Grapefruit League (the Arizona trainers are the Cactus League) still call Orlando or its environs their temporary home, and in the preseason you can watch them practice or play exhibition games. Unlike at season games, players often mingle with fans—in fact, some teams' facilities were built to cozy proportions (leave the binoculars at home), with interaction areas where you can collect autographs from athletes before or after practice. Sometimes it feels like the spirit of old-time baseball, the one supplanted by high-priced players and colossal arenas.

Tickets (usually $15–$25) go on sale in January. Pitchers and catchers report first, in mid-February, and by the end of the month, the whole team is on hand. They play against other teams through March before heading to their home parks by April.

- **Atlanta Braves** (Disney's Wide World of Sports, 700 S. Victory Lane, Lake Buena Vista; http://atlanta.braves.mlb.com; ✆ 407/939-4263). Since they took up residence in 1997 at Walt Disney World, the Braves can brag about having one of the nicest and largest (9,500 seats) training stadiums under the sun, where they play 18-odd games.

- **Houston Astros** (Osceola County Stadium, 1000 Bill Beck Rd., Kissimmee; http://houston.astros.mlb.com; ✆ 321/697-3200). The smallest training park in the Grapefruit League (5,200 seats—still hardly tiny) has hosted the Astros since 1985. Team members make themselves available for fan greetings in their Autograph Alley.

- **Detroit Tigers** (Joker Marchant Stadium, Al Kaline Dr., 2301 Lake Hills Rd., Lakeland; http://detroit.tigers.mlb.com; ✆ 866/668-4437). Lakeland, between Orlando and Tampa on I-4, has hosted the Tigers since 1934, the longest relations for any major league team, and the team is such a local institution that their so-called "Tiger Town" training complex, built on the site of a World War II flight academy, has grown up with them.

leisure travelers down the flume below at wedgie speed. But the best ride is **Disco H$_2$O,** in which cloverleaf-shaped rafts (two to four people) are accelerated in a tube and sent spinning around an enclosed chamber where disco music plays and lights spin. Universal, which owns it, is pulling to plug because it's building a state-of-the art park, Volcano Bay, to open in 2017.

6200 International Dr., Orlando. www.wetnwildorlando.com. ✆ **800/992-9453** or 407/351-1800. $57 adults, $52 kids 3–9, but online tickets good for 14 days are $10 less; parking $13. Hours vary, but it generally opens at 9:30 or 10am and closes at 5pm in winter and as late as 9pm in the summer.

WonderWorks ★ TOURIST MUSEUM   You know it's touristy because the facade looks like someone ripped a mansion out of the ground and turned it upside down. But the inverted motif doesn't continue very far into its doors.

You're locked in a room that looks like the set to a play—an office, a ship's hold—and given the clues hidden there, you must solve puzzles, crack codes, and find the key to get back out within an hour. Don't worry: There are no scary gotchas, and because of fire codes, the door's not *really* locked. If you're struggling with the mental challenge, staff is monitoring you via camera (don't pick your nose) and can nudge you in the right direction. It's much easier, and a lot more fun, to play with a group. Five escape rooms producers, all of them homegrown companies designed by puzzleheads, have flooded the Orlando market, and while each of them puts on games that look as if they were decorated using a gift card from Home Depot, some real gamer love goes into creating these challenges, and that adds to the fun. There may be an age minimum of about 12 and you're allowed to fail (many do).

America's Escape Game: 8723 International Drive, Suite 115, Orlando; www.americasescapegame.com; © 407/412-5585. Rooms: White House, Egyptian tomb, pandemic. Closed Mon. $35

The Escape Game: 8145 International Dr., Suite 511, Orlando; www.orlandoescapegame.com; © 407/501-7222. Rooms: art heist, terrorist threat, prison break; $28

Escapology: 11951 International Dr., Orlando; www.escapology.com; © 407/278-1515. Rooms: Western, pandemic, Cuban missile crisis, Chinese ship, $28

The Great Escape Room: 23½ S. Magnolia Ave., Orlando; thegreatescaperoom.com/orlando; © 386/385-8860. Rooms: Sherlock Holmes; $28

It's a Trap!: 6744 Aloma Ave., Winter Park; www.itsatrapgame.com; © 407/960-3824. Four evenings-only, fantasy-themed (wizards, superheroes) rooms with a live performer. $23

Instead, you get about 100 hands-on brainteaser exhibits not unlike what you'd find at a science museum or an arcade—an "earthquake simulator" box, a bubble-making area—all swarmed with children. Bring the Purell, because exhibits get smeary, and bring your patience, because some things will be broken. It's all about the children. And small kids love it—but then again, they have no concept of the value of your hard-earned dollar.

9067 International Dr., Orlando. www.wonderworksonline.com. © **407/351-8800.** $27 adults, $21 seniors over 54 and kids 4–12, $7 per game of Lazer Tag, $10 ropes course, $10 motion simulator ride. Daily 9am–midnight.

North of Universal & Orlando

Holy Land Experience ★ THEME PARK   The Trinity Broadcasting Network owns this peculiarly American park, a costume-party version of Jerusalem, which is far more attended by the faithful than by casual tourists. It has no rides, nor enough attractions to fill the hours, although performance times are spread across the clock to force completists to purchase a second day (which isn't necessary to do). For oddity, there will never be its equal. Will there ever again be a theme park where major attractions are a wax museum of the Passion, a model of Jerusalem in the year '66, and a "Garden of Eden" strewn with animal mannequins? A cutout photograph of a handsome Jesus is installed in the central pond as if he's walking on it, while the nearby Scriptorium houses a truly precious collection of rare specimens of Bible publishing. It seems wholesomely innocuous until late afternoon, when it turns into a gory snuff show: In an indoor amphitheater, an actor playing Christ, serenaded by contemporary power ballads and piped-in applause, endures a lingering beating and blood-spattered "crucifixion" by villainous Romans for an audience holding up their palms in testimony. The act of entertaining people with execution is actually more Roman than these guests perceive. There's no overt political context unless you're paying attention: recorded narration is all-male, Catholics are depicted as getting God wrong, concession stands serve Chick-fil-A, and Christians are portrayed as radicals persecuted in pursuit of freedom. If you have been to the real Holy Land, you will quickly grasp that this version of Israel is descended from the pomp of Charlton Heston movies.

4655 Vineland Rd., Orlando. www.holylandexperience.com. (℡ **800/447-7235** or 407/872-2272. $50 adults, $35 for children 6–12, $20 for kids 3–5, free parking. Tues–Sat 10am–6pm.

Mennello Museum of American Art ★★ MUSEUM A rare museum with live-in pets (two cats: Red and Black are feline hosts) the Mennello is a repository for the luridly vivid paintings of Earl Cunningham, a chicken farmer and folk artist whose conceptions sometimes seem refreshingly naive, and then a moment later become brazenly modernist. Cunningham, who died in 1977 while running a curio shop in Saint Augustine, is now considered so

Mennello Museum of American Art.

important that the Smithsonian devoted an exhibition to him. The museum also hosts exhibitions of fine American folk art.

900 E. Princeton St., Orlando. www.mennellomuseum.com. ⓒ **407/246-4278.** $5 adults, $4 seniors over 59, $1 students, kids 11 and under free. Tues–Sat 10:30am–4:30pm, Sun noon–4:30pm.

Orange County Regional History Center ★★★ MUSEUM   People who think Central Florida history began with Walt will have their eyes opened in this underrated museum in a handsome 1927 Greek Revival former court-house. Head first to the **fourth floor,** where the timeline starts 12,000 years in the past and work your way down. In 1981, a high school student rooting through lake muck found a Timacuan dugout canoe from around c.e. 1000, and now it is proudly displayed, as are mastodon teeth, pots from b.c.e. 500, and a 12-foot-tall oyster midden. As you advance through time, artifacts keep coming: saddles used by the forgotten Florida cowmen (the swampy ground made meat chewy, which Cuban customers liked), recipes for Florida Cracker delicacies (Squirrel Soup, Baked Possum), artifacts from the steamship tourist trade (in the 1870s, the St. John's River system was America's busiest one south of the Hudson), and a wall of gorgeous vintage labels from the many citrus companies that once dominated the area. The exhibitions are noticeably conflicted about the growth explosion wrought by the theme parks—the "Building a Kingdom" exhibition was created without Disney funding so it would have the freedom to be frank. An interesting sidelight is the retired Courtroom B, a handsome, wooden chamber out of "Inherit the Wind" silenced by cork floors and emblazoned with the slogan "Equal and Exact Justice to All Men." That was painted over the bench at a time when people were still being lynched here (there's a KKK robe in a nearby gallery), and until as late as 1951 in Orlando, black mothers had to give birth in the boiler

Orange County Regional History Center.

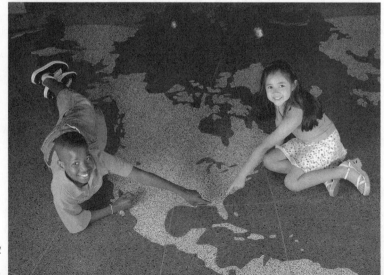

A TOWN OF psychics

George P. Colby was reared in the Midwest by Baptist parents, but incessant visions (and poor health) compelled him south, where in 1875, he came across land that, he said, appeared exactly as it had been shown to him by his spirit guide, Seneca. Soon after that, Colby enticed a group of refugees from chilly Lily Dale, New York—a town populated by spiritualists that still exists on the **Cassadaga** Lakes outside of Buffalo—to join him in the then-rural wilds of Florida. The winter "camp" of **Cassadaga ★★★** (exit 114 from I-4; www.cassadaga.org) was born. Nowadays, its residents offer a daily slate of services, laying-on of hands, and readings. The anachronistic village 40 miles northeast of Universal is untouched by development, and only accredited mediums may live among the ramshackle 1920s homes and Spanish moss. Tree-shaded, whitewashed, and more than slightly creepy, Cassadaga, on the National Register of Historic Places, is a bastion of metaphysicality in a region otherwise devoted to Christian fundamentalism.

Before setting out, check the town's website for the full list of events and psychics. When you arrive, consult the bulletin board in **Cassadaga Camp Bookstore** (1112 Stevens St., Cassadaga; ☏ **386/ 228-2880;** Mon–Sat 10am–6pm, Sun 11:30am–5pm) to see which mediums are available to take walk-in clients for readings or healings. Everything in town, including gift shops for gemstones and talismans, is within a few blocks, so park and explore. Because the rent's so cheap (the land is owned by the Southern Cassadaga Spiritualist Camp Meeting Association, which subscribes to a form of Biblical Spiritualism—Jesus is real, Satan isn't—services go for a fraction of what they cost in the outside world.

Wednesdays from 7:30–9pm at Colby Memorial Temple, mediums deliver messages from deceased loved ones ($5), and Fridays (except the first Friday of the month) from 7pm to 9pm, there's a workshop on how to be a medium yourself. Historic walking tours leave from the bookstore (Tues & Fri at 2pm and Sat at 3pm; $15), but the coolest ticket is the **Spirit Encounters Night Photography Tour,** Saturdays at 7:30pm ($25) where you bring your digital camera and go hunting for energy orbs. The next morning at 9:30, you can attend Lyceum—that's Sunday School for spiritualists—before Healing Service and church at the Colby Memorial Temple.

Residents shoo away outsiders at 10pm, so the only way to linger at night is to stay at the town's old-fashioned inn: The 1928 **Cassadaga Hotel** (355 Cassadaga Rd., Cassadaga; www.cassadaga-hotel.net; ☏ **386/228-2323;** $65–$75 Sun–Thurs, $80–$90 Fri–Sat, including continental breakfast; no guests under age 21), run by the New Age sect of the town and widely said to be haunted. Rooms (the cheapest ones don't have TVs or phone) are guaranteed to keep you anxiously listening for bump-in-the-night creaks. I asked the owner if I could take photos of the time-warp lobby. "Sure, you're welcome to," she said, "but most people get a kind of orb or white light instead." I haven't found those, but my shots *did* come out blurry. I'm just saying.

room of the hospital. Some justice *was* served here: In 1987, Courtroom B tried the first case in America in which DNA evidence obtained a conviction.

65 E. Central Blvd., Orlando. www.thehistorycenter.org. ☏ **407/836-8500.** $12 adults, $9 kids 5–12, $10 seniors over 59. Mon–Sat 10am–5pm, Sun noon–5pm.

Orlando Museum of Art ★ MUSEUM Although this fixture of local pride is touted as *de rigueur* in much tourist literature, OMA takes less than an hour to see. Most of it is not particularly important, just high atmosphere, but of note are Robert Rauschenberg's "Florida Psalm," a collage paean to the state's fading tourism emblems; Chuck Close's 1982 portrait of his wife done in fingerprints, and John James Audubon's Great Blue Heron. Temporary exhibitions up the par. Expect a pleasant outing, especially if you pair a visit with an amble around the surrounding Loch Haven Park, but not a milestone.

2416 N. Mills Ave., Orlando. www.omart.org. ☎ **407/896-4231.** $10 adults, $7 college students and seniors over 64, $5 kids 6–18. Tues–Sat 10am–4pm, Sun noon–4pm.

Orlando Science Center ★ MUSEUM The center is an excellent (if expensive) example of its type, but it's still just a science museum aimed at kids and school groups, and if you have one in your city, you should skip it. That's not to slam what it has: a dome that doubles as a movie theater; a Nature-Works area stocked with live baby alligators; a miniature KidsTown for kids under 48 inches tall to pretend to do grown-up things; a BeeHive Encounter area that feeds outside through a tube; a not-scary dinosaur zone full of reproduction skeletons and sandboxes where kids can dig for simulated fossils.

777 E. Princeton St., Orlando. www.osc.org. ☎ **407/514-2000.** Admission including exhibition $27 adults, $24 seniors age 55 and over and students with ID, $18 kids 3–11, parking $5. Sun–Thurs 10am–5pm, Fri–Sat 10am–9pm.

Winter Park & North Orlando

Winter Park has long been a bastion of wealth, particularly from New Money families who failed to find favor among the Old Money of the North. Its expensive tastes are represented by its lakefront mansions, red-brick streets, and a few wrongly overlooked gems for true masterpieces.

Charles Hosmer Morse Museum of American Art ★★★ MUSEUM The best museum in the Orlando area, and perhaps the finest in the state, presents an unparalleled cache of works by genius designer Louis Comfort Tiffany, from stained glass to vases to lamps, and even the lavishly decorated Daffodil Terrace and Reception Hall of his lost Long Island mansion, Laurelton Hall, and the bespoke fountains that ran through it. The Morse displays the best collection of Tiffany glass on the planet, including an entire room reconstructing the master's tour de force chapel, made for the World's Columbian Exposition in 1893. Once face-to-face with the uncanny luminescence of Tiffany's best work, even those previously knew nothing about him can't help but come away dazzled. The museum's founders also collected hundreds of other top-quality pieces from the Arts and Crafts movement, including sculpture, but the focus here is definitely Tiffany and his impeccable taste. Set aside an hour or more, though it's easy to combine a visit with a stroll through Winter Park's boutiques, because it sits among them.

445 N. Park Ave., Winter Park. www.morsemuseum.org. ☎ **407/645-5311.** $5 adults, $4 seniors, $1 students, free for kids 11 and under. Tues–Sat 9:30am–4pm, Sun 1–4pm, open until 8 on Fridays Nov–April. Free Fri 4–8pm Nov–Apr.

It's Not on the Tourist Maps

The standard tourist literature won't point them out, but pop history happened here:

- **Disney's Contemporary Resort, Walt Disney World.** On November 17, 1973, President Richard Nixon gave his "I'm not a crook" speech to a convention of Associated Press editors in the ballroom here, throwing gasoline on the fire of Watergate and bestowing him with his catchphrase of infamy.

- **Disney's Polynesian Resort, Walt Disney World.** While on vacation on December 29, 1974, John Lennon signed the document that officially dissolved The Beatles forever. Disney isn't sure exactly which room he was staying in.

- **1418½ Clouser Ave., in the College Park area.** In July 1957, 9 months before the publication of "On the Road," writer Jack Kerouac moved in with his mother, and he inhabited a 10×10-foot room with just a cot, a desk, and a bare bulb. Here, he wrote "The Dharma Bums," an exploration of personal spiritual renewal through a connection with nature. By the time he moved out in the spring of 1958, he was a literary superstar. The Kerouac Project (www.kerouac project.org) now owns the home and

invites writers to live rent-free in it for 3-month tenures.

- **1910 Hotel Plaza Blvd., Lake Buena Vista.** The very first building to be completed on Walt Disney World property was this low-slung glass-and-steel creation, considered painfully modern in January 1970. It was the Walt Disney World Preview Center, on what was then Preview Boulevard. Here, pretty young hostesses guided some one million visitors past artists' renderings, models, and films promoting Phase One of the resort that was being constructed. Naturally, the first souvenir shop at Disney World was also on the premises. The current tenant is a nonprofit organization promoting sports participation.

- **839 N. Orlando Ave., Winter Park.** In March 1986, the Canadian rock group The Band was in the middle of a disappointing reunion tour. After playing the Cheek to Cheek Lounge at the Villa Nova Restaurant, which stood here, pianist Richard Manuel, 42, returned to his hotel room at the Quality Inn next door and, when his wife briefly left the room, hanged himself. The lounge site is now a CVS drugstore, and the motel is the Best Western Winter Park Inn.

Cornell Fine Arts Museum ★ MUSEUM   Rollins College, whose graduates include Mister Fred Rogers, has long been a university of choice for parents with social aspirations for their children, and so it makes sense that its star exhibition hall would be bequeathed with such a fine collection in such a country-club setting. It's too small to showcase its impressive holdings, so even remarkable pieces (such as Vanessa Bell's portrait of Mary St. John Hutchinson) tend to rotate in and out of storage to make way for changing exhibitions, which spotlight a wide range of arresting works, from Matisse prints to 18th-century European portraits. A small but top-notch facility.

100 Holt Ave., Winter Park. www.rollins.edu/cfam. ⓒ **407/646-2526.** $5 adults, free for students, sometimes free thanks to grants. Tues–Fri 10am–4pm, Sat–Sun noon–5pm.

Bok Tower Gardens.

South & East of Disney

Diversions get populist as you go south, and their character says more about eccentric Florida than imported wealth; two of Central Florida's most authentic reptile parks are roughly between Disney and the airport.

Bok Tower Gardens ★★★ GARDENS/HISTORIC SITE   About an hour south of Disney, the elegant, 250-acre gardens—designed by Frederick Law Olmsted, Jr., who worked on the National Mall and the Jefferson Memorial—are not often visited, which is too bad, because it's a big reason you're in Orlando at all: It was one of Central Florida's first world-famous attractions. They're genuinely tranquil and among the best surviving remnants of early-20th-century philanthropic privilege. The gardens (don't miss the water lilies, big enough to support a child) and their 205-foot, neo-Gothic Singing Tower were commissioned as a thank-you to the American people by a Dutch-born editor, Edward William Bok, publisher of "The Ladies' Home Journal" and a pioneer in public sex education. Bok was buried at the tower's base in 1930, the year after its completion and dedication by President Calvin Coolidge. The 57-bell carillon on the tower's sixth level sounds concerts at 1 and 3pm daily, and its 1930s Mediterranean-style Pinewood estate ($6 more) is open for tours. The sanctuary was enshrined in 1993 as a National Historic Landmark.

1151 Tower Blvd., Lake Wales. www.boksanctuary.org. © **863/676-1408.** $12 adults, $3 kids 5–12. Daily 8am–6pm, last admission at 5pm.

Dinosaur World ★ TOURIST MUSEUM   An only-in-America roadside attraction, this is not someplace to pass hours—one will do, but it'll be a memorably weird one. Kids like to wander the jungle-y plot, happening upon more than 100 life-size versions of various dinosaurs, some 80 feet long. A labor of love by a Swedish-born man and his family, it's well kept, even if the foam-and-fiberglass models sometimes look more like aliens than reptiles. It's easy to catch on the drive to Busch Gardens.

5145 Harvey Tew Rd., at I-4's exit 17, Plant City. www.dinosaurworld.com. © **813/717-9865.** $17 adults, $15 seniors over 59, $12 kids 3–12. Daily 9am–5pm.

Fun Spot America—Kissimmee ★ AMUSEMENT PARK   Fun Spot's flagship property is near Universal (p. 172) but this southern outpost delivers the same well-kept carnival-ride playground experience. There's a selection of basic rides that wouldn't be out of place beside a circus (the Hot Seat swings seated riders on the end of a big stick), a wild mouse-style Rockstar Coaster with spinning cars, and a few multilevel Go-Kart tracks (the Vortex has 32-degree banking, the world's steepest, owners say) and racecar simulators. That 300-foot-tall skyline-scarring contraption is **SkyCoaster** ($40 a ride), which harnesses up to three would-be pants-wetters so that they're face-down, hoists them backward, and swings them forward at 80mph like wingless hang gliders.

2850 Florida Plaza Blvd., Kissimmee. www.fun-spot.com. © **407/397-2509.** Pay-per-ride $6–$9, unlimited ride armband $30–$40 (armband price based on height), discounts online. Generally daily 10am–midnight.

Gatorland ★★★ ANIMAL PARK   Back in 1949, the reassuringly hokey Gatorland became Orlando's very first mass attraction, featuring Seminole Indians wrestling the animals for tourists; the house-sized jaw at its entrance was a state landmark for Polaroids and Kodachrome. Back then, Florida was

Gator Jumparoo Show in Gatorland.

International Drive

crawling with alligators—you would see them basking by the sides of the roads—but these days, the reptiles have been mostly evicted by development, so sanctuaries like these are the best places to see the beasts (such as the newest resident diva, the 15-ft.-long, 1,400-lb. Bonecrusher II) in their ornery glory. Gatorland is rustic in a family-friendly way, as concrete pools have been replaced with natural-looking habitats, a sun-seared layout was molded into a pleasing nature walk, a kids' splash area, and stuff like a **wading bird rookery,** a **petting zoo,** and a five-stage **zip line** over gator ponds ($70; it's a good time) were added. At regular showtimes, good ol' boy gator rangers, buzzed on their own testosterone, wrassle, tickle, and otherwise pester seething gators, and for 10 bucks, they'll bring your children into the fray—safely, with a wad of duct tape around the critters' snouts—for snapshots. It's cornpone fun; signage is full of gags and every show is staged to contain a fake near disaster to titillate and thrill tourists. Most of the fun is trawling the 110-acre plot on walkways and docks as the critters teem ominously in murky waters underfoot. *Strategy:* It's easy to get the highlights in 2 or 3 hours, but don't miss the Jumparoo, when gators leap out of the water for suspended chunks of chicken meat. Bring a fistful of cash if you'd like to partake of extras such as feeding tropical birds and the miniature train. And save a few bills for one of its 1960s-era vending machines which press a toy alligator out of injected hot wax right before your eyes—it's just one of many unmissable throwbacks here.

14501 S. Orange Blossom Trail, Orlando. www.gatorland.com. ℰ **800/393-5297** or 407/855-5496. $27 adults, $19 kids 3–12. Daily 10am–5pm

Give Kids the World Village ★★★ LANDMARK Of the annual wishes granted by the Make-A-Wish Foundation and other wish-granting organizations for terminally ill children, *half* of them are to visit Central Florida. Make-A-Wish turns to this nonprofit to fulfill those dreams, which it does for 196 families at a time plus some 7,000 international families a year. No one is refused, and each family spends an all-expenses-paid week in their own villa, eating as much as they want (including ice cream for breakfast) and playing in a compound that looks like a second Magic Kingdom.

It's the most magical place you never knew existed. The 70-acre, gated operation is its own fantasy world with a 6-foot rabbit mascot, Mayor Clayton, who provides nightly tuck-ins. Perkins Restaurants and Boston Market discreetly support the dining pavilion, which looks like a gingerbread house, and there's an Ice Cream Palace where no child is ever refused a scoop. Christmas falls every Thursday, when there's a parade, holiday lighting, and an appearance by Santa, who gives everyone a toy provided by Hasbro. The carousel is the only one in the world that a wheelchair can drive right onto, plus there's horseback riding, a small-gauge train route, miniature golf, and more.

As you can imagine, it depends on volunteers—to the tune of 1,200 slots a week. You don't have to commit to anything longer than a few hours and if you're there for dinner, you'll eat; just apply online about 2 weeks ahead and be at least 12 years old, although exceptions can be made for families who want to volunteer together. Mornings or evenings are best because the kids want to spend their days at the theme parks, too. The workload is easy. That could mean turning person-size cards at the World's Largest Candy Land game, held Sunday nights on a board measuring 14,400 square feet. You could help at Mayor Clayton's surprise birthday party, thrown every Saturday, or at the "dive-in" movies screened weekly. You can spoon hash browns at breakfast (until about 11am), run the train, or serve dinner with a smile—the opportunities are virtually boundless and the staff matches talents with the right post.

Your mission is not to lavish pity or love, but to simply run the resort where families escape from hard times. You'll be a host, not a nurse. Not every child is sick—their brothers and sisters come, too, and many of them are starved for attention after their siblings' often long illnesses. You'll find that the village is quite a joyous place as families are, perhaps briefly, liberated from the burden of their lives. A favorite part of Give Kids the World is the Castle of Miracles, where the rafters are covered with thousands of golden stars. Each star is affixed by a child on the last night of his or her stay. Years later, moms and dads sometimes return and ask to see, one last time, the star their child left behind.

210 S. Bass Rd., Kissimmee. www.gktw.org. ℗ **407/396-1114.**

Machine Gun America ★ AMUSEMENT PARK Firearms fans finally have their own playground to fire guns of all types and eras. The staff, many of whom are ex-military, knows its stuff and puts you on a simulator before ushering you behind reinforced glass for your simulated slaughter. You may find it disconcerting to see people firing not at a target symbol but at a depiction of a man in a turban, and the most expensive package ($800) concludes with customers being presented with their "Man Card" (women have their own $180 package promising "to unleash their inner femme fatale"). Although safety is assiduously practiced, some guests report leaving with bruises—these are some powerful death weapons being used as playthings for thrills rather than in the context for which they were made.

5825 W. Irlo Bronson Hwy, Kissimmee. www.machinegunamerica.com. ℗ **407/278-1800.** Packages $100–$800. Sun–Fri 10am–8pm, Sat 10am–9pm.

Old Town ★ AMUSEMENT PARK Walt Disney tried to extinguish honky-tonk, but it lives on, cotton candy and all, at his doorstep. Old Town is the kind of low-rent entertainment center you'd find rusting near a small town somewhere. Built to look like 4 blocks of a Main Street–style town, expect Americana to the extreme: beer-soaked ale halls, Old Glory T-shirts, and a gauntlet of no-name stores peddling impulse buys from baseball cards to puppets to pins to Western gear, plus a variety of special events (Friday is for muscle cars, Saturday is Cruise Nite for pre-1975 classic cars), and go-karts and, bumper cars. You'll probably eat something fried.

5770 W. Irlo Bronson Hwy./U.S. 192, Kissimmee. www.myoldtownusa.com. ℗ **407/396-4888.** Daily 10am–11pm.

International Drive

JOIN THE club

Orlando is a world capital for miniature golf. Here, you play crazy golf under waterfalls, through caves, over motorized ramps, and even into volcanoes that "erupt" if you hit your shot. Putter around with one of these. The coupon booklets print discounts for all but Disney's courses; also check individual course websites for coupons.

○ **Congo River Adventure Golf** (www.congoriver.com): One of the best options, the challenging courses wind through man-made mountains speared with airplane wreckage—and there are live alligators in the pools! Play 18 holes for $13 adults, $11 kids. Two locations: 5901 International Dr., Orlando (☏ **407/248-9181**); and 4777 W. Hwy. 192, Kissimmee (☏ **407/396-6900**). Both open daily (Sun–Thurs 10am–11pm; Fri–Sat 10am–midnight).

○ **Disney's Winter Summerland** (outside Blizzard Beach, Walt Disney World; ☏ **407/939-7529;** $14 adults, $12 kids; daily 10am–11pm; 50% discount on the second round): Two cute 18-hole courses themed around Christmas. The Winter side, piled with fake snow, has more bells and whistles (love that steaming campfire and that squirting snowman). Combine it with Blizzard Beach without moving your car. Summerland beats the other Disney course, **Disney's Fantasia Gardens** (same rates), themed to the movie "Fantasia," with its two courses: Fairways and Gardens. The Fairways course has challenging shots; Gardens is sillier. Find it by the Swan and Dolphin hotel duo.

○ **Hawaiian Rumble Adventure Golf** (www.hawaiianrumbleorlando. com): These tropical courses are threaded with streams and waterfalls that could use a little upkeep. Play 18 holes for $10; 36 holes for $13. Two locations: 13529 S. Apopka Vineland Rd., Lake Buena Vista (☏ **407/239-8300;** daily 9am–11pm); and 8969 International Dr., Orlando (☏ **407/351-7733;** Sun–Thurs 9am–11:30pm and Fri–Sat 9am–midnight).

○ **Hollywood Drive-In Golf** (City-Walk Orlando, 6000 Universal Blvd., Orlando; www.hollywood driveingolf.com; ☏ **407/802-4848;** $15 adults, $13 kids 3–9; daily 9am–2am) The coolest 36 holes in town, CityWalk's "haunted & sci-fi double feature" is kitted out, hilarious, and always surprising. Spinning vortices! Corkscrew ball elevators! At night, the lighting effects are impeccable. You can even download its own scorecard app and putt with an eyeball.

○ **Putting Edge** (Festival Bay, 5250 International Dr., Orlando; www. puttingedge.com; ☏ **407/248-0700;** adults $11, kids 12 and under $8.50; Mon–Thurs 11am–9:30pm, Fri 11am–11pm, Sat 10am–11pm, Sun 11am–8pm). An 18-hole glow-in-the-dark course of fluorescent balls, holes, and decor.

○ **Pirate's Cove** (www.piratescove. net): Navigate wooden ships—a newly installed one is life-size—and falls of blue-ish water. Choose Captain's Adventure or Blackbeard's Challenge. Two locations: 8501 International Dr., Orlando (☏ **407/352-7378**), and 12545 S.R. 535, behind the Crossroads shopping center, Lake Buena Vista (☏ **407/827-1242**). Rates and hours the same: $13 adults, $12 kids 12 and under; open daily 9am to 11pm.

Reptile World Serpentarium ★★ ANIMAL ATTRACTION   Snake milking! What other enticement do you need? Truthfully, it's more of an unassuming biotoxin supply facility—and venom-collection wonderland—than a zoo. Begun in 1972 to collect poison for medical research and to save the lives of bite victims, its location 20 miles east of Disney tempted its operators into joining the ranks of tourist attractions 4 years later, and daily at noon and 3pm, you can thrill (safely behind glass) as George Van Horn grabs deadly serpents, plants their yawning fangs over the membrane of a venom-collection glass, and gets the creatures spitting mad. There are about 50 snakes on display (including an 18-ft. cobra and 11 types of rattlers) at any time, but obviously, this one's about venom spewing. Gotta admit—that's cool.

5705 E. Irlo Bronson Memorial Hwy./U.S. 192, St. Cloud. www.reptileworldserpentarium. com. ✆ **407/892-6905.** $8.75 adults, $6.75 kids 6–17, $5.75 kids 3–5. Tues–Sat 9am–5pm, Sun 10am–5pm.

KENNEDY SPACE CENTER

In the late 1960s, Central Florida was the most exciting place on Earth, thanks to the moon. **Kennedy Space Center ★★★**, which was established in 1958 and ruled the tourist circuit with Disney in the 1970s, was eventually eclipsed by attractions based on fantasy. These days, it's out of this world again.

It's on the Space Coast about an hour east of Orlando, and it's worth the trip. Start a full day near opening time. At the main Visitor Complex, many are waylaid by the retired rockets, IMAX films, and simulators, but that's not the best stuff—do them at the end of the day if you have time. Unless there's an **Astronaut Encounter** going on—that's an hour-long presentation in which an actual astronaut talks about his or her experience and answers questions—proceed instantly to the can't-miss **Bus Tour,** which leaves every 15 minutes until about 2:15pm, and takes most people around 3 hours. Be warned that the last buses don't leave you enough time to browse. Coaches, which are narrated by a live person, zip you around NASA's tightly secured compound. Combined with the nature reserve around it, the area (which guides tell visitors is one-fifth the size of Rhode Island and is home to 16 bald eagle nests) is huge but you'll be making one stop not too far away. You'll see the launch sites used by the shuttle and by the Apollo moon shots, and you'll receive an intelligent explanation of

NASA Kennedy Space Center.

the preparation that went into each shuttle launch. You'll buzz by eagles' nests, alligator-rich canals, pads now leased by private space-mission contractors SpaceX and Boeing, and the confoundingly titanic **Vehicle Assembly Building,** or VAB, where the shuttle—which NASA folk call "the orbiter"—was readied. It's just one story tall, but it's a doozy: The Statue of Liberty could fit through those doors with 200 feet left over. The main bus stop, the **Apollo/ Saturn V Center,** begins with a mandatory five-minute film and then a full-scale mock-up of the "firing room" in the throes of commanding Apollo 8's launch, in all its window-rattling, fire-lit drama—to skip that 30-minute show and get to the good stuff, pass through. The adjoining hangar contains a Saturn V rocket, which is larger than you can imagine (363 ft. long, or the equivalent of 30 stories)—but the new SLS rockets are even bigger. Don't overlook the chance to reach into a case to touch a small moon rock, which looks like polished metal. The presentation in the **Lunar Theatre,** which recounts the big touchdown, is well produced and even includes a video appearance by the late, reclusive Neil Armstrong. There's a cafeteria here, and look around for retired engineers and astronauts who are often on hand to answer questions.

After that, hasten back via the bus to the Visitor Complex for the grand finale: The $100 million home of the **space shuttle** *Atlantis.* Without giving too much away, the way in which it's revealed to you is perhaps the most spine-tingling moment in all of Orlando. Hanging 26 feet off the ground at an angle of 43.21° (like the numbers in a launch countdown), she's still covered with space dust, and she now tips a wing at everyone who comes to learn about her on the many interactive displays that surround her. Don't miss the commemorative **Forever Remembered,** quietly added in 2016. Alongside favorite mementos provided by 11 of the 14 families of their crews, you'll find respectful displays of a section of the hull of the *Challenger,* lost in 1986, and a slab of cockpit windows of the *Columbia* (2003), still encrusted with grass and mud from where it fell to Earth. You can also try the $60-million **Shuttle Launch Experience,** in which 44-person motion-simulator pods mimic a 5-minute launch with surprising (but not nauseating) clarity. The entire state-of-the-art, hyper-engaging space shuttle section can easily consume 2 hours.

Once you've completed the bus tour and *Atlantis,* it's up to you whether you want to plumb the sillier, kid-geared business at the Visitor's Complex. By this point, much of it will be redundant, and

Increased Access to NASA Secrets

The end of the space shuttle program has enabled previously off-limits areas to be opened for visits. Availability shifts, but on a variety of additional tours (generally $25 adults, $19 kids 3–11), there's always something that's not on the standard KSC Bus Tour. You can visit the shuttle's launch pad, the Launch Control Center used in the shuttle's last liftoffs, the core of the Mercury and Gemini missions, and find out what NASA's up to now, including the new SLS (Space Rocket System) that will carry the new Orion module into space for longer trips than ever before.

Although the Space Shuttle has flown into history, NASA still launches unmanned rockets—manned ones will resume in the early 2020s. Because launches are often postponed, it would be dangerous to plan a trip to Orlando just to catch one, but then again, if there's a launch when you're in town, it would a shame to miss it. Kennedy Space Center maintains an updated schedule online at **www.kennedyspacecenter.com/events**.

The general public is not permitted to flood NASA turf during the actual events, but Titusville, a town at the eastern end of S.R. 50, is a good place to get a clear, free view, because you'll be across the wide Indian River from the pad. Even if you can't leave Orlando for a launch, you can still see the fire of the rockets ascend the eastern sky from anywhere in town. Night launches are even more spectacular.

some of it is pure malarkey, but take the time to check the 42-foot-high black granite slab of the **Astronaut Memorial,** commemorating those lost; **Early Space Exploration,** where you'll see the impossibly low-tech Mission Control for the Mercury missions (they used rotary telephones!), plus some authentic spacesuits from the Gemini, Mercury, and Apollo series. (Astoundingly, the actual Mercury command building was torn down in 2010.) New in 2016, the **United States Astronaut Hall of Fame** moves here after many spending many neglected years 6 miles down the road.

Because the government commandeers the surrounding land as a buffer, there is nowhere else to eat within a 15-minute drive, and food is horrendous ($7–$9 a plate)—hamburgers taste like they were surplus from the Apollo program. Come on, NASA. Good hospitality isn't rocket science.

Route 405, east of Titusville. www.kennedyspacecenter.com. © **866/737-5235.** Admission $50 adults, $40 kids. Parking $10. Daily 9am to between 5 and 7pm, depending on the season. Astronaut Hall of Fame: open at noon and shares closing times with the Center. Bus tours every 15 min., last one at 3:30pm.

Kennedy Space Center Special Tours

Astronaut Training Experience ★★★ ACTIVITY KSC dubs the program ATX, but you could call it Space Daycamp. You'll test a few of the pieces of astronaut equipment, such as the Multi-Axis Trainer (which spins your body within a series of interlinked concentric circles to test your equilibrium), a ⅙th gravity chair, and a spell in a full-scale mock-up of the shuttle. Nothing is as intense as what astronauts experience, but it's still plenty rigorous for most terrestrials, and the facilitators can answer nearly any question you can launch at them. There's also a milder version, ATX Family, appropriate for younger children. The standard version is called Core.

Astronaut Hall of Fame, 6225 Vectorspace Blvd., Titusville. www.kennedyspacecenter. com. © **866/737-5235.** $175 age 14 and older, $145 age 7–11, includes admission to KSC, minimum age 7. 4½ hr.

5

MORE ORLANDO ATTRACTIONS

Kennedy Space Center

Lunch with an Astronaut ★★★   One of the coolest benefits of visiting the Space Coast is the chance to meet a real astronaut, many of whom have retired to the same area where they once worked. At times, you'll have seen headliners such as Jim Lovell and Story Musgrave making the rounds. Typically, these guys (and a very few women) love basking in fandom and in reliving old tales of glory—and unlike out-to-pasture sportsmen, these old-timers really did risk their lives the way heroes are supposed to—so these small-group sessions are geared toward questions. www.kennedyspacecenter.com. ℂ **866/737-5235.** $30 adult, $16 kids 3–11, not including required admission. Daily at noon.

NIGHTLIFE IN ORLANDO

After nightfall, the exertion of visiting theme parks has turned most visitors into exhausted puddles, and the resorts mop up the remaining energy at their on-premises nightspots. But these novel nighttime destinations are worth the rally:

Enzian ★★★ CINEMA   This thoughtfully programmed cinema would be the envy of any city in America. Before the movie, kick back at the Brazilian walnut patio bar, watching the sunset paint the Spanish moss red. Some of the drinks come from the private cellars of the Enzian's founder, the granddaughter of an Austrian princess. The relaxation continues inside at a large single-screen cinema, where a selection of art films and documentaries is shown, plus Hollywood biggies. Unlike multiplexes, there aren't rows of seats, but lollipop-colored levels of tables with cushy seating. Servers take your order (if you have one—eating's not required) before the movie and after the lights dim, your meal arrives surreptitiously and the air fills with the aroma of popcorn and truffled fries. After the show, a 20-minute drive has you back at Disney World. 1300 S. Orlando Ave., Maitland. www.enzian.org. ℂ **407/629-0054.** Tickets $11 adults, $9 seniors/students.

Howl at the Moon Saloon ★★ BAR   The 15-strong chain is good fun: a saloon delivered as a theme park experience, where dueling pianists outdo each other for laughs and virtuosity (expect to hear "American Pie"), and the patrons, mostly over 35 and white, clap earnestly to the beat. The theme resorts have their own dueling pianist joints: Jellyrolls at Disney's BoardWalk (p. 197) and Pat O'Brien's at Universal's CityWalk (p. 199). 8815 International Dr., Orlando. www.howlatthemoon.com. ℂ **407/354-5999.** Sun–Thurs 7pm–2am, Fri–Sat 6pm–2am, piano show starts 1 hr. after opening; cover $7–10.

Icebar ★ BAR   The gimmick: a bar made of 50 tons of ice, from the chairs to the frozen goblets. You're loaned gloves and a cape for warmth. The Arctic cocktailerie is only the size of a hotel room, dotted with ice sculptures, and aglow with cobalt lighting; when you've had enough, there's a larger, room-temperature lounge where you can continue the party. 8967 International Dr.,

Orlando. www.icebarorlando.com. © **407/426-7555.** $40 including 2 drinks, $20 without drinks, discounts online. Sun–Wed 7pm–midnight, Thurs 7pm–1am, Fri–Sat 7pm–2am.

Kings Bowl Orlando ★★ BOWLING ALLEY   Like Splitsville at Disney Springs, this new-brew nightspot in the shadow of the Eye turns a bowling alley into an all-evening party, with 22 ten-pin lanes, servers delivering surprisingly decent food (from pizza to ginger soy glazed salmon), serve-yourself beer, shuffleboard, bocce balls, billiards, ping pong, and dancing. Some nights it's for over-21s only, so if it's your family night, check first. 8255 International Dr., Orlando. www.kingsorlando.com. © **407/363-0200.** Bowling $6–$8. Daily 11am–2am.

Minus5° Icebar ★ BAR   Put on your parkas, because it's another frigid icebar. This newcomer, part of a chain with locations in Vegas and Manhattan, gradually changes color thanks to a flashy lighting system and ultimately, it depends not on local revelers but on convention crowds. Before 9pm, you can bring kids. Pointe Orlando, 9101 International Dr., Orlando. www.minus5experience. com. © **407/704-6956.** $40 including 2 drinks, $20 without drinks, discounts online. Sun–Thurs 5pm–1am, Fri–Sat 5pm–2am.

Orlando Brewing and Taproom ★★★ BREWERY   Because it's buried in an industrial area, you have to know about it to find it. There's no food served, either—if you want some, they've been known to hand you a binder of delivery menus—but that doesn't mean there isn't some delicious cooking happening. At least 24 beers (ales, IPAs, stouts—it changes according to how the brewers experiment) are on tap at 42°F and served at a copper-top bar. Most days at 6pm, the owners grant a free 30-minute tour of the beerworks, where quaffs are made without pasteurization (like the Old World) for sale within 2 weeks. The bar area is simple but convivial, like a rec room your dad might have slapped up in the basement, uncluttered by TVs or pool tables. 1301 Atlanta Ave., Orlando (just east of the Kaley St. exit off I-4, exit 81). www.orlandobrewing.com. © **407/872-1117.** No food; beer only. Mon–Thurs 3–10pm; Fri–Sat 1pm–midnight; Sun 1–9pm.

Parliament House Orlando ★★★ BAR/THEATER/DISCO   There's nothing else in America quite like it. In 1975, a dying Johnson-era, 130-room motel was revitalized as an amusement megacenter for gay folks. Its rambling size—10 acres, including a beach on a small lake out back—justifies it as a hangout not only for gay guys, but also for the friends who love them, women who want to dance without being accosted, and open-minded straight guys. Think of it as a fabulous entertainment mini-mall: There's the Footlight Theater for cabaret and drag hosted by longtime resident mistress Darcel Stevens; a diner; a pool; a disco, which gears up around 9pm; a video bar; and a scuzzy cubby called Western Bar, for leather-and-jeans-wearing guys who play pool. The scene is especially unexpected when you consider that its operators are a straight couple with six kids. It's considered a nucleus of Florida gay life, no matter how endearingly run-down it is. 410 N. Orange Blossom Trail, Orlando. www. parliamenthouse.com. © **407/425-7571.** Cover and hours vary.

Player 1 Orlando ★ BAR   Right outside the Disney Springs-area of WDW, is this spot where you can play video games all night long. Reasonable drink prices, a large beer selection, and a huge inventory of totally free games for superfans and nostalgics alike (consoles to cabinet), make it a fun secret of the Orlando leisure scene. All ages are permitted before 5pm, but kids under 18 must always have an adult with them. 8562 Palm Parkway, Lake Buena Vista. www.player1orlando.com. ✆ **407/504-7521.** Cover $5. Mon–Fri 5pm–2am, Sat–Sun 4pm–2am.

NIGHTLIFE AT THE RESORTS

After a long day trooping through the parks, your wish list for nightlife may begin and end with a hot bath. But if, once the fireworks fizzle, you're still ready to party, the amusement giants are happy to serve up to 1 or 2am daily. These playgrounds rock on every night, even if the dance floors happen to be desolate. Their offerings have been concocted by committee to appeal to as wide a spectrum of visitors as possible, and their playlists and decor alike are designed for the masses, but those who surrender to it are bound to have fun.

Walt Disney World

Between the Swan and Dolphin hotels and Epcot, **Disney's BoardWalk** (no admission required) is a lesser entertainment district (p. 96) though it's no match for the cocktails flowing at Disney Springs area. It can be reached from Epcot's International Gateway side entrance, but if you park at Epcot, be careful because once the park closes, you can't cut through to the parking lot. At the very least, BoardWalk is a scrubbed-down idealization of 1930s Atlantic City that makes for a pleasant backdrop for an evening stroll on the water. Most visitors grab an ice cream and stick around for a half-hour or so. Its two clubs thump along, sometimes in lonely desolation, although patronage depends greatly on what conventions are staying at the adjoining hotels.

Disney's BoardWalk.

Nightlife at the Resorts

MORE ORLANDO ATTRACTIONS

Disney Springs is more about food, cocktails, and entertainment and not about clubs, but a notable exception is **The Edison,** new in 2016. It adapts a concept that originated in an abandoned electrical substation in downtown Los Angeles, where dance floors and cabaret acts share space with rusty, century-old equipment. The Disney version, while still steampunk and free-spirited, is more about contortionists and palm readers than burlesque—but it's still a touch saucy and not for kids. Beyond that, there are tons of places to drink, including bars in pretty much every sit-down restaurant, highlights include **Jock Lindsey's Hangar Bar** (opened in late 2015 and themed after Indiana Jones's plane pilot), **Dockside Margaritas,** the waterfront **Lava Lounge** at Rainforest Cafe (p. 220), and an outdoor slushie bar attached to **Splitsville Luxury Lanes.**

Atlantic Dance Hall ★ Appearances to the contrary, it is not a place where they might shoot horses (that concept failed), but an under-patronized DJ dance club for Top 40, '80s, and videos. Its clientele seems to consist of tipsy trade-show attendees from the Swan and Dolphin hotels next door. Hip it's not, and nostalgic it ain't, which is too bad, because its Art Deco interior holds such promise and its spacious wood floor feels good to dance on. disneyworld.disney.go.com. © **407/939-2444.** No cover, minimum age 21. Tues–Sat 9pm–2am.

Jellyrolls ★ The brightest entertainment option at BoardWalk is Disney's challenge to the Howl at the Moon Saloon (p. 194): Dueling pianists jam, audiences sing along and try to stump them with requests, and the mood is light. Pianists start at 8pm and the space usually starts to fill up after 9pm, so arrive earlier for a table. There's no food beyond popcorn and the like. disneyworld.disney.go.com. © **407/560-8770.** $12 cover, minimum age 21. Daily 7pm–2am.

Trader Sam's Grog Grotto ★★★ At this terrifically fun tiki bar, which opened in 2015 at the Polynesian Village Resort, the rum drinks are curiously strong and the volcano out the window periodically erupts if you order a certain cocktail. Trader Sam's, named for the "head" salesman seen on the Jungle Cruise, is a spacious version of an older bar at the famous Disneyland Hotel in Anaheim, and people come just to collect its souvenir mugs—the Nautilus, shaped like Nemo's submarine, is exclusive to Florida. Kids are allowed until 8pm. Get there a bit before opening or you'll have to wait for one of the 51 seats inside, although the more spacious outdoor patio, while not nearly as fun and devoid of tricksy decor, is pleasant, too. The food is iffy, but since it's on the monorail, it makes for a boozy park break. disneyworld.disney.go.com. © **407/560-8770.** Daily 4pm–midnight.

Universal Orlando & CityWalk

CityWalk ★★   Universal Orlando's 30-acre nightclub mall takes fewer pains than Disney to present a wholesome face to the public: There's an upscale tattoo parlor and more nightclubs. Nights here, in the front yard shared by both Universal theme parks, were designed with jellybean colors and rock-concert panache but they attract locals as well as tourists and therefore have a sharper edge. The drinks seem stronger, too. The liveliness is bolstered partly by regular concerts at its Hard Rock Live venue. There is no charge to enter the common area, which is a boon because that allows anyone to tour around before deciding whether they want to pay to enter any clubs. Buying a $12 **CityWalk Party Pass** from any of the kiosks at the complex grants you unlimited admission to any and all of them on a given night; the clubs usually open after 9pm and are otherwise $7 a pop. Some of them serve food during the day and turn into nightspots late, and others open only in the evening. All Universal park tickets with multiday admission automatically come with one Party Pass. The Party Pass also is available with the addition of a movie ticket at the AMC Universal Cineplex, which is part of the complex. That combo costs $16. Finally, there's a package that buys a prix-fixe dinner at eight of CityWalk's restaurants with a ticket to the Cineplex for $22. Grab a "Times & Info" guide, which maps the stores and restaurants and lists the current happy hour times and specials. Many clubs only admit patrons 21 or older because drinking is permitted outdoors anywhere in CityWalk. 6000 Universal Blvd., Orlando, exit 75A coming on I-4 from the west, or exit 74B coming from the east. www.citywalkorlando.com. ✆ **407/363-8000.** $12 admission to all clubs; daily 11am–2am. parking $17 before 6pm, $5 6pm–10pm, free after 10pm, excluding event nights.

Blue Man Group ★★★   Three taciturn, bald, blue guys get into hilarious mischief, play with bizarre homemade toys, and trash their custom-made

Universal CityWalk.

theater—get a seat in the first four rows in the so-called "poncho section" (you'll get a plastic cloak) if you think it'd be a blast to be splattered with goo. (It is.) If you've gone to the parks for the day, the Blue Men won't require driving; guests can start drinking cocktails whenever they want and even bring them into the theater, accessible to both CityWalk and Universal Studios (it's practically beneath the Rockit coaster). www.universalorlando.com. © **407/258-3626.** Adults $69–$84, kids from $29, $10 discount online. Dinner packages for $15 more. 1 hr. 45 min.

Bob Marley—A Tribute to Freedom ★★ You often get live music for the $7 cover, but mostly it's an easygoing place to kick back, eat, and listen to recorded reggae—an antidote to the high-energy clubs around it. www. universalorlando.com. © **407/224-3663.**

CityWalk's Rising Star ★ This karaoke joint has a spin: You get a band and backup singers. Like all karaoke, the more you drink the more ridiculously fun it gets. Cover is $7, usually charged after 9pm. www.universal orlando.com. © **407/224-2189.**

the groove ★ Sleek and state-of-the-art; this DJ dance club is also middle-of-the-road; music skips from the '70s (Tues) to the '80s (Sat) to recent hits. The cover is $7, and it opens at 9pm. www.universalorlando.com. © **407/224-2165.**

Hard Rock Live ★★ A 3,000-seat, top-of-the-line live-music arena attached to the famous burger joint is one of Orlando's primary concert and comedy venues. The second-floor seating is spacious and has good sightlines; for some concerts, the first floor is converted to a dance floor or to standing room. You can't miss it—it looks like the Roman Coliseum. Check with website to see what'll be on during your visit. www.hardrock.com/live. © **407/351-5483.** Ticket prices vary.

Jimmy Buffett's Margaritaville ★★ Live music nightly in a touristy environment that's first about the cheeseburgers in paradise, secondly about margaritas (there are three bars), and thirdly about island music. Get there before the live music starts at 10pm to avoid the $7 cover charge. www. universalorlando.com. © **407/224-2155.**

Pat O'Brien's ★★ It's "an authentic reproduction of New Orleans's favorite watering hole," which is cool to see, and although its Hurricane rum drinks could make you see double, there are truly two dueling pianists playing nightly. O'Brien's serves good food, but if you can't get a seat (or don't want one), you can also grab a drink through a window facing the street. This spot is among the most popular here—the party starts at 4pm—and kids can join in. Cover is $7, usually after 9pm. www.patobriens.com. © **407/224-3663.**

Red Coconut Club ★★ A vanilla version of an ultralounge, it mixes stylish cocktails and cultivates the most intimate atmosphere at Universal Orlando. It's the district's most upscale venture. www.universalorlando.com. © **407/224-2425.**

OUTDOOR ORLANDO

Picture an old-fashioned steamship, not unlike the "African Queen," puttering along a narrow river of clear spring-fed water beneath a cool canopy of Spanish moss. Alongside, a few docile manatees nibble contentedly on river grass.

It's hard to believe, but that's what Central Florida really is. Well, was. When you tire of artificial rocks that conceal loudspeakers, remember that Orlando was adored first for natural beauty. Developers cleared everything but the lakes, ripping out natural vegetation. (And people wonder why they feel so hot.)

Central Florida's building explosion only kicked in a generation ago, and some people were smart enough to rope off land from destruction. Look around, and you'll find examples of the land's primacy—natural springs that Ponce de Leon once toured, swamps where alligators lurk beneath bladderwort and spatterdock, and marshy preserves thronged with migrating birds. And should all of that scenery bore, you can speed by it on bracing boat tours or observe it from above in a balloon or hang glider.

Blue Spring State Park ★★ NATURE RESERVE   You stand a fair chance of seeing manatees here, especially in the morning on a cold day. The creatures venture up the St. Johns River from the Atlantic Ocean to seek out the warmth of the springs of this 2,600-acre park, which maintain a constant 72°F temperature even in winter. From mid-November through March 15, all boating, swimming, and snorkeling are suspended while the big guys (more than 75 in some years) are in residence. An exception is made daily at 10am and 1pm, when a **2-hour guided boat tour** (www.sjrivercruises.com; 𝄢 **407/ 330-1612;** $22 adults, $20 seniors, $16 kids 3–12) is given, and the park also coughs up a few nature trails and canoe rental. Find it 60 miles north of Disney from exit 114 off I-4; go south on U.S. Rte. 17-92 to Orange City, and then make a right onto West French Avenue (there are signs).

2100 W. French Ave., Orange City. www.floridastateparks.org/bluespring. 𝄢 **386/775-3663.** $6 per car. Daily 8am–sundown

Manatees at Blue Springs State Park.

De Leon Springs State Park ★★★ NATURE RESERVE Florida has some 300 springs, and 27 of them discharge more than 60 million gallons of pure water a day. In fact, Florida has more springs than any other American state, so it's easy to conclude that natural springs are more authentically Floridian than pretty much anything else you might see in Orlando, and there's no more enjoyable place to experience them than here. The Spanish, Seminoles, and pre-presidential Zachary Taylor all fought over this spot of land, and Audubon saw his first limpkin here. (Remember *your* first time?) It's impossible to overstate the importance of the St. Johns River on the development of Florida—before rail, everybody used it—and, like the Nile, it's one of the few world rivers to flow north, not south. On this segment of the river, there are 18,000 acres of lakes and marshes to canoe (boats can be rented by the hour), a concrete-lined area to swim in, and 6 miles of trails to forge as you try to spot black bears, white tail deer, swamp rabbits, and, of course, 'gators. It gets cooler: At its general store–style **Old Spanish Sugar Mill** (www.planetdeland.com/sugarmill; ✆ **386/985-5644;** Mon–Fri 9am–4pm, Fri–Sat and holidays 8am–4pm), you make your own all-you-can-eat pancakes on griddles built into every table ($4.95 per person, but they'll cook you other things, too). Niftier still, the designated swimming area beside the Griddle House is in a spring-fed boil—30 feet deep in spots—that remains at a constant 72°F, year-round. To reach it, take I-4 north, exit for Deland, and 6 miles north of Deland on U.S. 17 turn left onto Ponce DeLeon Boulevard for 1 mile. Get there early, because when the weather sizzles, it gets busy.

601 Ponce de Leon Blvd., Deland. www.floridastateparks.org/deleonsprings. ✆ **386/ 985-4212.** $6 per carload. Daily 8am–sundown.

Harry P. Leu Gardens ★ GARDENS Botanical gardens seem dull on paper, yet once you find yourself within one, inhaling perfume and being warmed by the sun, you're in no hurry to leave. So it is with this 50-acre lakeside escape just north of downtown that gives visitors an inkling of why so many Gilded Age Americans wanted to flee to Florida, where the fresh air and gently rustling trees were a tonic to the maladies inflicted by the industrial North. Here you'll find Florida's largest formal rose garden (peaking in Apr); a patch planted with nectar-rich blooms favored by migrating butterflies; a large collection of camellias that bloom in late fall; and the lush Tropical Stream garden, crawling with native lizards and opening onto a dock where freshwater turtles swim and ducks bob.

1920 N. Forest Ave. www.leugardens.org. ✆ **407/246-2620.** $10 adults, $3 kids, free the first Mon of the month. Daily 9am–5pm.

Tibet–Butler Preserve ★ NATURE RESERVE Located more or less between Disney and SeaWorld (it's incredible it hasn't been turned into a golf course yet), it's the closest to the parks: about 5 miles north of the Lake Buena Vista hotel area. The 438-acre spread is combed by 4 miles of well-maintained boardwalks and trails (which close when flooded) that will give you respite among the cypress swamps and palmetto groves that once dominated this area.

8777 C.R. 535, Windermere. ✆ **407/876-6696.** Free. Wed–Sun 8am–6pm.

Outdoor Orlando

Canoeing in Wekiwa Springs State Park.

Wekiwa Springs State Park ★★★ NATURE RESERVE   The closest major spring to Orlando (just 20 min. north, off I-4's exit 94) is, despite encroachment by suburbs and malls, one of the prettiest preserves in the area. When you think of Florida, you don't normally picture rambling rivers, but the 42-mile Wekiva (yes, spelled differently than the park's name and pronounced "Wek-*eye*-va") is federally designated as "Wild and Scenic," meaning it hasn't been dammed or otherwise despoiled by development, despite the fact it's just northwest of Orlando's sprawl near Apopka. The springhead, fed by two sources, flows briskly and thrillingly over rock and sand, and some people come to fish, but most agree that its canoeing is among the most spectacular in the state. **Wekiwa Springs State Park Nature Adventures** (www.canoewekiva. com; ☎ **407/884-4311**) rents canoes ($20 for 2 hr.). Developers would love to sink their bulldozers' claws into this paradise; in fact, so much water is being siphoned from it that its flow is expected to diminish by 10% by 2025.

1800 Wekiwa Circle, Apopka. www.floridastateparks.org/wekiwasprings. ☎ **407/884-2008**. $6 per car. Daily 8am–sundown.

Boat Tours

The real Florida Everglades don't begin until south of Lake Okeechobee, which is why you'll hear Central Florida referred to as the *headwaters* of the Florida Everglades. Orlando-area swamps are still home to a wide diversity of life forms, though.

Boggy Creek Airboat Rides ★ TOUR   Airboats use powerful, backward-facing propellers to skip through shallow bogs, and they're a common form of eco-entertainment in Florida, particularly farther south in the Everglades. Though much wildlife is spooked by the din made by boat and plane alike (you'll get ear mufflers), many water snakes and alligators appear too thick-headed to care, so you should see a few on one of the continuously running 30-minute tours—boat skippers will cut the engine and float near the critters. The boats don't operate in the rain. The wildlife spotting is better in South Florida, but this'll is a long-running crowd-pleaser. Coupons are commonly distributed. One-hour night tours ($52 adults, $48 kids 3–12) are also available, but require reservations; check the website for times.

2001 E. Southport Rd., Kissimmee. www.bcairboats.com. (✆ **407/344-9550.** 30-min. tours $27 adults, $21 kids 3–12. Daily 9am–5:30pm.

Scenic Boat Tour ★★★ TOUR   This Winter Park institution has been showing visitors glorious lakeside mansions since 1938, when they were in their heyday of attracting wealthy snowbirds from the North. Three of Winter Park's seven cypress-lined lakes, which are connected by thrillingly narrow, hand-dug canals, are explored in a 1-hour, 12-mile tour narrated by salty old fellas. The lakes are flat and relaxing, with plenty of bird life, and your guide will pay particular attention to the works of James Gamble Rogers II, a virtuosic architect responsible for many of the area's finest homes. Among the high points is a glimpse of the modest condominium where Mamie Eisenhower spent her waning years, and 250-year-old live oaks. You'll find this charmer 3 blocks east of the shops on Park Avenue. Bring sunscreen: the pontoons are exposed.

312 E. Morse Blvd., Winter Park. www. scenicboattours.com. (✆ **407/644-4056.** $12 adults, $6 kids 2–11, cash only. Hourly departures 10am–4pm daily.

> ### Christmas Greetings
>
> **Christmas, Florida,** a blip on S.R. 50 between Orlando and Titusville, usually isn't much to write home about: farm supplies, roadkill. Unless, of course, it's the holiday season, when people come from far and wide to give their cards a Christmas postmark from the local post office. You'll find the P.O. at 23580 E. Colonial Dr./S.R. 50 (✆ **407/568-2941;** Mon–Fri 9am–5pm, Sat 9:30am–noon).

Golf

Golf courses do great damage to an ecosystem as precarious as Central Florida's, but the sport is nonetheless a major draw. Some of the brightest names in golfing, including Tiger Woods, Annika Sorenstam, Ernie Els, and Nick Faldo, have called Orlando home, as does cable's Golf Channel (which isn't open to visitors). In January, the Convention Center is home to the annual PGA Merchandise Show (www.pgashow.com).

Every self-respecting resort has a course or three, as do luxe condo developments. There are some 170 courses around town, and the competition has caused rates to plummet in recent years, although some still command around $150. The booking websites **TeeOff.com** and **GolfNow.com** both sell discounted tee times, driving rates down further. Some courses give priority to players who stay in their hotels through advantageous tee times, early reservations privileges, or cheaper fees. Prices can be steeper in high season (Jan–Apr), and they may be lowest in the fall and early winter. They usually sink to about half the day's rate for "twilight" tee times, which start around midafternoon. Club rentals cost $40 to $60. Reservations are all but required and most courses have a dress code and even an age minimum, so always ask.

DESTINATION COURSES

From pedigrees by well-known designers to clubhouses that operate more like spas, these fashionable courses are the theme parks of the fairway set. Tee times at these pricey greens fill quickly because the courses have national reputations. Count on paying about $10 per hole.

Arnold Palmer's Bay Hill Club & Lodge ★★★ Designer: Arnold Palmer, who owns it and also oversees the golf school. This guests-only course regularly receives the most accolades from experts. There's a full map of every hole on its website. The course was renovated under Palmer's direction in 2015.

9000 Bay Hill Blvd., Orlando. www.bayhill.com. ✆ **888/422-9445.** 27 holes.

ChampionsGate Golf Resort ★★ Designer: Greg Norman. Headquarters of the **David Leadbetter Golf Academy** (✆ **888/633-5323;** www.davidleadbetter.com), this resort and handsome high-rise hotel is 10 minutes south of Disney.

1400 Masters Blvd., ChampionsGate. www.championsgategolf.com. ✆ **407/787-4653.** 36 holes.

Mystic Dunes Golf Club ★★ Designer: Gary Koch. Located 2 miles south of Disney, it has steadily won "Golf Digest" praise. Elevation changes up to 80 feet over the course of play.

7600 Mystic Dunes Lane, Celebration. www.mysticdunesgolf.com. ✆ **407/787-5678.** 18 holes.

Reunion Resort & Club ★★ Designers: Jack Nicklaus, Arnold Palmer, Tom Watson. Top designers and a golf school overseen by Annika Sorenstam—all a 10-minute drive south of Disney.

7593 Gathering Dr., Kissimmee. www.reunionresort.com/golf. ✆ **866/380-8563.** 54 holes.

Ritz Carlton golf course.

The Ritz-Carlton Golf Club Orlando, Grande Lakes ★★ Designer: Greg Norman. This **Golf Digest School** (✆ **800/875-4347**) is taught by PGA and LPGA professionals. Family golf packages are often available.

4040 Central Florida Pkwy., Orlando. www.grandelakes.com. ✆ **407/393-4900.** 18 holes.

Shingle Creek Golf Club ★ Designer: David Harman. Near the convention center, Shingle Creek is also home to a school overseen by Brad Brewer.

9939 Universal Blvd., Orlando. www.shinglecreekgolf.com. ✆ **866/996-9933** or 407/996-9933. 18 holes.

Tranquilo Golf Club at Four Seasons Resort Orlando ★★★ Disney's former Osprey Ridge course, an Audubon sanctuary two miles east of the Magic Kingdom, was redesigned by its creator Tom Fazio in late 2014. Each hole has four sets of tees to appeal to all skill levels.

3451 Golf View Dr., Lake Buena Vista. www.tranquilogolf.com. ✆ **407/313-6880.** 18 holes.

Villas of Grand Cypress ★ Designer: Jack Nicklaus. This club, right next to Disney in Lake Buena Vista, was noted as one of Orlando's best golf resorts by the readers of "Condé Nast Traveler," who know about such things.

One North Jacaranda, Orlando. www.grandcypress.com/golf. ✆ **407/239-1909.** 45 holes.

Walt Disney World Golf Courses ★ Disney has been closing courses or parceling them to other resorts, but there are currently four left, including the Lake Buena Vista (once a PGA tour host), the recently refurbished Palm, and the Magnolia (the one with the sand bunker shaped like Mickey). Oak Trail (9 holes; $38) is the better choice for family outings. Greens fees include golf cart, when available, and kids under 18 get half-off full tee time rates at the 18-hole courses. All courses opened with the resort in 1971, and if truth be told, their maintenance is spotty.

Walt Disney World. www.golfwdw.com. ✆ **407/938-4653.** 63 holes.

MORE AFFORDABLE COURSES

Unlike the aforementioned courses, these don't have big marketing budgets and they don't always come attached to celebrity names, but they nevertheless are high-quality courses you can enjoy at sensible prices.

Celebration Golf Course ★★ In the Disney-built town next door to the Disney-built world, English master designer Robert Trent Jones, Sr. and his son pocked their course with water hazards on 17 of its 18 holes.

701 Golf Park Dr., Celebration. www.celebrationgolf.com. ✆ **407/566-4653.** 18 holes.

Falcon's Fire Golf Club ★ Designer: Rees Jones. Decently maintained and fairly priced (in the mid-$40s for prime tee times), this public course can be crowded, but holes are straightforward and a beverage cart makes the rounds.

3200 Seralago Blvd., Kissimmee. www.falconsfire.com. ✆ **407/239-5445.** 18 holes.

Hawk's Landing Golf Club ★ Because it's part of the Orlando World Center Marriott resort on World Center Drive by Disney, it crawls with convention-goers who keep prices high. Water is in play on 15 of the 18 holes, and the par-71 course carries a slope rating of 131.

8701 World Center Dr., Orlando. www.golfhawkslanding.com. ✆ **800/567-2623.** 18 holes.

Highlands Reserve Golf Club ★★   This highly praised public course, with a fair mix of challenges and cakewalks, is a strong value, charging a top rate of $45, and its twilight rates kick in as early as noon. It's about 10 minutes southwest of Disney.

500 Highlands Reserve Blvd., Davenport. www.highlandsreserve-golf.com. ✆ **863/420-1724.** 18 holes.

MetroWest Golf Club ★★   This Marriott Golf–managed course is the work of Robert Trent Jones, Sr., famous for tight greens protected on both sides by sand traps, trees, or water. It's one of the city's most popular courses, found less than 3 miles north of Universal Orlando.

2100 S. Hiawassee Rd., Orlando. www.metrowestgolf.com. ✆ **407/299-1099.** 18 holes.

Orange County National Golf Center and Lodge ★   At this wide-open complex (922 acres, unspoiled by houses—atypical around here), holes have five sets of tees, allowing you to choose a game that ranges between 7,300 yards and a little over 5,000. It's among the developments north of Walt Disney World, and it's cheapest early in the week.

16301 Phil Ritson Way, Winter Garden. www.ocngolf.com. ✆ **407/656-2626.** 45 holes.

Royal St. Cloud Golf Links ★★   Aiming to recall Scotland's great links—there's even a stone bridge that looks like it was built during the days of William Wallace, not in 2001—this affordable club, 25 miles east of Disney, has fairways are noted for being wide, well groomed, and firm, and planners promise you'll use "every club in the bag."

5310 Michigan Ave., St. Cloud. www.stcloudgolfclub.com. ✆ **877/891-7010** or 407/891-7010. 27 holes.

Timacuan Golf and Country Club ★★   There are five sets of tees, adapting this exceptionally well-groomed course from 7,000 to 5,000 yards, and unusually, designers were careful to leave its handsome Old Florida features (undulating fairways, Spanish moss, wetlands) mostly intact. Only 3 holes are riddled with water, which might make it easier for kids. The greens were renovated in 2013. Lake Mary is 10 miles north of downtown.

550 Timacuan Blvd., Lake Mary. www.golftimacuan.com. ✆ **407/321-0010.** 18 holes.

Up in the Air

Florida is well suited to hot-air ballooning for many of the same reasons that it's ideal for golf: flat, even topography and often placid morning weather. A trip involves a very early start—6am is common. You'll be finished with your hour-long ride by the time the theme parks get cranking. If balloons don't float your boat, there are other ways to see Orlando from up high as well.

Magic Sunrise Ballooning ★★ More intimate than its supersized competition, with just two to four people in the basket with the pilot, this company, flying since 1987, greets landings with a champagne toast.

603 N. Garfield Ave., Deland. www.magicsunriseballooning.com. ℂ **866/606-7433.** $215 per person for 2–4 people, $135 kids under 90 lb., no kids 5 or under.

Orlando Balloon Rides ★★ In business since 1983, its flagship balloon, launched as the world's largest in 2011, is 11 stories tall and its basket fits an incredible 24 people. It meets at a hotel near the main Disney entrance.

2900 Parkway Blvd., Kissimmee. www.orlandoballoonrides.com. ℂ **800/634-4774.** $225 adults, $109 kids 10–15, $10 less Mon–Fri.

Orlando Tree Trek Adventure Park ★★★ In some woods 3 miles south of Disney, eight fun and newly erected elevated obstacle courses, from 10 to 40 feet off the ground, challenge families to conquer their fear of heights. Sometimes you're stepping on boards, sometimes wires, sometimes nets, but you're always hooked into a safety line, and guides are always cheering you on.

7625 Sinclair Rd., Kissimmee. www.orlandotreetrek.com. ℂ **407/390-9999.** $50 adults, $40 seniors 65 and older, $30 kids 7–11, $39 kids 9–11. Daily 8am–dusk.

Wallaby Ranch ★★ In flat Central Florida, where there are no mountains that don't contain roller coasters, hang gliders can't soar from cliffs. Instead, they're launched by ultralight "aerotugs," to an altitude of 2,000 feet.

1805 Deen Still Rd., Davenport. www.wallaby.com. ℂ **863/424-0070.** Tandem flights $175.

SHOPPING

Orlando is a hotbed for outlet activity, partly because international visitors, with their often-stronger currencies, are prone to buying frenzies. Like most modern outlet malls, not all of the items you find for sale here will have come from higher-priced "regular" stores; much of the stock has been specially manufactured for the outlet market (although "Consumer Reports" doesn't think the quality is substantially different from retail). You'll usually find prices between 30% and 50% off sales at retail stores, and after the holiday rush, discounts go deeper. The best ones are village-style outdoor malls and most stay open Monday to Saturday from 10am to 11pm, Sunday 10am to 9pm.

Outlet Malls

Orlando Premium Outlets International Dr. ★★★ OUTLET MALL
The most dangerously tempting outlet in town is a stupendous 180-store (give or take) open-air village where it's very unlikely you'll come away empty-handed. Nearly every conceivable brand has a presence here, but the chief threats include Neiman Marcus Last Call—a clearance center that sells genuine department store castoffs from its namesake stores, Bergdorf Goodman, and the Horchow catalog—Saks Fifth Avenue Off 5th, Calphalon, Coach, Ann

Taylor Factory Store, Puma, Nike Factory Store, Guess? Factory Store, Eddie Bauer Outlet, Kenneth Cole, Fossil, Reebok Outlet Store, Hugo Boss Factory Store, Calvin Klein, Brooks Brothers Factory Store, Kate Spade New York, Tumi, and Victoria's Secret. There's a Disney's Character Warehouse to undercut your souvenir bill. Weekdays are quietest, and parking is most ample around back. The website lists sales by store. 4951 International Dr., Orlando. www.premiumoutlets.com. ✆**407/352-9600.**

Orlando Premium Outlets Vineland Ave ★★ OUTLET MALL Being just a mile east of Disney property has its perks—its owners tout it as the most productive outlet center in America, with sales exceeding $1,000 per square foot. That's why at press time, it was about to cut the ribbon on a 110,000-square-foot expansion of a property that already had 550,000 square feet and 150 stores. Among the goods: Armani Outlet, Banana Republic Factory Store, Barney's New York Outlet, Gymboree, and Burberry. One popular shop, because it's so close to the Mouse House, is Disney's Character Premiere, for cast-off official theme park souvenirs. Steel yourself during the weekend; the competition for parking approaches Olympian difficulty. It's 10 minutes from Disney Springs; the turnoff is just south of I-4's exit 68 on S.R. 535/Apopka Vineland, by Bahama Breeze. The I-Ride Trolley (p. 293) touches down here ostensibly every 20 minutes. 8200 Vineland Ave., Orlando. www.premiumoutlets.com. ✆**407/238-7787.**

Lake Buena Vista Factory Stores ★ OUTLET MALL The third-best outlet shopping in town is a strip mall–style collection of about 50 stores, not all of which are owned by famous brands. The offerings here, about 2 miles south of the Disney Springs gate, are not as shimmering as those at its two rival outlet malls, but they're decent, especially for kids. There are enough names you know (including Tommy Hilfiger Kids, Carter's for Kids, Old Navy Outlet, OshKosh B'Gosh, and Aéropostale) to warrant a quick trip. The Disney Character Outlet has some bargains (half-price mugs, shirts, toys, and some souvenirs dated from a few years ago), and there's a Travelex office for currency exchange. The mall provides a free daily shuttle to and from major hotels around Disney and I-Drive; they leave between 9am and 2:50pm and return in four batches from 12:55 to 7pm (6pm on Sun). 15657 S. Apopka Vineland Rd. (S.R. 535), Orlando. www.lbvfs.com. ✆ **407/238-9301.** Mon–Sat 10am–9pm and Sun 10am–7pm.

Disney Springs (Downtown Disney)

Disney Springs ★★, until this year called Downtown Disney—signs may not all be updated—is Walt Disney World's main free area for restaurants and shopping. Its unwieldy layout ambles along the shore of Village Lake a few miles east of Epcot in a traffic-clogged zone on the eastern edge of park property. At the easternmost section, the Marketplace section is dominated by stores selling every variety of Disney-themed merchandise you can imagine.

In 2016, it's at the tail end of a drastic, multi-year overhaul, with more corporate restaurants and shops added and the old, Disney-created Pleasure

Island concept extracted like a wart. Disney Springs remain a place to grab dinner (alas, no cheaper than elsewhere in the World), buy souvenirs, and maybe bowl or catch a Cirque du Soleil show, and now there's a lot more booze, too. Parking is free in two new, state-of-the-lot structures with overhead lights indicating at a distance if the space below them is free. "Orange," near the West Side, is most convenient to evening entertainment, and the other (open in mid-2016) is closer to the Disney-themed merchandise.

The district has four zones; because of the size, it's helpful to know which one you're heading for because the walk between them can be up to 15 minutes. The busiest and easternmost area is called the Marketplace (it's nearest to the DTS bus stop), and it's for shops and restaurants. The westernmost zone is the West Side, and it leans toward nightlife and entertainment, with a Cirque du Soleil show, **Splitsville Luxury Lanes** bowling, and a 24-screen AMC cinema (p. 198). Between them is the focus of the Disney Springs redevelopment, and it is divided into **Town Center,** for larger retail names, and **The Landing,** especially good for food. The major shops here are not likely to surprise you much if you've ever been to a mall: Zara, UNIQLO, Lilly Pulitzer, Tommy Bahama, and UGG are among the new additions—nice shops, and perhaps not new to you, but plenty to browse in between sips of margaritas.

Shops at the **Marketplace** (© **407/939-3463**) are almost pure Mouse, and nearly all of them sell candy, too. Stores are themed for maximum souvenir sales, including one for toys and games **(Once Upon a Toy),** one for Christmas and holiday decorations **(Disney's Days of Christmas),** one for high-end collectibles **(the Art of Disney),** one for kitchen tools **(Mickey's Pantry),** one for urban wear **(Tren-D),** one for stationery and albums **(Disney's Wonderful World of Memories),** and **Disney's Pin Traders,** a hub for collectors of the park's badges where you can also buy MagicBands. The most interesting is the **Marketplace Co-Op,** which contains some great mini-stores such as funky contemporary art versions of Disney characters at **WonderGround,** **D-Tech** for you-design-it smartphone cases, **Centerpiece** for homewares, and **Zoey and Pickles** fashion for little girls. For the Disney fan, there's a lot to discover.

The Marketplace's tent-pole is the big kahuna of Disney merch: **World of Disney,** the largest souvenir department store in the resort, crowned by a giant Stitch burping water onto passersby. It's a rambling cathedral-roofed barn stocked from rug to rafter with every conceivable Disney-branded item—a Villains room, a room for men, one for candy, one for the latest branding craze, and so on. You'll find stuff here you won't find at other Disney stores here or at home, especially if it's a "park exclusive." Despite its status as the chief Mouse mart, World of Disney still may not have what you want. That's because it's the only store that offers annual passholders a discount, which means the most obsessed fans clean the shelves here first. It also may not carry items that might be sold at another store at the Marketplace (tree ornaments, for example, or MagicBands).

One of the most special souvenir traditions on Disney turf is the collection of little enamel and cloisonné pins featuring every known character, ride, movie, and promotional event. When the Haunted Mansion was refurbished, pins were made that contained tiny snippets of Madame Leota's original crystal ball. Sometimes it seems it's easier to get your hands on a pin than it is to find a bottle of water—there's even a pavilion that sells nothing but pins at Disney Springs. They are usually worn on lanyards, and when cast members clock in for their shifts, they replenish their pin supply at a special window in the backstage area—a dozen to a lanyard at all times. The rule is that if a cast member is wearing almost any pin you want (barring ones commemorating employment milestones), you're allowed to ask them to trade it for one of your own and they're not allowed to refuse if the pin is legit. Universal sells a fair supply, too, but the craze is fiercest at Disney, where the backings are shaped, of course, like a mouse head.

Very few Marketplace stores sell non-Disney plunder. **Ghirardelli Soda Fountain & Chocolate Shop** is one of the few non–San Francisco locations run by the chocolate-making stalwart. It has a pricey sundae shop and a boutique where $1/12$-oz. samples are freely dispensed. Kids can't be separated from the **LEGO Store** (still here despite the fact the toymaker now brands a competing park, p. 168), where children can play with kits for free, or **Build-A-Dino** which does for reptiles what Build-a-Bear does for teddies. **Basin** sells bath products for those teeny hotel room tubs.

Bibbidi Bobbidi Boutique ★★★ SALON   Little girls bask in the star treatment as they are lavished with glittery, pink makeovers as princesses from $60 (Coach package with hair and a sash; add nails for $5) to several hundred (gown, wand, photos), overseen by a kindly "Fairy Godmother-in-Training." *Warning:* The dresses are hot and scratchy, so bring a change of clothes if the sun is strong. Boys are steered to the Pirates League in Adventureland, where similar gender roles are ascribed. There's also a salon in the Magic Kingdom in the Castle, but you'll need a park ticket for that and slots are scarcer. World of Disney, Marketplace. www.disneyworld.com/style. Ⓒ **407/939-7895.** Daily 8:45am–7:30pm. Minimum age 3. $60–$195 Reservations required.

Other Interesting Stores

If you feel moved to learn more about Florida history, the book selection isn't massive. The bookstore at the **Regional History Center** (Ⓒ **407/836-8594;** p. 182), however, is a good start. You'll find a well-stocked **Barnes & Noble** ★★★ (Venezia Plaza, 7900 W. Sand Lake Rd., Orlando; Ⓒ **407/345-0900;** daily 9am–11pm) among the terrific restaurants of Sand Lake Road west of I-4 and at the Florida Mall (8358 S. Orange Blossom Trail, Orlando; Ⓒ **407/856-7200;** Sun–Thurs 9am–8pm, Fri–Sat 9am–11pm).

Artegon Marketplace ★ MALL   This ongoing real estate tragedy at the top end of I-Drive is struggling to wake from a nightmare that began when it opened in 2001. In 2014, $70 million was sunk into reinterpreting a bleakly under-tenanted mall as a bazaar for 165 artisans making one-of-a-kind stuff, some of them interesting, some sad, but all keeping their own hours. No matter what happens with that scheme, the anchor stores remain interesting: The beloved **Ron Jon Surf Shop** out of Cocoa Beach; a **Sheplers Western Wear** for honing that proto-American look; a **Sky Zone** indoor trampoline park (not yet open at press time); and the camping-and-fishing explosion **Bass Pro Shops Outdoor World,** so gargantuan it must be seen to be believed. For minor entertainment, there's **Putting Edge** glow-in-the-dark minigolf course (p. 190) and **The Beef Jerky Outlet,** which sells nothing but that. 5250 International Dr., Orlando. www.artegonmarketplace.com. ✆ **407/351-7718.** Mon–Sat 11am–9pm, Sun 11am–7pm.

Eli's Orange World ★★ SHOP   Agra has the Taj Mahal and Sydney has its opera house—Orlando has a 60-foot-tall orange. Back when most of this land was orange groves, Florida roadsides were full of this kind of souvenir catch-all, stacked high with oranges and grapefruits in red mesh bags, but the citrus industry cashed out for McMansions. Fruit changes by the season: Fall is for navel and ambersweet oranges, January sees honeybell tangelos, and February through May sees a procession of oranges, honey tangerines, and Valencia oranges; Indian River grapefruit is available year-round. A timeshare hawker tries to pitch, and shelves teeter with the sort of corny Florida souvenirs that time forgot, including shellacked alligator heads and local jellies. Sure, there are *lots* of schlocky, fluorescent-lit barns selling junky souvenirs on U.S. 192 and I-Drive—but this is *landmark* schlock. 5395 W. U.S. Hwy. 192, Kissimmee. www.orangeworld192.com. ✆ **800/531-3182** or 407/239-6031. Daily 8am–9:40pm.

Theme Park Connection ★★ SHOP   There's no other junk shop like it. Here, Disney liquidates stuff it can't use anymore, including costumes, props, hotel dishes, name tags, retired souvenirs, signs, maps, hundreds of hard-to-find pins, and if you're lucky and loaded, entire ride vehicles. This merchandise is fascinating, and it's supplemented by some movie props. Find it in an industrial zone a few miles east of I-4 off Sand Lake Road. 2160 Premier Row, Orlando. www.themeparkconnection.com. ✆ **407/284-1934.** Mon–Fri 10am–5pm, Sat 10am–3pm.

CRUISES FROM PORT CANAVERAL

Cruise ships go from Port Canaveral (www.portcanaveral.com), an hour east of Orlando, so it's easy to combine a voyage with the theme parks. Parking costs about $20 a night or $120 a week, and there's nothing to do at the port.

As usual, you won't find many discounts from Disney, although MouseSavers.com tells which departures are going cheap. Quotes from specialty agents are often hundreds lower than those the lines themselves offer, and prices of $100 a night or less can be had if you book through a specialist. Check **Cruise Brothers** (www.cruisebrothers.com; ✆ **800/827-7779**), and **Cruises Only** (www.cruisesonly.com; ✆ **800/278-4737**). Don't quit before you consult a terrific site called **Cruise Compete** (www.cruisecompete.com), on which multiple cruise sellers jockey for your business by offering low bids.

Carnival Cruise Lines ★ CRUISE

Considered a bargain line, it's noisy and atwitter with neon, like the inside of a pinball machine. Think "Real Housewives of the Atlantic Ocean." Carnival is popular with families, teens especially like it, and there are few pretensions. Each ship has a twisting water slide that has also become a line signature. Carnival sails the *Sensation* and the *Valor* on 3-, 4-, and 5-night Bahamas runs. The *Sunshine* does weeklong Eastern Caribbean runs, and the *Magic* and *Valor* go to Mexico for 7 nights. www.carnival.com. ✆ **800/764-7419.**

Disney Cruise Line ★★★ CRUISE

These high-quality, casino-free ships, the newest of the port's fleet, include character appearances, fireworks at sea, and top-drawer entertainment. The hallmark is the kids' program, and in a brilliant touch, waiters follow you no matter the restaurant you're in (one restaurant, by the way, changes from black and white to full color as you dine). The *Magic,* DCL's original ship, and the *Dream* and *Fantasy,* the line's newer and larger additions, sail for weeklong Eastern and Western Caribbean trips and 3- and 4-night Bahamas jaunts. Disney packages trips with theme park stays and provides seamless transitions between the two, although because it's a Disney package it won't give you the best deal on the Walt Disney World portion.

www.disneycruise.com. ✆ **800/393-2784.**

Norwegian Cruise Lines ★ CRUISE

The family-friendly, middle-priced Norwegian brings its older *Spirit* to the port in early 2016, and its *Epic* (2010) arrives in November 2016 for a mix of weeklong Western and Eastern Caribbean cruises and 3- and 4-night Bahamas ones.

www.ncl.com. ✆ **866/234-7350.**

Royal Caribbean International ★ CRUISE

It's the line for young couples and teens, with active diversions such as rock-climbing walls. It hits the sweet spot between the gaudy tackiness of Carnival and the twee branding of Disney. The principal ship is *Enchantment of the Seas,* a Vision-class ship from 1996 (no ice rink, no wave machine) that's among the line's most manageable, at 2,664 passengers. It offers 3- and 4-night Bahamas runs, as does the *Majesty of the Seas. Freedom of the Seas* (2006) does 5-night trips to the Cozumel and 7-night runs to the Eastern Caribbean. At the end of 2016, the giant *Oasis of the Seas* starts making 7–night Caribbean trips.

www.royalcaribbean.com. ✆ **866/562-7625.**

DINING AROUND TOWN 6

You don't need a guidebook to decide if you want to eat at a chain restaurant—Orlando is crawling with those. But you can use help locating family-run small businesses or fledgling brands that aren't backed by multi-million-dollar ad campaigns. These are the worthy discoveries you might not otherwise have noticed among the clamor.

That's not to say corporate food can't have local provenance. In Orlando, even supersized brands have a pedigree: Darden, which owns Olive Garden and LongHorn Steakhouse, is based here, and so is Hard Rock Cafe. But for those, you know what you're going to get. We want to show you more flavors.

Pretty much every restaurant is open for lunch and dinner. Don't expect places to accept checks—credit cards are Orlando's cash. Also, this is a town where it bears asking for discounts.

In addition to our recommendations, check out Scott Joseph's Orlando Restaurant Guide (**www.scottjosephorlando.com**) by longtime food critic Scott Joseph, who reviews high-quality places to eat in the "real" Orlando north of the tourist zone. In September, dozens of area restaurants band together for **Orlando Magical Dining Month** (www.orlandomagicaldining.com), when three-course (appetizer, entree, dessert) prix-fixe dinners cost $33.

Prices are classified based on the price range for a main course at dinner:

- o Inexpensive: $10 or less
- o Moderate: $11 to $16
- o Expensive: $17 or over

OUTSIDE THE DISNEY PARKS

These are the restaurants on resort property or publicly accessible hotels but not inside a ticketed park. For places inside the theme parks, plus info on the Disney Dining Plan, see chapter 3. Disney's most affordable hotels don't offer much beyond food courts.

Reservations are a necessity for all of Disney's table-service restaurants. Walk-ins are accepted, but tables are often full. Bookings open 180 days in advance, and families throw themselves into

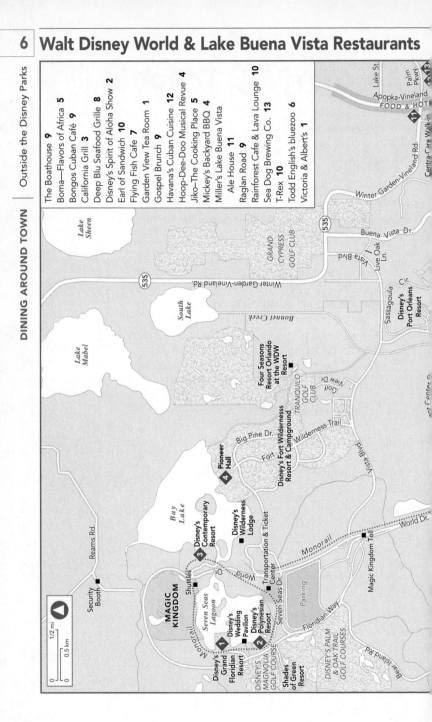

The Boathouse **9**
Boma—Flavors of Africa **5**
Bongos Cuban Café **9**
California Grill **3**
Deep Blu Seafood Grille **8**
Disney's Spirit of Aloha Show **2**
Earl of Sandwich **10**
Flying Fish Cafe **7**
Garden View Tea Room **1**
Gospel Brunch **9**
Havana's Cuban Cuisine **12**
Hoop-Dee-Doo Musical Revue **4**
Jiko—The Cooking Place **5**
Mickey's Backyard BBQ **4**
Miller's Lake Buena Vista
  Ale House **11**
Raglan Road **9**
Rainforest Cafe & Lava Lounge **10**
Sea Dog Brewing Co. **13**
T-Rex **10**
Todd English's bluezoo **6**
Victoria & Albert's **1**

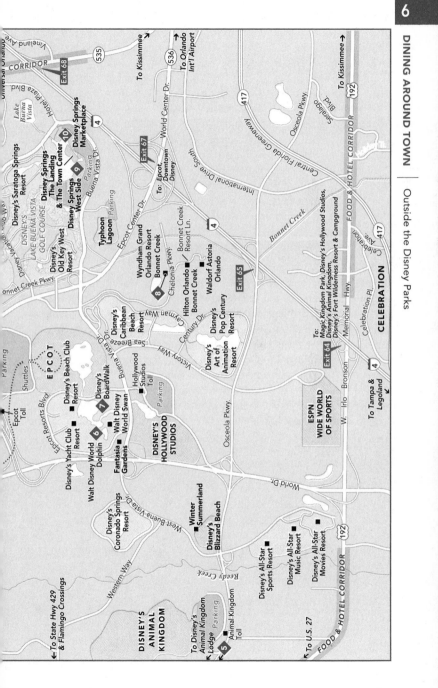

it early as if they're Panzer units invading Poland. Obnoxiously, Disney slaps you with a $10 per person fee if you fail to show up for your reservation, which is unfriendly, but the side benefit is that restaurants that seem impossible suddenly have space 24 hours ahead, when people dump bookings to avoid penalty. All Disney-run restaurants (disneyworld.disney.go.com/dining; © **407/939-3463** [DINE]) can be booked by phone, online, or using the My Disney Experience app. Non-Disney-run places can be booked directly or, usually, on OpenTable.

Parking is free with a reservation. Reservationists have schedules of other resort events (such as fireworks times) and will help you plan around them, but Disney's website withholds prices.

The nicest restaurants within Disney's hotels generally serve from 5 to 10pm, as it's assumed patrons will eat lunch in the parks. Some places are more special than others, and many have no culinary point of view or care mostly about processing the convention crowd, so focus your booking attentions on these recommendations (all unfortunately in the Expensive category).

EXPENSIVE

Boma—Flavors of Africa ★★★ AFRICAN   Make a reservation here and you get a bonus: a fine excuse to visit Disney's Animal Kingdom Lodge and pay a visit to the animals in its backyard paddocks, floodlit after dark—think of the high price as an admission fee for that. Dinner is a good time, too: A 60-item buffet menu, served in a dramatically vaulted dining room of thatching and bamboo, is not all African. It runs the gamut from roast chicken and beef to African-themed delights such as watermelon rind salad, curried coconut Indian *mater paneer,* and *bobotie* (a moussaka-like pie of ground beef from South Africa). There's an atmospheric wood fire, with plenty of chefs on hand to answer questions and plenty of options for less adventurous tongues.

Disney's Animal Kingdom Lodge, 2901 Osceola Pkwy., Bay Lake. www.disneyworld. com. © **407/939-3463.** Adults $39–$43, kids $18–$22. Daily 7:30–11am and 4:30–9:30pm.

California Grill ★★★ AMERICAN   For a blowout night with a view, the best choice is this beloved space on the 15th floor of the Contemporary Resort. The wine list is elaborate (250 by the bottle, 80 by the glass, 10 types of sake), and the California fusion-style menu, helmed by Chef Brian Piasecki, is bright and seasonal but hearty—swordfish, 24-hour braised short rib with truffle-whipped potatoes—and sushi and flatbreads are popular sidelines. Book as soon as you can—the maximum is 180 days before—and get a window seat for the fireworks. The music for the show is even piped in to the outdoor viewing platforms, which are practically on top of Tomorrowland. A dinner here is a fantastic excuse to stroll through the atrium of this most iconic hotel.

Disney's Contemporary Resort, 4600 N. World Dr., Lake Buena Vista. www.disneyworld. com. © **407/939-3463.** Main courses $34–$47.

Deep Blu Seafood Grille ★★ SEAFOOD A 2014 chef change hasn't done much to diminish this spacious resort restaurant's mandate for gourmet seafood-based creations. It repeatedly makes the list of the city's best choices for dishes such as crab mac and cheese, calamari "fries," and some divinely soft crab cakes that are plated as savory fall-apart patties, bucking most kitchens' tendency to over-fry. You can pair wines with every course, or try one of the house cocktails, most of which advance a tropical theme by being based on one fruit or another. You'll find Deep Blu in the massive Wyndham development close to Downtown Disney/Disney Springs on the south side of Disney property; turn left at the second Wyndham-marked entrance.

Wyndham Grand Orlando Bonnet Creek, 14651 Chelonia Parkway, Orlando. www. deepbluorlando.com.✆ **407/390-2420.** Mains $29–$45. Daily 5:30pm–10pm.

Garden View Tea Room ★★ HIGH TEA The pseudo-Victorian space with a garden gazebo feel delights little girls with its range of high teas—tea cozies, china, and all. The most extravagant option, the My Disney Girl's Perfectly Princess Tea Party, costs $334 for an adult and child together and includes a visit from Aurora.

Disney's Grand Floridian Resort & Spa, 4401 Floridian Way, Lake Buena Vista. www. disneyworld.com.✆ **407/939-3463.** High tea without characters $14–$38. Daily noon–5pm.

Jiko—The Cooking Place ★★ AFRICAN The a la carte fine dining room across the hall from Boma is considered by many to be one of the resort's most romantic spots. It serves entrees that are fairly good, too (plus flatbreads—all Disney's top restaurants have a love affair with flatbreads), but they often cost what the entire banquet does at Boma. The food coming from the open kitchen is pan-African, but waiters are sometimes too eager to pander to American palates. That said, there are some delicious twists such as sweet tamarind butter for the bread, frisky amuse-bouches (prosciutto-wrapped pineapple, cucumber sorbet), and crispy beef *bobotie* spring rolls. Animal Kingdom Lodge also has one of the largest lists of South African wines in all of North America. When you're here, you also get to see the animals in the view area at the Lodge. Wednesdays at 3pm, it puts on a wine tasting for $25.

Disney's Animal Kingdom Lodge, 2901 Osceola Pkwy., Bay Lake. www.disneyworld. com.✆ **407/939-3463.** Main courses $30–$46. Daily 7–11am and 4:30–9:30pm.

Todd English's bluezoo ★ SEAFOOD Todd English, known for rich flavors, won't be here but his stamp is. Eaten among witty colored-glass baubles that suggest being underwater, the menu changes but the focus is fresh fish. The nightly herb-rubbed "dancing fish" is grilled on a spinning skewer (watch them spin alongside the raw bar); the light clam chowder comes infused with bacon; and the 2-pound "Cantonese" lobster is painted in a sticky soy glaze that must be shared. The Lounge serves a bar menu.

Walt Disney World Dolphin Hotel, 1500 Epcot Resorts Blvd., Lake Buena Vista. www. swananddolphin.com/bluezoo.✆ **407/934-1111.** Mains $28–$60. Daily 5–11pm.

Victoria & Albert's ★★★ FRENCH   Disney's flagship restaurant is the destination for honeymoons, anniversaries, proposals, and gourmands. The company puts much stock in Chef Scott Hunnel, a multiple James Beard nominee who sources ingredients personally and also oversees the top-tier restaurants on Disney Cruise Line. Praised as the only AAA five-diamond restaurant in Central Florida, a citation it has earned since 2000, the adults-only, 65-seater lays on its indulgent seven-course menu (amuse-bouches, Osetra caviar, Iwate Japanese beef with oxtail jus, pheasant consommé) presented to you under cloches like a parade of debutantes. It's like the Very Fancy Restaurant where a character might take a date on a sitcom, which adds to the theater. The resort's most exclusive reservation is here: the four-table Queen Victoria's room, where a private 10-course meal is served behind closed doors for $210 per person before wine. It sells out. Reserve 180 days ahead.

Disney's Grand Floridian Resort & Spa, 4401 Floridian Way. Lake Buena Vista. www.victoria-alberts.com. ✆ **407/939-3463.** Prix-fixe from $150, wine pairings from $65. 10-course Chef's Table prix-fixe from $210, wine pairings from $105. 2 nightly seatings, 1 for Chef's Table and Queen Victoria's room. Jacket required for men (loaners available), no children under 10 permitted.

Disney Springs

In these restaurants (all in The Landing or on the West Side), food isn't as spectacular as the decor, and unless you come at lunch when prices drop by a third, you'll pay something to the tune of $16 for a burger. Welcome to Disney!

Disney Springs charges extreme prices ($30 at dinner, $22 at lunch) but doesn't return that money in skilled cuisine. Although no places serve foul food, most coast along by sponging from steady foot traffic. You can count these places out unless you're hungry and just don't care: **Fulton's Crab House,** in a mock riverboat berthed solidly in concrete since 1976; the fair-to-average **Portobello Country Italian Trattoria,** with an Italian theme; the Asian-fusion **Wolfgang Puck Grand Café** (it also has a walk-up window for quick bites); a **Planet Hollywood** (undergoing renovations this year to be renamed Planet Hollywood Observatory); **Paradiso 37** (tapas); and barbecue specialist **Crossroads at House of Blues. Ghirardelli Ice Cream and Chocolate Shop** is a rare offshoot of the San Francisco treasure, but it only does desserts (although its candy shop always gives away tablet-size free samples). A few semi-permanent **food trucks** on the West Side near Bongos sell hand-held stuff. All menus are available for perusal at Guest Services in the Marketplace area.

Disney Springs is emerging from a total makeover, and with the addition of so many new bars (margaritas, slushies—even the Starbucks serves wine after dark), suddenly it's even boozier than Universal's CityWalk. Several restaurants—**STK Steakhouse** (the only place in the Springs for rooftop dining), **Morimoto Asia** (overseen by Iron Chef Masaharu Morimoto)—were slated to open in The Landing after our press time. Give those a try, because as newcomers, they aren't yet jaded by the non-stop crowds and they're likely to be

NBA City at Universal.

on top of their game for a few years. **NBA City** also opens on the West Side, but that's more about interactive basketball games than about food.

EXPENSIVE

The Boathouse ★★★ AMERICAN   This convivial loft-like complex with three bars was immediately celebrated by locals upon its 2015 opening, and now the bar and dining room are elbow-to-elbow with people making a boozy evening out of its cocktails, craft beers, steaks, seafood, chops, and raw bar. The towering slices of baked Alaska are more daunting than the peak of Mt. McKinley. The nautical theme (there are rare boats affixed overhead) isn't superficial: After dinner, you can take a surf-and-turf ride (fee) from the boat ramp in an original 1961 Amphicar, a versatile vessel that transports passengers from the sidewalk to a 20-minute tour out on the lake. It is one of the top places to eat at Disney Springs.

The Landing, Disney Springs. www.theboathouseorlando.com. © **407/939-2628.** Mains $15–36. Bookable on OpenTable.com. Sun–Thurs 11am–1am, Fri–Sat 11am–2am. Reservations recommended. Free self-parking.

Bongos Cuban Café ★ CUBAN   This place proudly reminds you it was co-founded by Gloria and Emilio Estefan, the Cuban-born power couple of Latin music, and that boast is a portent that the focus will be on music and not on food. The dishes (ceviche, plantains, and lots of grilled or lightly fried fish and meats) are generally unsuccessful, and inattention to signature Cuban dishes is insulting when you've paid this much, but there's some festivity in the hyper-sugary decor (giant pineapples, palms, and bongo drums serving as barstools). At night, there's often a (loud) live band, and the upstairs patio is an appealing place to hang out with a rum drink—hence a gentle recommendation.

Disney Springs West Side. www.bongoscubancafe.com. © **407/828-0999.** No cover. Mains $18–$45. Bookable on OpenTable.com. Sun–Thurs 11am–11pm, Fri–Sat 11am–11:30pm. Free self-parking.

Raglan Road restaurant.

Raglan Road ★★★ IRISH One of the only restaurants at Disney Springs to win acclaim from food critics. Of all the chefs working Disney Springs, contemporary Irish chef Kevin Dundon has the most imagination and the most consistent standards. Here, Irish staples are turned into sprightly new visions, including glazed loin of bacon with cabbage, beef stew infused with Guinness, and good old fish and chips. Although the massive dining area is styled after an Irish pub, it's 20 times noisier. There's free live music most nights, and often step dancers. If you only want fish and chips, get it (plus beers) on the south side of the building for about $8 less at the counter-service hole-in-the-wall **Cooke's of Dublin ★**, run by the same people.

Town Center, Disney Springs. www.raglanroad.com. ℂ **407/938-0300.** Mains $17–$29. Bookable on OpenTable.com. Daily 11am–1am.

Rainforest Cafe ★ AMERICAN Another over-the-top themed doozy where families dine in a faux jungle with lions, pythons, elephants, and other robotic animals that periodically spring to life, interrupting dinner and stoking wild behavior in small children. Like so much in Orlando, it has no culinary specialization, instead opting to be all things to all eaters: burgers, salads, pizzas, capped by a volcano that steams and growls every half-hour. Its **Lava Lounge,** out on the water, is ideal for frozen drinks; it serves the same menu but rarely has the same line.

Disney Springs Marketplace. www.rainforestcafe.com. ℂ **407/827-8500.** Mains $16–$33. Sun–Thurs 8am–10:30pm, Fri 8am–midnight.

T-Rex ★ AMERICAN Nothing is a more surefire theme park-style diversion than life-size robotic dinosaurs planted among the tables. Every so often, the ceiling (at least, the one outside the simulated ice cave) is lit with a projected meteor shower and, for your amusement, the destruction of all prehistoric life forms is briefly simulated. Pass the ketchup. You can probably predict the fare: Bronto Burgers, Tar Pit fried shrimp, and to end it all, the $18 Chocolate Extinction, a fudge cake sundae for two or more people.

Disney Springs Town Center. www.trexcafe.com. *©* **407/828-8739.** Mains $16–$34. Sun–Thurs 11am–8pm, Fri–Sat 11am–midnight.

INEXPENSIVE

Earl of Sandwich ★★ SANDWICHES   The most affordable option at the Marketplace area, minus McDonald's, is located to its extreme east: a branch of a 27-location franchise based in Orlando. Grab a made-to-order 6-inch sandwich, made with fresh ingredients and toasted on the spot. There are more than a dozen hot and cold selections, from roast beef to turkey with stuffing, plus nine salads, and everything's six bucks. It's hard to believe such good prices exist in Disney World. Then again, Disney doesn't run it.

Disney Springs Marketplace. www.earlofsandwichusa.com. *©* **407/938-1762.** Sandwiches $7. Sun–Thurs 8:30am–11pm, Fri–Sat 8:30am–11:30pm.

Disney's BoardWalk

BoardWalk is a lakefront promenade that's notionally themed to an old-time pier. You'll find a few midway games, Surrey bike rentals, occasional buskers, and ice cream and margarita stores—not much, and most of its menus pander with the standard burgers-and-such variety. The **ESPN Club** serves food as an excuse to bask in the blare of countless TVs airing live sports while **Big River Grille & Brewing Works** serves mundane burgers, pastas, and salads (sound familiar?). It's a rare Disney joint that doesn't accept reservations, so if other places are full, try there. The newest restaurant here is **Trattoria al Forno,** an average place for $20 pastas, hand-made mozzarella, and Neapolitan-style pizzas. Post-meal strolls, as ferries serenely cross water and Epcot twitters in the near distance, are pretty, and they're reason enough to come. You can park at the BoardWalk Inn and get your parking validated or you can walk there via Epcot's World Showcase, 10 minutes away, where the dining is much more fun.

EXPENSIVE

Flying Fish Cafe ★★★ SEAFOOD   To say this is one of the most underrated restaurants on Disney property is not to say it's a knockout. But its kitchen is careful to source truly fresh food and deliver a good time in a theme-parky environment. Impeccably prepared seafood (grouper, mahimahi) is its principal domain, but it also does plenty of land-based meats. You can choose between a table or a stool facing the invigorating fire in its open kitchen. The entree of note is the memorable potato-wrapped red snapper, which should tell you about the carbohydrated concessions a fresh-ingredient kitchen must make to keep the booths packed in Orlando.

Disney's BoardWalk. www.disneyworld.com. *©* **407/939-5100.** Mains $30–$48. Reservations recommended. Daily 5:30–10pm.

Parents: I know you came to Orlando to spend some time with your family, but I also understand that you might need to get away from some of them for a few hours. If you're staying in a luxury resort hotel, the management may offer some kind of paid babysitting or supervised kids' club service. If not, there is always **Kid's Nite Out** (www.kidsniteout.com; 📞 **800/696-8105;** $18/hr. for the first child, $3 for each additional child, 4 hr. minimum). It is insured, bonded, and licensed, and it would appreciate a few days' warning for reservations for in-room sitting. Expect $10 to $12 in transportation fees. Five Disney resorts (the Polynesian, Dolphin, Yacht/Beach Club, Wilderness Lodge, and Animal Kingdom Lodge) operate supervised clubs (📞 **407/939-3463;** call at least 2 days ahead) for potty-trained kids ages 3 to 12 starting at 4:30pm and ending at midnight. These cost $15 per hour per child, 2 hours minimum, which includes a simple meal during dinnertime and a 10pm snack, and are sometimes open to people who aren't staying in a Disney hotel. The Four Seasons resort offers free babysitting as part of its nightly tariff. Although your kids would love it, I do *not* recommend depositing your offspring at the gates of the Magic Kingdom and speeding off rather than paying a babysitter, as actress Tracy Pollan's father once did to her.

Universal Orlando

Mythos (p. 152) and **Lombard's** (p. 137) are the only table-service restaurants inside the Universal theme parks worth a detour, but there are worthwhile dining options in Universal Orlando that are outside the parks—ones for which you don't need a park ticket. Universal's hotels have upscale restaurants (**Bice Ristorante** at Portofino Bay, **The Palm** steakhouse at the Hard Rock), while the CityWalk outdoor party mall, located between the resort's parking garages and the entrances to the parks, attracts locals who have no intention of proceeding to the rides.

After dark, CityWalk has windows serving stuff like Fat Tuesday booze slurpees, plus the slowest Burger King on the crust of the earth. Its table-service restaurants are loud, cavernous, family-friendly, often with faux antiques bolted to the walls. Arrive before 9pm, because some of these places charge covers after then. Everything closes by 2am. (For CityWalk's nightlife, see p. 198.)

If you intend to linger at CityWalk for the nightlife (parking is $5 from 6–10pm and free after 10pm unless there's a big event on), there are a few package deals that combine a meal, including a beverage, with a movie and entry to the clubs. The **Meal and Movie Deal** (📞 **407/224-2691;** $22) pairs dinner at one of seven restaurants with a movie at CityWalk's ABC multiplex, and can be purchased at the CityWalk Guest Services window. Conveniently, you don't have to enjoy both meal and movie on the same day.

Entrees cost more than they would outside Universal; they're mostly priced in the teens, with burgers sliding in around $14. So although none of these places are at the top of my list for a value meal, and only one of them is a true

Mythos restaurant in Universal.

gourmet experience, you may find yourself patronizing one after a long day at the parks. Call ℂ **407/224-3663** for more information, unless there's a different number listed. You know what you're gonna get at **Bubba Gump Shrimp Company,** the counter-service **Hot Dog Hall of Fame,** the Neapolitan-style **Red Oven Pizza Bakery**, or **Bread Box Sandwiches,** but these are the more interesting choices. **NBC Sports Grill & Brew,** themed to NBC Sports, is a self-explanatory option packed with HD screens and beer choices. You may (but don't have to) make reservations online for any CityWalk restaurant:

EXPENSIVE

Emeril's Orlando ★★ CREOLE   The highest standard of fare at City-Walk is a modern New Orleans menu with its heart in Southern classics and meats, with flavors typified by preparations such as gin and molasses brine (for its pork). The wine list could send you reeling even before you have a single sip—the back wall of this loftlike space displays a 10,000-bottle aboveground cellar built to dazzle. Happily, it offers a kids' menu (including a petite filet mignon), which makes adult pleasures more possible. Book ahead and you can sit along the chef's bar and watch your meal being created.

CityWalk. www.emerils.com. ℂ **407/224-2424.** Reservations suggested. Dinner mains $28–$38, 3-course lunch menu $22. Daily 11:30am–3pm; Sun–Thurs 5–10pm; Fri–Sat 5–10:30pm. Free valet parking for lunch.

Emeril's Tchoup Chop ★★★ PACIFIC RIM   Should Emeril's be full, Lagasse also oversees a restaurant at the Royal Pacific Resort, a few hundred yards away, that's more compelling. Pronounced "chop chop," it serves ostensibly Hawaiian creations, meaning there's a touch of Asian in the offerings

Emeril's Orlando.

including crunchy shrimp with hot and sour chili glaze and pineapple duck Penang curry. The daffy colors of the high-ceilinged dining room, exuberantly embellished by David Rockwell in rich orange and cobalt glass, are more a nod to boundless showmanship than a portent of a saccharine meal. The outdoor Tiki bar does a happy hour from 5pm to 8pm.

Royal Pacific Resort, 6300 Hollywood Way, Orlando. www.emerils.com. ℂ **407/503-2467.** Mains $18–$39. Daily 11:30am–2:30pm, 5–10pm.

MODERATE

Antojitos Authentic Mexican Food ★★★ MEXICAN   Beneath the day-glo pink bell tower, banish beany burritos and trashy Tex-Mex at this peppy place that conjures up the flair of Mexican street food. Downstairs is casual (food like tempura shrimp BBQ tacos with mango salsa, adobo chicken chimichangas), upstairs a little more refined (dry-aged coffee-crusted ribeye, slow-roasted pork loin).

CityWalk. www.universalorlando.com. ℂ **407/224-2106.** Downstairs mains $12–$20, upstairs mains $14–$29. Food daily 11am–midnight.

Bob Marley—A Tribute to Freedom ★ CARIBBEAN   Jamaican food (spicy jerk chicken, fried plantains, even oxtail) done passably, but stick around for when it turns into a reggae nightclub with a dance floor.

CityWalk. www.universalorlando.com. ℂ **407/224-3613.** Mains $10–$17. $7 cover after 9pm. Food served Sun–Thurs 4pm–10pm, Fri–Sat 4pm–11pm, bar open to 2am.

The Cowfish ★★ BURGERS/SUSHI   Sushi made with burger components, burgers made like sushi. This offbeat concept is rendered with a cocktail bar and some interactive screens to pass the time. It actually works, and it's fun. If there's a wait, head to the second floor for about 30 first-come, first-served bar seats; there are eight more on the third floor.

CityWalk. www.thecowfish.com. ℰ **407/224-3613.** Mains in the mid-teens. Daily 11am–midnight.

Hard Rock Cafe ★★ AMERICAN   Hey, look! It's . . . well . . . a Hard Rock Cafe. Granted, the world's largest (600 seats) and possibly the loudest. You've probably already sampled the Hard Rock shtick on offer at 163 of them: a casual tavern done up with music memorabilia (like Madonna's infamous "Like a Virgin" wedding dress and BOY TOY belt buckle, in the gift shop) and out back, a slab from the Berlin Wall. Fun fact: The company's headquarters is just 3½ miles north of here.

CityWalk. www.hardrock.com. ℰ **407/351-7625.** Mains $13–$32. Daily 11am–midnight.

Jimmy Buffett's Margaritaville ★★ AMERICAN   Because it's nearest to Islands of Adventure at the park's closing time, it gets jammed with park-goers clamoring for margaritas and grub like Cheeseburgers in Paradise. In late afternoon, there may be a strummer on the "Porch of Indecision" (not inside, not out), and after 10pm, the indoor area morphs into a three-bar club with a band and that $7 CityWalk cover. Across the way, under a 60-foot Albatross plane, the *Hemisphere Dancer,* is the **Lone Palm Airport** for margaritas and appetizers on the go.

CityWalk. www.margaritavilleorlando.com. ℰ **407/224-2155.** Mains $13–$25. $7 cover after 9pm. Daily 11:30am–2am.

Pat O'Brien's ★★ SOUTHERN   Like its bawdy Nawlins namesake, it does Cajun-style dishes such as shrimp gumbo, étouffée, and jambalaya, optionally served with a fat rum Hurricane cocktail in the hand. The potent drinks account for a clientele with fewer kids, but there is a kids' menu.

CityWalk. www.patobriens.com. ℰ **407/224-3663.** Mains $12–$18. $7 cover after 9pm. Food daily 4pm–2am.

Vivo Italian Kitchen ★★ ITALIAN   In a contemporary open-kitchen setting, dine on house-made pasta (from the classics to modern inventions such as fiochetti stuffed with Gorgonzola and pear), fresh mozzarella, braised short ribs, and cured meats.

CityWalk. www.universalorlando.com. ℰ **407/224-7223.** Dinner mains $11–$32. Sun–Thurs 4pm–11pm, Fri–Sat 4pm–midnight.

U.S. 192 & Lake Buena Vista

Around Disney, two major zones present every chain restaurant known to familydom. The Disney South zone, **U.S. 192**, goes both east and west from Disney's southern gate. The eastern zone, **Lake Buena Vista,** is a mile east of the traffic-snarled Disney Springs area. The two zones are linked by a few miles of Interstate 4, making it easy to shift from one to the other. Between them, you'll find all the usual suspects. Here are the best places you wouldn't otherwise know about.

EXPENSIVE

Columbia Restaurant ★★★ CUBAN Not everything in Celebration, the Disney-built town just east of Walt Disney World, is fake. The original location of this palatial restaurant opened in Tampa in 1905, and this outpost bustles as boldly as its daddy. The hot, fresh Cuban bread is so delicious you'll want to fill up on it, but don't, because portions are giant. Tampa was a major arrival city for Cubans, and their tradition holds sway with flavorful grilled steaks and chicken, sangria, paella, mojitos and sangrias, and big fish fillets. My favorite, the 1905 Salad, is mixed tableside with ham, cheese, lettuce, olives, greens, and a garlicky wine vinegar dressing that won't help you consummate any courtships, but is deservedly on sale by the bottle in the gift shop.

649 Front St., Celebration. www.columbiarestaurant.com. ✆ **407/566-1505.** Tapas plates $10; main courses $20–$27. Daily 11:30am–10:30pm. Reservations recommended.

MODERATE

Bruno's Italian Restaurant ★★★ ITALIAN A true find. Your temptation would normally be to drive past this place since it shares a building with dog-ugly gift shop that's garishly painted with killer whales, but inside, it's the food that's killer. There's a lot of junky pasta in the tourist zone, but it's the rare Italian table where the owner is not only cooking with pride, but he's also actually Italian. In this one modest room, Bruno loads his generous plates with garlicky goodness, from his puttanesca to his buttery rolls, and he also does pizzas, calzones, and fresh cannoli. Ask about the daily specials, which include braciole or a concoction called "eggplant Pavarotti," a rich piling of eggplant, ricotta, spinach, crabmeat, shrimp, and vodka sauce. Delivery is available to the vacation homes of Disney South.

8556 W. Irlo Bronson Hwy., Kissimmee. www.brunos192.com. ✆ **407/397-7577.** Main courses $10–22. Daily 11:30am–10pm.

Columbia's Quixote Dining Room.

Orlando Area Restaurants

International Drive

Agave Azul **19**
Arepas el Cacao **20**
Bruno's Italian
   Restaurant **25**
Bubbalou's Bodacious
   Bar-B-Que **19**
Café Tu Tu Tango **8**
Capone's Dinner
   & Show **29**
Cask & Larder **11**
Ceviche **17**
Christini's **22**
Columbia Restaurant **27**

Dandelion Communitea
   Café **15**
East End Market **13**
El Tenampa **30**
Ethos Vegan Kitchen **11**
Funky Monkey Wine
   Company **10**
Germans Restaurant
   & Bierhouse **26**
Hanamizuki Japanese
   Restaurant **6**
Hash House A Go Go **1**
Jerusalem Restaurant **28**

K Restaurant **14**
Le Coq Au Vin **18**
Lolailo the Original **5**
Maxine's on Shine **16**
McDonald's with world's
   largest PlayPlace **4**
Medieval Times **31**
Nile Ethiopian Cuisine **2**
The Outta Control Magic
   Comedy Dinner Show **9**

The Pharmacy **22**
Pirate's Dinner Adventure
   & The Three Musketeers:
   The Voyage Home **3**
The Ravenous Pig **12**
Rocco's Tacos **23**
Seasons 52 **23**
Sleuth's Mystery
   Dinner Show **7**

Taverna Opa **10**
Thai Thani **24, 27**
Treasure Tavern &
   The Cirque Magique **3**
Vietnamese District/Mills Fifty **15**
Wantilan Luau **21**

227

Germans Restaurant & Bierhouse ★★ GERMAN A giddy and welcome respite from the chain-dominated stretch of U.S. 192 west of Disney, this family-run 2014 newcomer celebrates everything authentically Teutonic, from bratwurst to strong German draught beers to cheese-and-meat plates, all with a fun-loving, family-friendly twist. The curry wurst, for example, is available in spicy or "what the hell," and a lunchtime option is the "schnitzel burger." Waitresses wear pigtails and lederhosen—in Orlando, there's Epcotty showmanship in everyone.

7868 W. Irlo Bronson Hwy., Kissimmee. www.germans-orlando.com. ℰ **407/507-2649.** Main courses $14–19. Mon–Sat 5–9:30pm.

Havana's Cuban Cuisine ★★ CUBAN It would be a shame to come to Florida without tasting authentic Cuban food. Disney only does touristy Cuban, but this modest family-run place nearby is hosting the real thing— tender *bistec palomilla* (thin-pounded steak with sautéed onion), aromatic *congri* (red beans and rice), and specials such as red snapper in garlic sauce. For dessert, the milk-soaked *tres leches* cake makes you wish you could start again for another round. It also does pressed sandwiches, a Cuban standard, for $9. Beware the green hot sauce—it'll knock you back. The decor is plain (rust-orange walls, reproduction travel posters), but there's heartiness in the food.

8544 Palm Pkwy., Orlando. www.havanascubancuisine.com. ℰ **407/238-5333.** Main courses $10–$25. Mon 5–10pm; Tues–Sat 11:30am–10pm; Sun noon–9pm.

Sea Dog Brewing Co. ★★ SEAFOOD Hidden in back of a strip mall facing I-4, this hails from Maine, where seafood matters but decorum doesn't. So expect a kid-friendly, relaxed joint serving good chowders (Bahamian conch, New England clam), conch fritters, salads, burgers, and dinners ranging from pot roast to broiled haddock. It's all designed to be served with more than a dozen Sea Dog beers by Shipyard Brewing Company in Maine, which you can also buy here by the case to fill your hotel room's fridge.

8496 Palm Pkwy., Orlando. www.seadogbrewing.com. ℰ **321/329-5306.** Main courses $10–$17. Mon–Fri 4pm–1am; Sat 11:30am–2am, Sun 11:30am–1am.

INEXPENSIVE

El Tenampa ★★★ MEXICAN From the outside, you'd swear it was just a grungy mini-mart best avoided, but inside, you discover a family-friendly hideaway of slotted-pot lanterns, hand-carved thrones, and big plastic cups in orange, magenta, and lime. Menus are bilingual but Spanish-first, which tells you about its main clientele, and because Mexican families show up in droves, you also know the food is authentic and good. The fresh *aguas frescas* (rejuvenating sweet water drinks, eight flavors ranging from tamarindo to limon) flow freely, and portions are big and reliable. You'll start with the free salsa and delicate corn chips that are still shiny and hot from the fryer, but don't fill up, because guacamole is a mere $4, whole fish $10, chicken mole with rice and beans only $8, and hefty burritos but $6.50. At its market next door, sample the Mexican popsicles at its *paleteria* and take away homemade pastries for under $1.75.

4565 W. Irlo Bronson Memorial Hwy./U.S. 192, Kissimmee. ✆ **407/397-1981.** Main courses $7–$13. Sun–Thurs 10am–9pm; Fri–Sat 9am–10pm.

Jerusalem Restaurant ★★ MIDDLE EASTERN   Unknown to tourists, a growing Muslim immigrant community calls Kissimmee home (you'll see a few halal grocery stores around this area), and this family restaurant is one of the benefits: a friendly choice hidden in an elbow of a quiet strip mall, embellished with bougainvillea, stone walls, and a gurgling fountain. Lunch specials (11am–3pm) get you kebabs for around $10, but wraps (including falafel, shawarma, and—in a nod to the tourists—Philly steak) start below that. I love the garlicky hummus, couscous dishes, and *kibbeh* fritters made of beef, cracked wheat, pine nuts, and seasonings.

2920 Vineland Rd., Kissimmee. www.jerusalemorlando.com. ✆ **407/397-2230.** Main courses $6–$17. Sun–Thurs 11:30am–10:30pm, Fri–Sat 11:30am–11pm.

Miller's Lake Buena Vista Ale House ★ AMERICAN   The Ale House has 70 locations and counting, so it's a chain, but I recommend it because this location has a unique twist of authenticity: It attracts Disney cast members who raise one of 75 beers after their shifts are finished. This is the kind of publike sports bar Florida does well—big room, lots of TVs, beers on special by the bucket—with a menu of finger foods like burgers, wings, nachos, and sandwiches. The Ale House's Zingers are boneless chicken wings, a trick of science to be rivaled only by the one conjured by your future cardiologist.

12371 Winter Garden Vineland Rd., Lake Buena Vista. www.millersalehouse.com. ✆ **407/239-1800.** Main courses $8–$10. Daily 11am–2am.

International Drive & Convention Center

This is a major hotel and entertainment center. The stretch of **Sand Lake Road** west of Interstate 4 is known, somewhat self-deprecatingly, as "Restaurant Row." It's true that some popular date-night restaurants for locals are scattered along this street. Meanwhile, **International Drive** is more the gamut of sit-down chains, from Applebee's to Cooper's Hawk to Yard House.

EXPENSIVE

Christini's ★ ITALIAN   Christini's, a fixture since 1984, is much more expensive than most Italian places and it doesn't permit young children. Those facts qualify it as a special occasion restaurant and not one to suck down a bowl of spaghetti. Picture a prototypical high-end Italian splurge and you've got it: Wandering accordion player, sommelier, lifetime waiters alert to your every twitch. It does pasta well, but guests tend to praise its meats, particularly the tender *osso buco*. Reservations are recommended, and the dress code is business casual at the least.

7600 Dr. Phillips Blvd., Orlando. www.christinis.com. ✆ **407/583-4472.** Reservations recommended. Main courses $23–$57. Daily 6–11pm.

Funky Monkey Wine Company ★ AMERICAN   The menu is ever-changing at this beloved locally owned eatery that stocks nearly eight dozen types of wine, and dabbles in sushi, but count on spry twists such as asiago fries, "Monkey Balls" of seasoned rice served with cream cheese and spicy mayo dipping sauce, pork chops, coffee-crusted steak, and a few fun lobster preparations. It's upscale without taking itself seriously, a mode that proves itself Fridays and Saturdays at 9pm when a highly amusing Divas Showcase show entertains diners. Service can be on the slow side.

9101 International Dr. at Pointe Orlando, Orlando. www.funkymonkeywine.com. ✆ **407/418-9463.** Lunch mains $10–18, dinner mains $27–38. Reservations recommended. Mon–Thurs 11:30am–11pm, Fri–Sat 11:30am–midnight, Sunday 5–11pm.

Lolailo the Original ★★ SPANISH   Lolailo's Galician cuisine rises above its mundane-appearing strip mall location, and its interior, with its burnished copper bar and Victoria Arduino espresso machine, elevate the mood, too. Both excellent tapas (grilled octopus, piquillo peppers) and mains (lamb, traditional cured ham) are available, but paella is not (unless you're there for Sunday brunch) because this is Spanish cuisine that celebrates delicate ingredients, not piles of rice. Finish with the *elogia al vino,* a surprising dessert of ice cream, custard, and red wine reduction.

7637 Turkey Lake Rd., Orlando. www.lolailo.com. ✆ **407/730-8948.** Tapas $7–$18, main courses $22–$40. Tues–Sat 11am–10pm; Sun 11am–3:30pm.

MODERATE

Agave Azul ★★ MEXICAN   Hidden in a strip mall, as so many of Orlando's most delicious places to eat are, Agave Azul cultivates a following with classic Latin dishes, from gourmet to Tex-Mex (ceviches, taqueria, a few types of guacamole including one with shrimp and goat cheese) in a soothing, modernist environment with lots of space, huge booths, and a gentle indoor fountain. The margaritas pack a wallop—the drinks here come stronger than the attentively measured pours elsewhere. It's around the corner from Universal.

4750 S. Kirkman Rd., Orlando. www.agaveazulorlando.com. ✆ **407/704-6930.** Main courses $9–$20. Mon–Thurs 11am–11pm, Fri–Sat 11am–midnight.

Bubbalou's Bodacious Bar-B-Que ★★ BARBECUE   Real barbecue done the way devotees like it, from cornbread to fall-off-the-bone ribs proven to stain shirts. There's no pretense at this tidied-up dive: Order at the counter and eat at picnic-style tables stocked with paper towel rolls and squirt bottles of sauce going from "sweet" to "killer." Get the standards: Texas brisket, pulled pork, ½ chicken, fried catfish, even gizzards. Sandwiches go for $8, but add any 4 sides (like baked beans, black-eye peas, Brunswick stew, or crunchy coleslaw) for a few bucks more. Or opt for meat by the pound ($11–$15), and take it back to the gang.

5818 Conroy Rd., Orlando. www.kirkman.bubbalous.com. ✆ **407/295-1212.** Main courses $8–$14. Mon–Thurs, Sat 10am–9:30pm; Fri 10am–10:30pm; Sun 11am–9pm.

Café Tu Tu Tango ★★ INTERNATIONAL   Fun, festive, and noisy in a good way, this casual tapas-style hangout flies high with an artist theme. Actual artists somehow concentrate on painting at easels amid the frolic of tables, cocktails, and nightly entertainment of belly dancing, salsa, or flamenco dancing. Their works fill the walls up to the rafters while boisterous diners spill out into the front patio. Despite the gimmick, the locally sourced food comes from sustainable ingredients and packs flavor. I love the guava BBQ ribs; the osso buco, Cajun chicken egg rolls, and brick oven pizzas are also popular. Sometime there are even alligator bites with key lime mustard—clichés aside, it tastes like chicken.

8625 International Dr., Orlando. www.cafetututango.com. ℂ **407/248-2222.** Tapas $8–$10. Sun–Thurs 11:30am–11pm; Fri–Sat 11:30am–midnight.

Hanamizuki Japanese Restaurant ★ JAPANESE   The theme parks never saw a fish they didn't want to batter-fry. So here, the fresh sushi, chicken and salmon teriyaki, and udon or soba noodle soups make for a refreshing palate-cleanser. The blonde wood and fabric decor conforms neatly to your expectations of a soothing Japanese restaurant—it draws a steady trade of Japanese visitors hungry for a taste of home—and so does the rest, from the greeting when you walk in the door to the deep bowls of flavorsome soup. The fun Ishiyaki Mix Steak allows you to grill meat and vegetables on a hot stone placed on your table. Best of all, because of a tucked-away location in a strip mall near the Kings Bowl Orlando, it's rarely crowded. At lunchtime, it adds ramen to the menu.

8255 International Dr., Ste. 136, Orlando. www.hanamizuki.us. ℂ **407/363-7200.** Main courses $8–$14. Tues–Sat 11:30am–2pm; Tues–Sun 5pm–10:30pm.

Hash House A Go Go ★ AMERICAN   Hash House's claim to fame is shocking immoderation. Dishes are laughably immense, piled as high as Jenga games, and the outcome could be just as messy if you attempt to eat all you are served. Everything on the down-home menu, which the restaurant calls "Twisted Farm Food," sounds like a good idea mostly in retrospect: 1-pound burgers (stuffed with the likes of bacon and cheese), towers of fried green tomatoes, a platter of fried chicken and waffles deserving of its own area code. This is destination food. The HH is an import from the casino culture of Vegas, where it began, which makes sense: This is a meal with a high risk-reward ratio, and you can bet there'll be leftovers.

5350 International Dr., Orlando. www.hashhouseagogo.com. ℂ **407/370-4646.** Main courses $11–$16. Sun–Thurs 8am–10pm, Fri–Sat 8am–11pm.

Nile Ethiopian Cuisine ★★★ ETHIOPIAN   Nile's owners are so friendly and eager to share their cuisine they have made themselves a devoted fixture on I-Drive. They even offer a few hutlike booths in which you can sit on the ground to eat, East Africa–style. It's a positive experience for families. Everyone tears off a piece of spongy injera bread to scoop up various stews and meats (beef, lamb, chicken, vegetarian) collected on a platter. You can even request a traditional coffee ceremony, in which beans are brewed in a *jabena* pot at your table and the eldest in your party is served first. Ethiopian cuisine is made with infused oil, not butter, so there are true vegan options; with advance notice, the injera can be made gluten-free. It's memorable and not daunting.

7048 International Dr., Orlando. www.nile07.com. © **407/354-0026.** Main courses $10–$15. Mon–Fri 5–10pm; Sat–Sun 4pm–11pm.

The Pharmacy ★ AMERICAN   Here, Orlando gets in on the speakeasy trend, but in a modern development: To find it, head to the west end of the shopping plaza, get to the first floor, and look for an elevator door marked for the 10th floor. Press the call button and you'll find yourself in an extremely echo-y room that, at least on the menu, riffs on the days of Prohibition when only your druggist could get you booze. Food is relentlessly rich: three-cheese mac and cheese, garlicky butter shrimp that arrives whole, roasted Cowart Ranch bone marrow. You may find the intensity of the flavors cloying (I did), but it's a popular joint, and the double-strong cocktails (lots of whiskey and gin) are crafted with much more care using a much more old-fashioned palate.

8060 Via Dellagio Way, Orlando. www.thepharmacyorlando.com. © **407/985-2972.** Main courses $12–$32 Mon–Sat 5pm–1am.

Rocco's Tacos ★★ MEXICAN   Every night's a party at Rocco's, a loud, popular, tequila-drenched upscale hangout where friends meet to kick back with margaritas and dig into guacamole mixed tableside. After sunset, flaming torches illuminate its lakeside terrace, and deeper into the night, a DJ spins, and occasionally Rocco himself appears to dance on the bar and pour tequila. It serves all kinds of Mexican entrées, but its specialty is the fajita-like *molcajetes,* marinated and slow-cooked for hours and served in a lava rock bowl to keep them hot longer.

7468 W. Sand Lake Rd., Orlando. www.roccostacos.com. © **407/226-0550.** Main courses $12–$24. Mon–Fri 11:30am–2am, Sat–Sun 11am–2am.

Seasons 52 ★★★ AMERICAN   This culinary experiment has spread nationwide, but this was its first location. The point of the menu, which changes to make use of seasonal crops, is that no dish clocks in at more than 475 calories (although none leave you hungry). Servings aren't particularly teeny—the food is just really good, thoughtfully made, and never sees a deep fryer. (Something you'll be thankful for after a long week in the theme parks.) The desserts come in single-serving shot glasses, but mind they don't catch you licking the glass.

7700 Sand Lake Rd., Orlando. www.seasons52.com. © **407/354-5212.** Main courses $13–$20. Sun–Thurs 11:30am–10pm; Fri 10am–11pm; Sat 11:30am–11pm.

Taverna Opa ★★ GREEK   It would be hard not to find something to eat, from tapas-like *meze* (hummus with garlic chunks and hot pita bread, *taramosalata, keftedes* meatballs), salads, hearty wood-fired and long-marinated meats and grilled fish, and *moussaka* (an eggplant lasagna with béchamel). There's no resisting the party that starts after 7pm or so—waiters and customers alike toss napkins and dance on the tables as belly dancers and "Zorba" dancers (their term) swirl. Kids really get into it. Lunches are more subdued, and mains are $10 cheaper.

9101 International Dr. at Pointe Orlando, Orlando. www.opaorlando.com. © **407/351-8660.** Meze $5–$12, main courses $15–$27. Sun–Thurs noon–11pm; Fri–Sat noon–2am.

Thai Thani ★★ THAI   A strip-mall anchor store by SeaWorld channels Chiang Mai with wood carvings, brass, and powerfully romantic private booths. Popular with locals (it recently added a Celebration location near Disney), it serves Thai food suited to newbies—the lemongrass soup is tame, with few chilies, which proves the chef is holding back—but more advanced eaters should choose from the "spicy dishes" section to get the full flair of the cuisine—I like the Thai chili jam stir-fried with veggies and your choice of protein. Finish with Thai Grandma Ice Cream: coconut ice cream with sticky rice and peanuts ($7). Lunch is about $5 less.

11025 S. International Dr. www.thaithani.net. © **407/239-9733.** Main courses $11–$16. Daily 11:30am–10pm. Second location near Disney: 600 Market St., Ste. 100, Celebration. © **407/566-9444.**

INEXPENSIVE

Arepas el Cacao ★★ VENEZUELAN   This local success story started in 2010 as a family-run food truck that rapidly cultivated a following that funded the launch of several brick-and-mortar locations. The specialty is simple: handmade white corn flatbread *(arepas)* that's overstuffed with slow-cooked meats, veggies, and your choice of sauce, from creamy to spicy. It's simple, filling, and honest, and it's made even more satisfying when you pair it with tropical juices such as blackberry or mango. You'll find it just east of the Universal complex, and it's open late for midnight binges.

5389 S. Kirkman Rd., Orlando. www.arepaselcacao.com. © **321/252-2226.** $7–$9.50. Sun–Weds 10am–3am, Thurs–Sat 10am–4am.

McDonald's ★ FAST FOOD   You've seen one McDonald's, you've seen them all, right? Not this one—otherwise why mention it? It serves the usual junk food, of course, but there's also a huge array of options such as burritos, pastrami, chimichangas, pastas, panini, and pizzas. That's odd enough, but it also claims to operate the largest PlayPlace in the world. Looks accurate: You'll find tube slides, a 500-gallon aquarium, and some 100 arcade games with a prize center. Keep kids wowed for the price of fries.

6875 Sand Lake Rd., Orlando. www.mcdonalds.com. © **407/351-2185.** Main courses $5–$8. Daily 24 hr.

Downtown Orlando

The neighborhood east of downtown, Thornton Park, hosts a few well-publicized bistros and sidewalk cafes, but with prices around $12 a plate for

Orlando's culinary culture club has a new playground with the arrival of the East End Market. Inspired by Chelsea Market in New York City, founders reclaimed an old industrial building with 10 stalls, each selling its own thoughtfully crafted specialties. **Florida Roots** sells local products such as beers and bath goodies, **Fatto in Casa** ("Made at Home") experiments with items such as mini mac and cheese muffins baked with bacon, **Houndstooth** does sauces, and **Kappo** is a seven-seat sushi counter that isn't fooling around with its quality—its $17 menu grants five types of fish while its $45 menu has 11. **Txokos** (www.txokoskitchen.com), at the side, devises Basque dishes from what's for sale here, while **Bookmark It** sells cookbooks and books by Florida authors. Find it between Winter Park and downtown Orlando (3201 Corrine Dr., Orlando; www.eastendmkt.com; ✆ **321/236-3316;** Tues–Sat 10am–7pm, Sun 11am–6pm).

lunch and $20 for dinner, there are no money-saving revelations among them. Instead, try these.

EXPENSIVE

Cask & Larder ★★ SOUTHERN Like its sister gastropub restaurant down the street, the Ravenous Pig (p. 235), it's dedicated to ever-changing dishes based on seasonal ingredients. The difference here is that Cask & Larder is less about picking meat off an animal's bones as it is about home-brewed beer by a resident brewmaster and a casual vibe. But you can eat, and comfort food is the thing—it could be fried chicken (a staple), country fried rabbit (yes), or an addictive potted pimento cheese topped with "ham jam" (ham that's been cooked down with honey). Rich touches prevail, such as the vanilla butter slowly melting atop the cornbread, which arrives in its own iron skillet, and the mac and cheese jolted with pickled mustard seeds.

565 W. Fairbanks Ave., Winter Park. www.caskandlarder.com. ✆ **321/280-4200.** Mains $19–$37. Daily 5–10pm, Sun 10:30am–3pm. Reservations recommended.

K Restaurant ★★★ AMERICAN Kevin Fonzo's mastery of rich flavors using Southern bistro classics and local ingredients made him a star of Orlando cuisine, and his upscale but casual showplace is one of the city's best. The menu changes but almost always includes a steak tartare (sometimes served with Brussels sprout kimchee), fried green tomatoes, and the K Filet dusted with wild mushrooms and accompanied by a wildly scrumptious cabernet sauvignon sauce. Ask to be served by the long-running and much-loved Rocky Mazza, who's famous in these parts. This uproariously flamboyant merry-maker carries with him a leather wallet full of photos from his colorful past, and he's got a hundred funny stories for each one. There's a big wine list, too.

1710 Edgewater Dr., Orlando. www.krestaurant.net. ✆ **407/872-2332.** Main courses $18–38. Tues–Fri 1:30–2pm, Mon–Tues 6–9pm, Weds–Sat 6–10pm.

Le Coq Au Vin ★★★ FRENCH   Longtime Chef Louis Perrotte hand-picked his protégé Reimund Pitz to take the reins at this classic French romantic restaurant, an Orlando institution since 1976. Diners, many of whom are here celebrating a special occasion, feel more like they're guests in a home than paying patrons, an illusion that's extended by its mostly residential neighborhood. Pitz is a classically trained French chef, so you get the complicated flavors (well-marinated coq au vin, daily selection of game meat, Grand Marnier soufflé) that the prices demand, plus Gallic staples such as frog legs and vichyssoise. Some dishes come in ample half portions that can cost two-thirds what larger servings do. A three-course prix-fixe menu is $35.

4800 S. Orange Ave., Orlando. www.lecoqauvinrestaurant.com. 📞 **407/851-6980.** Main courses $20–$40. Tues–Sat 5:30–9:30pm; Sun 5–8:30pm.

The Ravenous Pig ★★★ SOUTHERN   James and Julie Petrakis have won renown for knowing just when to deploy bacon and in what amount, a talent dear to me, and they have been rewarded by operating one of the city's most influential dining choices. Expect a beer-friendly yet sophisticated evening where the food is gourmet without pretentiousness. The menu changes seasonally but always features traditional farmhouse meats—in the form of frites, say—and some Southern comfort dishes with an upscale spin, like shrimp and grits with Gruyere biscuits. Get the Old Fashioned: bacon-infused Old Forester bourbon with vanilla and maple, garnished with candied bacon.

1234 N. Orange Ave., Winter Park. www.theravenouspig.com. 📞 **407/628-2333.** Mains $14–$30. Tues–Sat 11:30am–2:30pm, 5:30–10pm. Reservations recommended.

MODERATE

Cevíche ★ TAPAS   For a lively night out, head to Church Street Station, a revitalized pedestrian district of red-brick warehouses, gas-lit lamps, and late-night lounges. This rococo dining hall feels like it was plucked off Las Ramblas in Barcelona. The menu, also true to Spain, is piled with more than 100 tapas dishes, most $6 to $10, including daring-for-Orlando meats (quail, crispy chicken livers, oxtail), standard ones (chorizo, veal, lamb chops), and plenty of vegetable and fish choices. And, of course, there's ceviche (I like the tuna, with garlic, lime, onion, and a touch of jalapeño). Because everything's meant to be shared, the energy is social and vibrant. Things get loud when the flamenco band clacks and strums, so enjoy the evening on the front patio. Then club-crawl on Church Street late into the night.

125 W. Church St., Orlando. www.ceviche.com. 📞 **321/281-8140.** Tapas $8–$12. Sun–Mon 5–10pm; Tues–Thurs 5pm–midnight; Fri–Sat 5pm–2am.

Maxine's on Shine ★★ INTERNATIONAL   Hidden in a residential neighborhood (blink and you've passed it), it's a labor of love by its owners, who frequently emerge from the kitchen to party with guests. There's a good wine list plus a tiny stage hosting a roster of entertainment ('70s karaoke one night, classical piano the next). Chicken Maxine blends pan-seared diced chicken with shallots, mushrooms, a Marsala wine cream sauce with penne pasta, but on Sundays at 7pm, I go for the Serendipity Supper Club, when $25 buys three courses, plus a glass of wine, as long as you agree to let the chef serve you whatever inspires him that day. As you depart, a sign thanks you for helping "this little restaurant's dreams come true."

337 N. Shine Ave., Orlando. www.maxinesonshine.com. © **407/674-6841.** Mains $14–$24. Tues–Fri 5–10pm, Sat 10am–10pm, Sun 10am–9pm.

INEXPENSIVE

Dandelion Communitea Cafe ★★★ VEGETARIAN/VEGAN
When you hang out at Dandelion, you feel like you're a part of something. That's because it's as much a neighborhood hangout as it is a cafe. Once a private home, hardwood floors and cabinets were left intact, and now diners of all ages (including kids) roam. A huge selection of tea is served with menu items made with local ingredients. There's no meat, and nearly everything is gluten-free. The signature dish is the Giddyup (usually $9, but only $5 on Monday), a filling nacho bowl of tempeh chili piled with blue corn chips, diced tomatoes, scallions, and cheese. My favorite is the Homemade Hearty Chili, the most flavorful veggie chili I've ever had ($4). Twice a month, on the new and full moon, people gather here to "express your true self with music, rhythm, dance and trance." If you don't happen to travel with a bongo, they'll lend you one.

618 N. Thornton Ave., Orlando. www.dandelioncommunitea.com. © **407/362-1864.** Main courses $8–$9. Mon–Sat 11am–10pm; Sun 11am–5pm.

Ethos Vegan Kitchen ★★ VEGAN
As one of the only fully vegan restaurants in Central Florida, Ethos garnered such a loyal following it recently moved and expanded. That's because when vegan cuisine is all that you do (even the cheese qualifies), you have to be skilled at making it taste good, too—and Ethos succeeds. Among the favorites are pecan-encrusted eggplant, pumpkin seed pesto penne pasta, and 10-inch pizzas. Kelly and Laina Shockley, who run it, are assiduous about ingredient sourcing and proudly pay their servers a living wage (not minimum wage). Specials change according to seasonal crops, and there's always a soup of the day. About a third of the menu is gluten-free.

601-B New York Ave., Winter Park. www.ethosvegankitchen.com. © **407/228-3898** or 407/228-3899. Mains $8–$15. Mon–Fri 11am–11pm; Sat–Sun 9am–11pm.

Dinnertainment

Besides TV talent competitions, there may be no purer form of vaudeville left in America than the Orlando dinner show. Part banquet and part spectacle, most of these guilty pleasures involve stunts, audience participation, and plenty of noise. Most are mounted in arenas lined with bench seating and long tables, and while the show grinds on, waiters scurry, distributing plates of banquet food the way Las Vegas dealers deal blackjack cards. These shows are tacky to the extreme, but they're an intrinsic part of the Orlando scene. Nowhere else on Earth—at least not since Caligula's Rome—will you find so many stadiums in which to stuff your face while fleets of horses, swordsmen,

A GASTRONOMIC TOUR OF little vietnam

Just north of Orlando's downtown, along a stretch of 1950s storefronts around Colonial Avenue and Mills Avenue, a thriving Vietnamese area (variously called Little Vietnam, ViMi, or **Mills Fifty**) is flourishing. Many people fled here upon the fall of Saigon, and Vietnamese dissident Thuong Nguyen Cuc Foshee has been an Orlando resident since the time of the Vietnam conflict. Diners can find cheap meals here, true to Vietnam's reputation for nuanced flavors. Park anywhere (most buildings hide secret lots behind them) and explore on an empty stomach.

The quickest meal is *bánh mi*, addictive baguette-style sandwiches stuffed with thinly sliced veggies (cucumbers, daikon, carrots), cilantro, hot peppers, a buttery secret sauce, and meats such as roast pork, pâté, or meatball (or tofu). They're shockingly cheap: $3 to $4, hot, and made-to-order. The best are at **Bánh Mì Nha Trang,** hidden in an ancient strip mall (1237 E. Colonial Dr.; ☎ **407/346-4549;** Mon–Wed and Fri 10am–7pm, Sat–Sun 10am–6pm), where they barely speak English but are improbably friendly—every transaction ends with a chipper "See you tomorrow!" Also get them at the counter beside checkout at **Tiên-Hung Market** (1108 E. Colonial Dr.;

☎ **407/422-0067; **daily 9am–6pm), a catch-all for Asian groceries.

At most of the area's Vietnamese restaurants, where entrees range $8 to $12, menus drone on like a Russian novel, but if you're wise to it, each place has its specialty. **Phó 88** (730 N. Mills Ave.; www.pho88orlando.com; ☎ **407/897-3488;** daily 10am–10pm) excels with *pho* beef noodle soup; bowls seem as large as hot tubs, with many flavors vying for dominance. Its two enormous spring rolls could fill an average stomach for $3.25. The specialty at Ánh Hông (1124 E. Colonial Dr.; ☎ **407/999-2656;** daily 9am–9:30pm), on the corner of Mills, is tofu (especially fried), while **Viet Garden** (1237 E. Colonial Dr.; ☎ **407/896-4154;** Sun–Thurs 10am–9pm, Fri–Sat until 10pm) wows with its crispy noodle dishes. **Mamak** (1231 E. Colonial Dr.; www.mamakasianorlando.com; ☎ **407/270-4688;** daily 11am–11pm) does pan-Asian street food. Neophytes prefer the mass appeal of **Little Saigon** (1106 E. Colonial Dr.; www.littlesaigon restaurant.com; ☎ **407/423-8539;** daily 10am–9pm), which has dining areas with yellow walls and red tablecloths that place it as slightly more upscale than its utilitarian one-room neighbors.

and crooners labor to amuse you. Dinnertainments aren't top values, but they certainly represent the delight of Orlando's shtick.

Most times of the year, most of these shows kick off daily around 6 or 7pm, but during peak season, there may be two shows scheduled around 6 and 8:30pm. Upon arrival, crowds are corralled into a preshow area where they can buy cocktails and souvenirs, and endure hokey comedy routines—feel free to be slightly tardy, and feel free not to buy anything, because non-alcoholic drinks come with dinner. Most shows will be mopping up by around 9:30pm, so schedule a visit on a night when you don't intend to catch theme park fireworks. Most of them also serve kids' standards (chicken fingers, hot dogs, and so on) for picky children. Soft drinks, draft beer, and wine (the cheap stuff, watered down) are unlimited. Bring a sweater if you're sensitive to air-conditioning, and bring enough cash to tip your server because gratuities aren't included. *Money-saving tip:* The free coupon books and discount ticket suppliers should be your go-to for cheap prices on dinner shows. There are so many deals floating around for the banquets held off theme-park property that only a stooge pays full price. The ones thrown by the theme parks, though, generally don't discount. In fact, they tend to sell out, so book those as far ahead as you sensibly can.

IN ORLANDO & KISSIMMEE

Capone's Dinner & Show ★ ITALIAN   Kardashian-generation girls pretend to be 1920s flappers and warble to recorded music in this affordable dinnertainment effort. Dinner's a bog-standard steam table buffet of lasagna, spaghetti with meatballs, pizza, nuggets, and a few token non-pasta choices, such as a hot meat carving station. This troupe's own brochures and website promise half-off discounts, which grant the price I list, but I've never seen the so-called full price charged.

4740 W. Irlo Bronson Hwy., Kissimmee. www.alcapones.com. ℂ **800/220-8428.** $35 adults, $22 kids 4–12. Nightly, some 1pm shows.

Medieval Times ★ AMERICAN   The long-running coach-tour favorite, at which your waitress is called a "wench," is also an attraction in eight other North American cities, qualifying it as the McDonald's of dinnertainment. You eat spare ribs and chicken with your hands while the jousters compete in an arena. For $10 more, the Royalty Package gets you front-row seating, a free program, and a souvenir DVD. Its "castle" is located a few miles east of Disney on U.S. 192, in a downtrodden area of Kissimmee. It's also always greatly discounted by brochures to the tune of 30–50% less.

4510 W. Irlo Bronson Hwy., Kissimmee. www.medievaltimes.com. ℂ **866/543-9637** or 407/396-2900. $63 adult, $37 kids 12 and under. Nightly.

The Outta Control Magic Comedy Dinner Show ★★ PIZZA   More affordable and easygoing than its dinnertainment competition, the show mounted by the WonderWorks science/video playground targets kids—and parents weary of overproduced, overpriced glitz. Unlimited pizza, salad, beer, wine, and soda are distributed while buddy-buddy magicians engage in family-friendly jokes, tricks, mindreading, and improv. Discount coupons get $2 off.

WonderWorks, 9067 International Dr., Orlando. www.wonderworksonline.com. ℂ **407/351-8800.** $30 adults, $20 kids 4–12 and seniors. Daily 6 and 8pm.

Pirate's Dinner Adventure ★★ AMERICAN   For kids who just can't get enough Jack Sparrow–like misbehavior, there's this high-energy eye-popper, set on an 18th-century galleon with 40-foot masts amid a 300,000-gallon lagoon—the arena is the most spectacular of the Orlando dinnertainments. Expect a circus of rope swinging (lots of it), trampolining, singing, and arrrghing. Although the show provides opportunity for participation (each seating section roots for its assigned buccaneer, kids get onstage), it treats female characters like sexy livestock. That may account for why its most devoted demographic appears to be 13-year-old boys. Production values are fairly high. Buying online yields discounts, but the free brochures dispensed around town are good for even more off.

Pirate's Town, 6400 Carrier Dr., Orlando. www.piratesdinneradventure.com. ⓒ **800/866-2469.** $66 adult, $40 kids 3–11. Nightly at 7:30pm or 8:30pm.

Sleuth's Mystery Dinner Shows ★★ AMERICAN

After mingling with a few zany characters and watching this long-running show, which takes about an hour and contains at least one murder, you confer over dinner with your tablemates, grill the suspects, and, if you feel confident, accuse a killer. The cases change nightly, so you can attend several times without duplicating your experience. Actors seem to be having fun, and they'll even tone down the grown-up jokes if they see young children in the crowd, although these low-budget shows are clearly more suited to adults. As for audiences, they appear to be grateful for a rare chance to employ their brains in this town. Beer and wine are included, too. Lots of brochures offer discount rates.

8267 International Dr., Orlando. www.sleuths.com. ⓒ **800/393-1985** or 407/363-1985. $60 adult, $29 kids 3–11, $3–$7 less if booked online. Daily at 7:30pm.

The Three Musketeers: The Voyage Home ★ AMERICAN

The endurance of the Pirates Dinner Adventure inspired the same producers to put forth a similar show, priced identically, on the same ship set, with a plot just as flimsy, employing light stuntwork and recklessly butchering random

Sleuth's Mystery Dinner Show.

Broadway tunes for musical relief. The story is sketchy, the sorta-French-inspired food is pallid, but young kids usually don't notice all that. They love watching the rapier duels and acrobatics, and there are opportunities for them to get involved.

Pirate's Town, 6400 Carrier Dr., Orlando. www.3musketeersorlando.com. ℂ **407/206-5102.** $66 adult, $40 kids 3–11. Fri–Sat at 6pm, Sun 3:30pm.

Treasure Tavern ★★ AMERICAN   The people behind Pirate's Dinner Adventure also put on a 2-hour mix of burlesque, magic tricks, contortionists, ribald jokes, recorded music, and light dancing. It's allegedly for those 18 years old and over (although if you're older than 14, you can come with a grown-up). The adult concept is that Gretta, the bawdy proprietor of the Treasure Tavern, has assembled a band of misfits whom she puts to work entertaining you, and fortunately, most of them have talent. Think "Cabaret" meets "Benny Hill": Your main course arrives to "You Can't Beat the Meat," sung to the tune of "You Can't Stop the Beat," and your buxom servers are referred to as "jewels" (I said it was adult, not liberated). If you can release your inner juvenile and tuck into the rum, it can be fun. In late 2015, the same owners kicked off a new 6pm presentation in the same venue, **The Cirque Magique,** which is appropriate for the whole family: acrobats, magic tricks, prancing puppies—you're just spared the sophomoric jokes of its so-called adult version.

Pirate's Town, 6400 Carrier Dr., Orlando. www.treasuretavern.com. ℂ **407/206-5102.** Tickets $66. Tues–Sat nights, doors open at 7pm.

AT THE THEME PARK RESORTS

Disney's Grand Floridian resort does afternoon tea for little princesses (ℂ **407/939-1947**), but these are the parks' dinner shows for the whole family.

Disney's Spirit of Aloha Show ★ POLYNESIAN   The chicken-and-ribs luau presided over by fire twirlers, hula dancers, and the like has been going strong for years in an open-air theater on Seven Seas Lagoon. Bookings begin 6 months ahead, and usually the last people to reserve are shunted to the rear tables, which can feel like they're actually as distant as the Cook Islands; the tables that are farthest away are the least expensive. It bores some kids, but it has its adult adherents (although most of them cite not its educational qualities but its food—pineapple-coconut bread being at the top of their lists). It's on the monorail line from the Magic Kingdom, which means it's easy to catch the fireworks after early shows.

Disney's Polynesian Resort. www.disneyworld.com. ℂ **407/939-1947.** $59–$74 adults, $30–$40 kids 3–9. Tues–Sat 5:15 and 8pm.

Gospel Brunch ★ AMERICAN   There is no plot, and it's not sanctified, but the live music is jumping and the cuisine combines Southern and breakfast foods. The morning show fills first. Still, because so many House of Blues throw these, you can't say it's uniquely Orlando.

House of Blues, Disney Springs West Side, 1490 E. Buena Vista Dr., Lake Buena Vista. www.hob.com. ℂ **407/934-2583.** $53 adults. Sun at 10:30am and 1pm.

Hoop-Dee-Doo Musical Revue ★★ AMERICAN Book 6 months out, not necessarily because it's the best, but because it's Disney's most kid-friendly dinnertainment, which makes it crazy popular. Six-performer shows put on a hectic and helter-skelter music-hall carnival of olios and gags, which elementary-school age children usually find riveting, and much quarter is given to recognizing birthdays and special events. The headlining menu item is ribs served in pails—enough said? I prefer seats in the balcony, overlooking the stage (the cheapest, anyway).

Pioneer Hall at Fort Wilderness Resort. www.disneyworld.com. © **407/939-1947.** $59–$68 adults, $33–$37 kids 3–9. Shows scheduled from late afternoon to evening.

Mickey's Backyard BBQ ★ AMERICAN The dinner show choice for very young children features rope tricksters and taxi-dancing costumed characters wearing Western-style gear. More informal than the Hoop-Dee-Doo in that it takes place under an open-air pavilion (come dressed for humidity), the event serves passable buffet-style picnic food, but the toddler factor makes it chaotic, and for some cruel reason, seating is first come, first served. You might be less disappointed if you see this as a photo op with Mickey and not as a proper show.

The Outdoor Pavilion at Fort Wilderness Resort. www.disneyworld.com. © **407/939-1947.** $60 adults, $33 kids 3–9. Thurs and Sat Mar–Dec.

Wantilan Luau ★★★ POLYNESIAN Universal's weekly 2-hour luau is held in a covered pavilion. It, like Disney's Spirit of Aloha Show, has fire dancers and hula girls aplenty, but it trumps the rest for authenticity: Food includes pit-roasted suckling pig, with spiced rum–infused pineapple puree, and a Pacific catch of the day (which is not to say it was caught today in the Pacific); Mai Tais are included. Should kids be grossed out by carving meat off the pig, there's a tamer children's menu. The show is more culturally

Wantilan Luau at Royal Pacific Resort.

documentary than Disney's, too, as it's attentive to the differences between the various Pacific islanders it represents. You can walk from both Universal parks.

Royal Pacific Resort. www.universalorlando.com. ☏ **407/503-3463.** $73 adults, $40 kids 3–9. Sat at 6pm, some Tuesday nights.

CHARACTER MEALS

A character meal is a rite of passage. Usually all-you-can-eat and often buffet, it guarantees face-to-fur time with beloved costumed characters. Always, *always book ahead*—as soon as you can. If you can't, check 24 hours before, when people who can't honor their reservations cancel them to avoid the $10 penalty.

At Disney, meals are themed by location; at the Cape May Café, characters wear beach outfits, and at Chef Mickey's, they emerge in chef's aprons and do a towel-twirling dance. (Reading that, it sounds a little like a Chippendales show, not a Chip 'n' Dale show, but rest assured it's all preschool-friendly.) The characters (six to eight headliners make appearances) won't actually be eating with you, but they'll circulate, working the room the way a good host does, and signing autographs. This, as kids and grown-ups binge on a smorgasbord that would give Jillian Michaels apoplexy—Mickey-shaped waffles topped with M&Ms and all—comes the day's first sugar crash.

Prices vary, but they're a little cheaper at hotels than inside theme parks. When a breakfast is held inside a park, you'll still have to proffer an admission ticket. However, for breakfast, your name will be on a VIP list and you'll be admitted through the gates early (it's fun to walk through an empty park). Try to book the earliest seating available so that by the time you're done, you'll be among the first in line for the rides; you'll also have first crack at the stroller rentals. Tips are not usually included.

Cinderella's Royal Table, inside Magic Kingdom's Cinderella Castle, is the big "get"—there are some intense parents out there with freakishly fast speed-dial fingers, because that place always sells out 180 days early. Also try Chef Mickey's, which is a one-stop monorail ride away from the Magic Kingdom, and the Tusker House, a good start for the early day at Animal Kingdom. Less prestigious addresses, such as the buffet breakfast at the Beach Club near Epcot, can be smart choices, particularly because they tend not to be as crowded and you're likely to have lots more one-on-one time with the stars.

Inside Disney Parks

These are the regular meals, but during special events (such as during Star Wars Weekends in the spring), there may be temporary events that cost more.

Cinderella's Royal Table The most difficult reservation (reserve 6 months ahead at 7am Orlando time) features Cinderella, with possible appearances by her Fairy Godmother and other Princesses. The price includes five souvenir photos. See p. 65. Cinderella Castle, Fantasyland, The Magic Kingdom. www.disneyworld.com. ☏ **407/939-1947.** Meals $54–$72 adults, $35–$43 kids 3–9, plus park admission. All three meals.

Crystal Palace Winnie the Pooh and his friends, and a visible kitchen. See p. 63. Crystal Palace, Main Street, U.S.A., The Magic Kingdom. www.disneyworld. com. ✆ **407/939-1947.** Meals $25–$44 adults, $14–$25 children kids 3–9, plus park admission. All three meals.

Dining with an Imagineer When your kids have outgrown furry friends, there's still this exceptional mealtime meet-and-greet. Over a four-course meal, groups no larger than 10 hang out with a longtime Disney Imagineer— an art director, designer, or engineer—and have the chance to ask them any-thing about the mechanics of the resort. Hollywood Brown Derby, Disney's Hollywood Studios or Flying Fish Cafe, Disney's BoardWalk. www.disneyworld.com. ✆ **407/939-1947.** Lunch adults $74, kids 3–9 $42, plus park admission; kids under 14 not recommended.

Donald's Dining Safari Appearances by Mickey, Goofy, and Chip 'n' Dale. See p. 110. Tusker House Restaurant, Africa, Disney's Animal Kingdom. www. disneyworld.com. ✆ **407/939-1947.** Breakfast and lunch $30–$38 adults and $16–$20 kids 3–9, plus park admission.

Garden Grill Appearances by Mickey, Chip 'n' Dale, and Pluto. See p. 85. Garden Grill, The Land, Epcot. www.disneyworld.com. ✆ **407/939-1947.** Meals $38–$45 adults, $19–$22 kids 3–9, plus park admission. All 3 meals.

Disney Junior Play 'N Dine Appearances by Handy Manny, Jake, Doc McStuffins, and Sofia the First. See p. 98. Hollywood & Vine, Echo Lake, Disney's Hollywood Studios. www.disneyworld.com. ✆ **407/939-1947.** Breakfast or lunch $27–$35 adults and $16–$19 kids 3–9, plus park admission.

Princess Storybook Dining Appearances by the Princesses in the Nor-way section of Epcot. The price includes photos of your party. See p. 86. Akershus Royal Banquet Hall, Norway, Epcot. www.disneyworld.com. ✆ **407/939-1947.** Meals $41–$56 adults, $25–$30 kids 3–9, plus park admission. All 3 meals.

At Disney-Area Hotels

You don't have to be a guest at these hotels for these meet-and-greet meals.

Cape May Café Appearances by Goofy, Minnie, and Donald Duck. Cape May Café, Disney's Beach Club Resort. www.disneyworld.com. ✆ **407/939-1947.** Breakfast $27–$31 adults, $14–$17 kids 3–9.

Chef Mickey's Served by Mickey, Goofy, Donald Duck, and Pluto. Chef Mickey's, Disney's Contemporary Resort. www.disneyworld.com. ✆ **407/939-1947.** Breakfast, brunch, dinner $33–$42 adults, $18–$22 kids 3–9.

Cinderella's Happily Ever After Dinner Appearances by Cinderella, Prince Charming, Fairy Godmother, and others. 1900 Park Fare, Disney's Grand Floridian Resort and Spa. www.disneyworld.com. ✆ **407/939-1947.** Dinner $38–$44 adults, $19–$21 kids.

Garden Grove Appearances by Goofy, Pluto, and others. Garden Grove, Walt Disney World Swan. www.disneyworld.com. ✆ **407/939-1947.** Breakfast on weekends, dinner nightly. Breakfast: $25–$36 adults, $15–$17 kids, dinner a la carte (mains $30–$37, kids' menu $18, unlimited soup and dessert).

Good Morning Breakfast with Goofy & Pals Appearances by Goofy and friends, who (ssh!) usually include Mickey and Minnie. Strongly recommended for the high-quality food and lots of character face time. Ravello, Four Seasons Resort Orlando at Walt Disney World. 10100 Dream Tree Blvd. www.fourseasons.com/orlando. ✆ **800/267-3046.** Breakfast Thurs, Sat, and some Tues. $42 adults, $22 kids 3–12, including photo.

'Ohana Character Breakfast Appearances by Mickey, Pluto, Lilo, and Stitch. Disney's Polynesian Resort. www.disneyworld.com. ✆ **407/939-1947.** Breakfast $22–$27 adults, $13–$15 kids.

Supercalifragilistic Breakfast Appearances by a variety of characters, including Mary Poppins. 1900 Park Fare, Disney's Grand Floridian Resort and Spa. www.disneyworld.com. ✆ **407/939-1947.** Breakfast $23–$29 adults, $13–$16 kids.

Universal Orlando

Superstar Character Breakfast Universal's main character meal has characters from whatever's hot in its stable; the Minions are a good bet right now. In December, a Grinch-themed breakfast is often mounted inside Islands of Adventure. There's also a similarly priced character breakfast at the Royal Pacific Resort every Sunday morning, but there, Universal only promises appearances by "your favorite theme park characters." Hint: not Mickey. Cafe La Bamba, Universal Studios. www.universalorlando.com. ✆ **407/224-7554.** Breakfast $26 adults, $13 kids, plus park admission. Thurs, Sat, some Mons 9am.

ORLANDO'S HOTELS

Orlando has more than 118,000 hotel rooms, a staggering figure. It hosts some 62.3 million visits every year for theme parks, conventions, and outdoor recreation, making the city the world's most popular family vacation destination.

As you can imagine, with numbers that large, competition can be fierce, and at some properties, quality can be lax. A little too often, you find yourself shrugging and saying, "Eh, it does the job." Most of Central Florida's monolithic hotel architecture steals and inflates Europe's palatial traditions; often on such a scale that even a Texan would blush. You'll find arcades, frescoes, columns, Spanish tiles, arched windows, and marble . . . but knock on the columns. They're hollow. Get close to the marble. It's often painted on. That's why Orlando's resorts rarely achieve true opulence. Here, when you pay for a fine hotel, you're often paying for mood.

Following are a few key questions to ask:

How much space would I like to have? If you have kids with you, will a single room supply the elbowroom everyone needs? Disney's most affordable rooms, for example, have a maximum occupancy of four people in two double beds, so if your group exceeds that number, you'll have to rent two rooms or upgrade to something more expensive. For most families, renting a home or condo solves the space issue, and usually for less money.

Will I have a car? Unless you're a Disney-only type of person, you should have one. Cars can speed you away from its clutches, saving your sanity and your pocketbook. Cars enable you to see both Disney *and* Harry Potter as well as Orlando's many appealing diversions.

How much time will I spend at my accommodations? If your schedule is full, you'll only use a room to hit the sack. Do you *really* need a fitness center after slogging miles around theme parks for 15 hours a day? No, you don't.

Then grill your potential hotel: **Is there a resort fee?** It's common, and it dramatically increases the cost. **Is there a parking fee?** It's another way to hide the true price of a stay. **Is breakfast included?** If it's "continental", it could be instant coffee and a mound of stale muffins. **What's the view?** Properties boast a fireworks view—but don't mention it's from eight miles away.

GETTING THE BEST RATES

Ask any hotel what it charges, and you're unlikely to get a straight answer. They delight in changing rates according to how full they are. As a rule of thumb, prices are highest when kids are out of school (summers, spring break), and lowest in the light periods such as late January, September, October, and early December. Weekends see slightly higher prices, too, because Florida residents drop by. The prices in this guide represent an average rate.

The good news is that Orlando's average nightly rate is around $110, which is cheaper than the national average, so you're already working at an advantage. Primary websites that collect quotes from a variety of sources (whether they be hotel chains or other websites) include **HotelsCombined.com**, **Hotels.com**, **Kayak.com**, and **Mobissimo.com**. Always canvas multiple sites. The bidding areas on Hotwire.com and Priceline.com are more likely to get you the best rates in the month before you travel; hotels hold out for higher prices until then. Then call the local number of the hotel, not the toll-free one (which may connect to an office far away), to see if they'll do even better. Also check **Hotelcoupons.com** for discounted rates for some of the cheapest motels in town (no promises about their quality, and some hotels frequently refuse to honor the lowest rates if they hit 75%–80% occupancy).

Another reliable way to get a cheaper room is to use an **air/hotel package.** No domestic company operates charter flights to Orlando anymore, but several packagers buy cheap hotel rooms in bulk and sell them with scheduled airfare. Check **Lastminute.com** (✆ 866/999-8942), **Funjet** (www.funjet.com; ✆ 888/558-6654), as well as some of the vacation wings of major airlines such as **Southwest Vacations** (www.southwestvacations.com; ✆ 800/243-8372), **JetBlue Getaways** (www.jetblue.com/vacations; ✆ 800/538-2583), **Delta Vacations**

Theme Park Shuttles: Going Your Way?

Almost all of the hotels located off theme park property tout some kind of "free" shuttle service to the major parks (often covered by a resort fee). When they work, they're a dream, but you need to know that most are restrictive. Many run once or twice a day, on their schedule, and you must book ahead. A typical hotel shuttle may leave for the Magic Kingdom twice a morning and return at, say, 5 and 10pm. Shuttles may provide only one run per direction which drops after the park has opened for the day and returns before it closes, wasting valuable time and possibly costing you a fireworks viewing. Also, many hotels provide shuttles to only one area (Disney or Universal/SeaWorld) but not the other. **Ask.**

Many hotels share shuttles. They can be dirty, worn, and crowded, and you might have to stop at up to a half-dozen other places on your way. Not great if you're hungry, thirsty, tired, or your kids are restless.

Before settling on a hotel based on its advertised rides, ask questions:

1 What time do they leave and return?
2 Which theme parks are *not* covered or incur a fee?
3 How many other hotels share the same shuttle?
4 Is there a fee? (That $30 for two could have been used to rent a car.)

246

(www.deltavacations.com; ✆ 800/800-1504), and **American Airlines Vacations** (www.aavacations.com; ✆ 800/321-2121). Internationally, **Virgin Holidays** (www. virginholidays.co.uk) is a huge player, with lots of customer service reps available on the ground should things go wrong. Increasingly, these websites may sell hotel-only deals using their negotiated rates. Use properties highlighted on specials pages, though, because prices often come out higher in searches.

Few of these players will truly discount a Disney hotel, although they may package Disney products without discounts. If they do, be careful to parse the pricing and compare it to a la carte options—Disney packages are notorious for fees, wasting money, and including more than you need. Even if you do want a Disney hotel, price be damned, book your Disney hotel separately from tickets or airfare—"room-only," on a separate phone call—because it gives you more scheduling flexibility with Magic Your Way tickets and room-only cancellation rules are far kinder. Don't accept *any* package from a Disney receptionist, even if it's for harmless trinkets, unless you're okay with paying a $200 fee for cancellations made 30 to 2 days ahead; room-only bookings have no penalties for cancellations made fewer than 5 days ahead. When it comes to non-Disney hotels, though, package away, because that's where great deals live.

Conventions make last-minute bookings risky, but Orlando's **Official Visitor Center** (8723 International Dr.; www.visitorlando.com; ✆ **407/363-5872;** daily 8:30am–6:30pm) will help you find something. You're also likely to find a room (grotty though it may be) on U.S. 192 east of I-4.

ORLANDO'S HOTELS

Every hotel in this book has a swimming pool (because of liability issues, few are much deeper than 5 ft.), Wi-Fi, and ample air-conditioning, and almost every hotel offers shuttles to at least some theme parks, although fares around $5 to $10 may apply. Every hotel is kid-friendly. In fact, you should expect even top-end places to crawl with scampering, shouting children hopped up on a perpetual vacation-permitted sugar buzz. If you crave peace, steer toward a rental home or a splurge resort that leans toward the convention trade, in which case the rugrats will be replaced by phone-wielding conference-goers in chinos. If you stay in a unit with a kitchen, you may be in a timeshare that was rented to you because it was empty—this is normal, and it can be a good deal, but you may have to fend off "welcome" calls that are overtures to purchasing one.

Beware of trusting online hotel reviews in Orlando! Timeshare hotels are overpraised by owners who want people to stay there, and Disney hotels are overpraised because they're Disney.

Following are the categories and price ranges for this chapter:

o **Inexpensive:** Up to $95 a night
o **Moderate:** $96 to $175
o **Expensive:** $176 and up

Note: Prices in this book don't include taxes, which for hotels add as much as 14.5% to your bill depending on the municipality in which you're staying.

Orlando Area Hotels

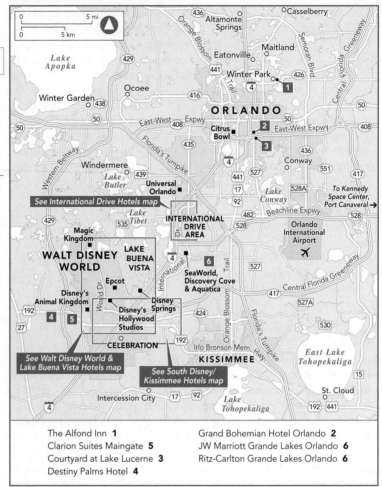

The Alfond Inn **1**
Clarion Suites Maingate **5**
Courtyard at Lake Lucerne **3**
Destiny Palms Hotel **4**

Grand Bohemian Hotel Orlando **2**
JW Marriott Grande Lakes Orlando **6**
Ritz-Carlton Grande Lakes Orlando **6**

Inside Walt Disney World

Some people don't mind spending twice Orlando's going rate so they can be on Disney property near the resort's storied "magic," although they are hard-pressed to explain what that precisely means. But strictly from a non-pixie-dusted, consumer-advice standpoint, there are advantages and disadvantages to staying on property in one of Disney's extremely busy hotels.

DISNEY PRICING SEASONS

Unlike most hotels, which price dynamically, Walt Disney World's hotel rates are fixed by a calendar. The seasons you need to remember are, in descending

How to Save on Lodging

- **Come when kids are in school.** Hotel prices are trimmed then.

- **Avoid holidays.** If the kids are out of school, you might pay double.

- **Make sure the room rules permit everyone in your party.** If you go over the guest maximum, you'll have to rent two rooms, doubling costs.

- **Always get a quote directly from the hotel.** It might be lower.

- **See what's on offer from a packager.** They have purchasing power.

- **Plug Kissimmee into Web searches.** It's cheaper than Orlando.

- **Good locations also save on food.** Are there affordable restaurants nearby?

- **Ask if there's a discount.** Disney reservationists will tell only if asked.

order of expense: **Holiday, Peak, Summer, Regular, Fall,** and **Value.** The major price spikes are around spring break, Easter, and the late December holidays—put simply, when more people can travel to Disney World.

Likewise, there are three categories of Disney hotel: **Deluxe, Moderate,** and **Value** plus Disney Vacation Club apartments. Ergo, for the cheapest room, book a Value room in a Value period.

SEASONS The dates for each season shift annually and are tweaked per property, but they follow the same pattern on the calendar. For 2015, the schedule generally shook out like this, including the weekday price of a Value hotel room so you'll know the bottom line of the lowest-priced room of each season (on weekends, prices pop up as much as 25%):

- **Value season:** Jan to mid-Feb, mid-Aug to Sept. Value price: $96
- **Fall season:** Mid-Sept to mid-Dec. Value price: $111.
- **Regular season:** Late Feb to early Mar, Late Apr to May. Value price: $123.
- **Summer season:** June to July. Value price: $153.
- **Peak season:** Mid-Feb, Mid-Mar to mid-Apr, Mid-Dec. Value price: $152.
- **Holiday season:** End of Dec, New Year's. Value price: $190–$226.

MouseSavers.com and **TheMouseForLess.com** post codes of all current known discounts. In general, AAA and military service may help cut costs.

STANDARD AMENITIES All Disney hotels, regardless of class, have touches that provide relief for families, including big pools and shallow kiddie pools, coin laundries, and playgrounds. Nearly all rooms have two double beds unless you pay for something more (like a bunk or a pull-out), but no microwave. Wi-Fi is free. There will always be somewhere to eat, although at Value resorts it will be a food court. Disney shuttle buses (p. 293) serve all resorts for free, and every property is protected by gated security. And, of course, every resort has at least one souvenir store—usually more. Check-in time is usually 3pm (you can use the pool while you wait) and you must check out by 11am.

Walt Disney World & Lake Buena Vista Hotels

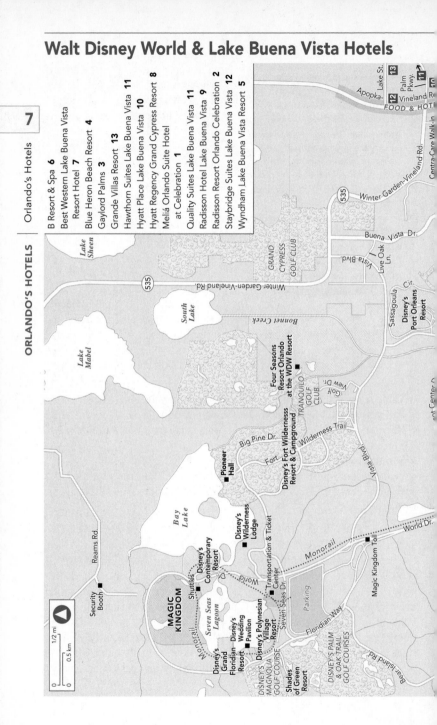

B Resort & Spa **6**
Best Western Lake Buena Vista Resort Hotel **7**
Blue Heron Beach Resort **4**
Gaylord Palms **3**
Grande Villas Resort **13**
Hawthorn Suites Lake Buena Vista **11**
Hyatt Place Lake Buena Vista **10**
Hyatt Regency Grand Cypress Resort **8**
Meliá Orlando Suite Hotel at Celebration **1**
Quality Suites Lake Buena Vista **11**
Radisson Hotel Lake Buena Vista **9**
Radisson Resort Orlando Celebration **2**
Staybridge Suites Lake Buena Vista **12**
Wyndham Lake Buena Vista Resort **5**

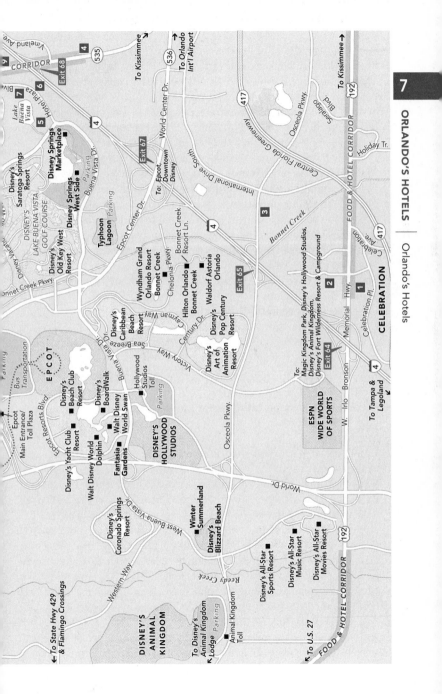

251

YAY! THE BENEFITS OF STAYING ON DISNEY PROPERTY

o For those without cars, there's **free bus, monorail, and ferry transportation** throughout the resort. This is the biggest consideration for most people. (Then again, it's free to *everyone* at Disney, guest or not.)

o **Free parking** at the theme parks (normally $17 per day for a car).

o The right to make **Fastpass+ reservations** 60 days ahead (instead of 30).

o Each day, during **Extra Magic Hours,** one or two parks open an hour early or up to 3 hours past closing for the express use of Disney hotel guests. The major attractions, but not all of them, will be open during this period, and lines tend to be shorter than when general admission is in effect.

o Free coach transfers to Orlando International Airport through **Disney's Magical Express** program. See p. 291 for its drawbacks.

o **Every room has a small balcony or patio** (except at Value resorts).

o The right to **charge purchases** on your room key card or MagicBand.

o The right to have in-park **shopping delivered to your room.** (The delivery lag time is such that you should be staying for at least 2 more nights.)

o Three or four timed **kids' activities** a day, albeit some at a charge.

o **Wake-up calls** featuring Disney characters.

o Sometimes staff (called "Mousekeeping") leaves **towels shaped like animals** (a Disney tradition).

o **Free wheelchair rental.**

o **Guaranteed admission** if parks are full.

o Option to purchase soft drink **mugs** ($17) that you refill endlessly while at the hotel (and not a minute more—they're embedded with computer chips).

BOO! THESE THINGS ABOUT STAYING WITH DISNEY STINK

o **"Free" resort transportation doesn't mean "fast."** Routes can be circuitous and require changing buses, waits can be aggravating, and you may have to stand.

o **Rates are 40%–70% higher** than off-property rooms of comparable quality.

o **Stingy occupancy limits.** Most rooms add $10 a night for each person past the limit of two up to the room's stated maximum capacity, so a $105 room will in fact be $125 if four people over 18 stay there. (One child under 3 can stay without being counted.) Value and Moderate resorts cap occupancy at four (not including a babe in a crib) and Deluxe cap at five. Families larger than four must rent two units, doubling the expense, but if you have seven or more people to accommodate, it gets ugly.

o **Haphazard room assignment.** In busy times, families with multiple rooms may get split apart. Requests for specific locations may not be honored.

o Disney resorts are so large (often 2,000 rooms) that **lines,** even for a cup of coffee, are an endless nuisance and **sprawling layouts are confusing** to small children, to say nothing of their parents. Disney has turned the failing into profit: It charges $15 more for "Preferred" rooms nearer the lobby.

- Counterintuitively, the more affordable a room is, they more you could use a rental car. Value rooms are about as **far from the action** as many off-property hotels. The Value resorts, in particular, are a good 15-minute drive from the Magic Kingdom (no farther than a decent vacation home).
- **Safes** are tiny (laptops won't fit). In-room cooking is made difficult in that the most affordable rooms lack **microwaves** or **coffeemakers.**
- The most affordable Disney hotels **don't have restaurants.** They have food courts (burgers, sandwiches, pasta—all at theme park prices of around $10) and the only room service item is pizza. This is less of a problem if you intend to save money by eating off property anyway.

DELUXE RESORTS

No one who has experienced a true luxury hotel can seriously attest that Disney's quality standards compare. They're 3-star hotels in fancy dress. Sure, they have sit-down restaurants, spas, lounges, and big pools. But rooms and service are nothing special. What Disney's Deluxe hotels mostly have is uplifting theming—a prevailing mood—that makes a stay fun, and it's a genuine thrill to be so near a theme park, to get such fantastic views of the Magic Kingdom or African animals—there's just something special about it. Yes, you can certainly pay less than the $300 to $1,100 you pay to sleep in only a standard room. But for many people, they're more than just a place to sleep.

Most Deluxes (standard room maximum guests: four unless noted) enable you to dart to the parks easily. Three are by the Magic Kingdom on the monorail line encircling the Seven Seas Lagoon: the Contemporary (the most iconic), the Grand Floridian (the fanciest), and the Polynesian (the most private and also nearest the stop for Epcot). A fourth, Wilderness Lodge, is linked to the Magic Kingdom by ferry, while the Beach Club, Yacht Club, and Board-Walk are walking distance from Epcot's side door. Only Animal Kingdom Lodge is marooned by roads, but it has other perks that counterbalance that.

For an extra $100 to $150, Disney sells "Club Level" concierge-style rooms with a private lounge stocked with free Continental breakfast, snacks, and beverages. In some hotels, it entitles you to better views or to buy additional experiences, such as a sunset tour of the savannah at Animal Kingdom Lodge.

Disney's Animal Kingdom Lodge ★★★ No grander lodge ever existed on the African veldt, and the higher tariff returns to you in the form of a 24-hour safari. The hotel, which has a dark wooden look and hand-carved furniture, is built within a system of paddocks, so if you've got a Savannah view (they start at $429—careful that you don't accidentally book a Standard one overlooking the parking lot), when you look out of your window, you'll hopefully see whatever genial African animal is loping by at that moment, be it a giraffe, an ostrich, a zebra, or a warthog. You'll find a game-viewing guide beside your room service menu. Because animals tend to be active in the early morning, when families are gearing up for their days, the idea works well. Anyone can visit, even if they're not staying here; there's even a public animal viewing area straight out the back door of the awe-inspiring vaulted lobby. Its

Interior of Animal Kingdom Lodge.

principal drawback is its distance from everything except for Animal Kingdom; all connections are by road. Standard room: 344 sq. feet.

2901 Osceola Pkwy., Bay Lake. www.disneyworld.com. ℗ **407/934-7639** or 407/938-3000. 1,293 units. $320–$652 non-club standard. 2-adult maximum, extra person $25. Children 17 and younger stay free in parent's room. **Amenities:** 2 restaurants, cafe, babysitting, supervised kid's program, Club Level rooms, health club & limited spa, heated outdoor pool, kids' pool, room service, valet parking $20, free self-parking, free Wi-Fi.

Disney's Beach Club/Disney's Yacht Club ★★★ Both excellent choices with 381-square-foot rooms, these adjoining sisters are on a pond across from the BoardWalk entertainment area (you'll need it since the hotels are short on decent choices for cheap food) and a short stroll out the International Gateway exit of Epcot's World Showcase, which brings the fun close to your room, although you can't watch IllumiNations from it. Their shared 3-acre pool area, Stormalong Bay, has a crazy water slide coming off the mast of a pirate ship, plus sandy shores. (It's easily the best pool on Disney property, and it's restricted to guests.) The difference between the two is nearly negligible—so much so that many guests think they're one giant hotel, but the Yacht Club has slightly nicer furnishings, bigger balconies, attracts slightly fewer families with kids, is a tad quieter, and is a 10-minute stroll from Epcot instead of 5 from the Beach Club. Other than that, it's a toss-up.

1800 Epcot Resorts Blvd., Lake Buena Vista. www.disneyworld.com. ℗ **407/934-7639** or 407/934-8000. Beach: 583 units. Yacht: 630 units. $400–$744 non-club standard. Extra person $25. Children 17 and younger stay free in parent's room. **Amenities:** 2 restaurants, grill, Club Level rooms, babysitting, children's program, character meals, health club & small spa, 3-acre pool and play area, 2 outdoor heated pools, kids' pool, room service, 2 lighted tennis courts, boat rental, $20 valet parking, free self-parking, free Wi-Fi.

Disney's Beach Club.

Disney's Contemporary Resort ★★★

Nothing says, "I'm at Disney World" more than the awesome sight of that monorail sweeping dramatically through its glassy Grand Canyon Concourse, which it does every few minutes on its way to and from the Magic Kingdom. The hotel, one of the first two to open in 1971, is now a midcentury architectural treasure, and indicative of the revolutionary methods that Walt Disney World hoped to pioneer: The United States Steel Corporation helped design it; its modular rooms were prefabricated down the road and slotted into place by crane. The current look: soothing putty and slate business-class colors. Best rooms (422 square feet, among the largest standard rooms at Disney) are high up in the coveted A-framed Contemporary Tower, but there are stylish low-level Garden Rooms along Bay Lake, too, near the surprisingly blah pool, that are about $150 cheaper. Rooms on the west of the tower face the Magic Kingdom itself (and, ahem, an intervening parking lot)—the 9th floor has the *ne plus ultra* of Disney views—and every water-view

Disney's Contemporary Resort.

room takes in the nightly electrical parade that floats after dark. Even if you can't stay here, this is the best hotel to tour. Drop by via monorail to see the 90-foot-tall mosaics of children by the visionary Imagineer Mary Blair, which encapsulate the late-'60s futurist optimism out of which the resort was born. If money is no object, this is a top choice for only-at-Disney panache.

4600 N. World Dr., Lake Buena Vista. www.disneyworld.com. ✆ **407/939-6244** or 407/ 824-1000. 1,008 units. $400–$803 non-club standard. Extra person $25. Children 17 and younger stay free in parent's room. **Amenities:** 3 restaurants, grill, 4 lounges, babysitting, Club Level rooms, character meals, small health club and spa, 2 outdoor heated pools, kids' pool, watersports rental, valet parking $20, free self-parking, free Wi-Fi.

Disney's Grand Floridian Resort & Spa ★★ It's strange to spend $600 a night on a hotel room and then have to walk outside in the rain to reach the building it's in, but from a value standpoint, that tells you a lot. This is the Disney hotel with snob appeal, since the whole point is to put on a costume of exclusivity and luxury (two things Walt despised, which is why *his* hotels had populist themes) and brag about it when you get home. So it's encrusted with upper-class affectation, from high tea to a pianist tinkling away in an outrageously pretty lobby (chandeliers, glass dome, wedding-cake balconies). It can't help but strum your imagination of what a true Victorian grande dame hotel might have felt like, but anyone can enjoy that on a day visit without paying insane rates for what amounts to a 3-star room. There *are* vacation-making pluses I'd unreservedly celebrate here if money were no object, such as next-door access to the Magic Kingdom, gourmet restaurants, and an atmosphere more romantic than at any other Disney hotel—in fact, you'll probably have to dodge a few wedding parties. Typical standard rooms are 440 square feet, although dormer rooms are smaller.

4401 Floridian Way. Lake Buena Vista. www.disneyworld.com. ✆ **407/934-7639** or 407/824-3000. 867 units. $549–$1,018 non-club double. Extra person $25. Children 17 and younger stay free in parent's room. **Amenities:** 5 restaurants, grill, character meals, babysitting, kid's program, Club Level rooms, health club & spa, heated outdoor pool,

Pool at Disney's Grand Floridian Resort & Spa.

Bungalows at Disney's Polynesian Village Resort.

kids' pool, room service, 2 lighted tennis courts, watersports rental, valet parking $20, free self-parking, free Wi-Fi.

Disney's Polynesian Village Resort ★★★

The 25-acre hotel, thickly planted and torch-lit by night, was one of the first two hotels built here, back when the South Pacific tiki craze was still swinging, and the longhouse-style thatched-roof complex remains one of the most transporting of the Disney resorts. The most expensive rooms glimpse the Magic Kingdom across the Seven Seas Lagoon (swimming in it is not allowed, but the newly renovated pool area is huge and lush), but most have greenery views. The Polynesian is a notch above for families as there's an on-site child-care facility, the monorail is steps away, and rooms are on the big side, sleeping five. An easy favorite. The downside is availability: In 2015, Disney converted several buildings into Disney Vacation Club "Studio" units, reducing the standard room count by several hundred, so it's harder than ever to enjoy this hotel now. (At least it also added Trader Sam's Grog Grotto (p. 197), one of the coolest cocktail bars in town.) When available, those studios cost $10 to $20 more than a standard room but include a mini-fridge and a microwave.

1600 Seven Seas Dr., Lake Buena Vista. www.disneyworld.com. © **407/939-6244** or 407/824-2000. 484 standard units 360 Studios. $483–$991 non-club double. Extra person $25. Children 17 and younger stay free in parent's room. **Amenities:** 3 restaurants, cafe, tiki bar, on-site babysitting, kid's program, Club Level rooms, nearby health club & spa (at Grand Floridian), 2 heated outdoor pools, kids' pool, character meals, room service, watersports rental, gas grills, free 7:30pm marshmallow roast, free 9pm outdoor movie, free Wi-Fi.

Disney's Wilderness Lodge ★★

This effective riff on Yellowstone's woody Old Faithful Lodge, swaddled by oaks and pines, is picturesque but disconnected from the rest of the park—the Magic Kingdom, 10 minutes away by ferry, is the only thing easy to reach if you don't have your own car (the other parks involve a laborious bus trek). Most of its tricks are in its dramatic atrium lobby: giant stone hearth, springs that flow to a thronged pool area out back—a geyser nearby spouts water 120 high on the half-hour from 7am to 10pm. Because of surrounding woods, rooms (340 square feet) are

Disney's Wilderness Lodge.

dark, but have adorable rustic touches such headboards carved with woodland creatures.

901 W. Timberline Dr., Lake Buena Vista. www.disneyworld.com. ✆ **407/934-7639** or 407/938-4300. 909 units. $325–$642 non-club standard. Children 17 and younger stay free in parent's room. **Amenities:** 3 restaurants, babysitting, club-level rooms, health club & limited spa, 2 spa tubs, 2 heated outdoor pools, jogging trail, boat rental, kids' pool, room service, valet parking $20, free self-parking, free Wi-Fi.

Walt Disney World Swan and Dolphin ★ Rewards points are a main appeal to the Starwood-run Swan and Dolphin, which are linked by a footbridge over the lake they share. Former Disney CEO Michael Eisner controversially allowed outside corporations to intrude on resort property, and the result was these dated designs distinguished mostly by splashy exterior set pieces—like the 56-foot tall dolphin statues. The ceilings are a little bit low,

Walt Disney World Swan and Dolphin.

the staff a little bit distracted, the incessant ferry horns vexing, but beds are fab and the location never quits: You can walk to Epcot in 15 minutes and Hollywood Studios in 20, avoiding the bus, which is a good thing because DTS sometimes arrives after having filled up at the Yacht, Beach, or Boardwalk hotels. Both are primarily business hotels for conferences, with lobby bars, steakhouses, and sushi counters to suit, although they strive to welcome families, too (rooms fit five and the waterfall in its shared grotto pool is inviting). Some rooms in the Dolphin's Center Tower have terrific distant views into Epcot. The Swan's rooms just enjoyed a modernizing renovation (blues, greys, chrome, more outlets) that contrasts the dated 1989 exterior; the Dolphin's rooms get the same treatment by the end of 2017. Everything lacks the tonal fantasy at Disney-run hotels, but guests get the same perks as at a Disney-run hotel including 60-day advance Fastpass+ bookings—except no Magical Express from the airport and no ability to make park purchases by room key or MagicBand.

1500 Epcot Resorts Blvd., Lake Buena Vista. www.swandolphin.com. ✆ **407/934-4000.** Swan: 756 units. $239–$505 non-club standard. Dolphin: 1,509 units. $219–$579 non-club double. Extra person $25. Both: Resort fee $23 per night. Children 17 and younger stay free in parent's room. Self-parking $18, valet parking $26. **Amenities:** 12 restaurants, cafe, character meals, babysitting, free domestic phone calls, kid's program, in-room coffee, game room, character meals, Club Level rooms, health club & spa, 5 heated outdoor pools, room service, 4 lighted tennis courts, Wi-Fi included with resort fee.

MODERATE RESORTS

The next category up from Value is Moderate. Compared to Value, what do you get for the extra dough? Put simply, the main pools have more elaborate themes with slides and there are usually a few additional, simple pools; rooms measure 314 square feet instead of 260 square feet (so 2 ft. wider); most have two sinks instead of one (both outside the shower/toilet room); all rooms have a small balcony or patio with seating (though most have no view to speak of); and you can rent a bike or a boat on the premises. The upgrade doesn't win you the right to fit more people: Rooms mostly fit four (only two adults) plus one child under 3, same as the Value class.

The grounds of Moderate properties feel more resortlike when compared to the glorified motels of the Values, but at heart, they're still glorified motels, with exterior corridors (close your drapes) and windowless bathrooms. You'll still be eating mostly in high-priced food courts located at a building that might be distant from your room. Although the bedrooms aren't much plusher than the Value properties, you will sense more breathing room and personality since Disney has been pouring money into glorifying its Moderate pool areas.

Disney's Caribbean Beach Resort ★

This resort sprawls around a central pond—1½ miles around!—with a loose island theme. Rooms (mostly full beds) are the Moderate category's largest (by a little); Disney spent a ton theming some rooms to "Pirates of the Caribbean" (beds like ships, carpet like decking) that cost $44 to $72 more than a regular room. The main Old Port

Royale pool area emulates a waterfront Spanish fort and has a giant tippy bucket, so you can see why families favor this property. The resort's principal drawbacks are a lack of elevators, bland food, a risk of being placed very far from the lobby and pool, and the fact no other major resort areas connect to it. At least Port Orleans, for nearly the same money, has boats to Disney Springs; from Caribbean Beach, all connections are by road, so it's strongly recommended to have a car here.

900 Cayman Way, Lake Buena Vista. www.disneyworld.com. ℰ **407/934-7639** or 407/934-3400. 2,112 units. $182–$308 standard double. Extra person $15. Children 17 and younger stay free in parent's room. **Amenities:** Restaurant, food court, arcade, heated pool, 6 smaller pools in the villages, kids' pool, free self-parking, free Wi-Fi.

Disney's Coronado Springs Resort ★

Built to attract convention crowds with a vibe to match, it nonetheless has fans for its subdued tone. The well-planted grounds, done in a hacienda style around a pond, are far-flung (some rooms are a 15-minute hike from the lobby, which gets old), and rooms, with kings (for 2) or queens (for 4), have a single sink, as at the Values. The food court is above average, though, as is the pool area (with a 123-foot slide) themed after a Mayan pyramid, and there's a cocktail lounge, Rix, with a semblance of sophistication. The hotel is 10 minutes' drive from any parks. If you need a room accessible for those with disabilities and the cheaper hotels are out of such units, you can try here, where there is an inventory of 99 rooms.

1000 Buena Vista Dr., Lake Buena Vista. www.disneyworld.com. ℰ **407/934-7639** or 407/939-1000. 1,921 units. $188–$314 double. Extra person $15. Children 17 and younger stay free in parent's room. Free parking. **Amenities:** Restaurant, grill/food court, arcade, health club and limited spa, 4 outdoor heated pools, kids' pool, free Wi-Fi.

Disney's Fort Wilderness Resort & Campground ★★

Not to be confused with the Wilderness Lodge, an imitation of Yellowstone Lodge, this 780-acre wooded enclave near Magic Kingdom consists of campsites and mobile home–style cabins with decks and grills that sleep six on a mix of beds, pull-outs, and bunks. Camping and RV parking under the thick pines are far and away the cheapest and most distinctive way to sleep on property, but it's twice the market rate, and without equipment (tents are $30, cots $4, if a group hasn't booked them first). The nightly marshmallow roast and outdoor Disney film screenings are perennial hits.

3520 N. Fort Wilderness Trail, Lake Buena Vista. www.disneyworld.com. ℰ **407/934-7639** or 407/824-2900. 784 campsites, 408 wilderness cabins. $56–$145 campsite/RV double, $336–$562 wilderness cabin double. Children 17 and younger stay free in parent's room. **Amenities:** Restaurant, grill, babysitting, extensive outdoor activities (archery; fishing; horseback, pony, carriage, and hay rides; campfire programs; boat rental; and more), 2 outdoor heated pools, kids' pool, character dining, 2 lighted tennis courts, free self-parking, free Wi-Fi.

Disney's Port Orleans and French Quarter ★★

An unwieldy name for an unwieldy property. It's actually two resorts, both built on a canal and awkwardly fused together. The French Quarter (1,000 rooms), built along right angles on simulated streets, purports to sorta imitate the real one in New

Orleans. Riverside (2,048 rooms), where buildings are more successful pastiches on magnolia-lined Mississippi-style homes (Magnolia Bend, where princess-themed "Royal Rooms" have touches such as headboards with push-button light shows; about $50 surcharge) and rustic cabins (Alligator Bayou, where trundle beds sleep five—good for a Moderate resort), is the nicer of the two, because it has more water for rooms to face (though the privilege will cost you another $30 a night) and is the locale for most activities for the two resorts. The main pool at Riverside is less elaborate than French Quarter's, and room windows all face an exterior corridor there, although it has five pools to French Quarter's one. The properties are far enough apart (about 15 min. walking) that many people choose to use the free boat service linking them. The boats will also take you to Downtown Disney—the trip is one of the most pleasant, least-known free rides at Disney World—but the parks are served only by buses.

2201 Orleans Dr., Lake Buena Vista. www.disneyworld.com. ℰ **407/934-7639** or 407/934-5000. 3,048 units. $182–$308 double. Extra person $15. Children 17 and younger stay free in parent's room. **Amenities:** 2 restaurants, grill/food court, 6 heated outdoor pools, 2 kids' pools, arcade, free self-parking, free Wi-Fi.

Shades of Green ★★★   Operated as a golf resort for 21 years before being handed to the military as the only Armed Forces Recreation Center (AFRC) in the continental U.S, it's the best deal on WDW soil if you or your spouse is an active or retired member of the U.S. military (a full list of eligibility requirements is posted online). Standard rooms are among the largest at Disney (just over 400 sq. ft.) and suites accommodate up to eight. All rooms have balconies or patios, and pool or golf-course views. Bonus: You can walk to the monorail and the Magic Kingdom.

1950 Magnolia Palm Dr. (across from the Polynesian Resort), Lake Buena Vista. www.shadesofgreen.org. ℰ **888/593-2242** or 407/824-3400. 587 units. $93–$131 double (based on military rank); $250–$275 6- to 8-person suite (regardless of rank). Extra person $15. Children 17 and younger stay free in parent's room. **Amenities:** 2 restaurants, café, health club, arcade, 2 heated outdoor pools, kids' pool, 2 lighted tennis courts, free self-parking, free Wi-Fi.

VALUE RESORTS

Although the Mouse pushes you toward its most expensive hotels by making them so cool, Disney, in fact, has more "Value" rooms: 9,504 of them, more than many midsize cities have in total—available mostly for $100 to $200. The T-shaped building blocks with outdoor corridors can feel at times like thin-walled battery hen hutches, gurgling with noisy plumbing and seething with kids who don't realize how sound carries (especially when school groups and cheerleader meets are in town). The walk to each hotel's lobby/food building can be a marathon. There are elevators.

FACILITIES   Value rooms are motel-style, often of standard cinder-block construction and exterior corridors. They come with two full beds, but a few have kings (request one when you reserve). Rooms fit four (there's a $10 daily charge for each third and fourth adult over 17), plus one child under 3—a full room would be a mighty tight squeeze. If your party is bigger, spring for a 6-person Family Suite, which is usually just two rooms with a door banged through and a mini-kitchen (little fridge, microwave, coffeemaker) added. Those are at the All-Star Music resort and Art of Animation, where the design is more spacious, but at $240 (lowest price at Music) to $303 (lowest price at Animation), you can do *much* better outside the World. There's no room service, but you can have pizza delivery from late afternoon until midnight.

The food court, front desk, and sundries shop are all in the same building by the bus stops to the parks, and some rooms are a 15-minute walk away unless you shell out $15 to $20 more for a "Preferred" room.

TRANSPORTATION No Value or Moderate resort is connected by monorail. Roads are your only option, be it a bus or your car.

Disney's All-Star Movies/Disney's All-Star Music/Disney's All-Star Sports ★

Depending on your point of view, at the Value resorts, Disney treats you either like a second-class guest or an average American family on vacation. The fun is in the outdoor areas, not in the rooms, which are only faintly themed. The setup of all three is identical—an expanse of concrete-block buildings at the edge of the property studded with enormous emblems, as if a giant had spilled the Legos in his toy box. But because they're older (they opened in the late 1990s) and there's no enlivening central pond, they are the last-choice Values. At the very least, sinks are outside of the toilet-and-shower room, which eases life for multitasking families. Of the three, I prefer Movies, not just because it's the youngest (opened 1999), but also because its exterior is laden with Disney-specific iconography while its sisters stick to dull musical and sports-equipment icons. Disney shuttle buses also tend to stop there last on their circuit of the three, which cuts transportation time. Then again, some choose Sports for the same reason, because it's the first stop and so it's easier to get a seat there. (That concern says a lot about the Value resorts.) The Music is the only one with suites fitting six people.

Buena Vista Dr., Lake Buena Vista. www.disneyworld.com. © **407/934-1936.** 1,920 units each. Standard rooms $96–$199, family suites $240–$445, 3rd and 4th adult $10. Children 17 and younger stay free in parent's room. **Amenities:** Food court, arcade, babysitting, 2 outdoor heated pools, kids' pool, free self-parking, free Wi-Fi.

Disney's Art of Animation Resort ★★★

This attractive 2012 addition benefits from theming more lavish than at other Values, including a spot-on Radiator Springs pool area. Family Suites have two bathrooms, convertible couches, and demi-kitchens (no stove). Standard "Little Mermaid" rooms are gorgeously and whimsically themed, too—better than at other Values. Suites draw on "Finding Nemo" (where there's the Big Blue pool, WDW's largest) and "The Lion King." Unfortunately, six-person suites cost three times more than basic four-person Value rooms, which is hard to justify.

1850 Century Dr., Lake Buena Vista. www.disneyworld.com. © **407/938-7000.** 1,120 suites, 864 standard units. Standard rooms $156–$224, 6-person family suites $303–$514. **Amenities:** 3 pools, food court, kids' pools, arcade, free self-parking, free Wi-Fi.

Disney's Pop Century Resort ★★
The largest Value resort (opened 2002) is a fair choice, with smallish (260 sq. ft.) rooms—one king bed or two queens—with one sink and one mirror, and for dining, a heaving central food court with quality akin to the average mall's. As if to counteract such dormlike austerity, the boxy sprawl of T-shaped buildings, some of which face a pleasant lake across from the Art of Animation Resort, is festooned with outsized icons of the late 20th century: gigantic bowling pins, yo-yos, and Rubik's Cubes—which kids think is pretty cool.

1050 Century Dr., Lake Buena Vista. www.disneyworld.com. © **407/938-4000.** 2,880 units. Rooms $107–$226. **Amenities:** Food court, 3 pools, kids' pools, arcade, jogging trail, free self-parking, free Wi-Fi.

DISNEY VACATION CLUB
Disney sells timeshares, too. Because this isn't a real estate guide, there's no need to go into the fact that after you crunch the numbers, **Disney Vacation Club (DVC)** is economical only for people who never want to vacation anywhere that isn't Disney. The company rents empty villa units to walk-up customers who have no intention of signing any dotted lines, but the best ones are usually claimed by the time you book. DVC properties are grafted onto the major hotels, plus there are stand-alone properties including **BoardWalk Villas, Saratoga Springs Resort & Spa** and its **Treehouse Villas** built on platforms above the ground, and **Old Key West,** serving hundreds of thousands of DVC investors. These units are heavily promoted around the resort and even inside the theme parks themselves, which Walt surely would have detested as a fantasy-killer. During value season, the simplest studio with a kitchen costs an insane $368 (at Old Key West, the cheapest) a night, and in Peak season, it costs $485 a night. One-bedrooms at the Contemporary Resort's Bay Lake Tower range $632 to $1,106. The new two-bedroom overwater Bungalows jutting into Seven Seas Lagoon from the Polynesian Village are truly sumptuous, and you can see Cinderella Castle from the spa tub on your private deck—but they cost $2,404 to $3,319 a night. This is, of course,

---

The "Good Neighbor" Policy

Scattered throughout town are properties that brag Disney has certified them as "Good Neighbor" (www.wdwgood neighborhotels.com). The appellation is mostly meaningless. It means that hotel will have shuttles, can sell Magic Your Way tickets, and screens a mesmerizing 24-hour "Must Do Disney" channel featuring the insanity-inducing Stacey Aswad, the world's most nose-wrinklingly perky Disney fan (to her, everything is "amazing"), and her Top Seven favorites at each park. To be brutally honest, most Good Neighbor hotels are mediocre. Only the Good Neighbor properties on the west side of Apopka Vineland Road (mostly on Hotel Plaza Blvd.) enjoy half-hourly shuttles; the rest don't. Legoland's version, with its own shuttles, are **"Bed & Brick"** hotels (© **800/979-9983**). So don't select a hotel just because it's a Good Neighbor hotel. Choose it because it's the hotel for you.

crazy, so I cannot in good conscience suggest the average family will find the best value in renting a DVC room. I have, though, now informed you they're available.

Non-Disney On-Property Hotels

The best way to think of these choices is "location without immersion." While some visitors find the Disney-run hotels cloying, these properties are permitted to run their own shows on Disney turf, supplying convenience and often, higher standards. Bonnet Creek-area hotels are newer, more remote, and nicer than ones on Hotel Plaza Boulevard, which are older and more tired, but run their own bus systems to the Disney parks and are often within walking distance to Disney Springs. (For nearby hotels that don't happen to be on Disney property, see Lake Buena Vista section on p. 278.) Technically, the Bonnet Creek resorts are not on Disney property, but you use Disney roads to get to them.

EXPENSIVE

Four Seasons Resort Orlando at Walt Disney World Resort ★★★
Orlando's most genuinely luxurious resort is deep inside the custom-built gated community of Golden Oak, within sight of the Magic Kingdom. Four Seasons' largest property in the world, and one of its best in years, is a stunner in both looks and service: Chandeliers were inspired by fireworks blooms and quiet, 500-square-foot rooms come with walk-in closets, concierge iPads, and marble bathrooms. The par-71 golf course, once Disney's Osprey Ridge but now renovated by Tom Fazio, is also a bird sanctuary, and the landscaped pool complex (with free sunscreen and valets bearing refreshments) goes on and on—adults-only pool, zero-entry family pool, lazy river with waterfalls, two water slides in a faux fort. To see the fireworks just two miles away from your balcony, you must spring for a "Park View Room," which are $200 more than

Lazy river and waterfalls at Four Seasons.

a "Lake View Room" on the lower floors, or opt for a meal at the rooftop Capa restaurant. As part of the sky-high rate, which is really no different from a Disney Deluxe hotel, daytime babysitting for kids 4 to 12 is free and kids 5 and under eat free. Its Goofy breakfast is one of the best character meals since it's less crowded and you get lots of photo time with him. If you can afford such pampering, it does it better than nearly any other property in town. The free shuttle is on a fixed schedule and doesn't go to Disney Springs, so if you want flexibility, have your own car.

10100 Dream Tree Blvd., Golden Oak. www.fourseasons.com/orlando. © **800/267-3046.** 434 units. From $399 for a standard double, no resort fee, valet parking $26 (no self-parking). **Amenities:** 3 restaurants, pool, children's pool, 5-acre "Explorer Island" splash zone and water slide, lazy river, spa, tennis courts, fitness center, sundries shop, character breakfast, kids' club, free Disney parks shuttle, free standard Wi-Fi, high-speed Wi-Fi ($18/day).

Hilton Orlando Bonnet Creek ★

Linked to the Waldorf Astoria by a convention hall and set in 482 mostly unbuilt acres, this is a favorite of large groups and one of Hilton's biggest properties. Rooms lack balconies, which is a real bummer, but they retain that reliable and unsurprising Hilton standard, and it's on Disney turf, which counts for a lot. Kids eat free for breakfast and dinner. The 3-acre pool area is done in contemporary stonework—a bit like riding a lazy river in a hotel bathroom—and is abuzz with cocktails and activities. Overall, it's a fine place to disappear but it's too large to be romantic. Shuttles to the Disney parks are plentiful and free.

14100 Bonnet Creek Resort Lane, Orlando. www.hiltonbonnetcreek.com. © **407/597-3600.** 1,001 units. $139–$309 for a standard king, plus $25/night resort fee. Parking $18/night (self) $26/night (valet). **Amenities:** 6 restaurants, coffee bar, pool bar, pool with activities, Disney shop, golf course, business center, fitness club, spa (at neighboring Waldorf Astoria), game room, free Disney shuttles, Wi-Fi ($17/night for high speed).

Waldorf Astoria Orlando ★★★

The first time the Waldorf expanded its brand outside of Manhattan it was in Orlando, and if the original's Upper East Side ethic was traded for Florida's tropical colors, the service standard is noticeably higher than at most other Orlando luxury hotels. Between the Rees Jones-designed par 72 golf course, the formally arranged adults-only swimming pool, the high-end Bull & Bear steakhouse, and the sink-deeper-into-slumber beds, this is the best choice of all the Bonnet Creek properties. If the price is similar to the Hilton, book here; for the same money you'll get perks such as bathrobes, better-aligned views of distant fireworks, and much more attentive service. You may use the lazy river of the Hilton next door.

14200 Bonnet Creek Resort Lane, Orlando. www.waldorfastoriaorlando.com. © **407/597-5500.** 498 units. $209–$449 double queen. $30/night resort fee. Parking (valet only) $26/night. **Amenities:** 5 restaurants, pool, kids' activities, spa, fitness center, golf course, golf club, free Disney shuttles, Wi-Fi free (standard) or $15 (high-speed).

Wyndham Grand Orlando Resort Bonnet Creek ★

This resort caps off a development of more than 1,000 timeshare villas around a pretty

10-acre lake at the south end of Disney property. When you stay here, you can roam the campus, dipping into pools themed after Caribbean fortresses and pirate ships, barbecuing on public grills. It's a sweet setup, and the fact that it's well-located among Disney's parks makes it better, but ho-hum rooms, aggressive timeshare sales, and a noticeably disaffected staff keep it from being a standout.

14651 Chelonia Parkway., Orlando. www.wyndhamgrandorlando.com. ✆ **407/390-2300.** 400 units. $149–$249 standard room, plus $20/night resort fee. Self-parking $18/night, valet parking $24/night. **Amenities:** 4 restaurants, coffee bar, pool with access to 5 others, 2 lazy rivers, spa, fitness center, kids' activities, gift shop, jogging trail, game room, free Wi-Fi.

MODERATE

B Resort & Spa ★★   The onetime Royal Plaza Hotel, convenient to both I-4 and Downtown Disney, completed a gut renovation in 2014. New threads and surfaces were laid on the old, finicky 17-story tower, and in place of a tired bed bunker you now have an airy Miami-flavored resort suffused in whites and clean lines. King rooms are much larger than double-queen ones, but all are sizable, and higher-floor "Stunning" (that's the name) ones claim views. Ringing the zero-entry pool, "Chic" rooms come with bunk beds. The Florida-based company that runs it wants to plow new Disney territory by providing a grown-up stay that's still family-friendly and affordable, and it succeeds with fun gimmicks such as loaner iPads and Aveda toiletries. The ground-floor restaurant, American Q, does a riff on barbecue; chandeliers are made out of Mason jars and diners pick buffet items from the flatbed of a Ford F1 pickup truck. It often offers 3-for-2 deals on its website.

1905 Hotel Plaza Blvd., Lake Buena Vista. www.BResortLBV.com. ✆ **407/828-2828.** 394 units. Doubles from $139–$189. Resort fee $23/night. Parking $17/night, valet parking $22/night. **Amenities:** Restaurant, pool, pool bar, tennis courts, spa, 24-hr. fitness center, sundries shop, free Disney shuttle, free Wi-Fi.

Best Western Lake Buena Vista Resort Hotel ★   Another motel-grade tourist machine on Hotel Plaza Boulevard, the congested road leading to Downtown Disney, this 18-story hotel is older and could use a brush-up (you have to request a fridge or microwave, for example, and there are few electrical sockets). But it distinguishes itself by having a balcony for every room and charging a resort fee of only $14 a day, which is better than the other joints on this strip. It's a fair mid-budget option if you can score a deal online (to pay three digits would be a stretch), and if you're lucky, your room will be high enough to offer fireworks views.

2000 Hotel Plaza Blvd., Lake Buena Vista. www.lakebuenavistaresorthotel.com. ✆ **407/828-2424.** 325 units. $89–$125 2-queen rooms, plus $10 for sleeper sofa. Resort fee $14/night. **Amenities:** 2 restaurants and a snack bar, pool with children's pool, arcade, fitness center, sundries shop, frequent Disney shuttle, free parking, free Wi-Fi.

Wyndham Lake Buena Vista Resort ★   The Wyndham gets passing, but not flying, marks. Rates bottom out at $84 but are usually in the low $100s

After years of economy-related delays, Disney-owned property a half-mile out its western gate is being developed into Flamingo Crossings, a hub for lower-cost hotels. The new affordable rooms, reached by Western Way, which runs west from Coronado Springs, will add welcome budget choices—practically on Disney property, but too far to walk. There's not much out there, not even flamingoes, except a ramp to a toll expressway (State Road 429), and getting to I-4 and the other attractions of Orlando will require driving across the busy Disney resort, but it may be worth it for 10 acres of freshly built, high-value, Marriott-flagged hotels. Two to look for: **SpringHill Suites Orlando Flamingo Crossings** (opening January 2016; www.marriott.com; ✆ **321/418-7250;** 13279 Flamingo Crossings Blvd., Winter Garden), where all rooms are junior suites (with microwave and mini-fridge) and include free breakfast, and the long-stay **TownePlace Suites Orlando Flamingo Crossings** with fully equipped kitchens (opening February 2016). Five more hotels, all decently priced, should open by 2017. Retail and restaurants are on their way too, but so far, they're only twinkles in a developer's eye.

for the full hotel enchilada, including an aging fitness center, two big pools, shuttles that depart every 30 minutes, minifridges in the rooms, and the only sanctioned Disney character breakfast on Hotel Plaza Boulevard (three mornings a week). The polished lobby makes everything seem more luxurious than it is, but the kid-friendly staff boosts the value. Ask for a Tower Room on the west side (floors 9–19) for a limited view of Lake Buena Vista.

1850 Hotel Plaza Blvd., Lake Buena Vista. ✆ **407/828-4444.** www.wyndhamlake buenavista.com. 626 units. $84 doubles with courtyard view, $115 doubles in tower. $19/night resort fee, $8/night parking. **Amenities:** Restaurant, 3 lounges, character breakfast (Tues, Thurs, Sat), babysitting, children's activity program, health club, spa tub, 2 outdoor heated pools, 2 lighted tennis courts, complimentary bus service to WDW parks, transportation to non-Disney parks for a fee, free Wi-Fi.

Inside Universal Orlando

As of 2016, there are five hotels on Universal property, totaling 5,200 rooms operated by the Loews hotel group, and they all feel more like true resorts, as opposed to Disney's busier profile properties. There are strong advantages that come with the higher prices. First, all hotels are within 15 minutes' walk of the parks, and three are connected by a free boat that runs continuously into the wee hours. Rooms have wet bars with coffeemakers, two phones, and turndown service (rare at Disney). Also, guests can use their room key to make charges throughout the resort, they get into Harry Potter an hour early, and at three hotels, they can join the Express line at the two parks' best attractions—that perk has the effect of freeing up a vacation schedule. Guests can also drink and dine all night at CityWalk next door without having to drive or wait for a bus. Use the hotels' website to find Hot Deals, which grants discounts of 20% to 30% on specified nights; the website also posts floor plans of all room types.

Guest rooms at Hard Rock Hotel.

The Universal property is hemmed in by lots of real-world restaurants where prices are realistic, and free shuttles to SeaWorld and Wet 'n' Wild are provided once a day. So unlike cloistered Disney, when you're at Universal, you're linked to the real Orlando, and there's more food flexibility. At Easter and during the December holidays, rates are $150 higher than the lowest price.

EXPENSIVE

Hard Rock Hotel ★★★   Besides being the city's most convenient hotel for any theme park—the two parks are both a 10-minute walk away—the Hard Rock has more perks for the money than most of the city's similarly priced hotels. Rooms have genuinely funky furniture, tons of mirrors, two sinks (one in and one out of the bathroom), two big beds, and music systems. The ginormous pool, which imitates a beach gently descending to depth, has not only a substantial water slide but also underwater speakers through which you can hear the party music. (They really bring out the finger cymbals in "Livin' on a Prayer.") Halls are lined with rock memorabilia (whoa: the gold-lion-head necklace Elvis was wearing when he met Nixon!). The Hard Rock truly walks the rock walk: The last Thursday of the month, the lobby is taken over by the rollicking Velvet Sessions (www.velvetsessions.com) concert series for well-known '80s acts, like Howard Jones, John Waite, and Survivor.

5000 Universal Blvd., Orlando. www.hardrockhotels.com/orlando. © **888/832-7155** or 407/503-7625. 650 units. Rooms $254–$394. Parking $20/night, valet parking $27/night. **Amenities:** 3 restaurants, cocktail lounge, Emack & Bolio's ice cream shop, babysitting, supervised children's program, club-level rooms, fitness center, pool with activities and bar, free Wi-Fi.

Loews Portofino Bay Hotel ★★   Universal's priciest and most romantic option faithfully re-creates the famous Italian fishing village, down to the angle of the boat docks, the bolted-down Vespas, and live opera music nightly

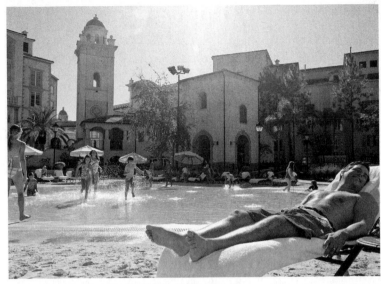
Beach pool at Loews Portofino Bay Hotel at Universal Studios.

along the waterfront. Beyond that spectacular gimmick (said to have been Steven Spielberg's idea, like much at Universal), rooms are of a particularly high standard—standard ones are a generous 450 square feet and have top-end beds. Because the resort is the farthest of the four from the parks (about 20 min. by boat or foot), it tends to appeal to couples, but a few suites are decked out in a "Despicable Me" theme to please your minions.

5601 Universal Blvd., Orlando. www.universalorlando.com. ℂ **888/430-4999** or 407/503-1000. 750 units. Double queen or king rooms $279–$474. Parking $20/night, valet parking $27/night. **Amenities:** 3 restaurants, Mandara spa, 3 pools with activities and bar, nightly opera show, free Wi-Fi.

Loews Royal Pacific Resort ★★★
The least expensive luxury option at Universal does an apt impression of the South Seas in the 1930s. It's more luxurious yet cheaper than the Disney Polynesian, with a lush pool area (sandy beach, winding garden paths, interactive water play area) and a sophisticated, wood-and-wicker look. The standard is high: very soft robes, cushy beds with fat pillows, and marble-top chests. It's right over the road from Islands of Adventure; many rooms have a panorama of it. In any other city, the Royal Pacific might be everyone's favorite resort. Here, though, its subtler charms get lost in the crowd.

6300 Hollywood Way, Orlando. www.universalorlando.com. ℂ **888/430-4999** or 407/503-3000. 1,000 units. Guest rooms $224–$329. Parking $20/night, valet parking $27/night. **Amenities:** 3 restaurants, sushi bar, cocktail lounge, pool with activities and bars, free Wi-Fi.

MODERATE
Cabana Bay Beach Resort ★★★
Universal's fourth hotel, a 2014 newcomer, is much larger and $100 cheaper than its sisters and it brilliantly plays

Loews Royal Pacific Resort.

the role of affordable family vacation hotel by embracing the genre: It kitsches it up as a retro 1950s beach hotel. Geometric fabrics, teals and lemons, swooping Space Ace architecture, a doo-wop soundtrack, a Jack LaLanne–branded gym, and a 10-lane bowling alley all wink at the midcentury vacation genre. Things may *look* old but they're decidedly modern, down to the ample outlets in the bedrooms, gated parking, and air-conditioning that's whisper quiet. In fact, this is the nicest "value" hotel the theme parks have to offer. Uniquely, bathrooms are lined up along the side of the rooms, galley-style, and the toilets are separate from the sink and tub, dulling noise and making mornings easier on families. On the north end of the complex, where a motor court theme prevails, you'll find 600 family suites with kitchen areas (microwave, no stove) that sleep six somewhat tightly, two on a sofa bed. The south courtyard, where the Miami Beach theme and lazy river are, you find standard rooms in 7-story towers. The music never stops in the two ginormous pool areas, fueling the family-friendly party. Its Bayliner Diner is better than it should be for a food court. All in all, the lower price opens Universal to a new group of visitors, but there's a trade-off: no Express pass privileges (you do get into the parks early), and to reach the action, you'll have to either walk 15 minutes or take a shuttle to CityWalk— there is no water taxi to this hotel. (Sapphire Falls, similarly priced, has that.)

6550 Adventure Way, Orlando. www.universalorlando.com. © **888/273-1311** or 407/ 503-4000. 1,800 units. Standard rooms from $119–$134, family suites $174–$284, with discounts for stays longer than 4 nights. Parking $20/night, valet parking $27/night. **Amenities:** Food court, 10-lane bowling alley with food, 2 pools, 2 pool bars, water slide, lazy river, fitness center, free standard-speed Wi-Fi (full-speed $15/day).

Loews Sapphire Falls Hotel ★★ Opening in the summer of 2016, the Caribbean-inspired Sapphire Falls is, along with Cabana Bay Beach, one of Universal's most affordable options. It's also the one most likely to be hosting conventions, which may affect the vibe. Most rooms have either a king or two queens (321 sq. ft.), but for $100 more you can have a King Suite with a separate sitting area (595 sq. ft.), and for $200 more there are Kids Suites with a separate double-twin bedroom for children. The 16,000-square-foot pool area is elevated and richly planted, but not true luxury-level. A stay comes with free water taxis (Cabana Bay only has buses) to the parks and early entry to The Wizarding World of Harry Potter, but not Express entry.

6601 Adventure Way, Orlando. www.universalorlando.com. ℂ **800/232-7827** or 407/503-5000. 1,000 units. Double queen or king rooms $199–$211. Parking $20/night, valet parking $27/night. **Amenities:** 2 restaurants, 2 bars, fitness center, pool with activities and bar, free standard-speed Wi-Fi (full-speed $15/day).

U.S. 192 Area Accommodations

The lowest rung in the Orlando tourist ladder both in class and price (with some exceptions), U.S. 192 is where you'll always find the cheapest (if often the most tired) motels close to the Disney zoo. Most were built in the 1970s boom and settled into the budget category. These places are technically located in the town of Kissimmee, which posts tourist info at **www.experience kissimmee.com**—check it for regular deals. In this region, shuttles are often available to Disney, but not always to SeaWorld or Universal.

MODERATE

Bohemian Hotel Celebration ★★ The Kessler Collection, which operates chic, art-laden boutique hotels in Savannah, Asheville, and other Old South enclaves, also runs this romantic fantasy come true. The civilized, full-service 115-room property evokes funky Florida and gets the pace and look just right. The lakeside setting is soothing and private—there's nothing on the opposite shore but trees and quiet. Furnishings are tropical, almost postcolonial (four-poster beds, wicker-paddle ceiling fans); the halls are filled with slightly skewed artwork that is a hallmark of the Kessler brand; there's a cool martini-style bar and frequent music on the waterfront terrace, but right out the front door is Celebration's easygoing downtown, ripe with non-chain boutiques and restaurants, and Disney is a 5-minute drive away, which is a good thing since there is no provided shuttle (another reason this place isn't suited to kids).

700 Bloom St., Celebration. www.celebrationhotel.com. ℂ **888/249-4007** or 407/566-6000. 115 units. $119–$199 king or queen. Daily $21 valet parking or $16 self-parking. **Amenities:** Pool, restaurant, fitness center, cocktail lounge, free Wi-Fi.

Meliá Orlando Suite Hotel at Celebration ★★ Curvy-walled and cloistered, this 240-room hotel, built in 2007, has fully equipped kitchens including full-size fridges plus dishwashers. Units also have a little patio, with a queen-size pullout to sleep more people. Protected by the hotel's four curving buildings, a perfectly round vanishing-edge pool ringed with funky red pyramid umbrellas recalls South Beach style, lending the sensation of an upscale resort, so it's not the best choice for rambunctious kids. Getting a pool view adds about $20. The location beside the jungle of U.S. 192 very near Disney is prime, but not a lot of people seem to know about it. Service can be lax and we're near the time when fixtures need a touch-up, but overall, it's peaceful for Orlando.

225 Celebration Place, Celebration. www.meliaorlando.com. ℂ **888/956-3542.** 240 units. $120–$219 1-bedroom suite sleeping 4, 2-bedroom suites sleeping 8 $30 more, $130–$269 family suite sleeping 8. Resort fee $15/night. Free parking. **Amenities:** Pool, breakfast-only restaurant, sauna, free park shuttles, fitness center (offsite), shuttles to Celebration village, bottled water, free continental breakfast, free Wi-Fi.

Orlando's Hotels

Kissimmee Hotels

WALT DISNEY WORLD

Disney's Hollywood Studios

Blizzard Beach

ESPN Wide World of Sports

CELEBRATION

KISSIMMEE

Lake Cecile

To Downtown Kissimmee

Barefoot'n Resort **13**
Bohemian Hotel Celebration **6**
Comfort Suites Maingate East at Old Town **14**
Disney's All-Star Movies Resort **3**
Disney's All-Star Music Resort **2**
Disney's All-Star Sports Resort **1**
Disney's Art of Animation Resort **4**
Disney's Pop Century Resort **5**
Gaylord Palms **12**
Hilton Orlando Bonnet Creek **10**
Meliá Orlando Suite Hotel at Celebration **7**

Nickelodeon Suites Resort **16**
Orlando World Center Marriott **17**
Palm Lakefront Resort & Hostel **18**
Radisson Resort Orlando Celebration **8**
Waldorf Astoria Orlando **11**
WorldQuest Resort **15**
Wyndham Grand Orlando Resort Bonnet Creek **9**

Radisson Resort Orlando Celebration ★★ Cheaper than its sister in Lake Buena Vista, this property aims squarely at families with a sports lounge, an active grotto pool area with a 42-foot rock slide, and rooms that have two double beds, one king, or come as family suites sleeping six. It's also one of the fresher choices in town, having enjoyed a 2014 renovation that poured $10 million into improvements, fitting it with pillow-top mattresses and granite-counter bathrooms. Adding to the convenience, it's a few hundred yards off U.S. 192, giving you all of its convenience but none of its nuisances.

2900 Parkway Blvd, Kissimmee. www.radisson.com/lakebuenavistafl. © **800/634-4774** or 407/396-7000. 718 units. Rooms $79–$175. Resort fee $20/night. Free parking. **Amenities:** Restaurant, pool, business center, game room, small 24-hr. fitness center, volleyball, lighted tennis and basketball courts, free Epcot shuttle, free Wi-Fi.

EXPENSIVE

Gaylord Palms ★ The Gaylord, run by Marriott, is geared to meetings, so although its scenery is extravagant, so are its incidental charges. Beneath its mighty glass atrium is a 4½-acre Florida-themed ecosystem of gator habitats, caves, indoor ponds, sand sculptures, restaurants, and a full-size sailboat—all that makes for an attraction unto itself, and to face it, you'll pay about $20 extra. Rooms sleep five and sport unusually nice granite-lined bathrooms. If it weren't nestled against Disney property, you could happily never leave, what with the on-site Cypress Springs mini water park, sports bar with two-story screen, adults-only pool, and the Relâche Spa & Salon. It also schedules family activities and an annual holiday ICE! extravaganza (p. 298). Look on its Web page for last-minute deals saving $25 or so.

6000 W. Osceola Pkwy., Kissimmee. www.gaylordhotels.com/gaylord-palms. © **407/586-2000.** 1,406 units. $169 king or double-queen rooms. $20 daily resort fee. $27 valet parking; $18 self-parking. **Amenities:** 2 pools with splash zone, fitness center, spa, 5 restaurants, sports bar, fitness center, arcade, room service, free local phone calls, park shuttles (Disney free), free bottled water, Wi-Fi $15 day, fast Wi-Fi $22/day.

Hyatt Regency Grand Cypress Resort ★★★ Probably the most complete resort campus near Disney, the stepped tower packs every conceivable amenity into a lush 1,500-acre campus located practically within Walt

---

Winning at Priceline Roulette

Instead of pecking around Priceline and making blind bids that may waste your money, use one of three secret-weapon sites, **BiddingTraveler.com**, **Better Bidding.com**, and **BiddingForTravel. com**, to find out what recent bids have been accepted. Then you'll get a sense of how low you can go. Using it one low season, I read about a $40 success story for an off-Disney two-star property. I dared to offer Priceline $29—and got my deal. Next, I shopped for rental cars. Although the major renters were offering around $25 a day on their own sites, Priceline accepted a bid of $16, through Alamo. That made for a total of $35 a day for both hotel *and* car—not bad. Three-star hotels go for $40 to $50, and four-stars for $60 to $70, even in summer.

Disney World. There's 45 holes of golf, an unforgettable waterfall-and-cavern-studded lagoon pool system (it's the best pool of any Orlando resort, and it recently added two new water slides), lush trails wrapping around a private pond, Lake Windsong, horses, and top-floor views of the fireworks at Epcot and the Magic Kingdom, even from the windows in the corridors. Resort fees are annoying, and this one's $25, but with so many extras (kayaks, paddleboats, mini-golf) this is a rare case where you can actually see where it's going. Contrary to its decidedly '80s atrium construction (and a snippy parrot, Merlot, who was allowed to remain in the lobby long after the previous tropical decor was retired), rooms—maximum guests: 4; 360 square feet—have an almost Asian sleekness with rain showers, chaise lounges, and adapter panels to play multimedia on the 37-inch HDTV. The spa, Marilyn Monroe, doesn't take itself too seriously—it also does haircuts for men—and the signature restaurant, Hemingway's, is in its own romantic courtyard pavilion and specializes in Florida ingredients. I've seen $85 Priceline bids accepted—such a steal.

1 Grand Cypress Blvd., Lake Buena Vista. www.hyattgrandcypress.com. ℂ **800/233-1234** or 407/239-1234. 815 units. $135–$369 king or double queen. Resort fee $25/day. Valet parking $25, self-parking $17. **Amenities:** Pool, babysitting, kids' club, business center, gift shop, babysitting, 2 year-round restaurants, 3 cocktail bars, coffee bar, game room, tennis courts, golf course, biking, trails, rock climbing wall, 24-hr. fitness center, salon, beach, free park shuttles, included Wi-Fi.

Nickelodeon Suites Resort ★

The multimillion-dollar hotel, with one- to three-bedroom suites arranged around two courtyards, has toned down its cartoonishness in the past year—gone are themed rooms with video games for kids, replaced by a more corporate feel, and renovations are ongoing, leaving this place something of a question mark. Still, the "Nick Suites" has facilities to make a kid's head turn. In the two slammed splashdown areas (noise alert: they're encircled by guest rooms, but they keep limited hours), water cannons blast, a 400-gallon bucket regularly spills water over squealing kids, and 13 slides and flumes twist. As you can imagine, it gets pretty noisy, so if you don't have kids, it may have you fleeing for the hills. The rest takes its cues from the theme parks: food court, 3,000-square-foot arcade, character breakfasts with Nick icons and a studio for "Double Dare" live game shows in which parents might get "slimed." The Lagoon complex rooms were just renovated, while the Oasis rooms will go under the paint brush from September to January 2017—at least one pool area will be open at all times during work. Three-bedroom suites (950 square feet), which sleep up to eight, come with equipped kitchens (so do one-bedroom kitchen suites), two-bedrooms (485 square feet) just have a microwave and mini-fridge. Everything has a pullout double, too. It's a fair, if expensive, choice if you plan to spend playtime back at base (it's wickedly close to Disney turf) and security is superb—it's gated and everyone wears wristbands. Don't forget that sky-high $35-a-day resort fee, which can bump this otherwise appealing option into the overpriced category.

14500 Continental Gateway, Orlando. www.nickhotel.com. ℂ **800/972-2590** or 407/387-5437. 777 units. Low-season rooms $109 (1-bedroom) to $350 (3-bedroom), high season rooms $209 (1-bedroom) to $599 (3-bedroom). $35-a-day resort fee. Free parking

Nickelodeon Suites Resort.

but $17/night for additional vehicles. **Amenities:** 2 pools with splash playgrounds and slides, arcade, souvenir shops, adult cocktail lounge, restaurant and food court, basketball court, kids' spa, 4-D cinema, character breakfasts, character appearances, free scheduled Disney park shuttle, babysitting, teen lounge, live entertainment, free Wi-Fi.

Orlando World Center Marriott ★   Mighty large, mighty busy, and mighty hard to ignore, the 200-acre World Center rises like a citadel over I-4, a straight shot into Disney on Epcot Center Drive. Although handsome and appointed as a Marriott resort should be—the pool and slide tower are among the best in town—it's the well-funded infrastructure that does all the work. In fact, if you need more than that, it operates with all the annoyances of a convention machine, meaning lines to get any service whatsoever, inflated prices ($8.25 for an egg sandwich at its Starbucks), and even a fee for Wi-Fi, which by now should be an archaic practice. Its Siro Urban Italian Kitchen uses fresh ingredients and is several notches above most hotel restaurants, but the World Center mostly has what I call "points appeal"—it's a fine place to cash in rewards for a vacation. Spring for the valet, because the parking structure is unforgivably far from the building—it requires a shuttle, if you can believe it.

8701 World Center Dr., Orlando. www.worldcentermarriott.com. ⓒ **800/380-7931.** 2,009 units. $135–$369 king or double queen. Resort fee $22/day. Valet parking $28, self-parking $18. **Amenities:** 2 pools with 3-water slide tower and bar/grill, 6 restaurants, 3 bars, 18-hole golf course, golf school, 24-hr. fitness center, spa, 4 tennis courts, 2 sand volleyball courts, kids' activities, Wi-Fi $15/day (throttled), $20 (high-speed).

MODERATE

Blue Heron Beach Resort ★   Ignore the deceptive "beach resort" part; you stay at this mid-priced condo-style property to get above it all. These two high-rise towers overlook Lake Bryan, furnishing the illusion that you're the only person in the city and not a mile off Disney property. Units are huge but not artistically furnished, have a private balcony, a washer/dryer, a sleeper sofa, two bathrooms (even in one-bedrooms), and a kitchen so well equipped it even has a blender (margarita time!). There are bunk beds in the hall to increase sleeping capacity for families. The best value is the two-bedroom units, which have perspectives of both the lake to the west and of Disney to the east; from high floors, you can see fireworks.

13428 Blue Heron Beach Dr., Lake Buena Vista. www.blueheronbeachresort.com. © **888/ 258-3684** or 407/387-2200. 283 units. $119–$149 1-bedrooms, $129–$199 2-bedrooms, plus $12 resort fee. Housekeeping $15–$25 per service. **Amenities:** Pool with hot tub and kids' area, Disney shuttle, fitness center, game room, free parking. free Wi-Fi.

Radisson Hotel Lake Buena Vista ★★★

Gleaming, professionally run, and consistently top-notch for a non-resort hotel. Rooms feel current and are packed with the latest modern conveniences such as HDTVs, iPod docks, free Internet, minifridges, and microwaves. Size is beyond the average, too: Bathrooms are spacious, balconies were long ago incorporated as sitting areas with pullout couches, so a superior room can sleep up to five. There are a few downers, such as a tricky entry that requires some U-turning, a dull but sunny pool area, and infrequent free shuttles, but those bummers are entirely offset by the quality of the rest and by the fact it's a short, safe walk to the restaurants of the Crossroads shopping center. Its website often offers the best prices.

12799 Apopka Vineland Rd. www.radisson.com/lakebuenavistafl. © **800/967-9033** or 407/597-3400. 196 units. Rooms $84–$165. Free parking. **Amenities:** Pool, small fitness center, restaurant, free Wi-Fi.

Staybridge Suites Lake Buena Vista ★★

Close to lots of restaurants, you'll find these apartment-like quarters (there are two TVs and the kitchens even have dishwashers). The three-level buildings don't have elevators, but overlook that fact and avoid the ground-floor rooms, which are darker and less private. The full breakfast is free and plentiful, and you can eat it indoors or out. There's also a well-used pool in one of the courtyards. Home or condo rentals are cheaper, but you won't find many of those so close to Disney grounds, and those also come with cleaning fees and minimum stays.

8751 Suiteside Dr., Orlando. www.sborlando.com. © **407/238-0777.** 150 units. $105– $145 1-bedrooms sleeping 4 and $120–$176 2-bedrooms sleeping 8. Free rollaways and cribs. Free parking. **Amenities:** Full breakfast, heated pool, spa tub, business center, sundries shop, free Disney shuttle, free Wi-Fi.

WorldQuest Resort ★★★

A richly appealing facility that feels like a luxury condo complex (it is—you're renting empty timeshares). Surrounded by nothing but trees and peace, yet only a mile from Disney property, its five-floor buildings gather around a lush, fountained pool area. Each unit is a fresh, contemporary apartment complete with full fridge and freezer, equipped kitchens you could bake a cake in, screened-in furnished balconies, DVD player, and a master bathroom the size of entire hotel rooms elsewhere in town. Here's the downside: It has no full restaurant and it's too isolated to walk anywhere, so you must use a car. Bookings made on Travelzoo waive the resort fee, and Expedia often packages it for less than you could get directly.

8849 WorldQuest Blvd., Orlando. www.worldquestorlando.com. © **877/987-8378** or 406/387-3800. 238 units. $139–$189 2-bedroom/1-bathroom suites, add $20 for a 3rd

And Now Two Warnings . . .

If you use a **debit card** (instead of a credit card) as collateral against any purchases you may make during your stay, your card may be temporarily charged $50 to $250 (or more) *per day*, whether you actually charge anything to your room or not. This policy can seriously deplete your account, leaving you with fewer funds than you might realize—and you won't see a credit back to your account until *up to 10 days after* you have checked out of your resort. Ask about your hotel's policy.

Also, Orlando police perennially fight the **pizza flyer scam** in which shady outfits put menus under your hotel room door and then rip you off if you order. If you want to order food in, always ask your hotel for its preferred vendors.

bedroom; 3-night minimum stay or a $39 fee; $16-per-night resort fee. Free parking. **Amenities:** Pool with cabana bar, security gate, fitness center, sundries shop, free continental breakfast, free Disney shuttle, free Wi-Fi.

INEXPENSIVE

Barefoot'n Resort ★   These lemon-colored one-bedroom villas a block off chain restaurant–lined U.S. 192 are everything you need in simple, condo-style accommodation. Rooms come with queen beds, washer and dryer, DVD players, and a sofa sleeper, but you choose between having a fully equipped kitchen with a dishwasher and bar seating or larger bedroom with a spa tub and a partial kitchen. You take care of your own cleaning. The very sunny pool area has a grill and also faces a pond that's home to brown ducks and a little alligator, Crocky. The tiny gated resort, which is in good shape and recently renovated but not plush, faces the Old Town amusement area, but the drifting music isn't bothersome. Book by phone and there's no minimum stay required.

2754 Florida Plaza, Kissimmee. www.barefootn.com. ⓒ **877/978-3314.** 42 units. 1-bedrooms $99–$123. Free parking. **Amenities:** Pool, hot tub, security gate, outdoor barbecue, free Wi-Fi.

Clarion Suites Maingate ★★   A superior-level motel organized around its pool, the Clarion has a quiet, pseudo-resort feel (it's set away from the bustle of U.S. 192 but near enough to its restaurants) that makes it popular with scrimpers. All rooms come with a small fridge, microwave, and pullout sofa (hence the "suites" distinction of the hotel's name), queen beds, and sleep up to six people. During the week, rooms facing the parking lot usually cost the least, and ones facing the landscaped, free-form courtyard pool cost $10 more. Prices on weekends are about $10 higher, and continental breakfast, with a few plusses such as waffles, is always included. Kids get excited when they look down its driveway and see the summit of Expedition Everest at Disney's Animal Kingdom peeking over the trees nearby.

7888 W. Irlo Bronson Hwy., Kissimmee. www.clarionsuiteskissimmee.com. ⓒ **888/390-9888** or 407/390-9888. 150 units. $83–$109 doubles. Free parking. **Amenities:** Pool, 2 restaurants, free Disney shuttle, free breakfast buffet, game room, barbecue grills, sundries shop, free Wi-Fi.

Comfort Suites Maingate East at Old Town ★★   A good choice for families, it's tucked just off the main drag of U.S. 192, a few miles east of Disney, with the restaurants and carnival-style amusements of Old Town mere steps from the door—but not so near that the noise is truly annoying. The best rates are for "standard rooms" with either a king or queen bed, but you can get a "deluxe" two-bedroom one for about $30 more, and all rooms are on the large side with mini-fridges, pull-out couches (to up your occupancy, if needed) and microwaves for basic meal preparation. The elevators can be overwhelmed when it's at capacity. AAA membership chops rates slightly.

2775 Florida Plaza Blvd., Kissimmee. www.comfortsuitesfl.com. ℂ **888/784-8379.** 198 units. $89–$179 1-room suites. Free parking. **Amenities:** Pool with poolside bar, 24-hr. fitness center, sundries shop, game room, business center, free park shuttles, free hot breakfast buffet, free Wi-Fi.

Destiny Palms Hotel ★   Standards are high considering this spot on 192 west of Disney is the cheapest end of the motel spectrum, and although the decor could use reviving (it could be termed "Early '80s Beige"), the staff keeps things spotless, and that's what you want. Rooms, all of which are nonsmoking, come stocked with a toaster oven, mini-fridge, free Wi-Fi, and a continental breakfast upgraded with eggs, oatmeal, pancakes, and waffles. King rooms face the north parking lot and are on the small side; double queen rooms look south on some pleasing old-growth Florida woods. The east-facing pool (it, too, is motel-simple) also faces the trees, which keeps this place from feeling hemmed in. Coupons from tourist circulars often halve prices to $30 to $40.

8536 W. Irlo Bronson Hwy./U.S. 192, Kissimmee. www.destinypalmshotel.com. ℂ **407/ 396-1600.** 104 units. $60–$70 doubles plus $3.50-per-night resort fee. Free parking. **Amenities:** Pool, free continental breakfast, free local calls, free Wi-Fi.

Palm Lakefront Resort & Hostel ★   Meet the absolute cheapest respectable option in town. The outdated cinder-block construction and past-its-prime stretch of U.S. 192 are not for pampered types—it's a youth-oriented, hostel-style joint with an international clientele. It backs up to Lake Cecile with its own dock, and there's a pool in the giant backyard, where there's also a barbecue pit. You'll find six-bed dorms, simple private rooms with cable TV, private bathrooms, and twin beds, plus a family room sleeping five ($15 per person). Across the street, there's a Publix supermarket for munitions (the hostel has an equipped kitchen), and the $2 city bus to Disney goes right past the front door. You can't hope for more for rock bottom.

4840 W. Irlo Bronson Hwy./U.S. 192, Kissimmee. ℂ **407/396-1759.** $36 doubles $36, $19 dorm beds. Free parking. **Amenities:** Pool, barbecue, shared kitchen, free Wi-Fi.

Lake Buena Vista

Roughly speaking, Lake Buena Vista is the area where the eastern end of Walt Disney World around Downtown Disney/Disney Springs meets exit 68 off I-4. LBV, as it's nicknamed, is more compact and higher-class than the comparable cluster of Kissimmee hotels along U.S. 192, a few miles south near Disney's southern gate. For breathing room, the best part of Lake Buena Vista is Palm

Parkway, a lightly trafficked, winding, tree-lined avenue that's a secret short-cut to Universal that avoids I-4. Drive north on it and you'll pass a turnoff for SeaWorld, a Walmart, a Whole Foods, and the restaurants of Sand Lake Road.

LBV has the highest occupancy rate in town, so you'll often pay higher prices (and meet lazier staff) than in Kissimmee or on I-Drive, and traffic stinks. Free shuttles around here tend to go to Disney but not to Universal or SeaWorld.

See the map on p. 250 for locations of the properties below. Also investigate the **Crowne Plaza Orlando—Lake Buena Vista** (12390 S. Apopka Vineland Rd., Orlando; www.ihg.com; © **800/439-4745**), which was slated to open after a gut renovation in October 2015, too late for review in this guide.

INEXPENSIVE

Grande Villas Resort ★   This dirt-cheap, aging complex of condo towers off Palm Parkway fits the bill for a budget—a one-bedroom with an equipped kitchen can be had for well under $100 on apps such as HotelTonight—which is why it's often full and chirping with the sounds of families on vacation. Units aren't glam, they possess the most durable of furniture; they measure just 524 square feet, and in that small area are packed a bedroom, a sizable bathroom, a full kitchen with microwave (you can cook and have a family dinner at a four-seat dinner table), and pull-out couch. Buildings cluster around a hoppin' pool area. The bathroom is off the main bedroom, so anyone sleeping on the couch has to troop past the bed, and you can hear your neighbors through the expansion door in the kitchen, but not from your pillow. There's no bar and no restaurant, but also no stress because you can walk or drive to tons of food choices around Lake Buena Vista. What *is* stressful are the relentless efforts to sell you a timeshare, including 8am phone calls, but for these prices, just unplug the phone and let them keep trying.

12118 Turtle Cay Circle, Orlando. www.diamondresorts.com/Grande-Villas-Resort. © **407/ 238-2300**. 408 units. One-bedrooms from $134. Resort fee $6/night. **Amenities:** Pool, hot tub, fitness room, tennis court, barbecue facilities, free parking, Wi-Fi ($5/day).

Hawthorn Suites Lake Buena Vista ★   The decor is a touch dated (no flatscreen TVs, for example), but the management is attentive and hard-working, so this L-shaped property, arranged around a quiet and uncompli-cated kidney-shaped pool, is a good pick. The special appeal of this place is its full kitchens, standard in all rooms, with dishwashers, stoves, cookware—what you need to cook for yourself and save. All suites are one-bedroom suites, and the cheapest ones have two queen beds. Monday through Thursday after-noons, free cocktails are served, and on Wednesday from 5:30pm to 7:30pm, there's a "Manager's Reception" serving a free hot dog or hamburger.

8303 Palm Pkwy., Orlando. www.hawthornlakebuenavista.com. © **866/756-3778** or 407/ 597-5000. $79–$159 double. 120 suites. **Amenities:** Pool, hot tub, small fitness center, breakfast buffet, park shuttle, game room, business center, sundries shop, free local calls, free Wi-Fi.

Hyatt Place Lake Buena Vista ★★   Opening in 2016, it has the ear-marks of the business-focused brand, which also happen to be useful for vacationers: rooms divided into sleeping and sitting areas (with pull-out couch) like low-cost junior suites, free breakfast, and free Wi-Fi. The pool's a little plain, but so what? Many other properties in the area date to the 1980s, so it's lovely to find something so new here again, and the staff is too fresh to be complacent yet. You can walk to many places to eat.

8688 Palm Pkwy., Orlando. www.hyattplace.com. ℂ **407/581-9000.** 196 units. $129–$179 double. Free parking. **Amenities:** Pool, free buffet breakfast, business center, 24-hr. fitness center, free Wi-Fi.

Quality Suites Lake Buena Vista ★★   Fronted by three-story-tall palm trees, these mini-apartments are simple but inviting. Probably because it's a pipsqueak among lions, its attentive managers charge a competitively low price and even throw in a cooked breakfast. All rooms, which are larger than the average, have two TVs and fully equipped kitchens with a big fridge, toaster, microwave, dishwasher, and stove—a rarity among hotels that usually make do with microwaves alone, and a lifesaver when it comes to saving money on dining. The hotel is close enough to the Disney parks to make for a realistic lunch break, and the basic pool is open until 11pm, lovely for end-of-day soaks.

8200 Palm Pkwy., Orlando. www.qualitysuiteslbv.com. ℂ**800/370-9894** or 407/465-8200. 123 units. $79–$139 doubles. $159–$249 2-bedroom units sleeping up to 8. Free parking. **Amenities:** Pool and hot tub, fitness room, Disney shuttle, free buffet breakfast, free local calls, business center, game room, grills, sundries shop, free Wi-Fi.

International Drive, Universal

I-Drive, a current target for rapid development thanks to the opening of the Orlando Eye, is a good place to stay if you don't have a car because it's central, well connected, and full of competing places to eat. It's also the only hotel zone with a semblance of street life. If you stay here, you'll be in the thick of the family-friendly come-ons, midway rides, souvenir hawkers, minigolf, and theme bars. You'll need wheels to reach Disney (most hotels offer shuttles, but not always to Disney, and not always free), although Universal is just across I-4 to the north and the dirt-cheap I-Ride Trolley (p. 280) links you with SeaWorld. Car traffic can clog I-Drive, but there's a workaround: Universal Boulevard, a block east, bypasses the mess.

EXPENSIVE

Hyatt Regency Orlando ★★   Hyatt's double skyscraper surpasses the expectations of a typical convention-center hotel, which it is, and delivers a luxurious if vaguely decorated stay above the gridlock of I-Drive. Expect space (415 square feet is the norm but the maximum is 3–4 guests), an echoing lobby of white stone and marble, sculptural waterfalls, richly appointed bathrooms, ankle-level lights that switch on when they sense your movement, and other high-end touches that appeal to business travelers who come for its massive meeting halls. The free-form pool is not as frenetic as some other kid-focused ones, the fitness center is extremely well-stocked, and a collection of business-expense restaurants (an "Italian steakhouse," seafood) and a casual diner-style joint round out the well-balanced menu of options. The windows

International Drive Hotels

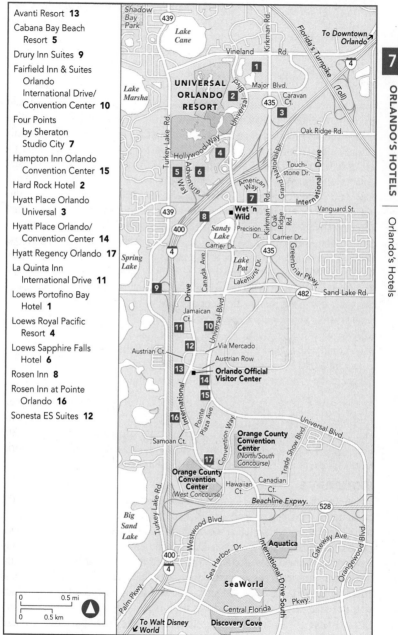

in the newer Regency Tower are larger, so ask for a View room there—you'll spy the distant Disney fireworks. All in all, it's not cozy, but it's a solid hotel.

9801 International Dr., Orlando. http://orlando.regency.hyatt.com. ✆ **407/284-1234.** 1,641 rooms. $139–$425 double or king for up to 4. Resort fee $22/night. $18 self-parking, $27 valet, **Amenities:** 3 restaurants, cocktail bar, pool with children's area and activities, hot tub, babysitting, spa, bike rental, 24-hr. fitness center, tennis court, free Wi-Fi.

JW Marriott Grande Lakes Orlando/Ritz-Carlton Grande Lakes Orlando ★★★

A true resort and a smart choice for a well-rounded vacation, the two luxury towers form a city unto themselves, and indeed, the JW's profile rises like a citadel in a 500-acre plot east of SeaWorld. The JW's 24,000-square-foot pool area, landscaped with fake rocks, jungle greens, and a ¼-mile lazy river, is the poshest outside of the Disney water slide parks, while the Ritz's is formal and refined. The JW's rooms have tile floors and slots for plugging your MP3 player into the plasma TVs. Yes, like many fancy convention hotels, it's a nickel-and-dime experience—everything costs you (the buffet breakfast is $28). As long as you know that in advance, the hotel's upscale amenities (gurgling lobby fountain, echoing bathrooms with separate bathtub and shower, palatial beds, narrow balconies on many rooms) are pleasing, even if the remote location means you'll have to drive somewhere every time your stomach rumbles if you want to escape resort pricing. At the Ritz-Carlton attached by a corridor, the three-level, 40,000-square foot spa is a winner, and in the rooms, the pamper factor is yet a notch higher. Both have unobstructed views of a Greg Norman–designed golf course and a nature reserve; west-facing rooms take in sunsets and SeaWorld in the distance. Stays come with two free hours at the kids' club. **Primo,** Chef Melissa Kelly's restaurant at the JW, and **Norman's,** Chef Norman Van Aken's ode to Florida flavors at the Ritz, are two top-of-the-line restaurants. Rates fluctuate wildly.

4040 Central Florida Pkwy., Orlando. www.grandelakes.com. ✆ **800/576-5760** or 407/ 206-2400 for the Ritz; ✆ **800/576-5750** or 407/206-2300 for the JW Marriott. JW: 1,000 rooms, Ritz: 584 units. $183–$799 double. Resort fee (both) $30. Both: Valet parking $26; self-parking $20. **Amenities:** 11 restaurants, babysitting, kids' activities, spa, club-level rooms, health club, golf course, 2 outdoor heated pools, kids' pool, 3 tennis courts, free local calls, transportation to non-Disney parks for a fee, free Wi-Fi.

MODERATE

Drury Inn Suites ★★★

A top pick. The popular, privately owned Missouri-based hotel group expanded to Orlando in 2012 on an ideal plot—drive around the corner to Universal, down Palm Parkway to Disney, or go on foot to the restaurants of I-Drive or Sand Lake Road. Design is fresh in rust browns and greens, rooms are wider than the industry average, and there are tons of free extras. So friendly is this brand that every day at 5:30pm, it hosts a "kick-back" with free food, beer, and wine. You could make a dinner out of it. The king-bed category has only a shower; the others have tubs.

7301 W. Sand Lake Rd., Orlando. www.druryhotels.com. ✆ **407/354-1101.** 238 units. $99–$146 1-king or 2-queen rooms. Free parking. **Amenities:** Indoor/outdoor pool, free hot breakfast, free soda and popcorn, 24-hr. fitness room, business center, free local calls, pets permitted for free, free Wi-Fi.

Four Points by Sheraton Studio City ★ Because it occupies one of those dated cylindrical towers that were briefly in vogue in the early 1970s, the ideally located property has a slight novelty that doesn't translate to luxury. It's just an interesting mid-priced choice. Because rooms are carved out of the floors like pie pieces, they're more spacious than the norm, and many have two queen beds. Request a room that doesn't face east, because the floodlights from the minigolf joint next door are blinding. The top floors have spectacular views of I-Drive, Wet 'n Wild (to the west), and Universal (just over I-4 to the north). It's not luxury, but it approximates it, and views in Orlando are rare at any price (particularly the $48 I've seen turn up in blind Hotwire bookings). Breakfast is $10, but there's an IHOP next door.

5905 International Dr., Orlando. www.fourpointsorlandostudiocity.com. ⓒ **888/625-4988** or 407/351-2100. 301 units. $104–$139 doubles. Resort fee $13/night. Free parking. **Amenities:** Pool, pool bar, restaurant, cocktail lounge, business center, park shuttles, free Wi-Fi.

Hyatt Place Orlando Universal ★★★ You check in at a kiosk that spits out your key, and without delay, head to a huge semi-partitioned room with giant beds and a sitting area, plus an extra pullout sofa. If you're not familiar with the standardized brand, it has up-to-date design, a 42-inch HDTV you can plug a laptop or an iPod into, granite bathrooms, wet bar, free continental breakfast, Wi-Fi, and plenty of space for five (six if two sleep on the pullout), all from $89. Seriously, why can't they all be like this? A second location at I-Drive isn't within spitting distance of Universal's gates as this one is, but it is nearer to more places to eat (**Hyatt Place Orlando/Convention Center;** 8741 International Dr., Orlando; http://orlandoconventioncenter.place.hyatt.com; ⓒ **407/370-4720;** 150 rooms, $127–$209 rooms two double beds). Both underwent 2013 renovations.

5895 Caravan Ct., Orlando. http://orlandouniversal.place.hyatt.com. ⓒ **407/351-0627.** 151 units. $89–$179 rooms with 2 double beds, $20 more for king bed. Free parking. **Amenities:** 24-hr. prepared meals, fitness center, free park shuttle, free breakfast, free Wi-Fi.

Rosen Inn at Pointe Orlando ★ One of the largest budget-priced properties outside of Disney's Value developments (so expect family noise), this former Quality Inn sprawls over 2 well-located city blocks and six Nixon-era buildings (renovated 2010). I-4 runs along the western side, resulting in a constant hum. Respectably affordable units, which come with a fridge, microwave, and two double beds, have smoked-glass windows, which helps create privacy given the external corridor construction, but doesn't help illuminate the bathrooms in the back. Rooms in the A building are near the lobby but suffer daytime noise from the sightseeing helicopter pad next door; opt for something in the F building, which is a 10-minute walk/2-minute drive from the lobby and has the most rooms hidden from I-4. Parking is gated but free. Many eateries are within walking distance on I-Drive. Universal is 10 minutes north, SeaWorld 5 minutes south.

9000 International Dr., Orlando. www.roseninn9000.com. ⓒ **800/999-8585** or 407/996-8585. 1,020 units. $89–$129 rooms with 2 doubles. Free parking. **Amenities:** 2 pools, playground, arcade, restaurant, bar, free local calls, free shuttle to Universal and Sea-World, charged shuttle to Disney, free Wi-Fi.

Sonesta ES Suites ★★   This well-located all-apartment hotel, across the street from the Eye and by plenty of places to eat, was recently lavished with a gut renovation, so there are fewer Moderate properties that are as current. All units, which are arranged around a courtyard pool, have new kitchens with new appliances, just-installed furniture, fresh carpeting, and bedding, a booth for family meals, and lots of added electrical outlets for recharging. Suddenly a dowdy '80s holdover has become a barely slept-in mid-priced darling. The staff is unusually dedicated, and some have been running this property for years.

8480 International Dr., Orlando. www.sonesta.com/orlando. ☏ **407/352-2400.** 146 units. 1-bedrooms $119–$189, 2-bedroom/2-bath $30–$40 more. Free parking. **Amenities:** Free breakfast, pool, spa tub, bar, sundries shop, small fitness center, free park shuttles (for Disney, connect via Epcot), free Wi-Fi.

INEXPENSIVE

Avanti Resort ★   Let's be frank: This is just an EconoLodge that got an extreme makeover. It still has the creaky bones of a motel, with small bathrooms, exterior corridors, and an echoing central pool. Yet because of its renovation, and those updated mellow colors and cool laminate floors, it's one of the fresher faces on I-Drive and consequently a good value. Double queen rooms sleep up to 4 and have fridges and microwaves, and the location makes it easy to walk to a slate of cheap places to eat. But it's not a "resort" by any stretch. It's an upgraded motel, and a nice one at that. A 2015 fire wrecked one of its buildings, but the rest was untouched and is going strong.

8738 International Dr., Orlando. www.avantiresort.com. ☏ **855/828-2684.** 652 units. Doubles $65–$119, plus $9/night resort fee. Free parking. **Amenities:** Restaurant, coffee bar, pool, fitness room, sundries shop, business center, game room, free local calls, park shuttles, free Wi-Fi.

Fairfield Inn & Suites Orlando International Drive/Convention Center ★★★   A 2013 new build, it has a terrific location by the Orlando Eye, which you can walk to. Expect large rooms in yellows and oranges, outlets galore, and large counters and desks to spread out on, On the east, rooms face nothing but greenery. True, the elevators and breakfast buffet can get a tad overwhelmed in the mornings and you have to ask for a room with a mini-fridge or you may not get one, but overall, it's a real find, as bright and as fresh as you could wish for an affordable hotel. The top rate is for an Executive Kitchen Suite, which has a whopping 625 square feet and a fully equipped kitchen.

8214 Universal Blvd., Orlando. www.marriott.com. ☏ **407/581-9001.** 160 units. $94–$159 doubles. Free parking. **Amenities:** Pool, free breakfast buffet, sundries shop, free Wi-Fi.

Hampton Inn Orlando Convention Center ★★   It may be just like every other Hampton Inn you've ever seen (they must make these buildings from kits), but that doesn't detract from the fact the place is in good shape; there are plenty of restaurants and a multiplex within walking distance; and the cheerful staff runs a tight ship. Stays include a bountiful all-you-can-eat breakfast, including a few hot dishes; there's also a 24-hour lobby booth selling snacks and sundries. I have personally witnessed front-desk clerks offering to beat competitors' prices. Ask for a room on the south side, because these don't face other nearby buildings.

8900 Universal Blvd., Orlando. www.orlandohampton.com. © **800/426-7866** or 407/354-4447. 170 units. $79–$229 doubles or rooms with 2 double beds. Free parking. **Amenities:** Pool, free hot breakfast, fitness room, sundries shop, free Wi-Fi.

La Quinta Inn International Drive ★   A veteran four-floor motel with external corridors and the usual minor noise inconveniences of the category, it's not a bad choice if you want a clean, basic place off I-Drive. Windows are on the large side, and most face an interior heated pool cloister instead of the whoosh of Interstate 4. The rooms facing I-4 tend to drive some guests nuts, so request accordingly. Don't believe the rack rate; you can get this place for $49 using the coupon books around town, which is why we vetted it for you.

8300 Jamaican Ct., Orlando. www.orlandolaquinta.com. © **800/753-3757** or 407/351-1660. 200 units. Doubles from $89. Free parking. **Amenities:** Pool, bar, free breakfast, free local calls, free Wi-Fi.

Rosen Inn ★   When you drive up to this concrete tower, you may be concerned. It is, after all, upgraded from what was once the largest Rodeway Inn in America. But fear not: This is dated, but this is value. It's clean and on a lively bend of International Drive that's 2 minutes' drive from Universal. The pool is heated when it's cold, security is always around, there's a pub, and all rooms have a microwave and refrigerator. The rate sometimes attracts noisy groups, but on balance, you can't do better at this price.

6327 International Dr., Orlando. www.roseninn6327.com. © **800/999-6327** or 407/996-4444. 315 units. Rooms with 2 doubles or king from $79; occasional two-night minimum. Free parking. **Amenities:** Pool, park shuttle, 2 restaurants, pub, park shuttles, arcade, business center, game room, free Wi-Fi.

Around Downtown Orlando

Because it's a 30-minute ride north of Disney on I-4 (yes, you should have a car for these), a hotel would have to be pretty special to convince a tourist to choose it over one that's nearer. Orlando has a few, where you can find respite from the hurdy-gurdy and plastinated smiles—or a breather from children.

EXPENSIVE

The Alfond Inn ★★   In 2013, Rollins College opened this boutique hotel using a $12.5 million donation; its income will endow a scholarship program. That makes it both the newest fine property in Winter Park and the one with the biggest incentive to keep quality high. Its restaurant and hopping cocktail bar, planted courtyard, and modern rooms striped in teal, wood, and lime, are designed to appeal to sophisticated palates, something that its fantastic public art collection underscores. These gleaming facilities are 3 blocks from the shopping of Park Avenue and the Morse Museum (p. 184), making it an instant keystone of the Winter Park scene. It's probably too far if you've got a heavy theme park schedule, but it's ideal for explorations around upscale Winter Park.

300 E. New England Ave., Winter Park. www.thealfondinn.com. © **407/998-8090.** 112 units. Doubles $159–$259. Valet parking $18, no self-parking. **Amenities:** Pool, restaurant, lounge, fitness center, pets permitted, free Wi-Fi.

Grand Bohemian Hotel Orlando ★★★ Yes, Orlando *is* sophisticated. Thanks to the hotel's collector owner, Richard Kessler, its common areas are decorated with eccentric artwork—it's part hunting lodge and part *commedia dell'arte,* including six original drawings by Gustav Klimt, and in the lobby, there's a storefront gallery. An L.A.–style pool terrace keeps sunbathers far above city traffic, and lighting is so muted in its rooms, the dark woods so dark and fabrics so indigo, that a dusky, drowsy atmosphere is created even on days when the Florida sun could blister pavement. By night the Bösendorfer Lounge is a stylish martini nightspot with a following and some epic neo-romantic paintings by William Russell Walker. For a city about fake Spanish country clubs and golf resorts, the Grand Bohemian's urban panache is welcome, and its lounge areas tend to attract local artists (and frequent wedding parties of young professionals) who live more like they're in Manhattan or San Francisco.

325 S. Orange Ave., Orlando. www.grandbohemianhotel.com. © **866/663-0024** or 407/313-9000. 250 units. Standard room $179–$349 for up to 4. Extra person $25. Valet parking $25, no self-parking. The garage is 2 blocks west on Jackson St. **Amenities:** Restaurant, 2 lounges, club-level rooms, health club, heated outdoor pool, room service, shuttle to the theme parks for a fee, free Wi-Fi.

MODERATE

Courtyard at Lake Lucerne ★★ Orlando just doesn't have rooms this individual anymore. South of downtown, near highways that go everywhere, you'll find a rare B&B, and rarer still, it preserves the feeling of Old Florida. There's a reason local couples favor it for weddings: Under Spanish moss, this hideaway of calm preserves four homey buildings of varied historic styles. Top of the line is the city's oldest documented house, 1883's Norment Parry Inn, which believe it or not has the cheapest rates here because not everyone likes sleigh beds and claw-footed tubs; you'll sleep in an elegant four-poster bed among Victorian-era European antiques. I. W. Phillips House recalls Key West because its wooden wrap-around verandah overlooks tropical plantings. Wellborn Suites is Art Deco, less elegant, but with kitchenettes. All rooms have TVs, phones, and private bathrooms. Note that there is not a pool here.

211 N. Lucerne Circle E., Orlando. www.orlandohistoricinn.com. © **407/648-5188.** 30 units. Doubles $110–$225. Some rooms do not permit kids. Free parking. **Amenities:** Free breakfast, free Wi-Fi.

Home Rentals

In most destinations, the main way to obtain a vacation rental is to contact the owner directly. This is an option in Orlando, and the prominent online databases operate here, including **Airbnb.com, FabVillas.com, FlipKey.com, HomeAway. com, Housetrip.com,** and **Vacation Rentals by Owner** (www.vrbo.com).

Legoland Hotel

In 2015, Legoland opened its own 152-room hotel ★★★, and it's a wonder—a fabulous, candy-colored property crammed with Lego models and structures, with Lego play areas, character breakfasts, a heated pool, and rooms with elaborately executed themes ranging from pirates to medieval times. It's also just "132 kid steps," as the owners put it, from the front gates of the park (p. 168). That makes it a dream for trips to Legoland, but hard to use as a base for Orlando, which can be an hour away depending on traffic. www.legolandhotel.com; ☏ **877/350-5346.** *Rooms start at $179 in low season, $249 in peak season.*

But here, there are many accredited companies that take the risk out of a rental—ones that actually inspect your potential home and give you support on the ground. In addition to being selected for their reputations, longevity, and inventory, these companies have satisfactory listings with the Better Business Bureau of Central Florida (www.bbb.org/central-florida).

Your credit card will usually be charged a deposit ($200–$300 or 1 night's rent is standard) a month or two ahead of time, and if you cancel, you're unlikely to see that again. You'll also have to pay a one-time fee that goes toward insurance or cleaning; $50 to $80 is normal, which makes short stays less economical. Perks like pool heat or grills may incur a surcharge, which is also normal. Also ask what supplies you'll need to buy. Clean bath towels and sheets are supplied, but maid service won't be unless you pay extra. Many rental agencies no longer require you to pick up keys. Instead, front locks are equipped with keypads and you're sent a code.

Alexander Holiday Homes The family-run outfit has been renting since 1981, when the industry was in its infancy. It reps some 250 properties, most of them within 10 miles of Disney. Using its website's Hot Deals, prices go as low as $65 for a two-bedroom condo, and you stay for less than a week. Annoyingly, its website doesn't reveal availability windows; you have to call. 1400 W. Oak St., Ste. H, Kissimmee. www.floridasunshine.com. ☏ **800/621-7888** or 407/932-3683. Wi-Fi $25. Pet-friendly.

All Star Vacation Homes My favorite vacation home renter by a mile has an in-house team that cuts no corners in furnishing each of its homes, with lots of woods, quality fabrics, and dried flowers. The completeness elevates the offerings above the haphazard competition. No matter the size of the home, it'll be keyless and have a pool (the heater can often be turned on in advance of your arrival remotely), free Wi-Fi, grills, and staff on call in an official vehicle for any problem. Most homes are within 6 miles of Disney. Three-bedroom condo units sleeping up to eight, with a themed kids' room, start at $129 a night, or half what it costs to squeeze eight into two Disney Value rooms. Or you could have a whole 3-bedroom house from $209. Prices go up as you add treats such as home cinema rooms, arcade rooms, multiple master bedrooms, and so forth. Full six-bedroom houses can go for

$309—you can split that among 14 people and pay just $23 a night each. I have found it nearly impossible to be unhappy with one of its rentals. I'm not alone: So successful has All Star been that it created a spinoff, **Fullhouse** (www.fullhousevr.com; ✆ **877/310-0669**), that designs and builds custom homes as large as 14-bedroom/14-bath mansions, unique in the rental market, with double-sized kitchens, in-home cinemas and arcades, themed kids' rooms and multiple washer/dryers. Nine-bedroom Fullhouse homes go for about $1,100, or $125 a night—remember that a single standard room at a Disney Deluxe can't often be had for less than $500.

1132 Celebration Blvd., Celebration. www.allstarvacationhomes.com. ✆ **888/619-2302** or 321/281-4966. No pets.

Florida Sun Vacation Homes   Another upfront business, it rents homes ranging from two to seven bedrooms in the Disney area (the Windsor Hills development in particular), with three-bedroom starting prices of $99 in low season and popping to $179 in high season. All of its properties have a pool or a spa (or both). Minimum stays of 3 nights are common, and like many companies, it asks that you reserve and pay at least 6 weeks in advance.

7802 W. Irlo Bronson Hwy./U.S. 192, Kissimmee. www.floridasunvacationhomes.com. ✆ **800/219-1282** or 407/938-0228. No pets.

IPG Florida Vacation Homes   IPG began by serving British vacationers before branching out into Florida; now it's among the largest, dealing in dozens of home developments south and west of Disney, particularly Bella Piazza, Highlands Reserve, Windsor Hills, and the Villas at Island Club. Two-bedroom condos run $120 to $160, often less; six bedrooms can cost a mere $143.

9550 W. U.S. 192, Clermont. www.ipgflorida.com. ✆ **800/311-7105** or 863/547-1050. Pets w/$400 fee.

Lowery's Vacation Homes   Around since 1985, Lowery's reps plenty of inexpensive, tasteful properties in the usual developments, and its website includes 360-degree tours of each property. It's a good fallback in busy seasons. Rates here can be sensational—how about $105 a night for a three-bedroom condo? The largest home available has seven bedrooms.

7864 W. Irlo Bronson Hwy., Kissimmee. www.moremouse.com. ✆ **800/569-3797** or 407/397-0088. Pet-friendly.

VillaDirect   Founded in 1998, it manages some 350 Orlando-area properties in a hodgepodge of styles and quality levels. Condos sleeping six start around $62, although prices in the $80s are more common. Its office is open 7 days, and a majority of its inventory is near Animal Kingdom, but it also has a few near SeaWorld. Helpfully, its website posts videos for each of its vacation home communities.

8132 W. Irlo Bronson Hwy., Kissimmee. www.villadirect.com. ✆ **877/259-9908** or 407/397-9818. No pets.

PLANNING YOUR TRIP TO ORLANDO

Orlando hosts some 62 million visits a year, and the people who run the airports, hotels, and theme parks are specialists in moving them from one location to another. You'll always find someone willing to sell you what you need. You will, however, need to take care of some nitty-gritty details, from flights to transportation.

GETTING THERE

BY PLANE Orlando is served by 44 airlines, so thankfully, competition keeps airfares among the lowest on the East Coast. Nearly 35 million people fly in or out of Orlando International Airport (MCO) each year, or nearly 96,000 a day. Strategies for finding a good airfare include:

Primary websites that collect quotes from a variety of sources (whether they be airlines or other websites) include **CheapOAir.com**, **Expedia.com**, **Kayak.com**, and **Momondo.com**. Each has odd gaps in its coverage because of the way they obtain their quotes. Some sites have small booking fees of $5 to $10, and many force you to accept nonrefundable tickets for the cheapest prices. You can often save money by booking between roughly 7 weeks in advance if you're flying domestically and 3 to 4 months ahead from abroad.

The main airport, **Orlando International Airport** (www.orlandoairports.net), is a pleasure. If, on the way home, you realize you neglected to buy any park-related souvenirs, fear not, because Disney, SeaWorld, Kennedy Space Center, and Universal all maintain lavish stores (located before the security checkpoint, so leave time). The airport, 25 miles east of Walt Disney World, was built during World War II as McCoy Air Force Base, which closed in the early 1970s but bequeathed the airport with its deceptive code, MCO. I don't know how they do it, but the late-departure rate of 17% is among the lowest in the country, even though the airport is America's 13th busiest. Midmornings and midafternoons can be crowded for outgoing passengers, weekends can be clogged with cruise passengers, and mid-afternoon summer thunderstorms sometimes create delays.

The main terminal is divided into two sides, A and B, so if you can't find the desk for your airline or transportation service open on one side, it may be on the other side. Several rental car companies are right outside, no shuttles required.

Rental car companies at MCO:

Alamo: www.alamo.com; ℭ **800/327-9633**

Avis: www.avis.com; ℭ **800/831-2847**

Budget: www.budget.com; ℭ **800/527-0700**

Dollar: www.dollar.com; ℭ **800/800-4000**

Enterprise: www.enterprise.com; ℭ **800/325-8007**

E-Z Rent-A-Car: www.e-zrentacar.com; ℭ **800/266-5171**

Hertz: www.hertz.com; ℭ **800/654-3131**

National: www.nationalcar.com; ℭ **800/227-7368**

Thrifty: www.thrifty.com; ℭ **800/367-2277**

Also keep in mind Hertz-owned **Firefly** (www.fireflycarrental.com; ℭ **888/296-9135**), which can offer lower prices than most of its competitors because its vehicles are older and well-used.

Very few airlines use **Orlando Sanford International Airport** (www.orlandosanfordairport.com), or SFB, 42 miles northeast of Disney. It's connected to the Disney area by the Central Florida GreeneWay, or S.R. 417—the trip takes about 40 minutes and there are tolls, so new arrivals should have U.S. dollars. European visitors might fly into **Tampa International Airport** (www.tampaairport.com), or TPA, 90 minutes southwest.

BY TRAIN   Amtrak's (www.amtrak.com; ℭ **800/872-7245**) Silver Service/ Palmetto route serves Orlando and Kissimmee. Trains go direct between New York City, Washington, D.C., Charleston, and Savannah.

Transportation to & from MCO

BY RENTAL CAR   Get a car. Otherwise, theme park resorts conspire to hold you prisoner. If you intend to experience the "real" Orlando or its rich natural wonders, get a car. If you want to save huge amounts of money on meals, if you ever want to take a breather from the theme parks' relentless plastic personalities—get a car.

Economy rental cars start around $15 to $25 a day. Test the waters at a site such as Kayak, Orbitz, or Travelocity, which compare multiple renters with one click. Priceline and Hotwire have been known to rent for as little as $15 a day.

If you rent a car from the airport, be alert as you **exit the airport**—you must decide whether to use the south exit (marked for Walt Disney World) or the north exit (for SeaWorld, Universal, the Convention Center, and downtown Orlando). Whichever route you take, you will pay a few dollars in tolls, so have loose change. Also, at toll booths, stay to the right, where the cash windows are; the others are for e-passes.

If you're staying on Disney turf, a budget-saving solution is to rent a car for only the days you'd like to venture off property. To that end, **Alamo** (www. alamo.com; ℭ **800/462-5266**) and **National** (www.nationalcar.com; ℭ **800/227-7368**) operate satellite agencies within the Walt Disney World Resort: one at the Car Care Center near the parking lot of the Magic Kingdom. Many giant resorts host a rental car desk from one of the major names. Renting away from the airport incurs taxes of around half of those charged by renting (or even merely returning) a car at the airport, where they're more than 20%. Always fill up *before* driving back to MCO because gas stations near the airport's entrance have been nabbed for gouging. Stations inside Walt Disney World charge a competitive price, but one not as low as outside the tourist zone.

Agencies may not rent to those under 25. **Action Car Rental** (3719 McCoy Rd., Orlando; www.actionrac.com; ✆ 877/535-7117 or 407/240-2700) goes as low as 18-year-olds, but it charges them $10–15 more a day. Most companies won't rent to anyone older than 85.

BY SHUTTLE Mears Transportation (www.mearstransportation.com; ✆ 407/423-5566 or 855/463-2776) is the 800-pound gorilla of shuttles and taxis; it sends air-conditioned vans bouncing to hotels every 15 to 20 minutes. Round-trip fares for adults are $32 ($24 for kids 4–11, kids 3 and under free) to the International Drive area, or $36 per adult ($27 for kids) to Walt Disney World/U.S. 192/Lake Buena Vista. You'll probably make several stops because the vans are shared by other passengers.

If you have more than four or five people, it's more economical to reserve a car service (do it at least 24 hr. ahead) and split the lump fee; an SUV for up to 7 would be $110 to $150. Try Mears, **Tiffany Towncar** (www.tiffanytowncar. com; ✆ 888/838-2161 or 407/370-2196), or **Quicksilver Tours** (www.quick silver-tours.com; ✆ 888/468-6939 or 407/299-1434), which often volunteers to toss in a free 30-minute stop at a grocery store so you can stock up on supplies.

If you have a reservation at a Disney-owned hotel, you have the right to take the company's airport motorcoaches (also known as **Disney's Magical Express,** run by Mears). By offering the perk, the Mouse makes it seem simple by sending you tags for your luggage, which you affix before leaving home, and telling you everything will be taken care of from there. By the time you even

Shuttle bus at Cabana Bay Beach Resort.

board the bus to the resort, you'll already have waited in two long lines—the first of many, many lines you'll endure, so get used to it—and then you'll stop at up to five other hotels first. Your bags may not meet up with you again for 6 to 8 hours, so hitting a park right away may be difficult (pack swimsuits in your carry-on). When you depart for home, you must be ready 3 to 4 hours before your flight. Magical Express is free, but it costs you. It lulls you into not renting a car, which means you'll probably never leave Disney property again. Seeing dollar signs, **Universal Orlando** is on the verge of launching its own system.

BY RIDESHARE   **Uber** and **Lyft** are currently banned from airport pickups (not drop-offs), but at press time they were fighting that.

BY TAXI   **Taxis** are not the best bargain. The going rate is $2.40 for the first ¼ of a mile or the first 80 seconds of waiting time, followed by 60¢ for each ¼ of a mile. Taxis carry five passengers. It'll be about $70 to the Disney hotels, $60 to Universal, not including a tip, which is cheaper than a town car but not a rental.

Traveling from Orlando to Other Parts of America

Orlando, while not an important air hub, is well connected to the cities that are, particularly New York, Atlanta, and Chicago. For advice on how to find cheap airfare, see "Getting There," p. 289.

The **USA Rail Pass** is the American equivalent of the Eurail Pass in Europe—although our national rail system, **Amtrak** (www.amtrak.com; ℂ **800/872-7245** or 215/856-7953), hardly compares to the European system. It barely compares to freight. The pass allows travel within the U.S. The cheapest pass is a 15-day pass, which grants eight trips ($459; $230 kids 2–12); the most expensive offers 45 days of travel over 18 trips ($899; $450 kids). Those on a grand tour of America may benefit from those rates compared to flying.

From late April to early June, some car renters redistribute inventory by offering **"drive-out"** deals for one-way rentals that originate in Florida and drop off elsewhere in the country. Rates can start at $10/day, so look for those.

For bus travel, Orlando is served by **Greyhound** (www.greyhound.com; ℂ **800/231-2222**) and **Megabus** (www.megabus.com; ℂ **877/462-6342**). Long-distance bus travel in the United States is a purgatorial experience. Don't.

GETTING AROUND

BY CAR   Probably 90% of what a tourist wants to do lies within a 10-minute drive of Interstate 4, or I-4, as it's called. That free highway runs diagonally from southwest to northeast, connecting Walt Disney World, SeaWorld, the Convention Center, Universal Orlando, and downtown Orlando. I-4 is technically an east-west road linking Florida's coasts, so directions are listed as either west (toward Tampa and the Gulf of Mexico) or east (toward Daytona Beach and the Atlantic Ocean). Once you've got that down, you'll be set. Exits are numbered according to the mile marker at which they're found.

Therefore, the Disney World exits (62, 64, 65, and 67) are roughly 10 miles from Universal Orlando's (74 and 75), which are about 9 miles from downtown (83). If you know the exit number, you can figure out distance.

If you stray much onto minor roads, it's a good idea to carry a map or turn on the Waze app or Google Maps. Roads can go by several names and be confusing. Disney World is a particular disaster, since its signage is intentionally incomplete to funnel traffic. Don't rely on free maps; laughably, some maps provided by Universal don't acknowledge that Disney exists at all. **Visit Orlando** (www.visitorlando.com/mapexplorer) has free marked maps.

Some Florida toll roads are cashless and require a transponder to pay. Fortunately for tourists, in Orlando only the Florida Turnpike has gone cashless. Rental cars will lend you a transponder for about $4 a day, even if you don't use it, plus the cost of tolls. Better to avoid the Turnpike instead.

SHUTTLES   Universal is easy: You walk, bus, or take a free boat everywhere. At Disney, though, hoofing it is impossible. It's so big as to require a fleet of nearly 300 buses, the **Disney Transportation System (DTS),** which anyone may use for free. Curiously, DTS qualifies as the third-largest bus system in the state, after Miami and Jacksonville's public services. Taking DTS to a theme park eliminates the parking tram rigmarole. However, add waiting time, which can be 20 to 45 minutes, plus the commute itself, which can be just as long and require standing as if it's rush hour on a Brooklyn subway. You might even have to transfer buses. All told, 90 minutes to 2 hours of a busy day can be devoured by DTS. So often, having a car is worth the expense.

DTS is particularly overwhelmed during the opening and closing of the theme parks, but dispatchers run extra buses around those times and keep routes rolling for about 2 extra hours before opening and after closing. If you're staying at a Disney resort that offers another kind of transportation—say, the monorail to the Magic Kingdom—then a bus won't be available for the same route. Also, since the system has a hub-and-spoke design centered on the theme parks and Disney Springs, *you must often transfer if you're going between two second-tier points,* such as between two hotels, a hotel and a water park, or a theme park and Disney Springs. It gets annoying.

The second shuttle variety is the **hotel theme park shuttles,** which go from independent hotels and are often free (or paid for by resort fees). The upswing is that, yes, you can save money by using them, but there are strong downsides, including wildly inadequate scheduling (you might miss fireworks) and rambling routes. These only go to the park gates, not to restaurants or the many worthwhile smaller attractions.

A third option is the **I-Ride Trolley** (www.iridetrolley.com; ℭ **407/354-5656;** adults over 12 $2 per ride, seniors over 65 25¢, kids 3–9 $1; day pass $5, 3-day pass $7, 5-day pass $9; passes not sold on board; daily 8am–10:30pm), an excellent shuttle bus with plenty of clearly marked and well-maintained stops, benches to wait on, and genuinely useful routes—except it doesn't go to Disney. Its **Red Line** (every 20 min.) plies International Drive from the shops and restaurants just north of I-4's exit 75 all the way to Orlando

Premium Outlets, near Disney; along the way it touches down at SeaWorld and the Orlando Eye. The second route, the **Green Line** (every 30 min.), takes in SeaWorld, too, but heads down Universal Boulevard, making it more of an express route, and turns around at Orlando Premium Outlets. It comes within a long block of the entrance to Universal Orlando. Visitors without cars may find it feasible to stay on I-Drive, use this dirt-cheap shuttle to see nearly everything, and then tack on the hated hotel shuttle or a city bus for Disney days.

BY PUBLIC TRANSIT   There's not much to love about public transit in Florida. Buses are infrequent (usually one or two an hour), shelters are often nonexistent, and when the sun's strong, the combination is dangerous. Distances are also fairly great, so journeys can take a while. The Central Florida Regional Transportation Authority runs the **LYNX system** (www.golynx.com), on which one-way fares are $2, day passes cost $4.50, week passes are $16, and transfers between lines are free. Up to three kids 6 and under ride with adults free, and you have to pay with exact change. In downtown Orlando, there's the free **LYMMO** (www.golynx.com; Mon–Thurs 6am–10pm, Fri 6am–midnight, Sat 10am–midnight, Sun 10am–10pm) bus service, which makes a loop between City Hall and the Controlled (including Church Street Station and the Orange County Regional History Center) every 10 to 15 minutes.

For tourists, here are the most convenient routes, many of which stop at Downtown Disney where you can transfer to Disney's free bus system:

- **Route 56** connects Kissimmee to the front gates of the Magic Kingdom, where you can catch DTS to the other parks. Buses run every 30 minutes, but the last one leaves at 10:53pm.
- **Route 8** does most of International Drive, including the Convention Center and SeaWorld. It duplicates the service offered by the I-Ride Trolley (p. 293).
- **Route 50** goes from downtown Orlando to Downtown Springs and to the gates of the Magic Kingdom. It stops at SeaWorld, where passengers can connect to I-Drive by Route 8.
- The lesser Disney areas are served by the 300-series lines. **300** goes to Hotel Plaza Boulevard from downtown; **301** to Epcot and Disney's Animal Kingdom from Pine Hills; **302** to the Magic Kingdom from Rosemont; and **303** to Hollywood Studios from the Washington Shores area. Bus **304** is the only one that connects with another tourist zone; it trawls Sand Lake Road, which bisects I-Drive. 301 and 302 pass within a few blocks of Universal Orlando, on Kirkman Road, so if you toss in about 15 minutes of walking, they could technically be used for Universal, too, but it wouldn't be fun.
- **Route 42** starts at the Convention Center on International Drive, and 75 minutes later, reaches the airport.

In 2014, Orange County added **SunRail** (www.sunrail.com; ⊘ **855/724-5411;** $2 one-way, $3.75 round-trip), running from DeBary, north of Sanford, to an obscure spot on E. Sand Lake Road near S. Orange Avenue. Tourists only care about the 16-minute jaunt between downtown Orlando and Winter Park, but as departures are widely scattered in the morning or evening, targeting commuters, few visitors see the point.

If you really want to be intense about your planning (for your sanity and relaxation, I don't recommend it), there are obsessive resources online that go into granular detail. They are:

- o **AllEars.net** and **WDWFans.com** offer encyclopedic compendiums of everything Disney, down to the menus, what's under renovation, and which rooms are best.

- o **OrlandoInformer.com** comprehensively reports Universal, including deals.

- o **WDWmagic.com** and **WDWinfo.com** (and its **DISBoards.com**) host some

of the most active message forums for news, Q&As, and Disney-positive posts.

- o The independently run **PartyThrough TheParks.com** rates drinking and nightlife and **DisneyFoodBlog.com** keeps track of meals.

- o **MouseSavers.com**, **TheMouse ForLess.com**, and **OrlandoCheapo. com** post current Disney deals.

- o **OrlandoAttractions.com**, **TheDisney Blog.com**, **JimHillMedia.com**—no one's better at staying on top of Disney Parks news and history.

BY TAXI Given so many alternatives, taxis are not a natural choice. **Uber** and **Lyft** operate in Orlando, although not as many as you'd hope. Lawsuits have prevented them from picking you up at the airport (they may drop you off there). You will still almost always find a taxi cluster outside of the theme parks' gates. If you spend more than $30 a day on taxis (a one-way ride from the Magic Kingdom to the hotel stretch on U.S. 192 east of Disney would cost about that), smack your forehead, because you could have rented a car for the same money.

Many companies accept major credit cards, but ask when you summon a ride, because your payment may need to be processed by phone. Companies are not carefully monitored, so only choose a recommended carrier. Call your own:

- o **Diamond Cab Company:** ✆ 407/523-3333
- o **Transtar:** ✆ 407/857-9999
- o **Yellow:** ✆ 407/422-2222

WHEN TO GO

The main consideration when it comes to selecting dates is balancing good weather with thin crowds. Crowds keep you from seeing everything. In the peak season (such as spring break or the week after Christmas), the Magic Kingdom's turnstiles spin like propellers. None of the theme parks close on **public holidays.** In fact, they do better business then. In late December, Disney parks sometimes hit capacity and seal gates. But in September and the week after Thanksgiving, you can do nearly everything in a day.

So when are the **peak seasons?** Put simply: when American kids are out of school. That means mid-spring, summer, and the holidays. Hotel rates rise then, too. If you want to **save cash,** early January, early May, late August, all of September, and the first half of December are prime. The flipside of low season

Which Day of the Week?

The busiest days at all parks are generally Saturday and Sunday. Seven-day guests are often traveling on these days, and weekends are when locals come to play. Beyond that: Tuesday and Thursday see an uptick in the Magic Kingdom;

Tuesday and Friday (and evenings) at Epcot; Wednesday is a tad busier at Disney's Hollywood Studios; and Monday, Tuesday, and Wednesday can be a zoo (forgive the pun) at the Animal Kingdom. Crowds tend to thin later in the day.

is that the theme parks trim services when it's quieter. January is a particularly tough month for missing out on rides due to rehabs. And especially in the winter months, you may find it too chilly to enjoy the rides that get you wet, which is a shame since Orlando has some of the best water rides in the world.

CLIMATE   June to September is the heaviest season for excruciating sun and brief torrential rain. Every afternoon at around 4pm, like clockwork, another heavy storm rolls in and shuts rides temporarily. Those storms usually roll out within an hour, just as reliably, but in the meantime, you'll see deluges and lightning. Central Florida suffers more lightning strikes than any other American locale. During that season, bring along a cheap poncho from home.

Orlando Average Temperature & Rainfall

	JAN	FEB	MAR	APR	MAY	JUNE	JULY	AUG	SEPT	OCT	NOV	DEC
HI/LOW DAILY TEMPS (°F)	72/49	73/50	78/55	84/60	88/66	91/71	92/73	92/73	90/73	84/65	78/57	73/51
HI/LOW DAILY TEMPS (°C)	22/10	23/10	26/13	29/16	31/19	33/22	33/23	33/23	32/23	29/19	26/14	23/11
INCHES OF PRECIPITATION	2.25	2.82	3.32	2.43	3.30	7.13	7.27	6.88	6.53	3.16	1.98	2.25

Orlando's Calendar of Events

Check the special events pages at the theme park websites to see if any themed weekends or smaller events are in the works. In addition, the events listings at **Visit Orlando** (www.visitorlando.com), **"Orlando Weekly"** (www.orlandoweekly.com), and the **"Orlando Sentinel"** (www.orlandosentinel.com) are comprehensive. You will also find a few listings at **"Orlando" magazine** (www.orlandomagazine.com).

JANUARY

Citrus Bowl. Now stickered by Buffalo Wild Wings—can *anyone* keep track of the square-dancing corporate naming rights anymore? Held New Year's Day at the Florida Citrus Bowl Stadium, it pits the second-ranked teams from the Big Ten and SEC conferences against one another. www.floridacitrussports.com.

ZORA! Festival. The folklorist and writer (1891–1960) was from Eatonville (a 30-min. drive north of Orlando), the country's oldest incorporated African-American town. This weeklong event includes lectures and a 2-day public art fair. www.zorafestival.org; ✆ **407/647-3307.**

FEBRUARY

Winter Park Bach Festival. This annual event at Rollins College began in 1935 and has evolved into one of the country's better choral fests. Although it has stretched to include other composers and guest artists (Handel, P.D.Q. Bach), at least one concert is devoted to Johann. It takes place mid-February to early March, with scattered one-off guest performances throughout the year. www.bachfestivalflorida.org; ✆ **407/646-2182.**

Silver Spurs Rodeo. Lest you doubt Central Florida is far removed from the American Deep South, it hosts the largest rodeo east of the Mississippi (with bareback broncs, racing barrel horses, rodeo clowns, and athletes drawn from the cowboy circuit) over 3 days in mid-February in an indoor arena off U.S. 192. 1875 Silver Spur Lane, Kissimmee. www.silverspursrodeo.com; ☏ **321/697-3495.**

Mardi Gras at Universal Studios. On Saturday nights, Universal books major acts (Bonnie Raitt, Hall & Oates, LL Cool J) and mounts a parade complete with stilt-walkers, jazz bands, Louisiana-made floats, and bead tossing—although here, what it takes to win a set of beads is considerably less risqué than it is in the Big Easy. It's included with admission. www.universalorlando.com/mardigras; ☏ **407/224-2691.**

Spring Training. See p. 179 for a rundown of which Major League Baseball teams play where. Mid-February through March.

MARCH

Epcot's International Flower & Garden Festival. This spring event, which lasts from March to May, transforms Epcot with some 30 million flowers, 70 topiaries, a screened-in butterfly garden, presentations by noted horticulturalists, and a lineup of "Flower Power" concerts (Chubby Checker, Petula Clark). It's free with standard entry. www.disneyworld.com; ☏ **407/934-7639.**

Florida Film Festival. This respected event showcases films by Florida artists and has featured past appearances by the likes of Oliver Stone, William H. Macy, Christopher Walken, and Cary Elwes. www.floridafilmfestival.com; ☏ **407/644-5625.**

APRIL

Epcot's International Flower & Garden Festival. See March for full listing, above.

Florida Music Festival. Some 250 bands over 4 days give exposure to up-and-coming musicians—at a pace of 50 per night, all over town. www.floridamusicfestival.com.

MAY

Orlando International Fringe Festival. This theatrical smorgasbord, the longest-running fringe fest in America, spends 14 days mounting some 100 newly written, experimental performances in Loch Haven Park. www.orlandofringe.org; ☏ **407/648-0077.**

Epcot's International Flower & Garden Festival. See March for full listing, above.

JUNE

Gay Days. What started as a single day for gay and lesbian visitors has bloomed into a full week of some 40 events managed by a host of promoters. It's said that attendance goes as high as 135,000, and it's become one of the biggest annual events in Florida. Held around the first Saturday in June, Gay Days are a blowout party with group visits to Disney's parks, an ongoing pool bash at Parliament House (p. 195), concerts (En Vogue, LeAnn Rimes), and several dance events including an all-night, after-hours RipTide dance party at Typhoon Lagoon. The overview is at www.gaydays.com.

Star Wars Weekends. Hollywood Studios' major annual do, held over 3 weeks in late spring, sees actors from the franchise arrive for signings, parades, and Q&As—and Mickey and Darth Vader in the same parade. It's not uncommon to catch Mark Hamill, Warwick Davis, or Ray Park. The finer points of the Lucas catechism are discussed, and much merchandise is traded at the Darth's Mall market. A regular ticket gets you in. www.disneyworld.com/starwars.

SEPTEMBER

Night of Joy. It's actually a long-running pair of nights of outdoor Contemporary Christian concerts—eight or nine acts—spread throughout the Magic Kingdom, which stays open late just for the occasion. Rides run all night, and it's separately ticketed. www.nightofjoy.com; ☏ **877/648-3569.**

Rock the Universe. Universal's festival of top-flight Christian rock bands who perform on stages around Universal Studios. Rides and performances continue past midnight, after regular patrons have gone home. It's separately ticketed, and goes on sale in June. www.rocktheuniverse.com.

OCTOBER

Epcot's International Food & Wine Festival. The World Showcase makes amends with the countries it ignores for more than 50 days by installing temporary booths selling tapas-size servings of foods and wines from many nations. That's supplemented with chef demonstrations, seminars, "Eat to the Beat" concerts by known acts (Hanson, the Go-Gos), and tastings by at least 100 wineries. A few of the more extravagant events are charged, but most are free. The festival lasts from late September to mid-November and the hotly awaited details are posted by Disney in the summer. www.disneyworld.com/foodandwine; ☎ **407/939-3378.**

Mickey's Not-So-Scary Halloween Party. The best of the Magic Kingdom's separately ticketed evening events, this one mounts a special parade with fiendishly catchy theme song, a few special shows, a fireworks display that surpasses the usual one, and stations where you can pick up free candy. Kids even show up in costume, although it's not required. The event happens on scattered evenings from mid-September through the end of October. Unfortunately, it's so oversold that you will barely be able to move. Halloween sells out early. Target audience: people who like lollipops. www.disneyworld.com; ☎ **407/934-7639.**

Halloween Horror Nights. Unquestionably Universal's biggest event, HHN is the equivalent of a whole new theme park that's designed for a year but only lasts a month. After dark, the Studios are overtaken by grotesque "scare actors" who terrorize crowds with chain saws, gross-out shows, and 7 or 8 big, walk-through haunted houses that are made from scratch each year. The mayhem lasts into the wee hours. Wimps need not apply; children are discouraged by the absence of kids' ticket prices. On top of all this, most rides remain open. HHN has legions of fans. Target audience: people who like to poop themselves in fright. (Busch Gardens' Howl-o-Scream event's scariness is somewhere between Universal's and Disney's.) www.halloweenhorrornights.com.

SeaWorld's Halloween Spooktacular. SeaWorld throws a sweet, toddler-approved weekend Halloween event of its own, with trick-or-treating (kids dress up), a few encounters with sea fairies and bubbles, and show starring Count von Count from "Sesame Street." Target audience: people who have a naptime. It's included in admission.

Orlando Film Festival. Like all festivals worth their salt, this one presents mostly mainstream and independent films in advance of their wider release dates. It lasts only a few days in mid-October or early November, screening at various downtown venues. www.orlandofilmfest.com; ☎ **407/843-0801.**

NOVEMBER

ICE! It debuted in 2003 at the Gaylord Palms hotel and has quickly become a holiday perennial. The hotel brings in nearly 2 million pounds of ice, sculpts it into a walk-through city, keeps it chilled to 9°F, and issues winter coats to visitors. Add synchronized light shows and you've got an event that charges $29 for entry—and sells out. www.gaylordpalms.com; ☎ **407/586-0000.**

The Osborne Family Spectacle of Dancing Lights. No, not Ozzy and Sharon, but Jennings, Paul, Mitzi, and Breezy (I swear I'm not making this up), whose preposterously overdone Christmas display at their Little Rock house was deemed so vulgar that neighbors went to the Arkansas Supreme Court to shut it down. Enter Disney's Hollywood Studios. Every 15 minutes, it twitters and "dances" to Christmas carols, all as foam "snow" gently wafts from above. It lasts until the first week of January.

DECEMBER

Mickey's Very Merry Christmas Party. This crowded night, which occurs on various nights starting even before Thanksgiving, is probably Disney's most popular special annual event. It requires a separate ticket from regular admission. What you get is a tree-lighting ceremony, a few special holiday-themed shows, a special fireworks display (very green and red), an appearance by Santa Claus, a special parade, and *huge* crowds. Meanwhile, Disney's warehouse for holiday decorations (it exists) empties out and its hotels deck the halls: The Grand Floridian erects a life-size house made of gingerbread. www.disneyworld.com; ☎ **407/934-7639.**

Holidays Around the World at Epcot. This one features holiday customs of many nations and a host of costumed storytellers, but its real showpiece is the daily, 40-minute candlelight processional, a retelling of the Christmas Nativity story by a celebrity narrator (recent names have included Sigourney Weaver, Whoopi Goldberg, Trace Adkins, and Neil Patrick Harris) accompanied by a 50-piece orchestra and a full Mass choir. The processional is a WDW tradition going back to its earliest days—Cary Grant did it! www.disneyworld.com.

Grinchmas & The Macy's Holiday Parade. Usual holiday traditions include a musical version of "How the Grinch Stole Christmas" and daily parades by Macy's, which brings some balloons and floats to Universal when Thanksgiving is over. That's included in the ticket price. www.universalorlando.com.

Russell Athletic Bowl. An ACC team battles a Big Ten team, usually a few days before New Year's and always at the Florida Citrus Bowl Stadium. www.russellathleticbowl.com.

New Year's Eve. Yahoo.com reports that Orlando regularly makes its list of top five most-searched New Year's Eve destinations. There's no shortage of places to party. At the parks: **CityWalk** lures top acts such as Cyndi Lauper. Three **Disney parks,** minus Animal Kingdom, stay open until the wee hours. **SeaWorld** brings in big-band music or jazz, plus fireworks.

Getting Attraction Discounts

For a full breakdown of Disney's ticketing, how it works, and how to ward against overspending, see p. 24.

One of the true discounted programs is the **FlexTicket.** For admission to five parks (Universal's pair, SeaWorld, Aquatica, Wet 'n Wild), you want the Orlando FlexTicket ($336 adults, $316 kids 3–9), which grants unlimited admission to all of the parks for a full 2 weeks. It's sold by those parks. Tack on Busch Gardens for $20 adults or kids. Considering 1-day admission to Busch Gardens alone is twice that, you don't have to get near a calculator to

Buyer Beware!

Before Magic Your Way made ticket expiration standard, pretty much every Disney ticket was good forever. That means there are a lot of unused days floating around. It's illegal to sell them, but that doesn't stop people. When you see a sign on the side of U.S. 192 promising discounted tickets, guess what may be for sale? Buying a ticket like this is a gamble, particularly if you don't have the expertise to recognize a fake or a spent ticket. Often, only a Disney laser scan can tell for sure.

Other organizations, such as timeshare developers, do offer legit tickets to theme parks and dinner shows, but to get them, you will have to endure heavy-duty sales presentations that may last several hours. The requirements for attendance can be tight: Married couples must attend together (gay couples may be excluded—that's legal in Florida), you both must swear your combined annual income is above a certain amount ($50,000, for example, for Westgate branded resorts—yes, owned by the timeshare baron in "The Queen of Versailles"), that you are in a given age range (23–65 is common), and that you commit to staying for at least 90 minutes, although being pitched for as long as 4 hours is also common. Even if you're fearless, an entire morning of your hard-earned vacation time is worth more than whatever discount is being promised. After all, how many days of working did it take for you to accrue those 4 or 5 hours? You also may not arrive at the parks until lunchtime, missing (in some cases) a third of the opening hours. Don't be so cheap and discount-obsessed that you throw away your time at a timeshare pitch.

see the savings, but you do have to go to as many parks as possible. Once you've paid for parking at your first theme park ($17 is the going rate), you can keep your ticket and avoid paying it again. Many hotel closed-circuit TV programs promise $10 off, so when you're buying a FlexTicket in person, claim you learned about it from your in-room programming and ask for the deal. FlexTickets are sold online, too (www.tickets.visitorlando.com, the area's official tourism bureau, gives small discounts on it).

Universal and SeaWorld discount the gate price if you book online, and all the parks discount per-day entry if you buy multiple days. SeaWorld and Busch Gardens also offer courtesy admission for members of the military and their families. Check www.herosalute.com to see if you are eligible. **Orlando Magicard** (www.visitorlando.com/magicard) grants discounts to heaps of attractions, meals, home rentals, and hotels. The participants are members of the local tourism bureau. Its discounts aren't much different from what the free coupon circulars promise, but they're still good deals. You will also find coupons through **OrlandoCoupons.com** and the discount circular **Hotel Coupons.com**.

A few outfits sell such faintly discounted tickets. **Maple Leaf Tickets** (www.mapleleaftickets.com; ✆ **800/841-2837**), **the Official Ticket Center** (www.officialticketcenter.com; ✆ **877/406-4836**), and **Ticket Momma** (www.ticketmomma.com; ✆ **866/996-7508**) are all accredited by the Better Business Bureau. So is **Undercover Tourist** (www.undercovertourist.com; ✆ **800/846-1302**), which also publishes a marvelous calendar that guesses, using as many statistics as possible, at what the best touring plans are for the days you're going. No Disney deals ever seem deep enough to offset shipping fees or the hassle of picking up your tickets at some third-party office; however, multiple purchases, stays of a week or longer, and third-tier diversions such as dinner shows ($10–$15 off) may work out for you. Tickets are nontransferable. A desk at the Orlando Official Visitor Center (p. 309) furnishes similar discounts on tickets you can trust.

One to be wary of is the **Go Orlando Card** (www.goorlandocard.com; ✆ **866/628-9036**), which offers admission to secondary attractions. The catch is you get an obscenely short time to use it. Rare is the person who can visit enough places to make the price (a 2-day card is $120 for adults) pay off.

[FastFACTS] ORLANDO

Accessible Travel

Nearly everything is accessible. This situation predates the Americans with Disabilities Act of 1990; as multigenerational attractions, the parks have always worked to be inclusive, and in response, guests with

mobility issues have long embraced them in return.

Upon arrival at Disney, anyone with a disability heads to Guest Relations to obtain a **Disability Access Service Card** that designates you as requiring consideration. No doctor's

letter is required. There was a time when guests in wheelchairs and ECVs were given special treatment and ushered to the front of lines, but when many guests abused the system, Disney (with the exception of Make-A-Wish Foundation kids and other special groups, by prior arrangement) required everyone to wait the same length of time. You will be given a reservation time that accounts for the current wait time (you can come back later as long as the time has passed, but you can't get another reservation until you've used the first one). Or part of your group might be asked to pass through the standard line while you wait in a special area and reunite with them before riding. There will usually be a place for you to wait for the special wheelchair-ready ride vehicle to come around. You might have to transfer to a manual wheelchair; the park maps indicate which rides will require you to leave your **wheelchair or ECV.** (There has been some controversy over whether this system properly accommodates people with autism and severe disabilities who cannot easily wait.) A very few, pre-ADA attractions, such as Tom Sawyer Island and the Swiss Family Treehouse, require you to be ambulatory. Those are marked, too. Oxygen tanks may not be permitted on rides. There is a special parade-viewing area for those with mobility issues so you can have good sightlines; arrive early and ask any cast member where it is. At Universal, go to the Guest Relations desk after the turnstiles for an **Attractions Assistance Pass**. If a ride's wait is less than 30 minutes, you'll scoot right on, and if it's

longer, you'll be issued a time to return, but you cannot get a new reservation time until that one is fulfilled. If that system won't work for you, Universal may choose to issue a **Guest Assistance Pass,** which grants Express access to all attractions, no appointment required, SeaWorld's version is the **Ride Accessibility Pass.**

Theme park hotels all can lend door knock and phone alerts, amplifiers, bed shakers, strobes, and TTY phones. For off-property stays, consider renting a house, which provides much more room; most home-rental companies also comply with ADA requirements.

All the parks have a full range of in-park services for guests of every need, including sign-language interpreters on scheduled days of the week. Service animals are permitted but aren't always allowed to ride attractions. Disney maintains a Special Services hotline to answer all accessibility needs, including full arrangements for the blind and captioning for the hearing-impaired with devices requiring a $25 refundable deposit (✆ **407/824-4321 (voice)** and TTY ✆ 407/827-5141; Disability.services@ disneyparks.com). Universal Orlando can be reached at ✆ **800/447-0672** [TDD] or 407/224-4233 [voice] (www. universalorlando.com); SeaWorld Orlando's number is ✆ **407/363-2400** (www. seaworld.com); Kennedy Space Center is at ✆ **321/449-4443**

(www.kennedyspacecenter. com). Try to contact those a few weeks ahead. Most parks can arrange sign language interpreters with a few weeks' notice; all furnish assisted listening devices or scripts for some, but not all, of the biggest attractions. There are plenty of accessible parking spots.

Medical Travel, Inc. (www.medicaltravel.org; ✆ **800/308-2503** or 407/438-8010) specializes in the rental of mobility equipment, ramp vans, and supplies such as oxygen tanks (be aware that many rides do not allow tanks). Electric scooters and wheelchairs can be delivered to your accommodation through these established companies: **Orlando Medical Rentals** (www.orlandomedical rentals.com; ✆ **877/356-9943**) also supplies oxygen, scooters, and the like. **Buena Vista Scooter Rentals** (www.buenavistascooters. com; ✆ **866/484-4797** or 407/938-0349), **Scootaround** (www. scootaround.com; ✆ **888/441-7575**), **CARE Medical Equipment** (www. caremedicalequipment.com; ✆ **800/741-2282** or 407/ 856-2273), and **Walker Medical & Mobility Products** (www.walkermobility. com; ✆ **888/726-6837** or 407/518-6000). All the theme parks, except the water parks, rent ECVs for about $50 a day and wheelchairs for about $12 a day. If your own wheelchair is wider than 25 inches, think about switching to the park model, because it is guaranteed to navigate tight squeezes such as hairpin queue turns.

Organizations that offer assistance to travelers with disabilities include the **American Federation for the Blind** (www.afb.org; *C* **800/232-5463**) and **Society for Accessible Travel & Hospitality** (www.sath.org; *C* **212/447-7284**).

Area Codes The area code for the Orlando area is **407** (if you're dialing locally, a preceding 1 is not necessary, but the 407 is), although you may encounter the less common **321** code, which is also used on the Atlantic Coast. The **863** area code governs the land between Orlando and Tampa, and the Tampa area uses **813** and **727.** The region west of Orlando uses **352.**

Business Hours Offices are generally open weekdays between 9am and 5pm, while banks tend to close at 4pm. Typically, stores open between 9 and 10am and close between 6 and 7pm Monday through Saturday, except malls, which stay open until 9pm. On Sunday, stores generally open at 11am and close by 7pm.

Car Rentals This topic is perhaps the most hotly debated issue in all of Disneydom. But the bottom line is there's only one reason to do without a car: You never intend to leave Disney. If you plan to fan out, such as visiting Harry Potter or the Space Shuttle, get wheels.

Disney guests often justify forgoing a car by saying they can't afford one. This is a fallacy. Disney hotels charge as much as twice what you'll pay to stay at a hotel of similar quality offsite. If you stay at a non-Disney property, you can afford a car and *still* pay less. A large inventory means rentals are cheaper here than in other American cities: $26 a day is common for a compact car.

One caveat is that **parking charges** can add up. Valet is often free in town, but the theme parks charge $17 a day for a space (Universal is $5 after 6pm). If you stay at a Disney resort, it is free. Also, if you pay for parking once at any Disney park, you won't have to pay again for another park on the same day. The bigger hotels now slap on $20-plus nightly fees for parking. In the rest of Orlando, parking is free, plentiful, and off the street.

Make sure your rental car locks by remote control fob; those are handy for making your vehicle honk and locating it in those confusing theme park parking lots.

Crime Disney may advertise itself as "the Happiest Place on Earth," but it's still on Earth. That means bad things happen. Never open your hotel room door to a stranger, and never give your personal details or credit card number to anyone who calls your room, even if they claim to work for the hotel. **Pickpockets** are virtually unheard of, but

they exist. Be vigilant about bags; you're going to be bumped and jostled many times—one of those bumps could be a nimble-fingered thief.

Customs Rules change. For details regarding current regulations, consult **U.S. Customs and Border Protection** (www.cbp.gov; *C* **877/227-5511**).

Doctors There are first-aid centers in all of the theme parks. There's also a 24-hour number for the **Poison Control Center** (*C* **800/282-3171**). To find a dentist, contact the **Dental Referral Service** (www.dentalreferral.com; *C* **800/235-4111**). **Doctors on Call Service** (www.doctorsoncallservice.com; *C* **407/399-3627**) makes house and room calls. If you don't have a car, **EastCoast Medical Network** (www.themedicalconcierge.com; *C* **407/648-5252**) makes "hotel room calls" to area resorts for $150 to $275 for most ailments. It's available at all hours and brings a portable pharmacy, although prescriptions cost more. Also see "Hospitals."

Drinking Laws The legal drinking age is 21. Proof of age is always requested, even if you look older, so carry photo ID. It's illegal to carry open containers of alcohol in any car or public area that isn't zoned for alcohol consumption (as CityWalk is), and the police may ticket you on the spot.

Driving Rules Americans drive on the right. In

Florida, you may turn right on red only after making a full stop unless the signal is an illuminated arrow, in which case you must wait for green. Many intersections are equipped with traffic cameras that will take a photo of your license plate, and rental car companies pass on fines along with hefty fees. If your plans take you outside the Orlando area, some toll roads (in Miami and Tampa, for example) are cashless and can only be paid by a Sun-Pass sensor that must be rented, for an extra daily fee, from your rental agency, otherwise you will incur large penalties. Last, Florida is full of visitors who don't know where they're going. These wandering souls will halt, cross three lanes of traffic, and barrel into the wrong lane without thinking. Keep a safe distance from the car in front of you.

Electricity The United States uses 110 to 120 volts AC (60 cycles), compared to the 220 to 240 volts AC (50 cycles) that is standard in Europe, Australia, and New Zealand. If your small appliances use 220 to 240 volts, buy an adaptor and voltage converter before you leave home, because these can be difficult to come by in Orlando.

Embassies & Consulates The nearest embassies are located in the nation's capital, Washington, D.C. Some consulates are located in major U.S. cities, and most nations have a mission to the United

Nations in New York City. If your country isn't listed below, call for directory information in Washington, D.C. (✆ **202/555-1212**), or log on to **www.embassy. org/embassies**.

Emergencies Call ✆ **911** for the police, to report a fire, or to get an ambulance. If you have a medical emergency that does not require an ambulance, you should be able to walk into the nearest hospital emergency room (see "Hospitals," below).

Family Travel All parks have a cool **baby care center** for heating formula, nursing, and so on, and diaper changing tables in the restrooms. But think carefully about whether your child is ready for the theme parks. Too many parents consider an Orlando vacation such a rite of passage that they rush into it too early without considering whether their child will find the experience overwhelming, or even if they'll *remember* it. I agree with many parenting experts who say that about 3 years old is the minimum age. It's not just that many younger children get wigged out when they see their first costume character, but also because it's no fun for a kid to get turned away from a ride they have their heart set on. Let kids take an active role in planning their vacation. Their excitement will make the going easier.

Some experts say kids are not truly ready for the rigors of theme parks until they can walk on their own

all day. Whether or not very young children are *advisable,* they are *possible:* Scarier rides have what's called a **child swap.** That provides an area where one adult can wait with a child while their partner rides and then switch off so the other gets a chance. Many rides also have a bypass corridor where chickens can do their chicken-out thing.

Your **stroller** will not be allowed inside most attractions, and it will not be attended in parking sections, so never leave anything valuable in it. Come prepared with a system for unloading valuables. Also have something that covers the seat; like in parked cars, they get sizzling hot in the Florida sun. Finally, tie some identifying marker (like a white flag, as in "I surrender") to yours so you can identify it amid the sea of clones. Some outfits deliver nicer models than Disney's to hotels: **Magic Strollers** (www.magicstrollers.com; ✆ **866/866-6177**) and **Baby Wheels** (www.baby wheelsorlando.com; ✆ **800/510-2480**) among them.

Health Your biggest concern is the **sun,** which can burn you even through grey skies on cloudy days. You will be spending a lot more time outdoors than you might suspect—rides take 3 minutes, but some lines will have you waiting outside for an hour. Hats are your friends.

Holidays Banks close on the following holidays: January 1 (New Year's), the third

- **Familiarize yourself with the height restrictions for all rides,** which are posted at the parks' websites and listed on the maps. Universal also keeps physical gauges in front of both its parks. Everything is measured in inches, so if your child is usually measured in centimeters, multiply by 0.393.
- **Bring supplies to kid-proof your hotel room.**
- **Slather your kids in sun lotion.** Florida sun is stronger than you think.
- **Dress kids in bright colors.** You'll spot them faster if you're separated. Some parents even put their phone number on their kids with temporary tattoos.
- **Dress kids to get wet.** There are water playgrounds, plus frequent rains.

- **Hotels offer "kids eat free" programs.** Ask.
- **Theme park strollers are easy, but basic;** they don't recline, and they won't secure kids younger than toddlers. Folding "umbrella" strollers have distinct advantages. They make getting onto trams, monorails, and into other tight spaces easier (not just for you—also for people waiting for you).
- **Bring a picture of your child** or keep one on your mobile phone in case you get separated.
- **Use a walkie-talkie app** such as Voxer or WhatsApp to communicate with your party; the phone carriers are often overwhelmed by the volume at the parks and text messages sometimes arrive with delays.

Monday in January (Martin Luther King, Jr., Day), the third Monday in February (Presidents' Day), the last Monday in May (Memorial Day), July 4 (Independence Day), the first Monday in September (Labor Day), the second Monday in October (Veterans Day), the fourth Thursday in November (Thanksgiving Day), and December 25. The theme parks are open every day of the year.

Hospitals **Dr. P Phillips Hospital** (9400 Turkey Lake Rd., Orlando; ✆ **407/351-8500**) is a short drive north up Palm Parkway from Lake Buena Vista. To get to **Florida Hospital Celebration Health** (400 Celebration Place, Celebration; ✆ **407/764-4000**), from I-4, take the U.S. 192 exit; then at

the first traffic light, turn right onto Celebration Avenue, and at the first stop sign, make another right. Clinics: **Centra Care Walk-In Care** in Lake Buena Vista (12500 Apopka-Vineland Rd., ✆ **407/934-2273;** Mon–Fri 8am–midnight, Sat–Sun 8am–8pm); near the vacation homes south of Disney (8201 W. U.S. 192, Kissimmee; ✆ **407/465-0846;** Mon–Fri 8am–8pm, Sat–Sun 8am–5pm); and northwest of Universal (8014 Conroy-Windermere Rd., Suite 104; ✆ **407/291-8975;** Mon–Fri 8am–8pm, Sat–Sun 8am–5pm). In addition, each theme park has its own infirmary capable of handling a range of medical emergencies.

Insurance Among many options, you could try

MEDEX (www.medexassist.com; ✆ **800/732-5309**) or **Travel Assistance International** (www.travelassistance.com; ✆ **800/821-2828**) for overseas medical insurance cover.

So what else may you want to insure? You may want special coverage for **apartment stays,** especially if you've plunked down a deposit, and any **valuables,** since airlines are only required to pay up to $2,500 for lost luggage domestically, less for foreign travel.

If you do decide on insurance, compare policies at **InsureMyTrip.com** (✆ 800/487-4722) or **SquareMouth.com.**

Internet & Wi-Fi Getting online isn't hard. Wi-Fi is now considered an essential amenity, like running water. Most hotels will have free access—sometimes in common areas, sometimes in guest rooms, and sometimes in both places. Walt Disney World's hotels have free Wi-Fi, and so do its theme parks, as do Universal's. (SeaWorld does not yet have free Wi-Fi.) Hotel connections aren't always fast enough to stream movies, but they're usually fast enough for standard uses. Nearly all home rentals come with Internet-connected computers and free Wi-Fi.

LGBT Travelers Orlando still has a conservative streak, but like most cities, it has come to realize that America welcomes every kind of person. The parks also employ thousands of gay people. As a consequence, gay visitors simply won't need special resources or assistance. Most hotels aren't troubled in the least by gay couples, and gay people can be themselves anyplace. The most intolerant attitudes will come from other guests at the theme parks, who, of course, mostly aren't from Orlando—public displays of affection there are not likely to be attacked, but don't expect a warm reception, either. Then again, sexual affection is not celebrated in the parks if you're straight, either. Use your intuition, your manners, and your common sense.

Mail At press time, domestic postage rates were 34¢ for a postcard and 49¢ for a letter. For international mail, a first-class letter of up to 1 ounce costs $1.20; a first-class international postcard costs the same as a letter. The post office most convenient to Disney and Universal is at 10450 Turkey Lake Rd. (✆ **407/351-2492;** Mon–Fri 9am–7pm, Sat 9am–5pm). If all you need is to buy stamps and mail letters, you can do that at most hotels. For more information, including locations nearest you, go to **www.usps.com** and click on "Calculate a Price." Ask at the theme park Guest Relations desks if mailing your items there will entitle you to a novelty postmark.

Mobile Phones Your phone will work in Orlando; it may not work in rural areas. To buy a pay-as-you-go SIM card, ask for a "no-contract" SIM card. Barring those suggestions, phones can be rented from **InTouch USA** (www.intouchusa.com; ✆ **800/872-7626**); some car rental outlets do it, too.

The theme parks' new reliance on programming your schedule via apps drains devices quickly. To have enough juice for a 13-hour day, carry a **portable charger,** such as the ones by **Mophie** (www.mophie.com) or **Jackery** (www.jackery.com).

Money This town exists to rake in money. Consequently, it places few obstacles between you and the surrender of it. Most ATMs are run by third parties, not your bank, which means that you'll be slapped with fees of around $2.50 per withdrawal (around $5 for international visitors).

Machines accept pretty much anything you can stick into them. Citibank customers can avoid the usage fee by using the fancy Citibank machines located at most 7-Eleven convenience stores. International visitors should make advance arrangements with their banks to ensure their cards will function in the United States. Also ask your bank if it has reciprocal agreements for free withdrawals anywhere. One institution known to charge international usage fees that are below the industry standard is **Everbank** (www.everbank.com; ✆ **888/882-3837**); another is **Charles Schwab** (www.schwab.com; ✆ **866/855-9102**), which reimburses ATM fees.

Credit cards are nearly universally accepted. In fact, you *must* have one to rent a car without a hassle. Most places accept the Big Four: American Express, MasterCard, Visa, and Discover. A few places add Diners Club, and some family-owned businesses subtract American Express because of the pain of dealing with it.

Before you leave home, let your issuer know that you're about to go on vacation. Many of them get antsy when they see unexpectedly large charges start appearing so far from your home, and sometimes they freeze your account in response.

Not only will Orlando clerks almost always neglect to check the purchaser's identification, but also, in the high-volume world of the theme parks, they don't even require signatures for purchases under a certain amount (as much as $50). You just swipe and go. That means you need to be doubly sure to keep your cards safe.

Try not to use credit cards to withdraw cash. You'll be charged interest from the moment your money leaves the slot. *Tip:* There is an exception that the resorts don't sanction, but I certainly do: Instead of using your credit card to draw cash from an ATM, use it to buy Disney Dollars (© **407/566-4985,** option 5). They're private scrip (sold at big shops and most guest services desks), valued precisely like U.S. dollars. But they are charged as a purchase, *not* as a cash withdrawal, so you'll see no additional fees. You can spend them like cash within the respective resorts. Pretty sneaky, sis! Universal sells its own version, Wizarding Bank Notes, sold at Gringotts Money Exchange in Universal Studios.

Because ATM withdrawals give better deals, old-fashioned exchange desks are few and far between, although you'll still find a few at the airport, at large hotels, at the **Travelex** at Lake Buena Vista Factory Stores (p. 208). If you need to change money, better rates come from banks during regular banking hours (Mon–Fri 9:30am–4pm).

Finding a bank isn't difficult in the "real" world of Orlando around SeaWorld and Universal, but at Walt Disney World, you could use a hand. The nearest bank is the **SunTrust** (1675 Buena Vista Dr., across from Downtown Disney Marketplace; © **407/762-4786;** drive-through Mon–Wed, Fri 8am–5pm, until 5:30pm on Thurs).

Newspapers & Magazines Business hotels distribute that shallow McNewspaper, "USA Today," to use as your morning doormat. The local paper, the "Orlando Sentinel" (www.orlandosentinel. com) is less widely available but much better for discovering local happenings. "Orlando Magazine" (www. orlandomagazine.com) is a glossy that covers trends and upscale restaurants. Also see the box on amateur-run websites covering the theme parks on p. 295; those are better for park goings-on.

Packing For the latest rules on how to pack and what you will be permitted to bring as a carry-on, consult your airline or the **Transportation Security Administration** (www.tsa. gov). Also be sure to find out from your airline what your checked-baggage weight limits will be; maximums of around 50 pounds per suitcase are standard. Anything heavier will incur a fee. Paying for the luggage at the airport is often more expensive than online.

If you forget something, there's nothing you can't buy in Orlando. It's hardly Timbuktu. But bring the basics for sunshine (lotion of at least 30 SPF, wide-brimmed hat, bathing suit, sunglasses), for rain (a compact umbrella or a plastic poncho, which costs $8 if you wait until you get into the parks), for walking (good shoes, sandals for wet days), and for memories (camera, storage cards, chargers).

Pets None of the Disney resorts allows animals (except service dogs) to stay on the grounds (the only exception being Disney's Fort Wilderness Campground, where you can have your pet at the full-hook-up campsites). The major theme parks offer animal boarding, usually for about $40 per day. Disney offers a single facility, **Best Friends Pet Care,** on the Bonnet Creek Parkway (www.wdw. bestfriendspet care.com; © **407/209-3126**). Overnight prices start at $41 for dogs and $28 for cats. Universal Orlando and SeaWorld will board small pets during the day only.

Universal's three Loews-run resorts allow pets on the property. So do Drury Hotels (p. 282). To find more pet-friendly hotels, two solid resources are **www.petswelcome.com** and **www.dogfriendly.com**.

Pharmacies The tourist area hosts mostly national chains. **Walgreens** (7650 W. Sand Lake Rd. at Dr. Phillips Blvd., Orlando; © **407/370-6742**), which has a round-the-clock pharmacy, could, at a stretch, be deemed an outfit with local roots; back in the day, Mr. Walgreen spent the cold months in Winter Park. **Turner Drugs**

Stuff You Never Thought to Bring (but Should)

Besides the usual toiletries, recharging cords, and drugs, you might not have thought of these good ideas, too:

- **Earplugs.** Orlando flights are swinging with kids going insane with excitement.

- **Hand purifier.** Turnstiles. Safety bars. Handrails. Furry mice. You're going to be handling a lot of dirty things.

- **Dark-colored clothing.** On almost all flume rides, the seating doubles as a step, so you're bound to stain your butt with a slightly muddy footprint. Also, it's hot and you'll be in lots of photos—and colored shirts show sweat stains.

- **Sandals that fasten.** Water-based rides soak regular shoes and cause pruning. Flip-flops won't always do because they're not hardy and they won't stay on.

- **Skin-tight underwear.** Hot, moist days can cause chafing even in people who rarely experience it. Under Armour or nonpadded bike shorts preempt that.

- **Sunscreen, a hat, and sunglasses.** Okay, so you probably thought of these, but it bears repeating.

- **A mobile phone battery recharger.** Between the My Disney Experience app, Wi-Fi, photos, and social media updating, you'll drain your battery quickly.

- **A superabsorbent shammy.** For lenses and wet children.

- **Pocket-size games.** People talk about rides, but they neglect to mention the hour in line before those exciting 3 minutes. Orlando *is* lines. Bring diversions.

(12500 Apopka Vineland Rd., Lake Buena Vista; www.turnerdrug.com; ☏ **407/828-8125**) is not a 24-hour pharmacy, but it delivers prescriptions to most Disney-area accommodations.

Police Call ☏ **911** from any phone in an emergency.

Safety Train kids to approach the nearest park employee in case of **separation.** Never dress kids in clothing that reveals their name, address, or hometown, and unless it's a travel day, remove any luggage tags where this information will be visible. If people can read your address off a tag while you're in line at Jurassic Park, then they'll know you're not at home. Don't leave valuables visible when

you park your car. Also, please keep your arms and legs inside the vehicle at all times. Thank you.

Senior Travel Just about every secondary attraction offers a special price for seniors, but the theme parks offer precious little. If you're over 50, you can join **AARP** (601 E. Street NW, Washington, DC 24009; www.aarp.org; ☏ **888/687-2277**) to find out what's being offered in terms of discounts for hotels, airfare, and car rentals. Before you bite, be sure that the AARP discount you are offered actually undercuts others that are out there. Elderhostel's well-respected **Road Scholar** (www.roadscholar.org; ☏ **800/454-5768**) runs classes and programs, both

inside the theme parks and around the Orlando area, designed to delve into literature, history, the arts, and music. Packages last from a day to a week and include lodging, tours, and meals. Most are multigenerational; bring the grandkids.

Smoking Smoking is prohibited in public indoor spaces, including offices, restaurants, hotel lobbies, and most shops. Some bars permit it. In general, if you need to smoke, you must go outside into the open air, and in the theme parks, smokers are quarantined to strictly enforced designated areas.

Taxes A 6.5% to 7% sales tax is charged on all goods with the exception of most edible grocery items and medicines. Hotels add another 2% to 5% in a resort tax, so the total tax on accommodations can run up to 12%. The United States has no VAT, but the custom is to not list prices with tax, so the final amount that you pay will be slightly higher than the posted price.

Telephones Generally, hotel surcharges on long-distance and local calls are astronomical, so you're better off using your **cellphone** or a **public pay telephone.** Many convenience groceries and packaging services sell **prepaid calling cards** in denominations from $10 to $50; for international visitors, these can be the least expensive way to call home. Many public phones at airports now accept American Express, MasterCard, and Visa credit cards. **Local calls** made from public pay phones in most locales cost either 35¢ or 50¢. Pay phones do not accept pennies, and few will take anything larger than a quarter. Make sure you have roaming turned on for your cellphone account.

If you will have high-speed Internet access in your room, save on calls by using **Skype** (www.skype. com) or another Web-based calling program.

For calls within the United States and to Canada, dial 1 followed by the area code and the seven-digit number. **For other international calls,** first dial 011, then the country code, and then proceed with the

number, dropping any leading zeroes.

Calls to area codes **800, 888, 877,** and **866** are toll-free. However, calls to area codes **700** and **900** can be very expensive—usually a charge of 95¢ to $3 or more per minute, and they sometimes have minimum charges that can run as high as $15 or more.

For **reversed-charge or collect calls,** and for person-to-person calls, dial the number 0, then the area code and number. If your operator-assisted call is international, ask for the overseas operator.

For **local directory assistance** ("information"), dial ℭ **411;** for long-distance information, dial 1, then the appropriate area code and 555-1212.

Time Orlando is on Eastern Standard Time, so when it's noon in Orlando, it's 11am in Chicago (CST), 10am in Denver (MST), and 9am in Los Angeles (PST). Daylight saving moves the clock 1 hour ahead of standard time. Clocks change the second Sunday in March and the first Sunday in November.

Tipping Tips are customary and should be factored into your budget. Waiters should receive 15% to 20% of the cost of the meal (depending on the quality of the service), bellhops get $1 per bag, bartenders get $1 per drink, chambermaids get $1 to $2 per day for straightening your room (although many people don't do this), and cab drivers should get 15% of the

fare. The Disney Dining Plan automatically includes gratuity. Elsewhere, don't be offended if you are reminded about tipping—wait staff are used to dealing with international visitors who don't participate in the custom back home.

Toilets Each theme park has dozens of restrooms that are clean (at least at opening time). Outside the parks, every fast-food place—and there are hundreds—should have a restroom you can use. Lobbies of large hotels also have some.

Visas Citizens of western and central Europe, Australia, New Zealand, and Singapore need only a valid machine-readable passport and a round-trip air ticket or cruise ticket to enter the United States for stays of up to 90 days. Canadian citizens may enter without a visa with proof of residence.

Citizens of all other countries will need to obtain a tourist visa from the U.S. consulate. Depending on your country of origin, there may or may not be a charge attached (and you may or may not have to apply in person). Be sure to check with your local U.S. embassy or consulate for the very latest in entry requirements, because these continue to shift. Full information can be found at the **U.S. State Department**'s website, www.travel.state.gov.

Visitor Information Orlando has one of the most responsive and question-friendly visitors' bureaus in America and it operates a storefront, **Orlando Official Visitor Center** (8723 International Dr.; www.visitorlando.com; ℂ **407/363-5872;** daily 8:30am–6:30pm), in a strip mall on the western side of I-Drive not far north of the Pointe Orlando shopping mall, that's stocked from carpet to rafter with free brochures. Although many, many other places in town (souvenir stands, mostly) claim to offer "official" tourist information, this is the only *truly* official place. Staff is on hand to answer any questions, and its ticket desk has the inside line on discounts.

Kissimmee, the town closest to Walt Disney World, maintains its own tourist office, the **Kissimmee Convention and Visitors Bureau** (215 Celebration Pl., Suite 200, Kissimmee; www.experience kissimmee.com; ℂ **800/333-5477;** Mon–Fri 8am–5pm). Its website also lists current discounts. The Kissimmee CVB works with the Orlando bureau, so you won't have to make two trips.

Water   Tap water has a distinct mineral taste. Your hotel's pipes are not to blame. Rather, think of Orlando as an island floating over a cushion of water. Most of the city's lakes started, in fact, as sinkholes. The drinking water is drawn from the aquifer, hence the specific flavor and odor. It's safe.

Index

Accommodations

Restaurants

Photo Credits